Myanmar's Rohingya Genocide

Myanmar's Rohingya Genocide

Identity, History and Hate Speech

Ronan Lee

I.B. TAURIS
LONDON • NEW YORK • OXFORD • NEW DELHI • SYDNEY

I.B. TAURIS
Bloomsbury Publishing Plc
50 Bedford Square, London, WC1B 3DP, UK
1385 Broadway, New York, NY 10018, USA
29 Earlsfort Terrace, Dublin 2, Ireland

BLOOMSBURY, I.B. TAURIS and the I.B. Tauris logo
are trademarks of Bloomsbury Publishing Plc

First published in Great Britain 2021

Cover design by Adriana Brioso
Cover image: Rohingya man carries a bamboo pole at Kutupalong refugee camp in
Ukhia on July 23, 2019. ((c) MUNIR UZ ZAMAN/AFP/Getty Images)

A catalogue record for this book is available from the British Library.

A catalog record for this book is available from the Library of Congress.

ISBN: HB: 978-0-7556-0246-9
        PB: 978-0-7556-0247-6
        ePDF: 978-0-7556-0248-3
        eBook: 978-0-7556-0249-0

Typeset by RefineCatch Limited, Bungay, Suffolk

To find out more about our authors and books visit www.bloomsbury.com
and sign up for our newsletters

To the Rohingya, with hope

Contents

List of Illustrations

Figure 1 Map of Myanmar

Acronyms

AA	Arakan Army
ANP	Arakan National Party
ARIF	Arakan Rohingya Islamic Front
ARSA	Arakan Rohingya Salvation Army
ASEAN	Association of Southeast Asian Nations
BJP	Bharatiya Janata Party
BROUK	Burmese Rohingya Organisation UK
DHRP	Democracy and Human Rights Party
EAG	Ethnic Armed Group
EIC	East India Company
EU	European Union
GDP	Gross domestic product
GNLM	Global New Light of Myanmar
ICC	International Criminal Court
ICJ	International Court of Justice
ICSPCA	International Convention on the Suppression and Punishment of the Crime of Apartheid
IDP	Internally displaced person
INGO	International Non-Governmental Organization
ISCI	International State Crime Initiative
MFA	Mayu Frontier Administration
NLD	National League for Democracy
NRC	National Registration Card
R2P	Responsibility to Protect
RIF	Rohingya Independence Force
RNDP	Rakhine Nationalities Development Party
RSO	Rohingya Solidarity Organisation
UEC	Union Election Commission
UK	United Kingdom
UN	United Nations
UNESCO	United Nations Educational, Scientific and Cultural Organization

UNHCR	United Nations High Commissioner for Refugees
UNSC	United Nations Security Council
US	United States
USDP	Union Solidarity and Development Party
VOC	Dutch East India Company/*Verenigde Oost-Indische Compagnie*

INTRODUCTION

Bamboo, Tarpaulin and Mud

Myanmar's Rohingya community experienced genocide gradually, and then suddenly. Decades of increasing human rights restrictions came to global attention during 2017 with a brutal army-led 'clearance operation' within Rohingya communities. Claiming to be seeking out militants in the northern reaches of Rakhine state, Myanmar's military, known as the Tatmadaw, engaged scorched earth tactics that targeted the civilian population, razed hundreds of Rohingya villages with fire, murdered at least 9,000 Rohingya men, and unleashed a monstrous campaign of sexual violence against Rohingya women and girls. These atrocities precipitated the largest forced migration in the region since the Second World War, with more than 700,000 Rohingya fleeing Myanmar in terror for the relative safety of Bangladesh.[1] Already extremely poor Rohingya refugees arrived in Bangladesh on foot carrying whatever possessions they could – cooking pots, sometimes rice, the occasional portable solar panel, and often infants or enfeebled elderly relatives. They also came with blood-curdling accounts of the sexual violence unleashed by Myanmar's military, and of how army helicopters were used to spread fire through the Rohingya's largely bamboo villages.

Along Bangladesh's frontier with Myanmar (a country regularly still known as Burma), land that had been unoccupied in late August by October had become a cramped shanty city of bamboo, tarpaulin and mud that stretched to the horizon. These new camps, within weeks of being established, became home to more people than cities the size of Dublin or Washington, DC. Humanitarian agencies struggled to provide the food, water and sanitation necessary for the rapidly growing and severely traumatized population. The scale of the forced displacement of Myanmar's Rohingya was horrifying. United Nations (UN) Secretary-General António Guterres characterized the crisis as 'a humanitarian and human rights nightmare', explaining how the 'situation has spiralled into the world's fastest developing refugee emergency'.[2]

In the immediate aftermath of the 2017 forced deportation I was encouraged by Rohingya friends to visit the Bangladesh camps to see for myself the consequences of Myanmar's latest military crackdown and, if possible, to check on the welfare of their family members. What I saw and heard left me with no doubt that the Myanmar authorities' ultimate aim was the obliteration of the country's Rohingya population – within just a few weeks more than half of Myanmar's Rohingya had been forced to Bangladesh and their former homes razed by fire. Myanmar's authorities quickly set about remodelling destroyed villages to remove evidence of former Rohingya residency.

My interviews with camp residents were invariably confronting, often distressing, and explained why so many Rohingya fled Myanmar so quickly. Newly arrived refugees painted a tragic picture, sharing heartbreaking accounts of murders, widespread sexual assaults and hundreds of villages laid waste by the Tatmadaw. One newly arrived camp resident, a farmer from Buthidaung township, told me how:

> I lost my two sons, and two daughters. At midnight the military come in my house and burnt the house, but first they raped my two daughters and they shot my two daughters in front of me. I have no words to express how it was for me to suffer, to look at my daughters being raped and killed in front of me. My two sons were also killed by the government. I was not able to get the dead bodies of my daughters. It is a great sorrow for me.

Descriptions of similar atrocities were shockingly widespread in August and September 2017. At Kutupalong, which had quickly become the world's largest refugee camp, residents also gave depressing accounts of their former lives in Myanmar. They described how the Rohingya had endured a decades-long pattern of odious rights abuses by the Tatmadaw and successive Buddhist-dominated governments, which continued after democracy icon and Nobel Peace Prize laureate Aung San Suu Kyi came to power in 2016. These events severely damaged Myanmar's reputation and Aung San Suu Kyi's international standing. The starkest indication that the country's fairy tale transition from brutal military rule to democracy was illusory came in December 2019, when Aung San Suu Kyi defended Myanmar against genocide accusations at the International Court of Justice (ICJ).

The Rohingya's situation was not always so bleak. For centuries prior to the British colonial period, the Rohingya's forebears – a mostly Muslim Indo-Aryan people – were a well-integrated part of the Arakan Kingdom, a sovereign state on the Bay of Bengal between the Burma Empire and Mughal India that roughly corresponds to Myanmar's modern-day Rakhine state and its surrounds. The Rohingya were integrated into Burmese society during the British colonial era and enjoyed full civil and political rights when Burma became independent in 1948. The Rohingya's situation deteriorated markedly after a 1962 military coup when the country came to be dominated by a xenophobic Buddhist nationalist military dictatorship. To rule a disparate and divided nation, the military government weaponized history, ethnicity and religion as tools of control. Collective citizenship rights were closely linked with prior recognition as a *taingyintha* or national race, akin to indigenous, for groups who traced ancestry in the country to before the start of the British colonial era in 1823. Many in Myanmar today regard recognition as a *taingyintha* as the peak of the country's rights hierarchy, surpassing even the value of an individually recognized citizenship.[3] In a legal sense, *taingyintha* status became pivotal to the Rohingya's collective citizenship and rights claims. By portraying the largely Muslim Rohingya as a population of more recently arrived migrants from neighbouring Bengal, Myanmar's Buddhist-dominated authorities denied them acknowledgement as a *taingyintha* and refused (frequently reversed) their citizenship claims. The consequences of this for the Rohingya have been dire.

From the 1960s, the Rohingya's rights were steadily restricted. They endured limitations on their access to education and healthcare, their ability to marry and have children, earn a living and travel – even short journeys between adjacent villages were strictly controlled. Rohingya increasingly found they could not rely on the authorities to acknowledge the validity of their identity documents, including passports, as proof of citizenship. Claims about history by Myanmar's government, military and nationalists that erase the Rohingya's long-term and legitimate presence in the country are central to the Rohingya's statelessness and the appalling rights abuses that have accompanied this. The Rohingya are now the world's largest stateless group, with a majority living as refugees in Bangladesh camps, while those who remain in Myanmar are subject to apartheid conditions, mass incarceration and genocide crimes.

In this desperately sad context, I undertook research with Rohingya communities in Myanmar, with newly arrived refugees in Bangladesh, and among the Rohingya's global diaspora. These Rohingya perspectives (presented in Chapters Six and Seven) are contextualized by the history, including new archival research, and citizenship law that is outlined in the book's early chapters. In Chapter Five, I show how the historical record and Rohingya views clash with official narratives about history that have been used to block Rohingya citizenship and to enable and justify human rights violations against them.

The Rohingya's situation is grim, but it need not be hopeless. My new archival research strengthens Rohingya claims to a long ancestry in Myanmar tracing back to ancient Arakan. I argue that the historical record shows the Rohingya are indigenous to Myanmar and thus ought to be recognized as a *taingyintha* and granted collective citizenship rights. I am strongly supportive of efforts to seek justice for the Rohingya through legal mechanisms like the International Criminal Court and ICJ, but believe too that a greater focus on Myanmar's domestic politics will be crucial for the Rohingya to achieve the domestic rights – including citizenship – they are entitled to.

This book involved research that I dearly wish did not need to be undertaken – the Rohingya deserve better than the bleak circumstances they have found themselves in. My hope is that clarity about Myanmar's history and the Rohingya's own perspectives will strengthen their citizenship and rights claims. I also hope that helping to give voice to the Rohingya community will contribute to the preservation of Rohingya historical memory – an increasingly important task as Myanmar officialdom aggressively works to erase it.

'We are Rohingya'

Disputes about names are central to the questions of history, identity and politics addressed throughout this book. I use names pragmatically to enhance meaning and avoid the confusion that might arise because of an intricate ethnic and religious context, multiple name and border changes, and differing translations over time.

The Rohingya are victims of serious human rights violations and they have also found the legitimacy of their identity and their name challenged (sometimes in academic circles). The Rohingya name continues to be aggressively rejected by the Myanmar government, the Tatmadaw and Buddhist nationalists, who believe it comes with implied and unacceptable political claims. These groups instead substitute the Rohingya name for the 'Bengali' label, which they use as a slur to identify Rohingya as recent and probably illegal migrants from Bangladesh or the Indian subcontinent. Misnaming the Rohingya as foreign has been used as a tactic to generate domestic political support for anti-Rohingya practices. Myanmar's former military dictatorship and the leaders of the quasi-civilian administration that followed it from 2011 stubbornly used the name 'Bengali' in place of Rohingya and encouraged others to do likewise. In a 2013 interview, Myanmar's President Thein Sein, an ex-general, dismissed Rohingya claims to a long-term heritage in Myanmar saying, 'There are no Rohingya among the races. We only have Bengalis who were brought for farming' [during British rule].[4]

Official portrayals of the Rohingya as foreign have had serious consequences for the group, contributing to domestic support for the Tatmadaw's anti-Rohingya actions, including the brutal 2017 'clearance operation'. Tatmadaw commander-in-chief Senior General Min Aung Hlaing justified his troops' actions by saying, 'The Bengalis were not taken into the country by Myanmar, but by the colonialists', 'They are not the natives' and 'The native place of the Bengalis is really Bengal'.[5] Min Aung Hlaing has also regularly depicted Rohingya as 'Bengalis' in his social media posts, which contributed to his 2019 Twitter ban.[6]

Aung San Suu Kyi has also avoided using the Rohingya name, a stance that appeared to briefly soften in mid-2016 when the Ministry of Information issued guidelines recommending the term 'people who believe in Islam in Rakhine state' in place of 'Bengali'.[7] This approach created tensions of its own. Ethnic Rakhine objected to the implication that Rakhine state's largest Muslim population (the Rohingya) should be identified as a 'community from Rakhine state' when they considered them interlopers. Adding further complication, another Muslim community, an ethnic group named the Kaman – a smaller Muslim group living in Rakhine state yet acknowledged by the authorities as indigenous and entitled to collective citizenship rights – worried this description linked them too closely to the Rohingya, jeopardizing their own status, and might in turn lead to their rights being restricted. Rohingya themselves were unhappy because the Ministry of Information's euphemistic term, once again, did not acknowledge their right to self-identify using their group's actual name.

Any hope Myanmar's government might have been relaxing its stance about the Rohingya's right to self-identify was misplaced. This was illustrated in May 2016, when Aung San Suu Kyi created a false equivalence between the Rohingya's desire to self-identify with others' desire to impose a foreign identity on them. She told visiting United States (US) Secretary of State John Kerry that, 'The Rakhine Buddhists object to the term "Rohingya" just as much as the Muslims object to the term "Bengali", because these have all kinds of political and emotional implications which are unacceptable to the opposing parties'.[8] Just as ex-general Thein Sein's government had done, Aung Sun Suu Kyi prioritized nationalist objections over the Rohingya's right to self-identify.

Sadly, government and Tatmadaw attacks on the legitimacy of the Rohingya identity have led some foreign actors to elide the Rohingya name from their public statements. The United Nations, whose agencies previously used the

Rohingya name in communications, from 2014 discouraged staff operating in Rakhine state from using the term, claiming it inflamed local tensions.[9] Far from reducing conflict, UN decisions to avoid using the Rohingya name potentially emboldened Myanmar's government and the Tatmadaw to further restrict Rohingya rights, believing UN agencies were unlikely to strenuously object.

During my research, Rohingya was the name routinely used by community leaders from Rakhine state's Muslim population, and it was the name they publicly asked to be identified by. 'Of course we are Rohingya' was how one Muslim community leader from Rakhine state described the group's identity when we spoke in 2015. There has been no public objection from within the Rohingya community to the application of the Rohingya name to the group. To put it simply – alongside calls to have their citizenship claims recognized and their human rights respected, Rohingya have asked to be called Rohingya.

That the Rohingya need to make this request is a strong indication of the hostility with which Myanmar's authorities and nationalists resist any acknowledgement of the legitimacy of Rohingya citizenship and rights claims. The perpetrators of rights abuses should never be allowed to dictate how their victims are labelled. To use a compromise name purely because the name Rohingya is objectionable to Myanmar's government, Buddhist nationalists or the Tatmadaw – which has undertaken a genocidal military campaign against the Rohingya – would be ridiculous. Alternative approaches such as surrounding the name Rohingya with quotation marks, to indicate the Rohingya's identity as disputed, detracts as well from the Rohingya's right to self-identify as they choose and plays into the hands of those who seek to curtail Rohingya access to human rights. This would represent a political rather than a scholarly approach, and would come with the high risk of adding further confusion to an already complicated and fraught situation by inadvertently aligning with the views of those who deny the Rohingya their choice of name, their right to a nationality and often their human rights. Consequently, like the international media, human rights organizations and most governments, I consistently use the Rohingya name to identify Rakhine state's principal Muslim population.

Human rights violations, intermittent local violence and poverty – Rakhine state has a poverty rate of seventy-eight per cent according to the World Bank – have contributed to a near constant flow of Rohingya refugees out of Myanmar since independence.[10] Rohingya migratory flows hasten when life opportunities are more marginal or when there is political or social unrest. This happened in the aftermath of major military operations conducted in the 1970s, 1980s and

1990s, following Rakhine state violence in 2012, again because of Tatmadaw operations in 2016, and spectacularly following the Tatmadaw's 2017 'clearance operation'. Precisely how many Rohingya in Myanmar have faced atrocity crimes has been made difficult to ascertain because of the lack of accurate demographic data from Rakhine state. The military-dominated government did not conduct a census between 1983 and the start of the quasi-civilian era. In 2014, a nationwide census was eventually undertaken. Controversially, as this census was funded by international donors including the British government and the UN Population Fund, Myanmar's government did not allow census-takers to enumerate those claiming Rohingya as their identity.[11] Identity data was not recorded for 1,090,000 people in Rakhine state, so for a time this was widely believed to be a close approximation of the Rohingya's population there.[12] More recent United Nations High Commissioner for Refugees (UNHCR) estimates suggest a larger Rohingya population, closer in size to 1,295,000 people.[13] By mid-2016, the Rohingya's worldwide diaspora was of a size comparable to the group's population within Rakhine state.[14] Forced migration between late 2017 and early 2018 – when an estimated 745,000, including 400,000 children, fled to Bangladesh (joining the estimated 300,000 victims of previous forced deportations already there) – means there are now more Rohingya living in refugee camps on the Bangladesh side of the international frontier than remain in Myanmar.[15]

Rohingya living outside of Myanmar and the Bangladesh refugee camps are commonly undocumented, making it necessary to rely upon estimates when assessing the overall size of the diaspora population. UNHCR data from 2016 indicated there were 31,759 Rohingya registered in Bangladesh, and 42,901 in Malaysia.[16] Since neither country is a signatory to the 1951 *Refugee Convention* or the 1967 *Protocol relating to the Status of Refugees*, a much larger Rohingya population in each country is unregistered. The UNHCR estimated 400,000 Rohingya refugees might have been resident in Bangladesh, and 100,000 in Malaysia, before the start of the 2017 forced migration.[17] The UNHCR also estimated that up to 200,000 Rohingya were living in Pakistan and 400,000 in Saudi Arabia, with many of these likely to be second- or third-generation Rohingya migrants.[18] International non-governmental organizations (INGO) like the Arakan Project, which monitors Rohingya refugee movements (including irregular maritime movements in the northern Bay of Bengal), believed these figures underestimated the size of the Rohingya diaspora population. Arakan Project population estimates from 2017 indicated there were 500,000 Rohingya in Saudi Arabia, 350,000 in Pakistan, 150,000 in Malaysia and 50,000 in the United Arab Emirates.[19] India's government has acknowledged 10,500 Rohingya living in the country but the actual figure is widely regarded to be closer to 40,000.[20] Rohingya diaspora populations outside of Asia are smaller. The US hosts the biggest with more than 10,000 Rohingya refugees settled.[21] There are around 3,000 Rohingya living in Australia, 400 in Canada, 300 in the United Kingdom (UK) and small yet politically active communities in Ireland and mainland European countries. Unrest within Rakhine state since 2012 generated large annual Rohingya refugee flows out of Myanmar. In the 2015 dry season alone, an estimated 25,000 Rohingya left Rakhine state by boat.[22] A 2016 Tatmadaw action was believed to have prompted around 90,000 Rohingya to seek refuge in Bangladesh, and while some of those refugees may have subsequently returned, the Tatmadaw's subsequent 2017 clearance operation likely ensured their return was brief.[23]

The Rohingya are not the only Muslim group from Rakhine state. Numerically much smaller than the Rohingya, an estimated 30,000 to 50,000 Kaman (Kamein) live principally in the south of the state.[24] The contemporary Kaman's ancestors are commonly believed to have been soldiers accompanying a Mughal prince, Shah Shuja, when he sought refuge in the Arakan kingdom during the seventeenth century.[25] The Kaman Muslims became influential at Arakan's royal court, but when their political power waned in the eighteenth century, they were exiled to Ramree Island.[26] The small Kaman Muslim population is regarded by Myanmar's government as a *taingyintha*, yet has frequently been treated by the authorities in a similar way to the Rohingya and subjected to rights restrictions, particularly limits on their freedom of movement, including confinement to their villages.[27] The Kaman's mistreatment indicates the centrality of anti-Muslim prejudice to official rights abuses in Rakhine state.

Burma or Myanmar?

Myanmar is today an overwhelmingly Theravada Buddhist country. Religious data collected for the 2014 census showed 87.9 per cent of the population identified as Buddhist, 6.2 per cent as Christian, and only a small minority of 4.3 per cent as Muslim.[28] The demographics of Rakhine state, the Rohingya's ancestral home, are different, with Islam accounting for 35.1 per cent of the 2014 population.[29] The majority ethnicity in Rakhine state is a Buddhist group, the Rakhine, for whom the state was named. Close to two-thirds of the state's population are ethnic Rakhine, and Rohingya account for much of the remaining third.

Nationwide, Myanmar's majority ethnicity is another mostly Buddhist group known as the Bamar (or Burman), which make up around two-thirds of the country's population. The names Burma and Myanmar are both derived from this group's Burmese language name: Myanmar represents the literary form and Burma its spoken equivalent. The British transliterated the spoken name, Burma (sometimes spelled using variations including Burmah), and this became the colonial name of the country. Debate about the country's legitimate name underscores tensions between ethnic minorities and the central government and military, which minority leaders argue – with considerable justification – have long been dominated by and operated for the benefit of the country's Bamar Buddhist majority.[30] Other Asian countries have changed their names over the course of the past century – Thailand, for instance, was known as Siam, and Sri Lanka as Ceylon – but few name changes have been as persistently controversial as Burma's 1989 name change to Myanmar (officially, Republic of the Union of Myanmar).

The military dictatorship argued that shedding the colonial name for the vernacular name was more inclusive of ethnic minority groups. Name changes were part of the military government's Burmanization strategy to dilute the cultural identity of ethnic and religious minorities and enforce Bamar Buddhist hegemony.[31] Many among the country's ethnic minorities and the political opposition mistrusted the military dictatorship's motives and disputed its legitimacy to change the country's name. They considered the Myanmar name as representing an exclusively ethnic Bamar designation, and for them, the choice of name became a political identifier and refusing to acknowledge it a political act.[32]

Controversy over the country's name has raged internationally too, fuelled by Aung San Suu Kyi, the National League for Democracy (NLD) and other opposition groups who did not acknowledge the legitimacy of the military dictatorship's change of the country's name. For a decade and a half, these groups and opposition leader Aung San Suu Kyi insisted on using the name Burma, and demanded the international community do likewise. During the military dictatorship, the UK, US and Western countries commonly followed Aung San Suu Kyi's lead and officially referred to the country as Burma, a practice widely adopted by academics. China, India and Japan adopted the name Myanmar, as did the UN and the Association of Southeast Asian Nations (ASEAN).[33]

As recently as 2012 Aung San Suu Kyi expressed her public disappointment with governments referring to the country as Myanmar: 'I shall always refer to this country as Burma, until the Burmese people decide what they want it to be called.'[34] Further confusing matters was Aung San Suu Kyi's apparently unprompted *volte-face* on this issue after becoming State Counsellor (the de facto Prime Minister) in 2016. Since then she has frequently used the name Myanmar, although there was no formal government announcement about this. With the NLD having formed the country's government, Aung San Suu Kyi's attitude towards the legitimacy of the Myanmar name seemingly changed, and she has indicated she now finds either name acceptable. In her first speech to the UN as State Counsellor in September 2016, she referred to the country as Myanmar.[35] She outlined some of her reasoning for this apparent change of heart in a speech to the foreign diplomatic corps: 'So it is up to you, because there is nothing in the constitution of our country that says that you must use any term in particular . . . I use Burma very often because I am used to using it. But it does not mean that I require other people to do that as well.'[36]

In recent years, the attitudes of international actors have also been inconsistent and changeable. For instance, the Australian government for years stuck with the name Burma, in 2012 officially acknowledged the country's name to be Myanmar, before partly reversing that decision in 2014. Since then, Australia has sometimes used a combination of both or either names dependent on the situation, and increasingly uses the name Myanmar in official documents.[37] In 2018, the European Union indicated the country should be identified as Myanmar/Burma, an update from its earlier guidance to use the name Burma/Myanmar. Recent US government practice has been just as flexible. Retaining an official US policy of calling the country Burma, President Barack Obama used both names on his country visits in 2012 and 2014.[38] President Donald Trump's administration has likewise frequently used the Myanmar name while sticking with Burma as the official designation.[39]

Differing domestic and international opinions about which name is most acceptable mean official and academic texts, and news reports, frequently use different names depending on the author's country of origin or political preference. Throughout this book, my focus is on maintaining clarity, so pragmatically I refer to the country by its official names – Myanmar from the time its name was changed in 1989, and Burma prior to that.

Contention over names has frequently been the case in parts of the country with ethnic, religious or political tensions like Rakhine state. The contested nature of Myanmar government name changes means towns, cities, geographic features and states are referred to and commonly known by their former, more familiar names. Rakhine state, for instance, is still regularly identified as Arakan, and alternative English-language spellings, like Rakhaing, are not uncommon.

Clarity can be made more difficult by multiple translations between the languages of Myanmar, official and unofficial, before an English-language name is agreed. Rakhine state achieved statehood in 1974 and underwent a disputed name change, from Arakan, at that time. Rohingya today often continue to refer to the area as Arakan, a name which they contend more accurately reflects its multi-ethnic and multi-religious history. I identify the area using its official names – Rakhine state from 1974 and prior to that as Arakan division, as it was known throughout British colonial rule and the early post-independence period. The area's pre-colonial history is examined in detail in Chapters One and Two, and I generally identify the area as Arakan or the Arakan kingdom, although others may use the names of its various historic urban sites and capitals (Dhanyawadi, Vesali, Lemro or Mrauk-U).

Far less controversial than Myanmar's name changes have been recent name changes in Bangladesh. In 2018, Bangladesh's government revised its official English spelling of Chittagong to Chattogram, which more closely aligns with how locals pronounce and write the name in Bengali. Since most references in this book are to the period long before its English spelling was officially changed it is the older spelling that generally appears.

My approach to Myanmar's personal naming conventions is worth outlining too. In Myanmar, names are frequently personal names. Families may not share any common name, although an unofficial surname might be used. In this book, Aung San Suu Kyi and others' Myanmar names appear in full, rather than being arbitrarily shortened to suit western naming conventions. In Myanmar titles can be added to names and become permanent fixtures. Common titles to appear here are 'U' (uncle), referencing a mature male, and 'Daw' (auntie), referencing a mature female. It is common practice in Myanmar to refer to individuals by their full name, including their title. To avoid confusion with names, I partly adopt this practice. Full names are used and titles like 'U' and 'Daw' are included in instances where common practice means the title has become accepted as part of the individual's name or when it is used in a direct quotation.

1

Rohingya Roots in Ancient Arakan

'From time immemorial' is how Rohingya usually describe their ancestors' lengthy residence in the Rakhine state area. While this is substantially true, migration during the first and second millennia contributed to their ancestor's presence in the land many still identify as Arakan, and to the introduction and growth of the Rohingya's majority religion, Islam. In this chapter, I examine pre-colonial history, from the early centuries of the first millennium until the late eighteenth century, when the independent Arakan kingdom was conquered by Burma. I outline key factors that contributed to the development of Arakan's Rohingya population by describing its first millennium links with Bengal and India, connections with regional and world trade networks, and the role played by slavery and involuntary migration. I also show how Islam had come to Arakan by the eighth century, likely through pre-existing trade links with Bengal and the Middle East, and how by the time of the Burmese invasion, the Rohingya's ancestors were a well-established community within a multi-ethnic and multi-religious kingdom.

The impenetrability of the Arakan Yoma mountain range, which separates Rakhine state from the flat central Irrawaddy River plains of Myanmar, has frequently been noted as a key explanation for the area's economic, political and social development independent of its neighbours to the east.[1] This physical boundary protected Arakan's kingdoms from land invasion by eastern rivals and helps account for the substantially different demographics of the lands on either side. Arakan's territory for the last two millennia has included land that is today Rakhine state – although there have been lengthy periods of time when territory north of the Naf River (areas now part of Bangladesh) was dominated by Arakan. Historically, there has been a much greater proportion of Muslims and of people with Indo-Aryan heritage living to the west of the Arakan Yoma than to its east. Geography, combined with the economic and military strength of Arakan's kingdoms, ensured that for much of the millennium preceding its eighteenth-century political decline and invasion by Burma in 1784, Arakan had largely avoided the authority of the Buddhist kingdoms east of the Arakan Yoma.[2]

Being bordered to the west by populous Muslim lands helps to explain too how today, Myanmar's Rakhine state could be home to a substantial Muslim minority. The Muslim population in Rakhine state is a consequence of trade links, multiple migrations (often involuntary) and conversions. Demographic patterns throughout the last two millennia account for the Rohingya's frequently (yet not always) darker skin tones compared with those of the ethnic Rakhine and Bamar. Skin tone differences, understood to reflect racial difference, have contributed to Myanmar government, military and nationalist assertions that the Rohingya are recent Bengali migrants.[3] Contemporary Myanmar newspaper cartoonists reflect this 'othering' of Rohingya by portraying Muslims from Rakhine state as having much darker skin than Myanmar's acknowledged *taingyintha*. Racial differences were regularly raised with me by ethnic Bamar and Rakhine as evidence that the Rohingya were foreigners and should not be considered indigenous to Myanmar. A simple explanation for differences of appearance between Rakhine state's confessional groups would be to generalize the Rohingya's ancestors as having come to Arakan from lands to the west and so having Indo-Aryan heritage, while the Rakhine and Bamar, with their Tibeto-Burman heritage, came from the east of the Arakan Yoma. Yet just as no single migration accounts for the Buddhist population in Rakhine state, neither does any single migration account for the Islamic or indeed Indo-Aryan presence there.

First millennium Arakan

Arakan's original inhabitants cannot be known with certainty. What is clear is that they were not the direct ancestors of the contemporary Rakhine and nor were they Theravada Buddhists. Archaeological evidence – coins and inscriptions of royal names and titles – in Sanskrit and the ancient languages of Pali and Pyu point to an Indo-Aryan first millennium population with close connections to the Indian subcontinent and Hindu religious traditions. Considered among the greatest scholars of old Arakan, Pamela Gutman traced this history in *Ancient Arakan*, describing the establishment of Arakan's first major urban sites in the northern fertile alluvial plains of the Kaladan and Lemro rivers.[4] In an era characterized by Southeast Asian trade with south India, first and second century Arakan became home to coastal trading centres from which hill tribes sold forest products.[5] Interruptions to China's overland trade with Europe, because of conflict between the Roman Empire and Middle Eastern polities including the Sasanian Empire (centred on Iran), further contributed to the expansion of Southeast Asian overland and sea trade routes.[6] This linked Arakan more closely with global trade networks.

By the fourth century, significant urban sites like Dhanyawadi (Dhannavanti), considered the capital of the first of Arakan's four major kingdoms (Dhanyawadi, Vesali, Lemro and Mrauk-U), could be identified. While there are traditional claims of royal lines dating back thousands of years, the historical record is regarded to begin around 729 with the Anacandra inscription in Sanskrit on the Shittaung Pillar.[7] Believed to have originated near the Vesali urban site, it is today housed at the Shittaung Pagoda near Mrauk-U (Mrohaung). Badly damaged in the Second World War, the Shittaung Pillar has since been restored and partly deciphered. The Anacandra inscription details Arakan's royal Candra dynasty and describes Dhanyawadi as 'a city adorned by surrounding walls and a moat', indicating it was a well-established and sizeable urban site.[8] Arakan at that time was strongly influenced by its interactions with India. Dhanyawadi was influenced not by Theravada Buddhism but by Buddhism's Mahayana branch, then popular in India. It was because of Bengal's influence – possibly conflict with emerging kingdoms there – that by the sixth century, Arakan's major urban centre moved southwards.[9] The new Vesali (Wethali) site, known as the 'city of stone chairs', is regarded as the most Indianized of Arakan's kingdoms, with rulers from the Indian Chandra dynasty, a Mahayana Buddhist group.[10]

Concurrent religious and political developments in Asia additionally contributed to changes in regional and global trade patterns that further meshed Arakan within these networks. The increasing popularity of Buddhism within China in the Six Dynasties period encouraged travel for religious purposes between China and India, and the further spread of Mahayana Buddhism.[11] China from that time would be home to the world's largest Buddhist population. Today, around 250 million people, more than half of the world's Buddhists and typically followers of the Mahayana school, live in China.[12] A measure of the popularity of Buddhism in China in the early first millennium is provided by reports that the Northern Qi dynasty was home to 40,000 temples and that three million clergy were defrocked after its conquest by the Northern Zhou in 577 – an indication that up to ten per cent of the population might have been in Buddhist religious orders.[13] Domestic political competition within China also disrupted trade on traditional silk road routes to Europe and the Middle East.[14] Trade was further unsettled by conflict between the Roman (western and eastern) and Sasanian Empires in the early and middle first millennium, which restricted Chinese access to trade routes south of the Caspian Sea and encouraged the more extensive development and use of land and sea routes through Southeast Asia.[15] China's overland routes to the Bay of Bengal were mostly unaffected by these developments, and in the early fifth century the monk Fa-Hsien (Faxian) documented his journey overland from China to India, which followed the course of the Ganges south through Bengal before he sailed to Sri Lanka.[16] Earlier Chinese chroniclers of the Han dynasty had documented an overland trade route from India via Assam and Burma from before the Common Era.[17]

Arakan's religious links, position on overland and sea trade routes between China and India, and close proximity to Bengal ensured it was far from a regional backwater. Mid-seventh century military treaties contributed to safer land routes between Arakan and India, which brought Arakan into closer contact with Mahayanist centres in northern India and contributed to the spread of Mahayanist Buddhism through Arakan.[18] Buddhist monks and pilgrims journeyed between India and China, over land and by sea. Buddhism spread along the land and sea trade routes, and as these routes were more frequently journeyed, trade too increased.[19]

Arakan and Bengal exercised significant influence on each other for much of the first millennium. Their overlapping frontiers were unmediated by the mountain topography that characterized Arakan's borderlands with its Burmese neighbours. Consequently, while Arakan's early links with Burma were often by necessity maritime, its links with Bengal were by both land and sea. This contributed to significant cultural interaction.[20] Archaeological and numismatic research attests to the strength of the first millennium links between Arakan and Bengal. One copper plate dated to the early sixth century and attributed to Arakanese king Bhuticandra suggests that Arakan's then leaders looked to Bengal for models of kingship, indicating the centrality of Bengal's civilization to Arakan.[21] Numismatic studies reveal that by the seventh century, Arakan communities as far south as Sandoway (Thandwe) maintained trade relationships with the Bengal Delta.[22] There is strong archaeological evidence of the connections between Bengal's ninth century Harikela kingdom and Arakan, with coinage and copper plates found at Harikela sites potentially copied from Arakan.[23] Southeast Asian coinage styles may even have been brought to Bengal via Arakan.[24] There is evidence too of Arakanese influence over Harikela coinage, including on specific aspects of their bull and trisula image designs.[25] The use of Arakanese letter forms on early Harikela coins (before giving way to Bengali lettering for later minting) indicates that people from Arakan may have migrated to Bengal and Assam in the late seventh century and established themselves there.[26] The potential seventh century migration of an Arakanese population to Bengal underscores Arakan's close historical links with Bengal and suggests that some among Bengal's contemporary population (or other first or second millennium Bengali migrants to Arakan) potentially trace ancestral links to first millennium Arakan.

Arakan's links with regional and world trade networks ensured the area was known far beyond the Bay of Bengal. Europe's sea trade with Asia expanded significantly from the early first millennium. Western coral, lead, copper, tin, glass, vases, lamps, wine and coinage were sent east, while Asian spices and cloth were brought to the west.[27] Strabo of Amasia, a Greek geographer from Asia Minor, in his *Geography* recognized and outlined the expansion of Asian trade during Caesar Augustus' rule, which he contrasted with the relatively small trade volumes that preceded it.[28] The *Pax Romana* that began under Augustus certainly contributed to the expansion of European and global trade in the early centuries of the first millennium, yet it was far from the sole reason.[29] Important too were the virtual revolution in shipbuilding technology and the diffusion of knowledge about how to use monsoonal winds for navigation.

Previously, Roman trade vessels had often been felucca, small open craft (similar to Arab dhows) that could load and unload in shallow water but lacked the navigability of later vessels and made ocean voyages challenging. Equipping western ships with fore and aft rigging made them much more manoeuvrable and increased their carrying capacity.[30] Roman trade ships' capacity increased so they could carry as much as several hundred tons of cargo.[31] While mariners had struggled to hold earlier craft to course when out of sight of land, and with compass navigational technology still centuries away, trans-oceanic voyages until the first millennium had been risky. Mariners might have navigated by the stars, observed the flight of birds or used trained birds to guide ships towards land.[32] Some adopted coast-hugging strategies, which slowed voyages, increased costs and restrained trade. The requirement to hug the coast diminished significantly between the first and third centuries, with improved shipbuilding methods and more widespread knowledge of monsoonal winds contributing to more active and further ranging maritime traffic and booming global trade.

Before the first century, few aside from Arab and Indian mariners had effectively used monsoon winds for navigation. This had provided them with the capacity for trans-oceanic travel and an immense commercial advantage. By the first century, monsoonal winds were increasingly understood by Roman sailors, who named them Hippalus Winds – naming them after the navigator Hippalus whom many, including the author of the *Periplus Maris Erythraei* (*Periplus of the Erythraean Sea*), attributed with discovering a direct trans-oceanic route from the Red Sea to India.[33] From that time, European mariners travelled to India and beyond with increased regularity. First century European arrivals to India found extensive pre-existing trade routes across the Bay of Bengal, including to Asia further east.[34] This prosperous trade along the Indian and Bengal coasts was acknowledged by early European geographers.[35] The first century Jewish and Roman geographer Titus Flavius Josephus (Joseph ben Mattityahu) described that precious stones and valuable wood products could be obtained from the 'Aurea Chersonesus' – an area he claimed as belonging to India and now understood to refer to the greater Malay peninsula.[36] Arakan's coast was known as well to Europeans from at least the first century. The Egyptian Claudius Ptolemaeus (Ptolemy), in his *Geography*, provided a comprehensive list of trading centres known to first century Rome, including details of urban sites, emporia and geographic features along the Arakan coast.

Bountiful Asian trade activities were portrayed in Indian texts, too. Sanskrit epic poems from before the Common Era, the *Mahabhārāta* and the *Ramayana*, depicted vigorous Asian trade activities that were reflected in later Buddhist legends.[37] First millennium Indian literature provided frequent accounts of trade networks in the Bay of Bengal and beyond, and characterized eastern trade as following the 'golden route'.[38] The *Jatakas*, Buddhist legends from around the fourth century before the Common Era, included tales of Indian traders journeying as far west as Baveru (Babylon) and east to Suvarnabumi (the 'golden coast', a likely reference to the greater Malay peninsula), from which travellers could 'bring back wealth'.[39] Tamil literature too identified Southeast Asia as 'Suvarnadvipa (island of gold) or 'Suvarnabhumi' (land of gold).[40] The second century Tamil poem *Paddinappalai* (*Pattapattu*) recounted established trade between Sri Lanka and the northern Bay of Bengal, including Burma.[41]

Contemporary Rohingya narratives refer to Arab and Persian sources to evidence well-travelled first millennium trade routes through the Bay of Bengal. Rohingya historian Tahir Ba Tha for instance, in *A Short History of Rohingya and Kamans of Burma*, listed more than half a dozen 'Arab geographers, Persian travellers, and merchants' (including Al-Musudi, Ibn al-Faqih, Ibn Khordadzbeh and Sulaiman), and set out how, 'They and many other travellers used route over Arakan Yoma to travel to Burma and then to China'.[42] British colonial-era historians, including G.E. Harvey, noted regular first millennium Arab travel to the northern Bay of Bengal. Harvey suggested they regularly applied the name

Burma simultaneously to Arakan and lower Burma in their descriptions of those journeys.[43] Modern translations of the tenth century works of Ibn al-Faqih and Ibn Khordadzbeh show them referring to Burma (Arakan and lower Burma) as *Rahma*.[44] This provides an explanation for the origins of a common Rohingya claim that their name derived from the Arabic for mercy – *Rahma* – used by Arab sailors shipwrecked on the Arakanese coast around the eighth century.

Today, Arakan's historical links with Bengal, the early influence of Hinduism, the presence of Mahayana rather than Theravada Buddhism, and connections to regional and world trade networks that give credibility to Rohingya claims about their heritage are disputed by Myanmar's government, military and nationalists. Although there is clear evidence that it was not the case, Buddhist nationalists commonly describe Rakhine state as overwhelmingly Theravada Buddhist for all of the last two and a half millennia. Popular Rakhine legends and the Rakhine Chronicles (state histories commissioned by the Burmese court in the eighteenth century) emphasize Arakan's Theravada Buddhist character and, ignoring its temporal impossibility, suggest Buddha visited Arakan's Dhanyawadi kingdom in his lifetime.[45] According to myth, the Mahāmuni statue or 'Great Sage' (or 'Great Image') was cast during Buddha's visit, and 'was enlivened – or consecrated – by the Buddha himself, in order to create a "living twin" who would counsel kings and, in his absence, preach sermons to the community'.[46] Known by its Pali name, the Mahāmuni statue contributed to Dhanyawadi becoming a pilgrimage site and in contemporary times the statue is venerated by Buddhists Myanmar-wide. The myths and rituals associated with the Mahāmuni statue serve two simultaneous and mutually reinforcing purposes: placing local actors and contexts within a universal Buddhist cosmology, and situating an ongoing biography of the Buddha in the Arakan and Burmese polities.[47] At various times, the Mahāmuni statue was claimed to have been an object of royal competition, and the failure of Burma's king Anawratha to acquire it through an eleventh century invasion is a source of ongoing pride for ethnic Rakhine.[48] The removal of the Mahāmuni statue to Mandalay (close to Burma's then capital at Amarapura) following Burma's 1784 conquest of Arakan represented both a religious and political blow, and symbolized the incorporation of Arakan into the Burmese Buddhist polity, spiritually and temporally. Today, the thirteen-foot-high statue is covered in a several centimetre-thick layer of gold leaf and displayed in a Mandalay monastery, alongside other artefacts looted from Arakan.[49]

These popular legends have been repeated by modern Rakhine archaeologists, who uncritically accept an uninterrupted two and a half millennium Buddhist heritage in Arakan. San Tha Aung, in *The Buddhist Art of Ancient Arakan*, argued,

'Two thousand five hundred years have passed since parinirvana of Gautama Buddha. Throughout the centuries, ever since the introduction of Buddhism up to the present time, Arakanese professed Buddhism without break.'[50] He further asserted that 'According to tradition and our historical annals Buddhism was introduced into Arakan during the life-time of Buddha himself.'[51] This underscores the way myth and history have frequently been intertwined to support contemporary Myanmar political narratives about history and identity. Perspectives like this are clearly historically inaccurate and downplay Arakan's long-term links with Bengal, any early influence of Hinduism, and the well-documented connections between Arakan and regional and world trade networks that would have brought Muslim traders to Arakan by the eighth century – before the major migration and settlement there of the ethnic Rakhine population.

Rather than ethnic Rakhine being present in the first millennium when Arakan was greatly influenced by Bengal, the Rakhine's first migration to Arakan likely occurred sometime in the ninth century, making them far from Arakan's earliest inhabitants. Indeed, as I outline in the next section, when the Rakhine migrated to Arakan they would have found Islam was already well established there. Nevertheless, the Rakhine's migration across the Arakan Yoma began a process that greatly altered Arakan's demographics – though whether it represented migration and assimilation or an invasion is yet unclear to scholars. Recent scholarship by the anthropologists Elliott Prasse-Freeman and Kirt Mausert indicated that after initial ninth century 'forays into Arakan', numbers leaving the Irrawaddy plain for Arakan increased through the tenth century, peaking in the middle of that century.[52] Drawing on contemporary genetic and linguistic studies, they outline how the Rakhine chronicles misrepresent the arrival of ethnic Rakhine in Arakan:

> Despite Rakhine chronicles and histories suggesting that either Shan or Mongol people invaded Arakan in the middle of the 10th century, the genetic population structure of Rakhine included in these surveys is strongly associated with the Burmic populations from Southwestern China. The divergences between the modern Rakhine and Burmese dialects show evidence of continuous exchange and influence, mostly of Burmese on Rakhine, and a mid-10th century basal dialectal split is also consistent with these findings.

This scholarship is important to contemporary understandings of demographic change within Arakan because it indicates that Arakan has certainly been, 'a site of churning cultures and peoples, and coincides with evidence from the archaeological record indicating that Arakanese civilization's earliest cultural and demographic links are to related neighboring Indic civilizations'.[53] The archaeological record and accounts from Chinese, Greek, Roman, Indian and Sri Lankan sources, and from the Arab world, demonstrate that from ancient times until the arrival of the antecedents of the contemporary Rakhine sometime in the ninth century, Arakan was part of a vibrant and well-integrated regional and world trade system and was closely linked with Bengal. These conclusions are consistent with the demographic reality of Rakhine state and of neighbouring Bengal. When the ancestors of today's ethnic Rakhine migrated from the Irrawaddy plains, Arakan and its people had already been closely connected to Bengal for centuries. For much of the first millennium, power in Arakan was centred in Bengal and Arakan could reasonably have been understood as a province of eastern India.[54]

Islam's arrival in Arakan

Rohingya origin stories often describe Islam as first introduced to Arakan by shipwrecked Arab sailors. That Arakan undoubtedly regularly hosted Arab, Indian, Malay and European mariners and traders in the first millennium significantly strengthens this claim. Since the seventh century, Islam had spread from Arabia through conquest, proselytization and trade. By the eighth century, Islam was the dominant Middle Eastern religion. Islamic governments stretched from Gibraltar to the Arabian Sea and beyond, encompassing former Sasanian Empire territory, as far as the Indus River and Chinese border.[55] Islam came to India early – Kerala's Cheraman Juma Mosque is believed to date from around 629, within a decade of Muhammad's *Hijrah* to Medina and during the Prophet's lifetime.[56] Arakan's connections to maritime and overland trade and religious routes, and its proximity to the Indian subcontinent, mean Islam potentially appeared there soon after it did in India.

While maritime traders have been claimed to be responsible for the earliest introductions of Islam to Arakan, geography – proximity to Bengal – probably played a bigger role in long-term regional settlement patterns and the spread of Islam. Unlike Arakan's separation from Burma's Buddhist kingdoms by a mountain range, there was no such barrier between Arakan and eastern Bengal. For centuries Arakan and eastern Bengal were part of the same political jurisdiction and when they were not, borders remained porous and conducive to migration. The relative freedom of people to voluntarily move throughout this region likely contributed, as did the Arakan kingdom's slavery practices, to the spread of Islam and people with Indo-Aryan heritage to Arakan. Significant Muslim political influence in Arakan is regularly associated with the establishment of the Mrauk-U dynasty.

By the fourteenth century, the Bengal Sultanate's emergence as a regional power ensured that Arakan's influential neighbour was Muslim ruled.[57] Bengal adopted similar administrative approaches to the Delhi Sultanate, using Persian administrative systems and Persian as the court language. Historian Aniruddha Ray described how after the establishment of the Bengal Sultanate, 'the conversion of occupational groups followed, thanks to the untiring efforts of the Sufis ... But these converts continued to keep their old customs and traditions.'[58] Ray noted too that Bengali poet Makundaram Chakrabarty (known as *Kabikankan* – 'a bracelet among poets') observed converts did not practice *Roza* (in Arabic, *Sawm* or fasting) and retained local traditions. Bengal's *penchali* literature, narrative folk songs, have suggested that Muslim converts in Bengal, particularly in the east, retained elements of their previous religious practice. This likely contributed, centuries later, to British confusion about religious affiliation in Bengal (discussed in Chapter Two). Bengal residents encountered by British East India Company (EIC) staff and colonial officials were assumed to be Hindus because of their cultural and religious practices but were later discovered to be Muslims.[59]

In 1406, Arakan's Lemro River cities had been invaded by the army of the Burmese Ava kingdom. The Arakanese ruler Min Saw Mon fled and sought the support of the Bengal Sultanate, a regional power with a growing Muslim population. Here he was claimed to have adopted the name Narameikhla and according to Rohingya accounts converted to Islam. Min Saw Mon/Narameikhla returned to Arakan with an army of soldiers provided by Bengal's ruler, reclaimed the throne and established the Mrauk-U dynasty.[60] The religious affiliation of the triumphantly returned Min Saw Mon/Narameikhla has been contested.

Rarely disputed is that this leader's return and the establishment of the Mrauk-U urban site and eponymous dynasty marked the beginning of the Golden Age of prosperity for Arakan. Arakan's economy boomed. It was a major exporter of rice and trader in slaves, and its territory expanded to include large areas of Bengal, including the city of Chittagong. Accounts of fifteenth and sixteenth century travellers suggest the lands in eastern Bengal around Chittagong were already home to a substantial Muslim population when the Arakanese took control of that area after 1459. Chittagong remained part of the Arakan kingdom for the next two centuries.

Mrauk-U's rulers used Muslim titles, Persian was a court language, and they minted coins adorned with local symbols and the *Kalima*, the Islamic declaration of faith. For many Rohingya, these symbols, and the construction of Mrauk-U's Santikan mosque (which now lies in ruins among rice paddies) by Bengali Muslim soldiers in the 1430s represented evidence that Arakan was at times a Muslim kingdom (regardless of whether the kings were themselves Muslims).[61] Unsurprisingly, Rakhine nationalists reject the assertion the Mrauk-U dynasty was ever Muslim ruled – they instead regard Arakan as always having Buddhist rulers and a Buddhist majority population. From their perspective, Mrauk-U's ruler Min Saw Mon was a Buddhist who, like the kings who followed him, assumed Muslim titles and adopted trilingual coinage bearing Arakanese, Bengali and Persian to acknowledge sometime vassalage to Bengal and to better interact with maritime trade networks, rather than to demonstrate a religious affiliation.

Travelogues from the Mrauk-U period describe this Arakan kingdom as one with a substantial Muslim influence and population. These accounts regularly describe how, from the fourteenth century, there had been a recognizable Muslim population in Arakan, and that Arakan-controlled Chittagong had become a key regional port for Muslim pilgrims and the export of manufactured goods. Among the foreign visitors to document their experiences in Arakan was Chinese official Ma Huan. Huan accompanied Admiral Zheng He (Cheng Ho) as a translator when Zheng He's Ming dynasty 'Treasure Fleet' visited what was then northern Arakan in the early fifteenth century. Writing of the Chittagong residents he encountered, Ma Huan declared, 'The people are all Muslims.' He identified them as speaking Bengali and occasionally Persian, and, 'As to the dress worn by the king of the country and the chiefs: they all observe the ordinances of the Muslim religion.'[62] Similarly, the Portuguese Duarte Barbosa's early sixteenth century account characterized a well-established and growing Muslim population in Arakan.[63] Barbosa wrote of the conversion of Bengali Hindus, particularly artisans, to Islam. He believed that conversions were frequently motivated by the desire to 'gain the favour of their rulers'.[64] Another sixteenth century visitor to northern Bay of Bengal territories controlled by Arakan was the Venetian merchant Cesare Federici. Federici depicted Sandwip Island, near Chittagong, as having a Muslim king.[65] The early seventeenth century Portuguese Augustinian monk Sebastião Manrique, who spent years resident at Mrauk-U and closely observed and documented local customs and politics, also claimed that Muslim power was firmly entrenched in the Delta area of eastern Bengal by the time of his travels there and to Mrauk-U early in the seventeenth century.[66] With Arakan's Mrauk-U kingdom having expanded to include territory around Chittagong, it became likely a majority of Arakan's population were ethnically Bengali and its largest religious affiliation was with Islam. Within Arakan's Golden Age borders, Buddhism represented a substantial, yet still minority, religion; south of the Naf River a majority would have been Buddhist, however.

Contemporary Mrauk-U is a sprawl of temples and palace ruins that Myanmar's authorities hope will soon receive an UNESCO World Heritage listing.[67] Mrauk-U's achievements and the old city's heritage values were commonly referenced by ethnic Rakhine and Rohingya I met while travelling there. Today, in Rakhine state, the Mrauk-U kingdom is still considered to represent the land's most glorious era. This status has contributed to disputed claims among Buddhists and Muslims as to its ethnic and religious complexion and the nature of its rule. That Min Saw Mon/Narameikhla and the royal line he began was sometimes politically subject to Bengal, and later came to dominate eastern Bengal, is rarely in dispute. Whether the court's use of Islamic titles like Sultan, its use of the Persian language and the inclusion on its coins of the *Kalima* reflected the religion of the kingdom's Muslim ruler, was an attempt by a Buddhist ruler to demonstrate fealty to Bengal, or was part of an economic or political strategy to better engage with Muslim-dominated trade networks or appease Muslim subjects, is disputed. These differences of opinion are central to much contemporary debate about whether a large Muslim population was resident in Arakan prior to hostilities with the British in 1823 or whether the Rohingya's ancestors might be overwhelmingly British-era migrants. Regardless of Min Saw Mon/Narameikhla's religion, there is strong evidence of a substantial Muslim population and Muslim cultural influence within Arakanese territory, as well as close ties between Arakan and its neighbour Bengal.

Arakan's Mrauk-U dynasty was multi-ethnic and multi-religious, and by the values of the time, its capital city was cosmopolitan. The religious affiliation of some of its rulers might remain disputed, but there were certainly well-integrated and sizeable Muslim and Bengali populations living in the Arakan kingdom for centuries before the colonial era. With the loss of Chittagong to the Mughals in 1666 Arakan's territory shrank to approximate the contemporary boundaries of Rakhine state, with its borderlands marked by the Arakan Yoma mountain range to the south and the Naf River to the north. From then onwards, Arakan's racial and religious composition would remain similar to that encountered by the colonial British 150 years later, with a Buddhist majority and a well-integrated and substantially sized Muslim minority.

Slavery and forced migration from Bengal

No matter whether mostly Buddhist, Hindu or Muslim, Arakan's influence on its neighbours was often far from benign. Involuntary migration provided the labour to build much of Arakan's wealth and construct its expansive complex of palaces and temples. This was particularly the case during the Mrauk-U dynastic period from the early fifteenth century. For centuries, slavery and rice production (which relied on slave labour) were central to Mrauk-U's economy and contributed to the growth of its Bengali and Muslim populations.

Contemporary Rakhine nationalists do not readily acknowledge their ancestors' role in bringing slaves to Arakan from Bengal and northern India, often Muslims, in the centuries before the British colonial period. Instead, nationalist narratives focus on Britain's role in altering Arakan's demography through migration from Bengal and the Indian subcontinent in the nineteenth and early twentieth centuries. Just as nationalists have been reluctant to face up to Arakan's history as a slave economy and the impact of slavery on Arakan's demographics, slavery has been underplayed by Rohingya historians.[68] Slavery was never central to the origin stories told to me by Rohingya, when it was frequently asserted that Arakan's Mrauk-U kingdom was once Muslim ruled. Responsibility for slavery and the involuntary movement of people from Bengal to Arakan – many of whom were the forebears of today's Rohingya population – rests with all Arakan's rulers and with the European powers involved and the European consumers of the goods slavery produced.

When the Arakanese engaged Portuguese mercenaries and other freebooters to raid neighbouring Bengal, Islam was already the religion of Bengal's leaders and, increasingly, its people. Superior weaponry allowed the Portuguese to successfully maraud through Bengal and northern India from their bases in Arakan and Sandwip Island (Sandvip) in the Bengal Delta. In the sixteenth and seventeenth centuries there was an established Portuguese community at Mrauk-U and substantial martial populations of Portuguese at Dianga near Chittagong and south-east at Syriam on the Gulf of Martaban.[69] Here, Filipe de Brito, a one-time mercenary serving the Arakanese king, by 1605 was styling himself ruler of a Portuguese territory, looting Buddhist monasteries (he sometimes looked to the Buddhist community for legitimacy and at other times accused them of idolatry) and brawling with his former Arakanese allies and other nearby powers. After initial military successes, De Brito was ultimately defeated in 1613 at Syriam (Thanlyin) in the Irrawaddy Delta by soldiers from the Burmese Ava kingdom. De Brito's death was gruesome – he was impaled on an iron stake for three days before being executed, while his wife and family were deported to the Burmese capital Ava as slaves.[70]

Portuguese slave-taking methods were no less brutal, and while De Brito's troops eventually struggled in battle against a major Burmese army, Portuguese freebooters achieved more success fighting Bengal Delta farmers and fishers on behalf of Arakan's rulers. Much of the Portuguese military success in the northern Bay of Bengal was likely attributable to their early adoption of matchlock-configured arquebus firearms, which were available from the Portuguese armouries at Goa and Malacca.[71] These weapons were more accurate, faster to reload and safer than earlier firearms, and became widely used in Asia, including by the Mughals in India, yet were not so easily accessible to the civilian farmers and fishers of Bengal's river deltas.[72]

Arakan's Mrauk-U kingdom became the northern Bay of Bengal's most prodigious slave makers. Historians have characterized Arakan's slavery practices as both brutal and effective, and contributing to the desertion of parts of Bengal by residents fearful of Arakanese raids. Bengali chronicler Shihabuddin Talish (Ibn Muhammad Wali Ahmad), in the mid-seventeenth century, outlined Arakanese (identifying ethnic Rakhine using a pejorative term, Magh) and Portuguese (*feringhi*, a term usually applied to Europeans or white foreigners) slave-taking practices in detail:

> The Arakan pirates, both Magh and feringhi, used constantly to come by the water-route and plunder Bengal. They carried off the Hindus and Mahemedans that they could seize, pierced the palms of their hands, passed thin strips of cane through the holes and threw them huddled together under the decks of their ships. Every morning they flung down some uncooked rice to the captives from above, as we fling grain to fowl. On reaching home the pirates employed some of the hardy men that survived such treatment in tillage and other degrading pursuits. The other were sold to the Dutch, English, and French merchants at the ports of the Deccan. Only the feringhis sold their prisoners. But the Maghs employed all whom they had carried off in agriculture and other services. Many high born persons and Saiyads, many Saiyad-born pure women, were compelled to undergo the disgrace of slavery or concubinage to these wicked men. Mahomedans underwent such oppression as they had not to suffer in Europe. As they continually practiced raids for a long time, Bengal daily became more and more desolate and less and less able to resist them.[73]

Precise numbers of slaves taken from Bengal to Arakan are impossible to ascertain, although a measure of the large scale of the trade in the 1630s was provided by Portuguese missionary Manrique. He had access to the Mrauk-U royal court and became acquainted with king Thiri-thu-dhamma who sanctioned the building of a church so Manrique could minister to Mrauk-U's Portuguese Christian community.[74] In *Travels*, a memoir of his years spent in Asia, Manrique recounted how annually, more than 3,000 slaves were brought to Arakan. This was a significant number of annual arrivals even considering the large population of the Mrauk-U urban site (estimated to be home to around 160,000 people).[75] In the early seventeenth century, this made Arakan's capital a large city by global standards, with Europe's then largest cities – London, Paris and Naples – estimated as being home to 200,000, 220,000 and 280,000 people respectively.[76] Accounts like those provided by Manrique, which indicated slaves from Bengal, largely Muslims, arrived in Arakan annually by their thousands in the seventeenth century, greatly strengthen contemporary Rohingya claims to ancestry that predates the British colonial period.

Contemporary Rakhine nationalist leaders are reluctant to trumpet Arakan's historic involvement with the slave trade and to admit to the large Bengali Muslim population that this transported to Arakan. Some, like nationalist historian Aye Chan, have acknowledged that Arakanese slave raids of Bengal were the 'conventional practice of the kingdom since the early sixteenth century'. Perhaps reluctant to admit Arakanese involvement with a transnational slave trade, he argued the Arakanese retained all captured slaves for themselves.[77] As evidence, Aye Chan cited the historian Talish, who had noted, 'only the Portuguese pirates sold their captives and that the Arakanese employed all of their prisoners in agriculture and other kinds of services'.[78] However, Aye Chan failed to recognize that Portuguese slavers were Arakanese residents and that their slave trading took place with the licence of Arakan's king, whose coffers certainly benefited from the trade. The argument that Arakan retained its Bengali slaves, perhaps unintentionally, strengthens contemporary Rohingya claims to ancestors who were resident in Arakan in the centuries before the British colonial era.

The Dutch East India Company/*Verenigde Oost-Indische Compagnie* (VOC) certainly understood that the Arakanese captured and traded slaves. Based on extensive research in the VOC archives, Wil Dijk pointed to Dutch records indicating that slaves could only be obtained if the king did not require them to stay in Arakan as labourers. A similar point was made by an eighteenth century British administrator in Chittagong, who recalled how Arakan's king levied taxation on plunder: 'Of the goods it is his allowed privilege to take half, and of the prisoners one fourth; but he generally exacts the lion's share.'[79] Stefan Smith's study of seventeenth and eighteenth century Portuguese Asian communities noted that it was labourers and skilled artisans who were regularly retained in Arakan.[80] Members of this artisan class were identified early in the sixteenth century by the Portuguese Duarte Barbosa as being among those Bengali Hindus readily prepared to convert to Islam.[81] This indicates that, of the Bengalis taken as slaves to Arakan, those more likely to have been retained in Arakan were Bengali Muslims with Hindu heritage.

Seventeenth century Arakan was a key provider of slaves to the VOC. Dijk described how, 'It did not take the Dutch long to discover that large numbers of slaves were to be had in Arakan, mainly brought there by Portuguese mercenaries and freebooters operating slave raids to Bengal.'[82] There was a VOC trading post in Mrauk-U by 1610, just eight years after the company's formation, with the purchase of slaves and rice its main business. Dutch archives indicate VOC slave purchases from at least 1624, although other trading interests (including among the English, French and Portuguese) likely bought slaves from Arakan before that time.[83] Arakan's slave economy served as well the European consumers of the goods slaves were forced to produce – spices including pepper, mace, nutmeg, cloves and cinnamon.

Some of those enslaved by Arakanese and Portuguese raids into Bengal were destined for onward sale to Dutch traders in need of human resources to work in the East Indies, meaning they may have spent a relatively short period of time in Arakan. Dijk attributed the VOC's appetite for slaves to the Dutch view that 'one slave could put in as much work as two or three Dutchmen, unaccustomed as the Europeans were to the intense tropical heat. Moreover, the Company men were wont to drink themselves into a stupor, what with the abundantly available cheap liquor.'[84] Contributing to labour shortages in the East Indies was brutal mistreatment of native populations there by colonial powers. The Dutch for instance, in 1621, slaughtered virtually the entire 13,000-strong native population of Pulau Run, an island in the Banda Sea now part of Indonesia, to gain unimpeded access to the island's nutmeg groves.[85]

Dijk's archival research identified a disturbingly large slave population brought to the East Indies via Arakan on board VOC vessels (excluding slaves transported on board independent ships). Between June 1621 and November 1665, 26,885 men, women and children were transported from Arakan to the East Indies on VOC ships – 1,379 (five per cent) did not survive the journey.[86] This mortality rate is small compared with the numbers of slaves who died following capture in the 1620s. A number of especially dry years in the first half of that decade contributed to a local famine in Bengal.[87] According to Dutch reports this coincided with a locust plague and an epidemic, so captives were likely already malnourished and weak when Arakanese slavers arrived – the consequences were devastating.[88] In 1625, more than half of the 1,300 captured died shortly afterwards.[89] In 1626, of the 10,000 captured, 4,000 soon died.[90] Dijk indicated that there was a debate within the VOC about whether they might achieve lower mortality rates were they to capture their own slaves rather than relying on Arakanese and Portuguese slavers. This may have been motivated more by commerce than altruism. Capturing their own slaves would likely have been cheaper than buying them, and there is little to suggest VOC agents would have expected to achieve this with fewer deaths.

Research about mortality among captured slaves in Africa also indicated an appallingly high rate of mortality. Studying the trans-Atlantic trade from Angola, Joseph Miller in *Way of Death* estimated only sixty to sixty-five per cent of Angolan slaves survived from capture until their arrival on the African coast, where a further ten to fifteen per cent died before boarding ships for onward transport.[91] Miller's African research indicated that (just as it was for captured Bengalis) the deadliest time for a slave was the period between capture and embarkation on a slavers' ship. These high rates of death strongly indicate the brutality of slavery practices in Africa and point to a northern Bay of Bengal slave trade that was just as brutal and degrading as elsewhere.

The impact of Arakanese slave raids on Bengal's population was apparent to Bengal's eighteenth-century political power, the British East India Company. By the time Britain was first undertaking detailed mapping of the Bengal area in 1776, James Rennell, the Surveyor-General of India, tellingly included a note on one section of the Bengal Delta, explaining that, 'This part of the Country has been Deserted on Account of the Ravages of the Muggs.'[92] While today 'Mugg' is considered a pejorative term, it was routinely used by the British in the colonial era to describe the Rakhine and people from Arakan. The colonial British also applied this label to Bengali-speaking Buddhists living in Chittagong.[93] Rennell's comment ought not be assumed to represent the British or EIC's moral disapproval of Arakan's practices of slavery. Indeed, slavery was widespread in EIC territory (including Bengal) and British interests were key funders of the international slave trade decades after it had been outlawed by Britain's parliament.[94]

The EIC was often more concerned with suppressing the slavery practices of others than addressing the underlying causes of slavery within its own territory, which were frequently attributable to its own economic policies.[95] British policies in Asia were focused on commercial gain, made EIC shareholders rich and greatly contributed to the poverty of ordinary Bengalis. Contemporaneous with Arakanese raids ravaging delta communities, British policies were themselves clearly driving residents of inland Bengal towards slavery. One British judge in Bengal reported, 'The chief cause of slavery in the district may perhaps be ascribed to the extreme indigence of the lower class of inhabitants, many becoming slaves through necessity by selling their persons.'[96] EIC archival records indicate that by the early nineteenth century, extreme poverty was regarded by British administrators as a key cause of slavery within upper Bengal and that slaves were being transported from the inland to cities including Dhaka and Calcutta. The inconsistent British attitude towards slavery was succinctly summarized by one EIC director's 1796 comment that Bengal's salt workers ought to be released from slavery because, 'slaves cannot work so cheap as free men, besides we ought to give all our subjects liberty.'[97] Rather than local British anti-slavery practices, a decline in Dutch demand for Arakanese slaves most impacted this trade and further depressed an Arakanese economy still struggling from the 1666 loss of its territory around Chittagong to the Mughals.

For centuries, the slave trade had been responsible for forcibly migrating a substantial population of Muslims from Bengali to Arakan. Seventeenth-century military reversals and Arakan's economic decline contributed to internal political turmoil and likely led disgruntled nobles to invite a Burmese invasion. In 1784, the conquering army devastated Mrauk-U and deported thousands across the Arakan Yoma to Burma as slaves. In the face of the Burmese conquest, 30,000 refugees fled to British-controlled Bengal. Arakan would never again be an independent sovereign state. Mrauk-U's destruction at the hands of the Burmese invaders means reliable records from the period immediately preceding the conquest are scarce. Post invasion, the Burmese court commissioned histories placing Arakan within Burma's orbit and legitimizing their rule. In response, Arakan's Buddhist monks, still supportive of an independent Arakan, wrote their own histories that privileged the historic role of Rakhine Buddhists.[98] These chronicles have helped shed light on various aspects of Arakan's history, but the obviously political nature of both canons diminishes their evidential value. A further complication is that in the immediate aftermath of the invasion, Muslim religious and political leaders did not produce their own accounts of Arakan's history. This allowed narratives that minimized the historic influence of Islam, while privileging Theravada Buddhism and Buddhist groups like the Rakhine to predominate.

The conquering Burmese army encountered a multi-ethnic and multi-religious kingdom that was home to a substantial and well-integrated Muslim population, yet Arakan's Muslims subsequently found themselves largely written out of locally produced histories. The consequences of this invisibility endure to contemporary times, with nationalists frequently disputing the reliability of any histories that acknowledge Arakan's sizeable eighteenth-century Muslim population. This is especially problematic for the Rohingya because the earliest accessible evidence for their specific identity as a Muslim population in Arakan dates from the decade after the Burmese invasion.

British Colonial Rule and Rohingya Identity

Myanmar today occupies a strategic position between China and India, and also shares land borders with Bangladesh, Laos and Thailand. The Myanmar–Bangladesh frontier represents a political division that is traditionally regarded as separating South from Southeast Asia. This area is often identified as Myanmar's *anouk-taga* or 'western gate', a reference to the Rakhine state area that links Myanmar with the Indian subcontinent and is separated from the remainder of Myanmar by a mountain range.[1] The Arakan Yoma runs roughly north-south and provides a physical barrier that contributed to political separation and parallel cultural development on either side. Today, Rakhine state's Buddhist residents speak an archaic Burmese dialect as their mother tongue. This old-fashioned language, agrarian economy and grinding poverty have given rise to contemporary Myanmar narratives of Rakhine state as unsophisticated and its residents as yokels.

Symbolically, the 'western gate' represents the westernmost expansion of the Konbaung dynasty, Burma's last royal house, and the westernmost expansion of Burmese Buddhism. Konbaung kings who ruled from the 1750s oversaw a militaristic and expansionist empire that claimed territory in areas that are today parts of Bangladesh, India, Laos and Thailand.[2] Known as 'Kings who rule the universe', their Burmese subjects treated Konbaung rulers as demi-gods.[3] Myanmar's state-controlled textbooks describe the Konbaung dynasty's creator Alaungpaya as a founder of the nation, and he is lauded by the Tatmadaw. At the main military parade ground in Myanmar's capital, Naypyidaw, stands a ten-metre-high statue of Alaungpaya alongside two other empire-building Burmese Buddhist warrior kings, Anawratha and Bayinnaung.[4]

The Konbaung dynasty's 1784 conquest of the Arakan kingdom extinguished Arakan's sovereignty and brought the Burmese into close proximity with British-controlled Bengal. This had disastrous and long-lasting consequences for Arakan's population and for the Burmese. An immediate consequence of Burma's invasion of Arakan was the emergence of a disputed international frontier. The

Arakan kingdom had contracted considerably during the previous two centuries, with its former possessions in Bengal having fallen first to the Mughals and then to the British. By 1784, British control of Bengal stretched south to the Naf River. Burma's king Bodawapaya did not regard the Naf as marking the full extent of his new territorial gains, understanding that Arakan's former holdings in Bengal had rightfully become new Burmese possessions too. Ironically, the lands and mostly Muslim population that King Bodawpaya asserted were Burmese territory and subjects are today regarded by Myanmar's government, military and nationalists as utterly foreign.

Before the Burmese invasion, the EIC had been reluctant to pursue engagement with Arakan or Burma, in large part because other trading companies had beaten them to it. There were Portuguese traders and mercenaries in the northern Bay of Bengal from the sixteenth century and the VOC had a trading post in Arakan from the early seventeenth century.[5] In the aftermath of Arakan's loss of Chittagong, isolated efforts to woo Arakan's king (whom the British addressed using his Persian title 'King of Reccan') had resulted in few new trade opportunities.[6] Independent British traders had been resident in Arakan and Burma by the late eighteenth century, but until Burma's annexation of Arakan, the EIC had not committed significant resources to dialogue with either. The newly shared border changed the situation markedly.

Tens of thousands of refugees fled to Bengal in the aftermath of the invasion, and with Burma's soldiers firmly in control of Arakan and making regular incursions north of the Naf, the EIC was presented with a strong motivation to negotiate with the Burmese leadership. British priorities included protecting their commercial and political position in Bengal, repatriating the tens of thousands of refugees from Arakan who had become reliant on the material support of the EIC, and, as always, seeking new commercial opportunities. Concurrent events in Europe contributed to British interest in reaching favourable trade and political agreements with the Burmese. Conflict with France, after the revolution there, stoked fears among Britain's India-based leadership that the French might gain a military advantage in the Bay of Bengal, and access to important shipbuilding resources, including quality teak timbers, port facilities and commercial benefits, through agreements with the Burmese.

In 1795, the EIC tasked Colonel Michael Symes with facilitating diplomacy and trade with Burma, making him Britain's first official emissary to the Burmese Court at Ava.[7] Symes was accompanied by the polymath Francis Buchanan (later known as Hamilton or Buchanan Hamilton), a medical doctor and botanist, who diligently recorded details of the geography, local politics, and the characteristics and habits of the people he encountered.[8] Buchanan became a key gatherer of intelligence for the EIC in Asia and was subsequently engaged by the Company to undertake other strategically important research, including a study of Chittagong in 1798, surveys of Mysore in 1800, Bengal in 1807–14, and to join a mission to Nepal in 1802.[9] Tens of thousands of people from Arakan had been forcibly resettled in upper Burma in the aftermath of the conquest. Throughout their Ava trip, Buchanan and Symes met many former Arakan residents and likely first encountered people identifying themselves using a label clearly linked with the contemporary Rohingya – Rooinga. Buchanan documented in detail his journey to Ava, including his meeting with people from Arakan who identified themselves as Rooinga. Understandably, because Myanmar citizenship rights are today based largely on indigeneity – defined as resident in the country before 1823 – Buchanan's writings have become central to contemporary Rohingya historical narratives.

Arakan's Rooinga community in 1795

Buchanan's research findings form the cornerstone of Rohingya assertions about the group's history in Myanmar. His evidence greatly enhances Rohingya claims to settlement that predates the colonial period. In 1799, years after the Ava mission and indeed after his subsequent study of Chittagong, Buchanan published *A Comparative Vocabulary of Some of the Languages Spoken in the Burma Empire*. In this article he described how 'The *Mahommedans* settled at *Arakan*, call the country *Rovingaw*.'[10] Buchanan presented the languages of Burma: 'I shall now add three dialects, spoken in the *Burma* empire, but evidently derived from the language of the *Hindu* nation. The first is that spoken by the *Mohammedans*, who have been long settled in *Arakan*, and who call themselves *Rooinga*, or natives of *Arakan*.'[11] Rovingaw and Rooinga strongly indicate similar foundations, pointing to the Muslim group using their own Rooinga language to identify their place of origin, Rovingaw (their name for Arakan). By deriving their group's name from where they were native, the Rooinga clearly asserted their indigeneity to Arakan.

Buchanan's work represents seemingly undeniable evidence of Rohingya residency in pre-colonial Arakan and that is certainly how the Rohingya's contemporary leadership regard it. Buchanan is almost universally referenced by Rohingya as providing incontestable evidence their forebears had lived in pre-colonial Arakan and had characteristics (including their own language) that should entitle them to be recognized as indigenous to Myanmar and a *taingyintha*. Nonetheless, perhaps unsurprisingly, nationalists (and some commentators) have been reluctant to accept Buchanan's work as evidence for Rohingya indigeneity. They instead argue that Buchanan recorded meeting with a group identifying only their place of origin rather than their ethnic identity.[12] This is a mistaken reading of Buchanan's work that is only possible by ignoring Buchanan's own efforts to pre-empt such errors – he made clear Rovingaw referred to the place of origin, while Rooinga referred to the group. This highlights the way clear documentary evidence of Rohingya indigeneity is readily brushed aside by nationalists and others keen to diminish the strength of the Rohingya's contemporary rights claims.

Debate about the meaning of Buchanan's work has often focused solely on his publications, but these represent only a small subset of the information he gathered and recorded. The Rohingya's case for recognition as a *taingyintha* is further strengthened by Buchanan's unpublished material. Buchanan's many manuscripts, reports and letters are available in the EIC's archive held at the British Library. Among kilometres of shelves housing EIC documents are considerable archives of Buchanan's research, including copies of his journal from the Ava mission. These manuscripts, when read in tandem with Buchanan's published work, clarify his understanding that the Rooinga he identified represented a well-established population in eighteenth-century Arakan.

In his journal entitled *Journal of Progress and Observations During the Continuance of the Deputation from Bengal to Ava in 1795 in the Dominions of the Barma Monarch*, Buchanan did not distinguish between the legitimacy of Arakan's Buddhist and Muslim populations – for him, they were equally settled communities. His manuscripts indicate these views were based on conscientious research. He met with numerous people from Arakan and developed a detailed knowledge of the land and its people. His understanding and description of Rooinga as a discrete language, for instance, was informed by the Bengali-speaking servants from Chittagong with whom he travelled. They would certainly have noticed the difference between Bengali-dialect speakers from Arakan and those from elsewhere. Buchanan additionally recorded being able to fact-check his research with local English-speaking authorities, including gathering information from at least one English-speaking trader, Mr Beaudre, whose business had been in the independent Arakan kingdom and who continued to trade there after the Burmese annexation.

Buchanan's previously unpublished journal explains that both Rovingaw and Rooinga were recorded in the dialect of the Bengali language that he identified as

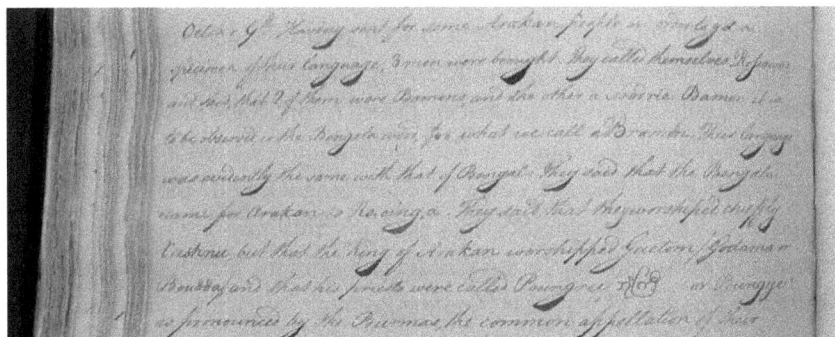

Figures 2 & 3 East India Company employee Francis Buchanan visited Burma in 1795 and identified Rooinga as a Bengali language name for Arakan.

Rooinga. He further noted how, while staying at the then Burmese capital, Amarapura (near modern Mandalay), he met with a group of men from Arakan (who had likely been deported by the conquering Burmese). They were Hindus who he portrayed as having been formerly 'long settled' in Arakan and calling themselves Rossawns. Buchanan recorded how, 'They said that the Bengala name for Arakan is Ro.oing,a.'[13] Buchanan clearly presented the Rooinga as a Muslim group from Arakan whose identity derived from their place of residence, Rovingaw. Both names – Rooinga and Rovingaw – are indicative of the group's indigeneity.

Buchanan identified Rooinga and Rovingaw as deriving from a Bengali dialect, although he did not address their etymology. However, clues about this can be found in Buchanan's identification of Rovingaw as a reference to the land of Arakan. A compelling explanation is that Rooinga and Rovingaw both derived from local names for Arakan's Mrauk-U or Mrohaung dynasty. Arakan, like Burma, was often identified by the name of its ruling dynasty or capital. It is plausible that Arakan's Bengali-speaking Muslims, over time, corrupted the Mrauk-U/Mrohaung name to an approximation of the Rovingaw or Rooinga identified by Buchanan in the late eighteenth century, and that this has evolved into the contemporary Rohingya name. At the time of Buchanan's writing, a proximate English language description might have been 'Arakan Muslim' or simply 'Arakanese', although Buchanan made clear the Bengali name, Rooinga, was applied only to Muslims, so there was a clear religious specificity to the label. A further possibility is that Rooinga or Rovingaw derived from the Arabic or Persian name for Mrauk-U/Mrohaung – Rohang – as some Rohingya leaders have also indicated.

Buchanan's published and unpublished accounts, when considered together, present a compelling case for the origin of the Rohingya designation and greatly strengthen contemporary Rohingya claims to indigeneity. They provide an explanation for why subsequent British records did not record Arakan's Muslim community as *Rooinga*, instead using various labels including Arakanese Muslim, Musalman and Mohammadan. British records were made in the English language, not Bengali (or Burmese, Rakhine or Rooinga). Consequently, Bengali-derived names like Rooinga would have been anglicized by the British for the purposes of record-keeping. So, while Arakan's Muslims were not identified as Rooinga in British census reports, this did not mean the British were unfamiliar with their Rooinga identity. Far from the Rooinga designation being unknown to the British who administered Arakan as some commentators have asserted, most nineteenth-century British administrators, especially those working in Arakan, were likely familiar with Buchanan's work, including his references to the Rooinga.[14] In modern times scholars have come to rely on Buchanan's published and easily accessible work, yet his unpublished reports – including his Rooinga references – would certainly have been known to British colonial administrators, for whose benefit they were written.

Throughout my research, Buchanan's Rooinga meeting was referenced frequently by Rohingya as proof of Rohingya residency in Myanmar prior to

1823 and of the group's indigeneity and entitlement to be considered a *taingyintha*. An explanation for the contemporary Rohingya's reliance on Buchanan's account can of course be found in Myanmar's citizenship laws, which privilege indigeneity (these laws are examined in detail in Chapter Three). Importantly, Buchanan referenced a Rooinga group he understood to be native or indigenous to Arakan and speakers of a Bengali dialect that he identified as the Rooinga language. This represents the oldest documentary evidence for the origins of a specific Rohingya name and identity, and clearly points to the group being resident in pre-colonial Burma. Rather than accepting that Buchanan's Rooinga represented the forebears of the contemporary Rohingya (and were a *taingyintha* with their own language who were resident in Burma before 1823), nationalists and commentators have rejected this seemingly obvious reading of Buchanan's work. This highlights the bind the contemporary Rohingya often find themselves in – every piece of evidence about their claim to indigeneity is scrutinized very differently to the histories of other groups and seemingly incontrovertible evidence is rejected.

Vocal critics of the Rohingya's reliance on Buchanan's writings have included academic Jacques Leider, Rakhine nationalist author Khin Maung Saw, and ex-British diplomat and commentator Derek Tonkin. For Leider, the lack of alternative British era references to Rooinga or Rohingya contributed to his criticism of the contemporary Rohingya's reliance on Buchanan's account.[15] Leider ignores the obvious anglicization of names like Rooinga by British administrators to English language variants such as Arakan Mohammadan or Arakan Muslim. Rohingya leaders claim a centuries-long heritage in Arakan, but Leider has painted Rohingya identity as a mostly 1950s creation that is a 'political project of the Rohingyas' rather than a legitimate Myanmar ethnic minority like the Chin, Karen or Rakhine.[16] Leider has curiously argued that the Rohingya name was 'unfamiliar to large parts of the Muslim community of Arakan that it is supposed to name', and suggested the way the word Rohingya 'is used today by some members of the Muslim community in Rakhaing State to refer to themselves is of a fairly recent origin. Most Muslims in Rakhaing State – which includes many non-Rohingya Muslims – do not like or use the term'.[17] These are extraordinary claims that warrant evidence – Leider provided little to back his assertions, which are wildly at odds with my own research among the Rohingya community. While I found some Rohingya might, in a desperate effort to protect their basic rights, be flexible about the name applied to their group, the overwhelming majority expressed a strong desire to be known as Rohingya. Leider's assertions about Rakhine state Muslims' dislike of the Rohingya name appear to be based more on his own rejection of the name.

Rakhine nationalist author Khin Maung Saw has been similarly critical of contemporary Muslims' use of the Rohingya name.[18] His extreme views greatly undermine his scholarly credibility. Khin Maung Saw's extreme attitudes towards the Rohingya are evidenced by the cover art of his book *Behind the Mask: The Truth Behind the Name 'Rohingya'*, which features a demon-like red-eyed beast removing a blank mask – presumably to warn that acceptance of Rohingya identity and rights claims would be extremely dangerous. This represents the kind of dehumanizing narrative that paints Rohingya as a danger to Myanmar's national fabric and gives licence to rights abuses against them. Nonetheless, Khin Maung Saw's writings have been approvingly referenced by prominent commentators, including Derek Tonkin, and used as well by Leider. Like Leider, Khin Maung Saw argues that the use of the Rohingya name represents a 'hijacking' or 'kidnapping' of 'the name of the real natives of Arakan (Rakhaings) in Bengali language'. In a somewhat contradictory manner, he has also argued, 'The term "Rohingya" is neither a name of an ethnic group nor a historical name, instead the name was invented for the sake of a political movement and to define a political movement.'[19] Even with clear evidence that a substantial and well-integrated Muslim population lived in Arakan before British rule, Rakhine nationalists like Khin Maung Saw, and some scholars, do not accept that Rohingya are a Myanmar *taingyintha*. They instead present Rohingya identity as a relatively modern, mostly post-Second World War creation, and that Rohingya leaders have used what they regard as tenuous links to Buchanan's Rooinga to legitimize their group's claim to indigenous citizenship rights. They are sceptical too about the likelihood that the modern Rohingya population in Rakhine state, which was estimated to have numbered around 1.29 million at the time of the 2014 census, could have grown from the Muslim population believed to be living in Arakan at the time of the British takeover without large-scale immigration in the intervening period. However, the historical record indicates the opposite and points to a Rohingya population in Arakan with a strength that has remained consistent between the early colonial period and modern times.

Arakan's pre-colonial population

Arakan had regularly dominated areas north of the Naf River, including Chittagong, and Arakan's capital at Mrauk-U had grown into a thriving and populous city. Visiting Mrauk-U in the early seventeenth century, Portuguese missionary Sebastião Manrique documented a city of around 160,000 people.[20]

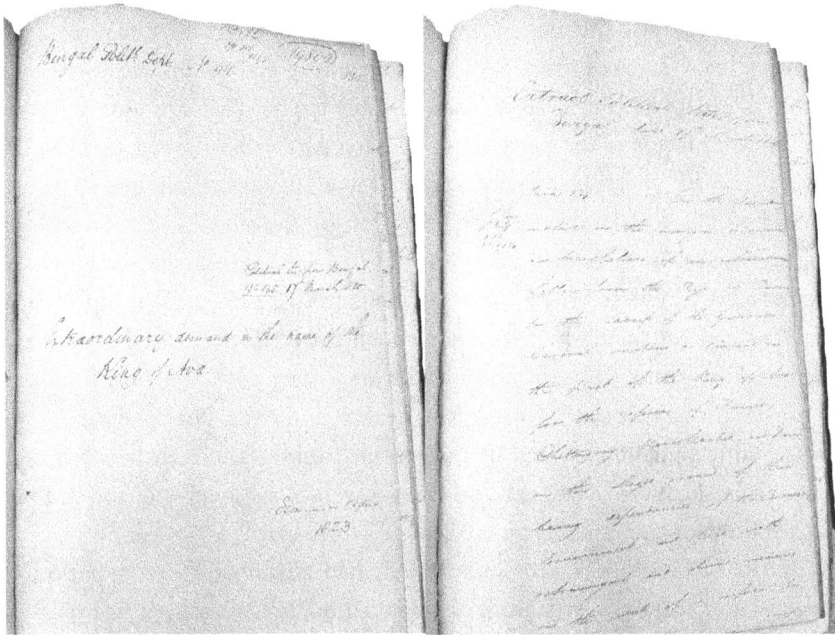

Figure 4 In 1823, the East India Company recorded Burma's demand for the cession of Arakan's former possessions north of the Naf River, including Chittagong and Dacca.

A VOC employee, Wouter Schouten, depicted Arakan in 1660 as heavily populated and the city of Mrauk-U as larger than Amsterdam, then a city home to around 200,000 people.[21] By the seventeenth century, Arakan was in economic and political decline, losing Chittagong to the Mughals in 1666 before being annexed by Burma in 1784. By then, the EIC had established effective company rule in India, made its capital at Calcutta, and considered territory to the north and west of the Naf River to be its own. The Arakanese, having ceded their northern possessions, including Chittagong, only relatively recently because of military defeat, maintained a claim to lands north of the Naf. This claim was subsequently reiterated by the Burmese after the 1784 invasion of Arakan.[22] In 1799, the EIC recorded 'Inroads made by a body of the Burmah troops into Chittagong under pretence of seizing the emigrants who had fled to that country from Arracan.'[23]

Myanmar's authorities today reject citizenship claims by people believed to have ancestry from the north of the Naf River (which forms much of Myanmar's frontier with Bangladesh), although when the Burmese kingdom invaded Arakan the case was different. Burmese officialdom strongly asserted their claim as the rightful rulers of former Arakanese territory and considered the people living there to be Burmese subjects.[24] This territorial claim was a major contributing factor to the outbreak of the first Anglo-Burma War in 1824, the start of a series of conflicts that would lead to all of Burma falling into British hands by 1885.[25] Arakan and Bengal being part of the same jurisdiction with no international frontier between them would be repeated just four decades after the Burmese conquest. British victory in the first Anglo-Burma War in 1826 and the *Treaty of Yandabo*, which formally ended the conflict, resulted in Arakan's incorporation into EIC-controlled India and later into the British Indian administrative apparatus.[26] Once again, Arakan and Bengal became part of the same political jurisdiction and their residents could move freely between each place. This situation continued until Burma gained its independence in 1948, broken only for a period during the Second World War.

By the late eighteenth century Arakan had already suffered a period of political and economic decline and its population had fallen from its Mrauk-U dynasty peaks. Burmese rule in Arakan was harsh and contributed to further population decline as Arakan's residents sought to avoid punitive taxation, forced labour or deportation to the Burmese capital. Arakan's new Burmese rulers forcibly resettled tens of thousands to Burma proper. Scholars have chronicled how the Burmese deported Arakan's political and cultural elite to their capital at Amarapura, and that deportations to Upper Burma for forced labour precipitated an exodus to Bengal.[27] Rakhine nationalist writer Aye Chan believed, 'A considerable portion of the Arakanese population was deported by Burmese conquerors to Central Burma. When the British occupied Arakan, the country was a scarcely populated area.'[28] These forced migrants likely included many of those Buchanan met when accompanying Symes on the 1795 mission.

Historian Michael Charney estimated that because of Burma's invasion, between twenty to twenty-five per cent of Arakan's population migrated north of the Naf River.[29] EIC officials in Chittagong reported how refugees from Arakan – Buddhists and Muslims – had been 'impelled by acts of oppression and cruelty in their own country'.[30] In 1800, an EIC *Report on the State of the Colony of Arracan Emigrants in Chittagong* described how,

> ...from twenty to thirty thousand of these unfortunate people claimed the protection of the Company. Both policy and humanity required that they should

not be compelled to return to Arracan, we therefore entirely approve of their having been formed into a colony, with certain portions of waste or forest lands appropriated to them for the purpose of being brought into a state of cultivation, previously supplying them with rice for their sustenance, and with implements of husbandry to enable them to procure subsistence for themselves, with an exception from the payment of any rent for the space of three years.[31]

With the EIC having estimated that as many as 30,000 people sought their protection in the aftermath of the Burmese invasion, this would have placed Arakan's pre-invasion population at between 120,000 and 150,000 people. Leider meanwhile has suggested that both the number seeking refuge and the pre-invasion population of Arakan might have been much larger than Charney or the EIC themselves estimated, believing 80,000 people may have fled from a pre-invasion population of between 250,000 to 300,000 people.[32]

Buchanan's unpublished manuscripts also indicate the presence of a substantially sized Muslim community in Arakan in the late eighteenth century. He recorded meeting with an Arakan Buddhist who identified as a 'Yakain' (Rakhine) and illustrated the differences between Buddhists and Muslims in Arakan, describing 'vast numbers' of Muslims settled there:

> A vast number of Musselmans and Hindus from Bengal have settled in Arakan, they call Yakain kula probably adopting their own phrase of Kulaadami or black man, as the natives of Hindoostan are more swarthy than the inhabitants of these countries. Great numbers of both kinds of Yakain have, since the conquest been dispersed through the Empire.[33]

Two centuries ago, Buchanan recorded 'kula' as a description to differentiate Bamar and Yakain from others. Buchanan described how the term Kula was then applied – 'Kŭlá. This includes all the people from Hindoostan, Europeans, Hindoos, Armenians, Moormen & Shan.'[34] The kalar term has come to be used in Myanmar as a slur, often against darker skinned people, Muslims and those perceived to have Indian heritage. In 2020, Myanmar anti-racism activists, inspired by the Black Lives Matter movement, launched the social media campaign 'Don't call me Kalar' to curtail the term's use.

Colonial Arakan

Border disputes between the Burmese and the British festered, and in 1824, within four decades of invading Arakan, the Burmese were engaged in the first of three Anglo-Burma wars. Burmese defeat in the first conflict and the ceding of Arakan to the British in 1826 marked the beginning of more than a century of British colonial influence over Burma. In the distant future, ethnic groups considered to have been resident in Burma prior to the start of this war would be considered a *taingyintha* and entitled to group rights to Myanmar citizenship. This ensured that the consequences of Arakan's history of migration – trader settlement, forced migrations of slaves, voluntary migrations encouraged once the British took control and numerous movements of refugees in the wake of conflict – would continue to be influencing life in Rakhine state, and the region, nearly 200 years later. As I address in Chapter Three, Myanmar's privileging of groups recognized as indigenous makes it important for the Rohingya to be recognized as a *taingyintha* in order to claim group citizenship rights. To do that they must demonstrate that their ancestors were resident within the borders of the country before 1823. In the Rohingya's case, much of the debate about the legitimacy of their claim to indigeneity has centred around questions of British colonial era migration and whether there was an established Muslim population in pre-colonial Arakan that could account for the size of the contemporary Rohingya population in Rakhine state.

Burma's forces lost all three wars with the British, and following each relinquished swathes of territory to British control. Defeat in the third war saw the entire country's sovereignty ceded to the British, who governed Burma as a province of British India from their capital in Calcutta and later Delhi.[35] For Burmese Buddhists, the ultimate humiliation was the abolition of the monarchy and the exiling of the last Konbaung king, Thibaw Min, to India.[36] Burma's Buddhist kings had served important symbolic and practical roles as patrons of Buddhism. The removal of Thibaw and his family from the palace grounds by bullock cart represented a serious religious snub.[37] The monarchy's abolition was a spiritual and political destabilization that created a significant legitimacy vacuum which the colonial British administration never adequately filled.

Burmese pride was greatly bruised by these military and political reversals. The country's Buddhist majority were often resentful of their British rulers and of those perceived to have benefited from British rule. In recent times the Rohingya and other Muslim groups in Myanmar have borne the brunt of this bitterness. Animosity was fuelled by often valid perceptions that the British administration privileged those of Indian origin, frequently Muslims with darker skin than the country's Buddhists, for plum jobs within the colonial apparatus.[38] The British considered Burma underpopulated for their commercial purposes, imported large numbers of administrators and encouraged the inward migration of low-income labourers from the Indian subcontinent who undercut the wages of locals. Indian moneylenders arrived too. Through loan defaults Indians became major landowners in colonial Burma, contributing to the economic alienation of the indigenous population from their ancestral lands.[39] This experience of colonial-era migration contributed to attitudes that persist to contemporary times that Indian, often Muslim, migrants flooded colonial Burma and subsequently gained economic advantage over the mostly Buddhist indigenous population. These narratives contribute greatly to the ethnic and religious tensions in modern Myanmar.

There have been differing estimates of Arakan's pre-1823 population, and these have been reflected in differences of opinion about the relative size of Arakan's Muslim population at that time. In 1826, British Sub-Commissioner of Arakan Charles Paton's *A Short Report on Arakan* claimed Arakan's total population to be around 100,000 people rather than the more than 200,000 people Leider suggested might have been living there immediately before the Burmese conquest. Paton's 1826 report estimated Arakan's Muslims to account for 'three-tenths' of the total population.[40] He wrote, 'The population of *Aracan* and its dependencies, *Ramree*, *Cheduba*, and *Sandoway*, does not, at present, exceed a hundred thousand souls, and may be classed as follows: Mugs, six-tenths. Musselmans, three-tenths. Burmese, one-tenth.'[41] This figure is close to the proportion of Muslims estimated to be living in Rakhine state when the 2014 census was undertaken almost 200 years later.[42] Paton made efforts to ensure the accuracy of his estimates, and first undertook 'a tour made through its [Arakan's] several subdivisions, and such communication, with the people of the country, as an imperfect command of the language would permit'. The British colonial practice of identifying populations using inconsistent and changeable labels was displayed in Paton's work – he identified just three major groups in Arakan, conflated ethnic and religious groups, and used the term 'Mug', which would today be regarded as a pejorative description for ethnic Rakhine. Paton noted too how Arakan's Muslims spoke a dialect similar to southern Chittagonian:

> The Musselman Sirdars generally speak good Hindustani, but the lower orders of that class, who speak a broken sort of Hindustani, are quite unintelligible to those who are not thoroughly acquainted with the jargon of the southern part of the Chittagong district. The universal language of the provinces is the Mug, which, although differing in some respects from the Burma, particularly in pronunciation, is written and spelt in the same way.[43]

This was likely the dialect of Bengali referred to by Buchanan when he identified Arakan's *Rooinga* group – an antecedent of the modern Rohingya language.

Some scholars have been sceptical of Paton's population figures, pointing to a lower estimate for the proportion of Muslims in Arakan made in 1841 by colonial administrator Arthur Phayre.[44] Phayre's *Account of Arakan* indicated that Arakan's Muslims made up less than fifteen per cent of the total population.[45] This was consistent with the first British census undertaken in 1872, which indicated an Arakanese Muslim population of a little more than thirteen per cent.[46] Of course, for Phayre and the 1872 census to have been accurate, Paton's population estimates made decades earlier do not need to have been inaccurate. Indeed, the British undertook an enumeration for tax purposes in 1829, three years after Paton's report, which indicated Arakan's population was 121,288 – a figure clearly consistent with Paton's earlier estimate, strengthening the credibility of his research about the size and make up of Arakan's population.[47] Paton's estimates strengthen contemporary Rohingya assertions that the proportion of Muslims in Rakhine state in modern times has changed little from the one-third of the population Paton reported as Muslim in 1826. There were certainly demographic changes in Arakan in the decades immediately following Paton's report, and these changes overwhelmingly involved the arrival of Buddhists, which consequently diluted the proportion of Muslims in Arakan by the time of Phayre's visit and the 1872 census.

The administration's enumerations for tax purposes, as well as censuses, clearly demonstrated that a Buddhist influx rather than Muslim immigration was the cause of much of Arakan's nineteenth-century population increase. The 1872 census report clarified this:

> There is not a doubt that on the acquisition in 1826 of Arakan and Tenasserim there must have been a great influx of immigrants from the intervening province of Pegu [Bago], as exemplified by the rapid increase of population in Arakan, and people who had fled to the Chittagong and other neighbouring districts consequent on Burmese oppression in Arakan previous to the first Burmese war, must have returned to their homes; but the great bulk must have come in between 1826 and 1832. From 121,288 in 1829, the population increased to 195,107 in 1832, or 60.86 per cent in four years . . .[48]

Population data compiled by the British administration in the half century prior to the 1872 census reflected this too, with the greatest proportional increases in Arakan's population consistently being in the southern parts of the state where the Muslim population was smallest. Sandoway district's population increased by 43.4 per cent between 1832 and 1842, by 55 per cent between 1842 and 1852, 24 per cent between 1852 and 1862 (when parts of Sandoway were temporarily transferred to another division), and by 57.98 per cent between 1862 and 1872. By comparison, throughout the same periods, Akyab (Sittwe) district (albeit starting with a larger population), where most of Arakan's Muslims lived, increased by just 18.6 per cent (1832–1842), 55 per cent (1842–1852), 12.67 per cent (1852–1862) and 23 per cent (1862–1872).[49] This evidence indicates that while many who fled the Burmese conquest returned to Arakan after the British took control, the defining demographic feature of nineteenth century Arakan was an influx of Buddhists from east of the Arakan Yoma into southern Arakan.

Arakan's biggest demographic shock during the first half century of British rule, between 1826 and the 1870s, involved a flood of Buddhists into the division. This runs contrary to nationalist narratives about Muslim migrants swamping the country once the colonial British arrived. A consequence of disputes about the meaning and reliability of demographic data from the colonial period is that today, rather than resolving arguments about the complexion of Arakan's nineteenth-century population, they contribute to them. Two contested demographic issues have key relevance for the Rohingya's contemporary claims – the size of Arakan's population when the British took control, and the relative strength of the then Muslim population. Estimates of Arakan's early 1820s population have ranged from around 120,000 to 300,000, and estimates of the proportion of Muslims living in Arakan in the early years of EIC control range from the low teens to thirty per cent.

Importantly, considering Myanmar's legal reliance on indigeneity, there was widespread acknowledgement by the colonial British of the indigeneity of Arakan's Muslim population. Arakan was the only place in Burma where the British considered a Muslim group to have been indigenous: 'Mahomedans, as noticed below, are indigenous only in Arakan, where two-thirds of the total number for the province reside.'[50] All of Arakan's Muslims were identified in the 1872 census as 'indigenous', with the census including them in the section 'Nationalities and Races of the People' and reporting that,

> There is one more race which has been so long in the country that it may be called indigenous, and that is the Arakanese Mussulman. These are descendants partly of voluntary immigrants at different periods from the neighbouring province of Chittagong, and partly of captives carried off in the wars between the Burmese and their neighbours. There are some 64,000 of them in Arakan,

differing from the Arakanese but little, except in their religion and the social
customs which their religion directs.[51]

The 1881 census similarly acknowledged that, 'there is an indigenous Mahomedan
population in Arakan'.[52] This evidence points to a substantial Muslim minority
having been present in pre-colonial Arakan – and Buchanan's unpublished
journal indicated that this group identified as *Rooinga*.

The principal explanations for Arakan's Muslim population at that time were:
organic growth as Islam spread geographically from west to east through
conversion and migration; a Muslim population who settled in Arakan to
facilitate maritime trade or because of shipwreck; involuntary migrants
taken to Arakan as slaves; and the settlement of mercenaries. Similar factors
that brought Islam to Arakan contributed to a local population mix that
included large numbers of people with Indo-Aryan heritage. This process
would have been aided by the long periods of Arakanese control of lands to the
north and west of the Naf River, including Chittagong, that today form part of
Bangladesh.

The early decades of British administration were provided by the EIC, whose
interests were overwhelmingly commercial. Working to maximize financial
returns from territories under its control, the EIC sought to greatly expand
the area of Arakan's land under agriculture. The EIC regarded Arakan as
underpopulated for its commercial purposes and they encouraged the inward
migration of agricultural labourers, administrators and other workers from
Burma proper and from the subcontinent to fulfil its administrative and
economic requirements.[53] There is little dispute that both Burma's overall
population and its Muslim population increased greatly in the British colonial
era, and that much of this is attributable to migration. This was particularly
evident from the latter part of the nineteenth century, when Indian migrants
began to dominate cities like Rangoon (Yangon).[54] In Arakan, Muslim agricultural
labourers frequently stayed only for the harvest season, returning to their homes
north of the Naf River before the authorities undertook enumerations that
would have required them to pay annual taxes. Arakan had a centuries-long
history as a multi-religious polity – Burma proper was not so accustomed to
Muslim influence. For the millennium prior, freedom of movement between
Arakan and Bengal had been the rule, rather than the exception. The political
consequences of colonial era migration still reverberate in Myanmar more than
a century later, and have contributed greatly to nationalist fears about the
encroachment of Islam into Myanmar's Buddhist character.

After the 1872 census and the influx of Buddhists into Arakan, some among the Chittagonian agricultural labourers who had been annually returning to work Arakan's harvest began to settle permanently. Contemporary Rohingya leaders have contended that the bulk of those settlers were descendants of Arakan natives that fled the Burmese conquest, and so indigenous. Nineteenth- and early twentieth-century migration was legal, although nationalists have not accepted the legitimacy of Muslim migration to Arakan over that time. Significantly, temporary agricultural labourers were predominantly male. A 1941 British report on Indian immigration identified a nationwide 'acute disequilibrium due to the presence of a large excess of immigrant males'.[55] The disparity would have been less in places with a fully settled population such as among Arakan's Muslims. Over time, a number of temporary agricultural workers settled in Arakan permanently. Data from the 1931 census pointed to a striking difference between Arakan's male and female 'Indian' population (as Arakan's Muslims and Hindus had been labelled by British administrators). Just seven per cent of Arakan's 'Indian' women had been born outside of Burma, with the figure for men exceeding forty per cent – an indication of the inward migration of male labourers.[56] Of course, even as legal arrivals, the gendered nature of this immigration would have important consequences for the migrants' descendants. As will be outlined in Chapter Three, because Myanmar's citizenship laws privilege membership of indigenous groups, the children of male colonial era migrants whose mothers were likely to have been from the overwhelmingly locally born female Arakanese Muslim population would be indigenous, and thus entitled to citizenship rights.

One perspective presented by both nationalists and ordinary Myanmar residents is that the ancestors of Muslims today identifying as Rohingya arrived throughout the nineteenth and twentieth centuries with the encouragement of the country's British colonial rulers and so cannot be regarded as indigenous.[57] Rohingya authors frequently avoid discussion of the migration that occurred in this era, and whether these migrants were temporary or permanently settled there is disputed.[58] Historians like Mohammed Yunus in *A History of Arakan (Past & Present)* suggested that many colonial era Muslim arrivals were actually returning residents who fled Arakan in 1784.[59] Rohingya historian and political leader Kyaw Min claimed colonial migrants were mostly seasonal labourers who never took permanent residence, instead returning home when their job was complete.[60] Virtually all colonial migration was legal, so any arrivals from Bengal came to Arakan or Burma proper legally and had a right to remain indefinitely. Today their descendants ought to be citizens of Myanmar, and because of the gendered nature of colonial migration are likely also descended from the indigenous Muslim population.

Colonial era migration did create tensions in Burma. Government administrators of Indian origin, frequently Muslim and ethnic Bengali, were considered to occupy a higher place in the British colonial pecking order than members of the country's other ethnic groups, and this contributed to an animosity towards them from both the Bamar and Rakhine Buddhist communities that persists to contemporary times. Indian Chettiar moneylenders were deliberately encouraged to migrate to Britain's new Burmese territories to help provide the capital necessary to improve the under-developed agricultural sector. Economic adviser to Aung San Suu Kyi, Sean Turnell, writing with Alison Vicary argued that the Chettiars were crucial to the transformation of Burma into the 'rice bowl of Asia'. They outline how because of loan defaults and land confiscations Chettiars would become 'widely demonised and made scapegoats for the vices of colonialism'.[61] The International Crisis Group recounted how this Indian group was considered to have taken advantage of Burma's Buddhist population, and became 'particularly hated figures' that were widely reviled, providing more fuel for anti-Indian and anti-foreigner attitudes.[62] Anti-foreigner attitudes contributed to the outbreak of violence in Rangoon (Yangon) in the 1920s, 1930s and early 1940s. Nyi Nyi Kyaw set out the anti-Muslim character of this violence, which has commonly been characterized as anti-Indian.[63] By the 1930s, these animosities were exacerbated by the severe economic pressures caused by the Great Depression. In one instance, in May 1930, low wages paid to Indian dock workers led to industrial action, the use of Bamar strike breakers and consequent violence between these groups. Charney identified how other factors, including the arrest in India of Mahatma Gandhi and the authorities' slow response to an earthquake that had struck Rangoon at that time, contributed to a combustible political atmosphere that ultimately led to riots.[64]

The British administration appointed a commission of inquiry to examine Indian immigration, led by colonial official James Baxter. Baxter's *Report on Indian Immigration* was published in 1941, and again clearly identified the indigenous nature of Arakan's Muslims. The report made numerous references to 'indigenous Mohamedans in the Arakan Division' and noted early on that, 'There was an Arakanese Muslim community settled so long in Akyab District that it has for all intents and purposes to be regarded as an indigenous race.'[65] Despite this, the report's methodology defined 'Indian' broadly to include most of Burma's Hindus and Muslims. This reflected the way British colonial administrators had from the late nineteenth century enthusiastically embraced methods of classification of people that would be rejected by former colonial powers today. Unfortunately, similar attitudes towards the classification of people have endured in former colonial dominions like Myanmar.

Baxter's report has sometimes been misrepresented as problematizing migration into Arakan – it did not, although Baxter did recognize the pressures to restrict immigration throughout Burma. Baxter pointed to the settled nature of Arakan's Muslim (and small Hindu) community, noting the high proportion of 'Indians' in Arakan born in Burma – nearly seventy-seven per cent – compared with the just twenty-seven per cent for Indians living elsewhere in Lower Burma.[66] The descendants of this population should today be entitled to Myanmar citizenship rights. Importantly, the report acknowledged as well that immigrants to Burma were predominantly male. Expressing sentiments that are familiar eighty years later, the report noted, 'In this country for generations Burmans and Indians have grown up side by side, joint contributors to a progressive economic development.'[67] The report's recommendations focused on streamlining immigration processes, giving certainty – and documentation – to Indians who had permanently settled in Burma. Had Baxter's recommendations been implemented, there is a chance the Rohingya's plight today might not be so bleak, but within months of the report's publication, war had broken out. Japanese bombing raids of Rangoon began, and Aung San's Burma Independence Army moved through the country claiming territory from the British. By mid-1942 the British colonial administration had retreated *en masse* to India.[68]

Today, ethnic Bamar commonly regard Aung San as the father of Myanmar's independence. When I travelled around Myanmar his image, dressed in the overcoat gifted to him by Jawaharlal Nehru and worn to the post-war independence negotiations in London, was frequently proudly displayed in homes, tea shops and taxis. Although Aung San is revered by Bamar for the pivotal role he played in achieving independence, his actions made him a controversial figure among the country's ethnic minorities. Aung San's politics were changeable, and he was at various times in his life a communist and a social democrat, and cooperated with the fascist Japanese and colonial British. He was made a Major General by the Japanese military and is often known by the Burmese honorific *Bogyoke* (General), which has become something of a nickname. He has been labelled a revolutionary nationalist, and Aung San Suu Kyi described her father as a man of 'strong character who led his country to independence with single-mindedness and a high sense of purpose'. These are adjectives that might easily be applied to Aung San Suu Kyi's political approach today. She acknowledged 'Accusations of ruthless ambition, unreasonableness, and duplicity' (criticisms that might likewise be made of Aung San Suu Kyi), but these claims are brushed aside as unfair criticisms made by those who 'saw his fight against the foreign rulers of his country as "treachery"'.[69]

Ethnic minorities, particularly wartime supporters of the British rather than the Japanese, recall atrocities committed against their people by Aung San's Burma Independence Army and their Japanese bosses. Myanmar's ethnic minorities have increasingly come to regard Aung San as symbolizing the Bamar-dominated central authorities' policies of Burmanization and aggressive Tatmadaw military actions against minority communities that treat their refusal to submit to Bamar hegemony as disloyalty to the nation.[70] In recent years, activists in Chin, Kayah and Mon states have resisted the erection of statues of Aung San, which they believe represent cultural violence and symbols of Bamar supremacy that diminish the historic achievements and political legitimacy of Myanmar's ethnic minorities.[71] In 1947, as the country stood on the threshold of independence, Aung San and six members of his cabinet were assassinated by a political rival.[72] This tragedy denied the country important political leadership at the time of its independence, undermined its nascent democracy, and contributed to the Tatmadaw's entry into politics and the subsequent decades of brutal military rule. Myanmar's residents commonly believe military rule could have been avoided had Aung San not been gunned down. Consequently, much of Aung San Suu Kyi's early political legitimacy, particularly among the Bamar majority, derived from her father's wartime reputation as a hero of the independence movement.

The legacy of the Second World War continues to have a strong influence on the politics of Rakhine state. During the war, Arakan's Muslim population generally supported the British, and Rakhine Buddhists and Bamar supported General Aung San's Burmese nationalists and, consequently, the Japanese.[73] A power vacuum left by the retreating British – all effective state authority collapsed – was exploited to aggressively settle old scores, and significant inter-communal violence became a feature of wartime life.[74] There are conflicting accounts of what occurred, and both the Rohingya and Rakhine claim their people were the victims of violence at the hands of the other that caused the deaths of tens of thousands from each community.[75] Estimates place the death toll at around 100,000, with hundreds of villages destroyed.[76] A key demographic consequence of this violence was the mass movement of people within Arakan. By the war's end, Muslims were living mostly in Arakan's north, and Buddhists in the south. This settlement pattern endured, and in contemporary Rakhine state Buddhist and Muslim communities are commonly geographically separated. In the decades following the war, and with Buddhist and Muslim communities leading overwhelmingly separate lives, mixing mostly in the marketplace, large parts of Rakhine state have come to resemble the plural society portrayed by colonial historian John Furnivall, where different groups mixed without merging.[77] Some scholars, including Anthony Ware and Costas Laoutides, believe serious unresolved tensions existed between Rakhine and Rohingya from the colonial period, and they present the contemporary conflict as a tripartite dispute involving the Bamar, Rakhine and Rohingya.[78] As an analytical lens, this greatly overplays the agency of Rakhine and Rohingya and minimizes the overwhelming dominance of Myanmar's central authorities. Throughout my research, principal responsibility for the Rohingya's mistreatment was clearly identifiable as Myanmar's government and military (two mostly Bamar institutions). The contemporary consequences of Rakhine–Rohingya political disputes appeared minor when compared with the government's apartheid restrictions and the Tatmadaw's semi-regular and brutal forced deportations of Rohingya civilians. Government and military mistreatment, rather than conflict with the Rakhine, will also be shown as central to the lived experiences of Rohingya victims of rights abuses that are presented in later chapters.

Wartime demographic changes have had serious consequences for the Rohingya. Dense Muslim population of Rakhine state's north, adjacent to Bangladesh, and sparse Muslim settlement in the south, have contributed to a widespread perception among Myanmar's Buddhist community that Rohingya represent a recently arrived foreign population encroaching on Myanmar's territory. In recent years, Myanmar's authorities weaponized this belief. By disregarding Arakan's longer-term settlement patterns, they have convinced many among Myanmar's Buddhist majority that Rohingya have little legitimate claim to indigeneity. Problematic too has been the physical separation of Rakhine state's Buddhist and Muslim communities. Over the course of decades this led, little by little, to increasing distrust between these communities, diminishing their shared sense of identity. The decades of physical separation that followed the war ultimately led Rakhine state's Buddhist and Muslim communities to increasingly consider each other strangers in the land they shared for centuries. Pre-colonial Arakan had been a multi-ethnic and multi-religious polity, and while differences between ethnic and religious groups became more salient under colonial rule, post-war separation greatly contributed to the development of the Rakhine and Rohingya as groups with distinct political interests. A consequence for the contemporary Rohingya has been that their exclusion from Myanmar's mainstream political life has often been achieved with the support of the ethnic Rakhine leadership.

Citizenship Laws: Making Rohingya Stateless

In Myanmar, history has a daily impact on people's lives, influencing individual and group access to citizenship and the rights and protections that should accompany it. In this chapter, I examine Myanmar's citizenship laws and practices since independence in 1948, and outline how the country's politics interacted with these laws to make the Rohingya the world's largest stateless group. Clarity about when and how the Rohingya lost their citizenship rights will help to explain whether there is a genuine legal basis for the Rohingya's collective claims to Myanmar citizenship, and to the assertion made by many Rohingya that they were acknowledged as citizens in the 1950s and have subsequently had those legal entitlements wrongly denied by the authorities. This belief has contributed to the strategy of many contemporary Rohingya leaders to focus on the strength of their historical and legal claims to Myanmar citizenship rather than adopting alternative approaches. Addressing the legal means by which the Rohingya's citizenship claims have been denied will help explain when the legal recognition of their citizenship rights ceased and whether the Rohingya's legal rights were altered solely by citizenship law changes in 1982.[1]

Since independence, Myanmar has commonly been regarded as having two citizenship regimes. These distinct legal frameworks correspond with the citizenship laws and practices built around the 1948 post-independence *Constitution of the Union of Burma* and laws, and the framework created by the post-1962 military administration, built around the 1974 Constitution, and now legally based on the *Burma Citizenship Law (1982)*, which remains in force today.[2] Each citizenship framework privileged ethnicity and indigeneity, yet they also provided avenues to citizenship based on residency. In practice, a third citizenship regime likely operated between the time of the military's 1962 *coup d'état* and the enactment of the *Burma Citizenship Law*. This accounts for how the Rohingya's collective rights were increasingly restricted throughout the 1960s and 1970s, and explains official actions around the Tatmadaw's *Nagamin* operation in the late 1970s and the authorities' subsequent reluctance to acknowledge the citizenship of Rakhine state's Muslims post *Nagamin*. This explains as well why Rohingya frequently claim they were once acknowledged as legal citizens and in many cases possess old identity documents to prove this.

Independent Burma's citizenship regime

In light of the Rohingya's present day situation, where the authorities do not consider them to be a *taingyintha*, yet Rohingya claim that members of their group were previously acknowledged as citizens, it is worth considering whether the recent ancestors of the contemporary Rohingya would have qualified for citizenship at independence in 1948 if they had come to be resident in Burma after 1823, as has often been claimed. Such an analysis is important for the citizenship claims of those identifying as Rohingya because the authorities consider their ancestors to have mostly arrived within Myanmar's borders since that time.

In 1948, the *Constitution of the Union of Burma* and the *Union Citizenship Act (1948)* together provided a range of legal pathways towards Burmese citizenship.[3] This citizenship framework recognized indigeneity but was far from exclusionary, providing multiple pathways for residents who might not be regarded as indigenous. The Constitution intended citizenship for,

> 11. (i) Every person, both of whose parents belong or belonged to any of the indigenous races of Burma; (ii) every person born in any of the territories included within the Union, at least one of whose grand-parents belong or belonged to any of the indigenous races of Burma; (iii) every person born in any of territories included within the Union, of parents both of whom are, or if they had been alive at the commencement of this Constitution would have been, citizens of the Union; (iv) every person who was born in any of the territories which at the time of his birth was included within His Britannic Majesty's dominions and who has resided in any of the territories included within the Union for a period of not less than eight years in the ten years immediately preceding the date of the commencement of this Constitution or immediately preceding the 1st January 1942 and who intends to reside permanently there in and who signifies his election of citizenship of the Union in the manner and within the time prescribed by law, shall be a citizen of the Union.[4]

Acknowledging Burma's recent wartime chaos, the constitution even ensured a pathway to citizenship for those who might have temporarily fled the country during the conflict. While most who fled Arakan during the war (Buddhists and

Muslims) would readily qualify for citizenship through other provisions of the constitution or citizenship law, this nonetheless serves to highlight the constitution's intention of making citizenship inclusive rather than limiting access to citizenship rights. The constitution also ensured that birth within Burma to parents who were (or would have been) citizens was enough to qualify an individual for citizenship (via Section 11, iii).[5] Consequently, citizenship matters should not have needed to be revisited by members of each subsequent generation – once an individual qualified for citizenship, their children, if born in Burma, were citizens. This would have been the case whether the parents' citizenship rights were derived from their lengthy residency in Burma or by virtue of their membership of an indigenous group. The constitution made no distinction in rights between citizens of the Union and did not attempt to create a citizenship hierarchy. Section 10 declared, 'There shall be but one citizenship throughout the Union; that is to say, there shall be no citizenship of the unit as distinct from the citizenship of the Union.'[6] With no hierarchy of citizenship groups all citizens were considered equal before the law, whether their citizenship entitlement was derived from indigeneity or ancestral residency.

The 1948 citizenship law made no specific accommodation for those who temporarily left the country during the war, but cast an even wider net, indicating – like the constitution – an inclusive approach to citizenship rights. Section 4.2 stated: 'Any person descended from ancestors who for two generations at least have all made any of the territories included within the Union their permanent home and whose parents and himself were born in any of such territories shall be deemed to be a citizen of the Union.'[7] This clarified that residents of Burma with three generations of ancestry there could expect to become legal citizens, and that these citizenship rights accrued regardless of whether individuals were considered members of an indigenous group. The descendants of Buchanan's Rooinga population – whether accepted as indigenous or not – would certainly have qualified for citizenship, as would virtually all colonial-era migrants. Considering their mistreatment and forced deportation by Ne Win's military government in the years that followed, it is worth noting that the 1948 Constitution and citizenship law would likely have provided Burma's long-term Chinese and Indian residents with citizenship rights.[8] The only residents of post-independence Burma clearly excluded from citizenship were non-indigenous, very recent arrivals.

The practical implications of this citizenship framework were that virtually all long-term residents of Burma at the time of independence could have been considered legal citizens. This would have included the long-term Muslim residents of Arakan division, who traced their ancestry to the pre-colonial era and from whom today's Rohingya leaders often claim their group's ancestry. It would have included as well British colonial era migrants from Bengal or other parts of the Indian subcontinent who have been described by Myanmar officials, including former president Thein Sein, as the ancestors of Rakhine state's contemporary Rohingya population.

With a widely cast citizenship net, in 1948 the constitution and associated laws nonetheless privileged members of 'indigenous races'. Section 11 (i) of the 1948 Constitution granted citizenship to children if both their parents were considered part of an 'indigenous race'. There was no requirement for the indigenous race of both parents to be the same, and neither the 1948 Constitution nor the 1948 *Union Citizenship Act* clarified what assumptions the authorities might subsequently make about the specific identity of an indigenous mixed-race resident, other than that they would likely be considered to be a member of an indigenous race. Individuals born in the territory of the new nation, meanwhile, were granted citizenship by Section 11 (ii) of the 1948 Constitution so long as they had at least one indigenous race grandparent. The matter of which groups should be considered indigenous for the purposes of Section 11 was partly clarified by the *Union Citizenship Act.*[9] This Act included a non-exhaustive list of 'indigenous races':

> For the purposes of section 11 of the Constitution the expression "any of the indigenous races of Burma" shall mean the Arakanese, Burmese, Chin, Kachin, Karen, Kayah, Mon or Shan race and such racial group as has settled in any of the territories included within the Union as their permanent home from a period anterior to 1823 A.D. (1185 B.E.).[10]

Crucially important to those groups not listed was the included caveat, 'and any such racial group as has settled in any of the territories included within the Union as their permanent home from a period anterior to 1823 A.D.' This kept open the possibility that if a group's status as a pre-1823 indigenous population could be established or simply accepted, their members could have a collective path to citizenship and so avoid the need to individually prove long-term residency in Burma.

While no majority Muslim group was explicitly named within Section 11, strong evidence indicates the authorities during the civilian government period after 1948 did consider the Rohingya to be indigenous. In Burma's first period of democratic rule (1948–1962), official acknowledgement of the Rohingya as a legitimate Burmese identity group was the norm. At that time, key national political figures, including from within the military, were comfortable acknowledging the status of the Rohingya as legitimately indigenous. Burma's post-1962 governments rejected this approach, did not treat the Rohingya as a *taingyintha* and increasingly, aggressively resisted using the Rohingya name.

Burma's first post-independence prime minister, U Nu, whose twelve years in that office between independence and Ne Win's 1962 coup make him the country's longest serving civilian leader, told a 1954 radio audience, 'The people living in Maungdaw and Buthidaung regions are our nationals, our brethren. They are called Rohingyas. They are one of the same par in status of nationality with Kachin, Kayah, Karen, Mon, Rakhine and Shan. They are one of the ethnic races of Burma.'[11] Similar attitudes were expressed by Burma's first president, Sao Shwe Thaike, who said, 'Muslims of Arakan certainly belong to the indigenous races of Burma.'[12] On that point, independent Burma's second prime minister, U Ba Swe, concurred: 'The Rohingya has the equal status of nationality with Kachin, Kayah, Karen, Mon, Rakhine and Shan.'[13] In the year immediately preceding the 1962 coup, the Rohingya language was broadcast by the Burma Broadcasting Service's radio station, and the central government acceded to Muslim demands for the creation of a special zone, centrally administered, within the promised Arakan state.

The establishment of the Mayu Frontier Administration (MFA) zone in 1961 was designed to allow northern Arakan's Muslims to be administered by the country's central authorities rather than by a majority ethnic Rakhine Buddhist administration in Akyab (Sittwe). This act of carving the Muslim-majority townships of Buthidaung, Maungdaw and parts of Rathedaung away from the locally based and overwhelmingly ethnic Rakhine administration served to reinforce ethnic Rakhine fears that a Muslim agenda included exclusive control of territory which they believed rightfully belonged to the Rakhine, and contributed to tensions between Arakan's Buddhist and Muslim communities. These fears had been given some credibility in the aftermath of the Second World War, when Muslim *Mujahideen* militants, for a time, controlled territory in northern Arakan division. Some among these militants, notably Jafar Hussain (or Jafar Kawwal), are claimed to have harboured a desire for Muslim majority areas of northern Arakan to be incorporated into Pakistan rather than remaining part of the recently independent Burma.[14]

Secession was certainly not a widespread desire among Arakan's Muslims – a point underscored in 1948 documents from Burma's Police Special Branch. Burma's police bosses in Rangoon acknowledged they had 'no coherent report' about the activities of Muslim groups in northern Arakan, and instead their assessment of Muslim politics was 'prepared from disjointed sitreps' (situation reports).[15] This assessment claimed Muslim militants, 'declared that one of the aims and objects of their movement was to demand inclusion of Buthidaung and Maungdaw in Pakistan.'[16] This official assessment appears to have been based more on supposition than evidence, because the same report included a list of claims they had actually received from Muslim militants that did not include the demand to join Pakistan. Rather, Muslims asked Burma's government to create a majority-Muslim state in northern Arakan ('similar to the Shan States in Burma') and 'To recognise all Arakanese Moslems as Burmese', indigenous like the Bamar, Shan and Kachin.[17] Tellingly, the police reported their inability to curtail militancy in Arakan: 'Due to pre-occupation elsewhere no action could be taken by the authorities to suppress the lawlessness.'[18] With Burma's central authorities believing they were losing (or had already lost) control of Arakan's borderland security, a Muslim group there making strong political claims about the newly independent country would have understandably contributed to fears about Burma's ability to maintain its territorial integrity. Concerns about containing this insurgency likely contributed to the government's decision to create the MFA in the early 1960s.

This political concession to Muslim aspirations in Arakan is noteworthy because it was an acknowledgement by the government of the legitimacy of Muslim political claims. Military figures also acknowledged the legitimacy of the Rohingya identity at that time – in a 1961 speech accepting the surrender of Muslim *Mujahid* insurgents in northern Arakan (whose political demands were seemingly adequately satisfied by the creation of the MFA), the Army's Deputy Commander-in-Chief Brigadier General Aung Gyi said,

> The people living in Mayu Frontier are Rohingya. Pakistan [now Bangladesh] is located west of Mayu Frontier and Muslims are living there. The people living in the west are called Pakistani and the people living here are called Rohingya. This is not the only border that has same people on both sides; border with China, India and Thailand also have the same phenomenon.[19]

Arakan's Muslims unquestionably had political rights in the democratic period preceding the 1962 coup, were free to vote in elections, and counted among their number elected members of Burma's parliaments, including government ministers and parliamentary secretaries.[20] Rohingya retained voting rights until their disenfranchisement by Thein Sein's government prior to the 2015 national election.

Arakan's Muslims were also uncontroversially granted identity documents and passports just like other Burmese citizens. This fact would, in later years, be a source of much frustration and confusion among older Rohingya, who considered the question of their citizenship long settled and the routine grant of National Registration Cards (NRC) and passports to be irrefutable proof of this. Rohingya frequently showed me their family documents from this era. During my 2017 visit to Bangladesh's Rohingya refugee camps, Rohingya who had recently fled Tatmadaw destruction of their villages commonly expressed frustration that their right to Myanmar citizenship was denied by the authorities who ignored their identity documents proving their legitimate citizenship claims. One older Rohingya man I met in the Kutupalong camp showed me documents including his grandfather's passport, issued in 1961, which he considered ample proof his family had already been officially acknowledged as citizens of Burma at that time. He described how his family's situation began to change after the 1962 coup, from which time the authorities rejected official documents that had acknowledged Rohingya citizenship – effectively making them stateless.[21] This was far from an isolated example and I met many camp residents who showed me official Burmese identity documents, including passports and NRCs which they hoped would one day help them regain the citizenship rights they were adamant their family members once enjoyed in Myanmar. These documents were often preserved by being wrapped in plastic to protect them through the arduous journey to Bangladesh. Considering the few possessions these refugees managed to bring with them from their homes in Myanmar, this demonstrated the importance they attached to identity documents that proved they had already been acknowledged as citizens.

There is clear evidence that in Burma's first period of democratic government the Rohingya were acknowledged as an indigenous group by government practice, by the public statements of senior national political and military leaders, and by the country's constitution and laws. The Rohingya at that time were collectively acknowledged as citizens either because they were an indigenous group, or because their residency in Burma qualified them all for citizenship rights. However, independent Burma's political situation was such in its early years that the central authorities lacked the capacity to strictly enforce law and order, let alone citizenship regulations. There are two principal explanations for this. Firstly, since the 1948 Constitution and citizenship law provided citizenship rights for virtually all who might desire to claim them, there was little necessity for the government to strictly enforce citizenship regulations. This lack of enforcement contributed, in later years, to government claims of widespread citizenship fraud and would feed official mistrust of identity documents, including NRCs. There would be a reluctance by the authorities to accept NRCs as legitimate proof of citizenship or residency, particularly where Muslims in Arakan/Rakhine were concerned. The narrative that migrants could illegally cross a porous border into Burma from East Pakistan (now Bangladesh), to escape internal conflict, natural disaster or to seek economic opportunity, persists to contemporary times and was given further credibility in the wake of the 2015 Bay of Bengal irregular migration crisis, when returned trafficker boats included some passengers originating in Bangladesh but claiming to be Rohingya.[22] Census data from the 1970s, when political conflict and natural disasters were at their most challenging in Bangladesh, demonstrated a stable population in Rakhine state, however – certainly not evidence of widespread immigration.

Secondly, the political situation within Burma in the years following independence meant the central authorities' ability to enforce laws were severely limited. The capacity of the central authorities were impaired by the requirement to maintain Burma's territorial integrity in the face of a range of interconnected conflicts with ethnic insurgents (which included both a Muslim *Mujahid* insurgency and ethnic Rakhine fighters), communist revolutionaries (there were two communist armies in Arakan), and the remnants of Republican China's *Kuomintang*, who set up camps in the north-east of Burma and were using them as staging posts to attack the new People's Republic of China government.[23] The *Kuomintang's* incursion was so destabilizing for the recently independent country that scholars, including Mary Callahan (in *Making Enemies: War and State Building in Burma*), identified it as a threat to Burma's very sovereignty.[24] The military shared this view, and this catalysed the institutionalization and professionalization of the Burma army. So serious was the threat to the central authorities' power that between 1949 and 1951 the government controlled little more than urban centres like Rangoon (Yangon).[25] Efforts to tackle the *Kuomintang* incursion, communist insurgencies and widespread ethnic conflicts gave the Tatmadaw increased authority to define who were loyal citizens of Burma and who ought to be considered the country's enemies. This was crucial power in an ethnically diverse state like Burma, and ultimately contributed to the military's consolidation of state power and takeover of government in 1962. Prior to this coup there was little warning to Arakan's Muslim community that their citizenship circumstances would be soon markedly and irrevocably changed.

The 1948 citizenship regime is widely acknowledged to have come to an end, in a legal sense, during General Ne Win's post-1962 rule. Precisely when and how this occurred is unclear. The 1982 *Burma Citizenship Law* has commonly been regarded as the most significant legal change for Arakan's Muslims, although recent scholarship has focused on the way Myanmar's polity has increasingly come to privilege matters of *taingyintha* over other factors when determining citizenship rights. *Taingyintha* is certainly central to contemporary domestic understandings of who ought to be entitled to citizenship rights in Myanmar. I believe the increasing focus on *taingyintha* might well account for why national public opinion is today opposed to the Rohingya being collectively granted citizenship rights, but this does not adequately account for how those who were acknowledged as citizens in the 1950s came to lose those rights, or when this might have occurred. Rather than focusing exclusively on the role of the *Burma Citizenship Law (1982)* as the instrument that stripped the Rohingya of their citizenship rights, I instead argue that it was decisions made early in the tenure of General Ne Win's post-1962 coup government that altered the citizenship standing of Burma's residents and effectively stripped Rohingya of the citizenship rights they had enjoyed, by law and by official practice, since independence.

Citizenship after the 1962 coup

On 2 March, 1962, Tatmadaw leaders successfully undertook a *coup d'état* and gained control of the Burmese state. Civilian politicians were variously detained, arrested or murdered. Ousted Prime Minister U Nu was held in 'protective custody' for years and President Sao Shwe Thaike died in military detention (soldiers had already shot dead his sixteen-year-old son Myee). General Ne Win was empowered at that time with all state authority – executive, legislative and judicial. Ne Win's whim could represent the law of the land.[26] His decisions about ethnic and religious issues were often motivated by xenophobia and religious prejudice, if not outright racism. The policy transformations Ne Win's government undertook had widespread and lasting consequences and a particularly negative impact on groups the authorities, and Ne Win, considered to be foreign. Most ethnic minority groups were adversely affected by the government's Burmanization policies, but it was the Indian (both Hindu and Muslim), Chinese and Anglo-Burmese communities that arguably were the key targets in the early years of military rule.

Unfortunately for the Rohingya and other ethnic minorities, Ne Win's xenophobic rule closely followed decisions made in the 1950s, after the country emerged from colonial rule, to 'reinvent' themselves, helping to reify previously loosely adopted ethnic identities and identity labels that might not have been well known in other parts of the newly independent country. This point was made to me by Harn Yawnghwe, a son of Burma's first president Sao Shwe Thaike, the last Shan hereditary ruler of the principality of Yawnghwe (based around the town of modern Nyaung Shwe on Inle Lake). His father helped draft the 1947 *Panglong Agreement*, which formed the basis of the independent Burmese state. Today, he is the Executive Director of the Euro-Burma Office, a non-profit organization working to promote the development of democracy in Myanmar, and while understandably he has little positive to say about Ne Win, his analysis of Myanmar history is nonetheless insightful. Yawnghwe told me in 2015 that,

> ... Ne Win is the ultra-nationalist. When he kicked out thousands of Indians, Hindus, Chinese, foreigners, everybody. So that mindset, I would say, gained the upper hand in the '60s and it's been here since. And it really also affects the ethnic struggle because basically, the ethnic struggle is based on rights, equal rights. And the reason they are fighting for equal rights is because the Union of Burma came into being in 1948 as a result of the '47 Panglong Conference so they feel they are equal owners so they have equal rights, but the military concept, the majority Bamar concept is that this whole nation is a continuation of Anarawtha's rule ... So, because of that, the military is the guardian of this empire, and the military is the one who decides on what happens. And so, in that sense everybody else is subordinate to the Bamar and to Buddhism. And that is the main underpinning of this military mindset.

Yawnghwe traces the roots of the Rohingya's contemporary crisis to the period of Ne Win's rule, and while we mostly discussed the formation of Shan ethnic identity, academics including Mandy Sadan have traced the reification of Kachin identity to a similar period. Sadan's *Being and Becoming Kachin: Histories Beyond the State in the Borderworlds of Burma* described the development of modern Kachin ethno-nationalism from around that time.[27] Yawnghwe suggested the politics of the 1950s led Arakan's largest Muslim group to embark on a similar process, leading to the widespread acceptance of the previously less widely used Rohingya identity label among the state's Muslim community. He told me, 'In the 50s everybody was reinventing themselves ... To me it's a right of the Rohingya to call themselves whatever they want.' He noted that in the 1950s the Rohingya were recognized as a legitimate part of Burmese society and pointed to state radio broadcasts in the Rohingya language from that time. He asked, 'In the 50s there was the Burma Broadcasting Service with the Rohingya language – if Rohingyas don't exist and they are not citizens, why did they have that?' From Yawnghwe's point of view, the Rohingya's situation changed markedly, and for the worse, under Ne Win's rule.

Ne Win's military administration treated their suspension of the 1948 Constitution as an opportunity to revisit the entire question of who ought to be considered a Burmese citizen. Since all government authority was vested in the personage of Ne Win, the administration could adopt any position it wished on citizenship matters. Ne Win could include or exclude any individual or group he wished from the citizenship framework. There is compelling evidence that from the military government's perspective, the period between the suspension of the 1948 Constitution and the enactment of a new constitution in 1974 was regarded as representing a time when the only officially acknowledged citizens were those the military administration deemed to be citizens. This was certainly how the authorities behaved. The national government did not act as though the 'existing laws' the new constitution purported to respect (by Article 145, b) included the citizenship framework created by the earlier constitution and the *Union Citizenship Act (1948)*. Instead, the coup leaders' decision to suspend the 1948 Constitution was treated as if this had erased the citizenship rights that would have accrued to Burma's residents under previous laws. I believe that this period represented a new citizenship regime that later allowed Ne Win's administration to apply the provisions of the 1974 Constitution to a virtual citizenship 'clean slate', in which Burma's residents were not able to rely upon a prior government's recognition of their citizenship rights or official identity documents to prove their citizenship entitlement. Rohingya frequently identify this period of military rule under General Ne Win as the time when their group's rights began to be eroded before being ultimately denied by the country's authorities.

The enactment of a new Burmese Constitution in 1974 should have been an indication that the citizenship framework was being altered, although where citizenship was concerned, the military's revised constitution did not appear to deviate greatly from the values underpinning the 1948 Constitution or the *Union Citizenship Act (1948)*. If anything, the military's 1974 Constitution appeared to rely less on notions of ethnicity than the previous version. Article 145 read: '(a) All persons born of parents both of whom are nationals of the Socialist Republic of the Union of Burma are citizens of the Union. (b) Persons who are vested with citizenship according to existing laws on the date this Constitution comes into force are also citizens.'[28] The implication of Article 145 (b) is that existing citizens would maintain their citizenship rights. Yet this is not how the authorities acted. Ne Win's regime did not acknowledge rights that had accrued according to the 1948 Constitution or the *Union Citizenship Act (1948)*. Instead, the government acted as though 'existing laws' noted in the new constitution were a reference to the Ne Win administration's citizenship framework – a reference to the administration's *practice* from the time of the coup and prior to the enactment of the 1974 Constitution.

In that context, the question of who was a legal citizen of Burma when the 1974 Constitution came into effect was settled by the authorities by assuming most Muslims in Rakhine state, despite holding official identity documents and having been treated as citizens by the authorities in the decades previous, were likely not citizens. People in that category would need to prove their citizenship claim again, this time based on evidence of legitimate residency and according to the 1974 Constitution's provisions (without being able to retain rights that accrued according to the 1948 framework). In practice, Arakan's Muslims would be required to make their citizenship claims without being able to use their previous Burmese citizenship (circa 1948–1962), possession of identity documents or a Burma passport as proof of their existing citizenship rights. Consequently, the claim by Rakhine state's largest Muslim group to be an indigenous group (whether called Rohingya or by an alternate name) was rejected outright by the authorities. In practice, individual claims to citizenship rights by Rakhine state Muslims were also rejected by the authorities.

Rakhine state's Muslims commonly considered that the Burmese citizenship their group had undoubtedly been entitled to from independence remained in place throughout military rule. In modern times, Rohingya will commonly refer to government practices in the 1950s and 1960s that acknowledged them as citizens, and to official documents previously issued to them or to their family members (which they frequently still possess) which they believe proved their citizenship. They believe they should still possess the citizenship rights their group accrued by virtue of the 1948 legal framework – because subsequent constitutions and laws made clear existing citizenships would be respected. This explains much of the frustration and confusion among the contemporary Rohingya community, who believe their identity documents, often granted originally under the terms of the 1948 system, continue to represent proof that the government had already accepted them as citizens. While it is true many had been accepted as citizens by the authorities, the military administration, by suspending the constitution and empowering Ne Win with all official authority, appears to have reassessed those citizenship claims.

Ne Win's administration did not explicitly state the citizenship laws had been altered, but the 1948 citizenship framework would never again provide reliable legal support for a citizenship claim by Arakan's Muslim Rohingya. The evidence that the country's existing citizenship laws (based on the *Constitution of the Union of Burma ,1948* and the *Union Citizenship Act, 1948*) had been nullified in the early years of Ne Win's post-coup rule is based on my analysis of the government's actions during that time and their consequences. There were of course inconsistencies in the policy approach adopted by the authorities during Ne Win's lengthy tenure (he continued to lead the country until the 8888 Uprising in 1988), but the examples I consider next demonstrate a pattern and present a strong case that Ne Win's administration regarded the legal citizenship status of some Burma residents to have changed after the 1962 coup and before the enactment of the 1974 Constitution.

Shortly after Burma's 1962 military *coup d'état* the authorities ended the special status of the MFA. This represented a dramatic reversal of the rights Rohingya had routinely enjoyed under Burma's civilian-era administrations. During U Nu's final years in office, Muslim political influence in Burma was strong enough that concerns about the potential for ethnic Rakhine domination of a promised state led to a political compromise – the creation of the MFA, which was expected to ensure that Muslim-majority communities in northern Arakan (the townships of Buthidaung, Maungdaw and parts of Rathedaung) would be administered by the central authorities after statehood was granted. The coup delayed statehood until 1974 and the MFA was abolished by the new military government in 1964. Historian Moshe Yegar believed the civilian administration had already drafted legislation for the creation of an Arakan state that excluded the MFA when the coup occurred in 1962.[29] However, when Arakan was granted statehood in 1974, Muslim-majority communities that were formerly part of the MFA were included within it, and were subject to a state administrative apparatus based in Akyab (Sittwe) and dominated by ethnic Rakhine. Ethnic Rakhine domination of the bureaucracy in the newly created Rakhine state had serious consequences for the Muslim community, who were often victimized by an administrative apparatus that increasingly acted as if its role was to defend ethnic Rakhine privilege against Muslim demands.

It was not only the state-level bureaucracy that undermined Rohingya rights. The national military government's policies privileged Bamar ethnicity and the Buddhist religion through a process of cultural assimilation known as Burmanization, which aimed to reinforce and privilege Bamar and Buddhist identity as the national norm.[30] The Burmanization policies undertaken by the military government frequently involved discrimination against ethnic minority groups in areas of culture, language, religion and education.[31] Onerous restrictions were placed on members of non-Bamar ethnic groups and the authorities actively silenced alternative historical narratives. Ethnic minorities frequently complained that the government prevented the teaching of their history and languages in schools, and treated overt expressions of ethnic identity such as language, dress, dance and festivals as bordering on sedition. The policies and practices of Burmanization have been widely criticized by non-Bamar ethnic groups and there is little doubt that those populations Ne Win considered to be foreign were among the key targets of discriminatory policies. The question of who might be considered foreign was determined by the attitudes of Ne Win rather than reference to Burma's civilian era laws.

The xenophobic nature of Ne Win's administration and the military government's arbitrary application of the country's citizenship laws were clearly demonstrated by the way in which legitimate citizenship rights were routinely ignored, and policies adopted to force 'foreigners' from the country. Even after being settled in Burma for generations, and so entitled to citizenship under the provisions of both the *Constitution of the Union of Burma (1948)* and the *Union Citizenship Act (1948)*, Ne Win's administration took steps to expel those it regarded as 'foreigners'. Central to this strategy was the nationalization of private enterprises, which undermined the ability of Indian, Chinese and other groups regarded as foreign to earn a living. The consequence was a widespread forced migration of Indian and Chinese people out of Burma. Often described as a 'repatriation', this was little more than the compulsory expulsion of communities at the behest of the military government. It is estimated around 300,000 Indians and 100,000 Chinese left Burma in the 1960s.[32]

Burma's military rulers did not seek to expel Arakan's large Muslim population at that time. Considering the military authorities' abolition of the MFA and their subsequent mistreatment of the Rohingya, this was not because Ne Win considered the Rohingya had a legitimate right to stay. In its early years, Ne Win's government might have had the authority to expel Chinese and Indian populations (principally from urban centres, including Mandalay and Rangoon), but seeking to force a well-established population of Muslim citizens out of a potentially unstable and recently contested Burma border region risked triggering instability there which the central authorities could ill afford. In the 1950s and 1960s, Karen ethnic fighters had regularly routed Tatmadaw troops in battle, Kachin soldiers had defected from the Tatmadaw in large numbers to support their own ethnic insurgency, and communist militancy continued to be a concern, as were the *Kuomintang*, whose long-term incursion destabilized the Shan highlands. In Arakan, *Mujahid* fighters had only recently formally surrendered (in 1961) and there remained a looming threat that this militancy could be reignited. Under Ne Win's rule, a Burmese state in which ethnic minorities had previously considered themselves equal partners with the majority Bamar was actively replaced by a Bamar- and Buddhist-dominated entity. Policies based on the Tatmadaw's perspective about the history and nature of the Burmese nation would become increasingly dominant.

The most striking indication the government had altered Burma's citizenship framework came through a national citizenship verification process known as *Nagamin* (King Dragon) undertaken in 1978. *Nagamin* was an attempt to register foreigners prior to a planned nationwide census and was conducted by immigration and military staff.

Nagamin was conducted in the aftermath of the 1971 Bangladesh Liberation War, a series of devastating natural disasters including major floods, and the 1974 Bangladesh famine.[33] In recent years, some scholars have suggested these events contributed to fears of illegal immigration into Burma during the 1970s.[34] Yet, as with previous migrations, perceptions have been powerful and facts subservient to mythological beliefs about history. In Rakhine state, relatively recent events can be subject to wildly divergent interpretations. Rohingya leaders commonly argue that any war and climate refugees were only temporarily resident in Burma.[35] Far from creating an influx of migrants to Burma, Bangladesh's Genocide Archive characterizes the overwhelming majority of wartime refugees as having entered India rather than crossing Burma's frontier.[36] Researchers examining those migrations outlined how most returned to their former communities soon after hostilities ended.[37] The worst effects of the flooding in Bangladesh and the subsequent famine were felt in northern districts, far from the Burmese frontier.[38] Lending further credibility to Rohingya assertions are census data from 1973 and 1983 that do not point to any large inward migration to Rakhine state.[39] The evidence indicates fears about illegal 1970s migration from Bangladesh were greatly exaggerated. Regardless of the facts, the *Nagamin* operation was undertaken in a context where the authorities evidently feared they were not adequately maintaining the security of the western borderlands – the 'western gate'. This would likely have been particularly vexing for the military administration, since maintaining the stability and sovereignty of the Union of Burma had been a key motivation and justification for the 1962 coup.

The military authorities were concerned too about continued militancy in Rakhine state involving communists, Rakhine and Muslim insurgents.[40] Concurrent with *Nagamin*, the Tatmadaw undertook an aggressive counter insurgency operation, *Ye The Ha*, using its unyielding 'four cuts' strategy, which aimed to sever militants' links with resources (food, funds, recruits and information). 'Four cuts' operations adopted similar scorched earth tactics to the

Tatmadaw's contemporary 'clearance operations' and over the years have forcibly displaced millions of people, mostly in the borderlands of Kachin, Karen, Rakhine and Shan states. In the *Nagamin* operation, Burma's military adopted a heavy-handed approach, acting as if they were searching out militants and militant sympathizers or investigating potentially violent illegal immigrants. This approach sparked a mass panic among Rakhine state's Muslim population and more than 200,000 Rohingya fled Rakhine state to Bangladesh.[41] This reaction was treated as an indication that Rohingya wanted to avoid scrutiny of their migration status rather than feared mistreatment by security personnel – further fuelling official fears over illegal migration and giving credibility to the common nationalist trope about illegal Bangladeshi migration. From the authorities' perspective, the large number of people who seemingly objected to having their residency status scrutinized indicated they had been resident in Burma illegally.[42] From the perspective of many Rohingya, in 1978 they fled violent military action against a civilian population, a point echoed by numerous reports from the UN, international humanitarian actors, and domestic and international non-governmental organizations (NGOs) that described appalling Tatmadaw mistreatment of Rohingya civilians. Sadly, similarly conflicting narratives would emerge frequently in the decades after.

Following a protracted negotiation, the *1978 Repatriation Agreement* was reached between the governments of Bangladesh and Burma. Burma's government acceded to the repatriation of nearly all refugees yet did not acknowledge them as Burmese citizens. Instead, it was noted that 'lawful residents of Burma who are now sheltered in the camps in Bangladesh' were being accepted back to Burma, and required their 'presentation of Burmese National Registration Cards'.[43] Those repatriated had their NRCs – strong evidence that their citizenship had previously been officially acknowledged – taken from them, ostensibly for verification purposes. These NRCs were not subsequently returned. Instead Temporary Registration Cards were issued by Burma's authorities. These cards marked the holder as a temporary resident and are not the same as a citizenship verification document. These Rohingya were still commonly holding temporary registration cards almost three decades later when President Thein Sein's government cancelled all 'White Cards' in 2015. The Burmese authorities' actions indicated that they did not consider the repatriated Rohingya to be entitled to their NRCs but were prepared to accept their return and identify them as 'lawful residents' to keep peace with Bangladesh. The subsequent actions of Burma/Myanmar's authorities suggested that these returnees, accepted as 'lawful residents', were not accepted as having rights to citizenship.

The consequence of the *Nagamin* operation for the Rohingya was that rather than confirming their citizenships, which had been acknowledged in the civilian era, it helped enforce – often violently – a new citizenship regime altogether. Rohingya who possessed documentary evidence of citizenship such as NRCs or other official documents showing residency were mistrusted by the authorities, and NRCs were not accepted as proof of a legitimate citizenship claim. The systematic way in which the Burmese authorities confiscated NRCs from the repatriated 1978 refugees indicated that removing NRCs from the possession of Rakhine state's Rohingya population was a government priority. Since the military came to power in the 1960s, the authorities have actively diminished the Rohingya's ability to demonstrate evidence for their citizenship claims by removing documents like NRCs from their possession. Frequently, Rohingya would then (as they still do now) rely on having once possessed a properly issued NRC as proof of their citizenship entitlement. Yet providing evidence that the authorities had previously treated an individual as a citizen was not enough to convince the military government that an individual should continue to be entitled to citizenship rights. Repatriated Rohingya were required to relinquish their NRCs, and those who had not fled the *Nagamin* operation simply had their NRCs confiscated. Since the government was redrafting the citizenship laws throughout that time, it appears likely that the confiscation of Rohingya NRCs prior to the enactment of a new law in 1982 was a deliberate government strategy to diminish the strength of future Rohingya citizenship claims. Both events and their consequences came to be closely associated for many Rohingya (and for scholars). Today, the confiscation of NRCs and other rights restrictions around that time are commonly blamed on the citizenship law changes brought by the enactment and enforcement of the 1982 law.

These examples – the abolition of the MFA, Burmanization policies and the expulsion of Chinese and Indian populations, and the aggression of the *Nagamin* operation – illustrate a pattern of action by Ne Win's administration that could be attributed to either his government ignoring existing laws or to believing laws had changed to make their actions legal. Considered in isolation these examples might be regarded as merely reflecting the practice of a discriminatory or xenophobic government that believed itself above the law, but when examined collectively a clear pattern emerges, providing strong evidence that the government's attitude towards the legal standing of its Muslim residents in Arakan/Rakhine state changed markedly from the attitudes of pre-1962 civilian administrations. This is not to suggest other groups with citizenship claims of similar strength to the Rohingya would necessarily lose rights post-1962, but rather that Ne Win's government believed citizenship recognition was entirely within their gift – and there is strong evidence that this government decided the Rohingya population were no longer to be treated as legal citizens of Burma. Because of the inconsistent way Burma's bureaucracy administered citizenship and other laws, it would be years before the full legal consequences of Ne Win's rule would become clear for the Rohingya.

The possibility that Ne Win's administration considered the country's citizenship laws to have been changed after 1962 and before the enactment of the 1982 citizenship law has been underexamined by scholars. Instead, research has more commonly focused on the implications for the Rohingya of the *Burma Citizenship Law (1982)*. A widespread assumption that Ne Win's administration unfairly administered existing citizenship laws before altering them in 1982 has contributed to a debate about the impact of the *Burma Citizenship Law (1982)* on the Rohingya that frequently ignores other legal possibilities. Rohingya activists, media commentators and researchers have suggested the 1982 law as key to the Rohingya's collective statelessness. I believe the evidence demonstrates this is not the case. Instead, the Rohingya ought to be understood as having been citizens in the 1950s and losing those rights, in a practical – and potentially in a legal – sense, early in Ne Win's tenure rather than following the enactment of the 1982 law. Instead of accepting the widely held view that Burma/Myanmar has had just two citizenship regimes since independence, I believe that a third regime came into force under Ne Win's rule, operating between the time of the 1962 coup and the start of the current citizenship framework in 1982. This explains official actions towards the Rohingya associated with the *Nagamin* operation, the authorities' subsequent reluctance to acknowledge their citizenship rights post *Nagamin*, and accounts for how it is that Rohingya today commonly believe they were citizens in the 1950s yet found their collective rights restricted in the 1960s and 1970s before the enactment of the *Burma Citizenship Law (1982)*.

1982 Citizenship Law

The Rohingya's citizenship was not removed because the authorities were unaware of the strength of their claims to be a *taingyintha*. Rather, the history of Arakan and of the Rohingya sat uneasily with the historical narrative of Burma as an exclusively Buddhist state that Ne Win and the military authorities promoted. With the enactment of the *Burma Citizenship Law (1982)* the stripping away of the Rohingya's civil, political and economic rights was given a legal rationale. The long-term practices of Ne Win's administration gained public legal clarity with the enactment of this law. Made under the military's 1974 Constitution, the citizenship law has been widely, and inaccurately, identified as the legal instrument that stripped the Rohingya of their citizenship, making them stateless. The key provisions of the 1982 law relied much more heavily on notions of ethnicity than the 1974 Constitution, and despite similarities with the previous citizenship regime, its reliance on ethnicity greatly narrowed the scope for attaining citizenship.

The citizenship law may have come into force during the period of military dictatorship, but there has been little domestic political momentum for it to change when compared with constitutional provisions such as those related to the qualifications for the presidency or the role of the military in the legislature. Since coming to power with a handsome parliamentary majority, Aung San Suu Kyi's NLD government has provided little indication that it would ever seek meaningful alterations to the *Burma Citizenship Law (1982)*. Instead, the NLD prioritized changing the 2008 Constitution – for which they did not have sufficient parliamentary support – coordinating petitions of voters calling on the legislature to make more than one hundred constitutional amendments, including to limit military influence in the parliament and to make Aung San Suu Kyi eligible for the presidency.[44]

The 1982 law spells out the criteria for each of the three categories of present-day Myanmar citizenship, with the key provisions based on ethnicity. Full citizenship rights in Myanmar are granted collectively to members of ethnic groups believed to have been living within the boundaries of the country in 1823, before the first Anglo-Burma War, associate citizens are those born in the country after 1823 and there is a provision for citizenship by naturalization. As with the 1974 Constitution, the 1982 law specifies eight major indigenous groups, and makes clear those who are, 'Kachin, Kayah, Karen, Chin, Burman, Mon, Rakhine or Shan' are citizens.[45] These are the groups that are widely understood in Myanmar as being *taingyintha*. Importantly, the law states that this list is not exhaustive, and empowers the Council of State to 'decide whether any ethnic group is national or not'.[46]

The question of just how Myanmar's government determines whether residents comprise a distinct ethnic group that can acquire citizenship rights is opaque and highly controversial. In 1990, the Myanmar government clarified which groups it considered 'national' by publishing a list of 135 ethnic groups.[47] Larger groups on the list, such as the Bamar, include tens of millions of Myanmar residents, while other groups, the Moken people for instance, may include just a few thousand. The Rohingya were excluded from this list. Understandably, there has been considerable human rights-led criticism of the 1982 citizenship law's reliance on potentially arbitrary notions of ethnicity and the provision that allows the Council of State to decide whether any ethnic group represents a *taingyintha*. The government can readily remove citizenship rights from any group or grant *taingyintha* status and citizenship rights to any group. This happened in the dying hours of the Thein Sein administration in 2016. The Mone Wun, generally seen as ethnically Chinese – they are mostly Chinese speakers and descendants of migrants from Yunnan – were granted citizenship as a Bamar subgroup.[48] The decision was widely regarded as rewarding the Mone Wun for their cooperation with Tatmadaw actions in northern Shan state.

Robert Taylor, a sympathetic Ne Win biographer, noted the possibility that the government, in compiling its list of *taingyintha* groups, might have made use of British-era colonial census records: '67 years after independence, people are still discussing a nearly hundred year old list created by British colonial officials and amateur linguistics [sic] and ethnographers.'[49] The problems with such an approach are manifold. The challenges of ethnic classification created by language were addressed in Chapter Two to explain why labels like Arakan Muslim were more commonly recorded by British chroniclers than Rooinga/Rohingya. However, regardless of which label the colonial British used to note Arakan's Muslim population as indigenous, in 1990 Myanmar's authorities excluded them from the list of 'national' groups. This suggests that even if Myanmar's government did rely on colonial records, their intention nonetheless was to exclude the Rohingya. Another problem with relying on British-era data is that, particularly by the late nineteenth century, they were often compiled by colonial administrators who lacked a thorough understanding of the country they were surveying and may have been biased towards recording ethnicities with which they were already familiar.[50] An obvious criticism of this approach is that groups excluded from one study are readily excluded from subsequent studies – ignorance is compounded and contributes to the ongoing invisibility of potentially large populations. The colonial administration's demographic knowledge was often far from comprehensive, as was evidenced by India's 1871–1872 census, which revealed a Muslim population in Bengal of tens of millions more than colonial administrators had previously been aware of. However, even familiarity with the people and places being studied did not guarantee that wild generalizations based on the racist pseudoscience common at the time would not be made by officials.

Europe's colonizing powers aimed to subdue, control and exploit the people unfortunate enough to have come under their rule. To advance their political and economic domination, colonizers typically divided humanity along arbitrary lines, affixing labels and hierarchies of ethnicity and race. The British who colonized Burma between the 1820s and 1940s categorized using a range of measures, including language, religion, place of residence and skin tones. Key among Britain's categorizing officials was an ethnologist and scientific racist, Herbert Risley, who was made responsible for the 1901 Census of India and Burma (his innovation was applying the caste system to all of India's population).[51] Risley undertook data collection based on perceived racial hierarchies and he supported making classifications according to the discredited 'nasal index'.[52] A reliance on 'race science' as a classification and governing tool encouraged colonial administrators to identify clear and unchanging boundaries between groups, where locals at that time might have considered identity labels fluid or unimportant.

British-era classifications and associated hierarchies contributed to processes of identity group reification that continued after independence. Sadly, in Myanmar today, ethnicity is frequently regarded in much the same way as it was by the colonial British census-makers of the late nineteenth and early twentieth centuries, as something that is inborn and unchanging.[53] Language clouds and confuses this issue further still. Taylor believed, 'The confusion over ethnicity and race in Myanmar is compounded by the fact that one word, *lumyo*, is normally used to express both concepts. Literally, *lumyo* means variety or kind of human'.[54] This conflation of ethnicity, race and religion has created obvious challenges for those wishing to make a claim of ethnicity based on newer or less familiar ethnic descriptors, as has been the case for the Rohingya.

A heritage within Myanmar predating 1823 is crucial to obtaining citizenship rights according to the *taingyintha* provisions of the 1982 citizenship law. Yet having ancestors who lived within the boundaries of the Burma Empire in 1823 is not necessarily enough to obtain collective citizenship rights, otherwise people living in parts of the Indian states of Assam (then Ahom) and Manipur, over which Burma claimed sovereignty at that time, would be entitled to claim Myanmar citizenship today.[55] The citizenship law refers to the present-day borders of Myanmar – not the 1823 boundaries – so having been governed by someone else altogether in 1823 is not necessarily a disqualification to citizenship: portions of the Shan highlands for instance were not under Burmese control in 1823 yet do form part of present-day Myanmar.[56]

Complicating matters further, some parts of Burma's 1823 empire had only recently come under Burmese control. This was the case with Arakan, which was conquered less than forty years before the Burmese subsequently lost control of it to the British. At the time of the Burmese invasion, the Arakan kingdom's territory was at its smallest for hundreds of years and had it not been for the invasion may have attempted to regain lost territory north of the Naf River (which today marks the international frontier between Bangladesh and Myanmar). As it was, the newly arrived Burmese claimed British-occupied lands beyond the Naf (now part of Bangladesh) as rightfully belonging to them – a factor that inflamed tensions with the British and contributed to the first Anglo-Burmese War.[57] In recent times, Aung San Suu Kyi noted concerns about the location of this border when she told the ICJ in December 2019 that, 'The historical Kingdom of Arakan had at times extended much further to the north than the River Naf, including what is today Chittagong District in Bangladesh. Members of some Rakhine communities therefore felt that the border drawn by the British was too far south; others, that it was too far north.'[58] She might have added that Burma's king Bodawapaya also regarded the border to have been drawn too far south. Yet, while Aung San Suu Kyi may have acknowledged disputes about the proper siting of the border, she has made no effort to alter Myanmar's citizenship law to reflect this. Instead her government defends the 1982 law, including its *taingyintha* provisions.

The alternative pathways to citizenship provided by the *Burma Citizenship Law (1982)* – as Associate or Naturalized citizens – have been equally problematic for the Rohingya and involve a high risk of future statelessness. Diminishing the Rohingya's enthusiasm to seek citizenship recognition individually is their fear that these citizenships could be later arbitrarily revoked. Section 8 of the *Burma Citizenship Law (1982)* makes it easy for the government to do precisely that: '(b) The Council of State may, in the interest of the State revoke the citizenship or associate citizenship or naturalized citizenship of any person except a citizen by birth.'[59] The limitations of this approach were also made clear by President Thein Sein in 2012, when he described it as the pathway to citizenship for Muslims living in Rakhine state.[60] He outlined how this would apply only to those whose ancestors arrived in Burma between 1823 and 1948, and suggested the Rohingya group were all post-Second World War arrivals and therefore illegal migrants – and ominously indicated future plans for the mass deportation of Myanmar's Rohingya, saying, 'The solution to this problem is that they can be settled in refugee camps managed by UNHCR, and UNHCR provides for them. If there are countries that would accept them, they could be sent there.'[61] In light of presidential statements like this, and the Rohingya's collective experience of discrimination by Myanmar's authorities, the prospect of seeking any form of citizenship that could be arbitrarily revoked was hardly inviting and this no doubt contributed to Rohingya resistance to this citizenship path. Regarding the Rohingya identity as a post-independence creation, official Myanmar often treated those claiming it to be post-independence immigrants unentitled to citizenship rights. Consequently, individuals claiming to be Rohingya and accompanying their claim with documentary evidence of prior official recognition of their Burmese citizenship, have frequently been treated by the authorities as presenting proof of likely citizenship fraud. Thein Sein succinctly summarized official perspectives: 'We will take care of our own ethnic nationalities, but Rohingyas who came to Burma illegally are not of our ethnic nationalities and we cannot accept them here.'[62] The authorities even rejected the Rohingya's right to self-identify in the 2014 nationwide census, leaving more than one million residents of Rakhine state unenumerated.

Yet, even with Associate and Naturalized citizenships being so precarious, those Rohingya prepared to make a claim to such citizenships have commonly found Myanmar's state institutions unwilling to advance their residency and citizenship applications.[63] These processes have been controversial, characterized by administrative inertia making progress frustratingly slow, and do not allow applicants' individual citizenship claims to simultaneously recognize their identity as Rohingya, with the 'Bengali' label routinely applied by officials. These factors mean those claiming their identity as Rohingya have collectively been left without citizenship of Myanmar (or any place else) and lack the rights and protections that a citizenship should provide. The 1982 citizenship law has generally been characterized as a key roadblock to Rohingya access to both citizenship and human rights – a situation representing the significant change in government attitudes towards Rohingya citizenship claims from those of the 1950s.

The 1982 citizenship law did not of itself made the Rohingya stateless – instead, its provisions have provided the government with a law to keep them that way; the human rights consequences of this for the Rohingya have been dire. In 2017, the Kofi Annan-led Advisory Commission on Rakhine State (commonly known as the Kofi Annan Commission) highlighted the negative impact of the citizenship law and called for, 'Re-examining the current linkage between citizenship and ethnicity.'[64] A similar recommendation was made by the UN's Fact-Finding Mission in its 2018 report, which highlighted the centrality of *taingyintha* narratives to the Rohingya's plight:

> Successive laws and policies regulating citizenship and political rights have become increasingly exclusionary in their formulation, and arbitrary and

discriminatory in their application. Most Rohingya have become de facto stateless, arbitrarily deprived of nationality. This cannot be resolved through the citizenship law of 1982, applied as proposed by the Government through a citizenship verification process. The core issue is the prominence of the concept of "national races" and the accompanying exclusionary rhetoric, originating under the dictatorship of Ne Win in the 1960s. The link between "national races" and citizenship has had devastating consequences for the Rohingya.[65]

Rohingya, because of their statelessness, have routinely endured rights abuses, including official restrictions on travel (even between villages), marriage, pregnancy outside of marriage and economic activity, stipulations on work and forced labour.[66] Yanghee Lee, the UN's Special Rapporteur on the situation of human rights in Myanmar, was strongly critical of these rights violations, explaining that,

> By virtue of its lack of legal status, the Rohingya community continues to face systematic discrimination, which includes restrictions on the freedom of movement, on access to land, food, water, education and health care, and on marriages and birth registration. The human rights violations faced by the Rohingya community … include summary executions, enforced disappearances, torture, forced labour and forced displacements, as well as rape and other forms of sexual violence.[67]

Lee demanded that, 'These allegations should be investigated and addressed, with perpetrators held to account.' This point has been echoed by Human Rights Watch, who have argued, 'Burma's discriminatory citizenship law not only deprives Rohingya of citizenship, but for decades has encouraged systematic rights violations.'[68] Amnesty International apply the apartheid label to the Rohingya's circumstances.[69]

Deriving from the Afrikaans meaning 'apartness' or 'separateness', apartheid represented South Africa's policy of racial segregation operating in that country from 1948 until it was dismantled in the early 1990s.[70] South Africa's apartheid system was justifiably criticized as discriminatory and racist, and this eventually led the UN, during the 1970s, to agree on the text of a convention to suppress and punish apartheid as a crime. In recent years the term has been used to describe racist and discriminatory policies in states including China, Israel and Saudi Arabia.[71] The 1973 *International Convention on the Suppression and Punishment of the Crime of Apartheid* (ICSPCA), which came into force in 1976, provided a definition of the racial segregation and discrimination common to apartheid as a crime against humanity, and outlined how 'those organizations, institutions and individuals committing the crime of apartheid' are declared criminal.[72] ICSPCA Article Two describes how the crime of apartheid will include 'similar policies and practices of racial segregation and discrimination as practiced in southern Africa'.[73]

Myanmar's discrimination against the Rohingya includes key elements of the apartheid crime set out by the ICSPCA and has been made possible by the operation of the country's discriminatory citizenship regime. The apartheid conditions imposed on the Rohingya include: the deliberate imposition of living conditions designed to cause the destruction of the group; preventing the group's meaningful participation in the country's political, social, economic and cultural life; and dividing the population along racial lines by creating separate reserves or ghettos. This was the subject of a 2017 Amnesty International report, *Caged Without A Roof*, which examined apartheid affecting the Rohingya in Rakhine state, and asserted,

> What Amnesty International has uncovered in Rakhine State is an institutionalized system of segregation and discrimination of Muslim communities. In the case of the Rohingya this is so severe and extensive that it amounts to a widespread and systemic attack on a civilian population, which is clearly linked to their ethnic (or racial) identity, and therefore legally constitutes apartheid, a crime against humanity under international law.[74]

Myanmar's authorities have utilized a range of tactics to enable their apartheid regime. This has involved downgrading Rohingya identity documents so that their ability to prove their legitimate residency in Myanmar and citizenship claims are diminished. For instance, Rohingya victims of a forced deportation in 1991 and 1992 found their return to Myanmar required them to relinquish their identity documents to the authorities, a process that was achieved at that time with the cooperation of the government of Bangladesh and the UN (the UN signed a controversial 1993 Memorandum of Understanding with Bangladesh to cooperate with the 'safe and voluntary repatriation' of Rohingya to Myanmar). Returnees were given temporary 'White Card' documents, which they held until cancelled in 2015, although their original identity documents – demonstrating evidence of previously acknowledged citizenship and legitimate residency in Myanmar – were removed from them.[75] Denying the legitimacy of Rohingya residency in Myanmar has enabled the authorities to place restrictions on Rohingya rights and has been central to the development of the apartheid system in Rakhine state.

Discriminatory outcomes were likely a key motivation when the citizenship law was enacted in 1982, but creating a law specifically to deny nationality or citizenship rights to any group contravenes state obligations under international law.[76] In 2014, the UN General Assembly passed a resolution calling on Myanmar to bring its citizenship laws into line with international standards.[77] Myanmar's government has ignored this and persisted with approaches to limit Rohingya citizenship rights by practice as well as law. Myanmar's justice system is characterized by long delays and arbitrary decisions, with its day-to-day functioning subject to political and military influence.[78] The politicized nature of Myanmar's legal system has allowed the authorities to weaponize laws to restrict Rohingya rights. Arbitrarily applied laws, citizenship impediments and rights restrictions consequently became the norm for the Rohingya throughout the period of military rule, and when the military stepped away from total political control and Myanmar began a move towards quasi-civilian government, the Rohingya were already the world's largest stateless group.[79]

Myanmar's Failed Political Transition

For decades, the Rohingya's statelessness was used to justify far-reaching practices of discrimination and human rights violations. Myanmar's purported transition towards democracy – and a 2010 general election – was cause for optimism that the Rohingya's lot might improve. Sadly, this has not been the case. During two terms of quasi-civilian government new communication technology and political freedoms have given nationalists opportunities to spread hate speech portraying Rohingya as a threat to Myanmar's Buddhist character and licence to brutal Tatmadaw violence against the group. The authorities, reluctant to alienate Buddhist voters, allowed anti-Rohingya speech to proliferate with devastating consequences. Key international actors, including the UN, were similarly hesitant to criticize the civilian administration's handling of the Rohingya's situation lest this undermine momentum for democratic change. In this chapter, I will outline key factors relating to Myanmar's politics in the recent civilian era. This will provide important context to the Rohingya perspectives presented in the chapters that follow.

Political change in the Golden Land

As recently as 2010, foreign entry to Myanmar was strictly controlled. Visitors commonly arrived through Yangon's (formerly Rangoon) international airport, having found other entry points either forbidden or allowing only short trips. Long-running economic sanctions meant arrivals were greeted by posters advertizing local brands like Max Cola and Grand Royal whisky, mostly unknown outside of Myanmar, rather than the global brands more familiar at international airports. Signs cheerfully declaring 'Welcome to the Golden Land' referenced the abundant use of gold to adorn Buddhist temples and shrines nationwide. The golden spire of Myanmar's most sacred site, the Shwedagon Pagoda (literally Golden Dagon Pagoda), towers 100 metres over Yangon and is claimed to be 2,500 years old, which would make it one of Buddhism's oldest monuments. The Shwedagon is said to contain important relics, including strands of Buddha's hair, and to be encrusted with 4,531 diamonds and around 20,000 gold bars.[1] The Shwedagon's spire is visible from central Yangon and marks the city as unusual among modern Asian commercial capitals, where skyscrapers rather than religious edifices more commonly define skylines. In 2010, the Shwedagon's predominance pointed to the centrality of religion, specifically Theravada Buddhism, to Myanmar life. It also underscored Myanmar's decades of self-isolation under military rule and Yangon's underdevelopment compared with cities like Bangkok, Kuala Lumpur or Singapore.

Throughout five decades of military dictatorship – whose rule was as brutal and arbitrary as it was economically inept – Myanmar had been one of the world's poorest countries.[2] Amid fears elected politicians could not be trusted to maintain the territorial integrity of the then recently independent nation, General Ne Win declared, 'parliamentary democracy was not suitable' and seized power in a 1962 military *coup d'état*.[3] The five decades that followed saw the military in continual conflict with the country's ethnic minorities.[4] Myanmar's ongoing domestic conflicts have been labelled the world's longest running civil war and appear far from ending (there are at least two dozen active insurgencies nationwide).[5] Under the military's stewardship the country was brought near bankruptcy, and close to the point of complete economic collapse.[6] In 1987 the UN designated Burma 'Least Developed Country' status, making Ethiopia (then a recent beneficiary of Bob Geldof's Band Aid charity), Sudan and Chad its economic peers.[7] By 2010 the economy had barely improved, and with reliable economic statistics continuing to be notoriously difficult to come by, experts like Australian academic Sean Turnell (a future special economic consultant to Aung San Suu Kyi) believed it accurate to describe Myanmar's economy as 'dismal'.[8] Yangon's streets bore a closer resemblance to early 1960s Bangkok or Kuala Lumpur than those of a modern Asian city. The poverty rate in rural Myanmar had reached shocking levels. Asian Development Bank research showed how only sixty-five per cent of rural residents could access safe drinking water, only thirty-four per cent could access electricity, and while seventy-seven per cent could access sanitation, in Rakhine state this figure was only fifty-four per cent.[9]

Surprisingly, with the wretched state of the economy, many of the people I met in Myanmar in 2010 were optimistic about their country's future. Much of their optimism derived from the hope that if only the popular opposition leader Aung San Suu Kyi could become the nation's leader, she would change things for the better. They hoped the promised transition to democratic rule would lead to Aung San Suu Kyi's release from house arrest and eventually to her taking up the reins of government. This hope may well have dampened enthusiasm for revolutionary change among Myanmar's ethnic Bamar majority, encouraging patience with military rule because of the expectation political change was already on the way. Myanmar's claimed transition to democracy took place within a legal framework constructed by the military to cement their ongoing influence on the country's government and avoid civilian oversight. The military-drafted 2008 Constitution ensured the armed forces' Commander-in-Chief, Senior General Min Aung Hlaing, could directly appoint the government ministers for Border Affairs, Defence and Home Affairs, as well as a quarter of the parliament's members (these members of parliament [MPs] would sit together in parliament wearing military regalia), giving the military a veto over future constitutional change.[10] Myanmar's voters would choose the remaining three-quarters of the *Pyidaungsu Hluttaw* (national parliament), the dual-chambered national assembly that would select a president to lead Myanmar's first notionally civilian administration for almost five decades.[11]

The first election to take place under the 2008 Constitution was boycotted by Aung San Suu Kyi and her NLD party.[12] Even with the chance to exercise a democratic franchise at an election for the first time since 1990's annulled poll, nationwide turnout estimates for the November 2010 general election were low.[13] It was an overcast morning in Myanmar's commercial capital when polls opened, and as voting began, Yangon's streets were uncharacteristically quiet, perhaps because seven million eligible voters did not participate. There were tight restrictions on campaigning and a common perception that the election was not 'free and fair', with the results being a foregone conclusion.[14] To avoid close scrutiny of the 2010 poll, Myanmar's government barred international media and foreign election monitors, save for those few diplomats already in the country.[15] Ex-general and then-Union Election Commission (UEC) chairman Thein Soe justified this approach, saying, 'We are holding the election for this country. It's not for other countries.'[16] Comments like this were suggestive that the UEC believed there was something to hide and it was their responsibility to hide it. As little as thirty-five per cent of eligible voters may have participated.[17] This figure was much less than the seventy-two per cent turnout in 1990, yet the government claimed a higher participation rate of seventy-seven per cent.[18]

There were low expectations for immediate political change because of the election – the military, it was assumed, would retain effective political control. The new constitution had been written to achieve precisely that outcome.

Nonetheless, there was excitement at the prospect that Aung San Suu Kyi might soon be released from house arrest and a genuine belief and hope she might be able to deliver meaningful political change in the future. In Yangon on election day, I noticed residents' unenthusiastic embrace of their democratic rights. There was a subdued mood around polling places in the city, and little excitement about the election and the prospect it might give Myanmar the elected officials and political change the people had long desired. I heard resigned sentiments about the likely election outcome time and again as I moved around the country, but I experienced as well people's optimism about Myanmar's prospects if Aung San Suu Kyi could be released and become the nation's leader.

Aung San Suu Kyi remained under house arrest throughout the election period, as she had been for fifteen of the previous twenty-two years. Since emerging as a political leader during the 8888 Uprising (named because protests began on 8 August, 1988) she had been championed as the voice of the people and regarded as a 'symbol of popular opposition to the government'.[19] Ironically, Aung San Suu Kyi's house arrest was in the colonial-era villa gifted to her family by the state following the assassination of her father, independence hero Aung San. Armed guards from the military her father founded were stationed outside and blocked traffic along a formerly busy thoroughfare to keep press and well-wishers away. Recognized internationally as political prisoners, Aung San Suu Kyi and a further 427 jailed NLD members were considered 'criminals' by Myanmar's military-led government, preventing them from participating in elections.[20] Unhappy with the election's rules Aung San Suu Kyi had announced, 'she would not even think about registering'. The NLD duly refused to expel members serving a jail term, an official requirement for continued party registration, and did not participate in the 2010 poll.[21]

In Rakhine state, a thousand kilometres away from Aung San Suu Kyi's lakeside home, Rohingya did participate in the 2010 poll. Not formally recognized as citizens and enduring terrible rights abuses, around 700,000 Rohingya, mostly long-term holders of 'White Card' temporary identification documents, could still cast votes. They elected Rohingya representatives to the lower house of the national parliament, the *Pyithu Hluttaw*, and to Rakhine state's assembly. Curiously, all were members of the ruling, military-aligned Union Solidarity and Development Party (USDP), whose leaders, once serving military officers, had overseen decades of rights violations against the Rohingya. The NLD's absence from the poll guaranteed a nationwide election victory for the USDP and Rakhine state's ethnic composition complicated party allegiances there considerably.

Claiming to exclusively represent ethnic Rakhine interests, the Rakhine Nationalities Development Party (RNDP) attracted considerable electoral support and advocated tighter rights restrictions on the Rohingya community than the authorities had already imposed. In those circumstances, Rohingya politicians like Shwe Maung (also known as Abdul Razak), a Buthidaung representative who became a vocal parliamentary advocate for Rohingya interests, hoped USDP connections might prevent further rights erosions and bring the Rohingya closer to Myanmar's political mainstream. Highlighting the central importance of citizenship rights to the Rohingya, Shwe Maung said, 'My election promise was based on one thing: I said I am not state authority or immigration, but I will do my utmost best and make my voice as loud as possible until our rights are restored, if you elect me. Apart from this, I did not promise anything, because this is the key issue for the people.'[22] The USDP's motivations were more craven. They used Rohingya voters, hoping to stave off what was ultimately an embarrassing electoral rout in Rakhine state at the hands of the RNDP. Nationwide, the USDP were comfortable winners, claiming almost sixty per cent of the national vote. On election night 2010, Rohingya communities knew they would again have a Rohingya voice in parliament and must have felt optimism that their collective circumstances in Myanmar might soon improve.

The military-controlled government released Aung San Suu Kyi from house arrest one week after the 2010 election – the new quasi-civilian administration would not take up office until March 2011. In anticipation of her release, expectant crowds gathered outside her Yangon home chanting 'Long live Aung San Suu Kyi,' a sentiment echoed by millions of her supporters nationwide.[23] Like many visitors to Myanmar I had read her books, knew her remarkable story and supported the campaign for a return to democratic government. A few days after her release, I was pleased to meet 'The Lady' and have a chance to thank her for years of courageous commitment to democracy in Myanmar. In the years to follow my attitude towards Aung San Suu Kyi's politics and her policies, like that of large numbers of her one-time admirers and supporters, changed markedly.

Waiting to meet Aung San Suu Kyi at the NLD's run down Yangon headquarters it was as easy to be inspired by the optimism of her supporters as it was to be impressed by their political commitment. Scores of these NLD activists had been jailed for their political activity, more than 400 NLD members were still behind bars, and it was not yet clear whether the authorities would again clamp down on opposition political activity as had happened when Aung San Suu Kyi had last been briefly free in 2003.[24] At that time, she narrowly escaped assassination when her entourage and local supporters were set upon by military-sponsored thugs near the town of Depayin (Tabayin) in central Myanmar's Sagaing division. Her bodyguards were not so lucky, with at least four murdered alongside possibly dozens of NLD supporters in what came to be known as the 'Depayin Massacre'. Aung San Suu Kyi's rearrest and another crackdown on opposition activists followed. A repeat of the events of 2003 was a very real concern for Aung San Suu Kyi and her supporters as they enjoyed the early days of their new-found political freedom.

An ominous and permanent fixture at the tea house opposite the NLD's office were plain clothes government security personnel, likely military intelligence, closely monitoring the comings and goings of opposition supporters, media and diplomats. Doubtless there were more plain clothes government agents mingling amongst the crowd inside. If they were paying attention, they would have noticed the same optimism I experienced from NLD activists and their freed leader. And they would have heard the stories of numerous political activists, previously jailed for their beliefs, who remained determined to work for the return of democracy to Myanmar. Here, Aung San Suu Kyi was surrounded by scores of activists who shared her political commitment and experience of incarceration. After conducting an election and releasing Aung San Suu Kyi, government surveillance was yet to retreat from everyday Myanmar life. This was demonstrated to me once I left the NLD office and found myself followed around the city by various goons on foot, in cars and using the authorities' ubiquitous orange motorbikes. For me this was an alien experience; for Myanmar's residents it was a fact of everyday life and had been for decades.

The coming to office in March 2011 of a quasi-civilian administration was understood by key international actors as an important step in a democratic transition, and it opened the door to the lifting of Western economic sanctions, new foreign investment and political engagement. The new president, Thein Sein, was an ex-general with a long track record as a military loyalist. He had been a high-ranking figure in the military dictatorship, chaired the national convention which drafted the controversial 2008 Constitution that embedded 'discipline-flourishing democracy' and military influence on domestic politics, and was already the country's prime minister when the 2010 election was held.[25] His elevation to Myanmar's presidency represented the continuity of military-infused rule rather than a break with the military-ruled past.

Thein Sein has been claimed as a 'reformer', although much evidence – including his suppression of the 8888 Uprising and his actions in the aftermath of Cyclone Nargis –suggests otherwise. He entered parliament with a record as a Tatmadaw true believer, who had chaired the National Disaster Preparedness

Central Committee that rejected offers of international humanitarian assistance in the aftermath of the 2008 cyclone calamity.[26] In May 2008, Cyclone Nargis devastated the Irrawaddy Delta and Yangon. The cyclone killed an estimated 140,000 people, made 2.4 million people homeless and left more than 50,000 people missing. Fearing foreign intervention might precipitate future regime change, the military government retarded the relief operation, refusing visas for international disaster relief experts and aid workers and blocking crucial aid for days. Two million people needlessly waited weeks for assistance to arrive. Military junta decisions in the aftermath of the cyclone's landfall unnecessarily cost the lives of thousands of victims who might have been saved had assistance been allowed to reach them. Leaked US diplomatic cables also indicated Thein Sein's key role in the suppression of the 8888 Uprising, explaining that as commander of the elite military 55th Light Infantry Division, from the perspective of the junta 'he distinguished himself . . . in the crackdown against the 1988 Uprising'.[27]

Having risen to prominence amid Myanmar's most repressive periods of military rule, Thein Sein was the hand-picked successor of the brutal dictator Than Shwe.[28] When Thein Sein assumed the presidency few would have predicted that between 2011 and 2016 his government would undertake a series of monumental national policy reforms, including liberalizations of the notoriously insular economy, freeing the telecommunications and media sectors, opening space for increased political participation and releasing political prisoners.[29] Despite these reforms, Thein Sein's administration was subject to legitimate criticisms from domestic and international actors over aspects of its agenda, particularly its failure to settle disputes with ethnic minorities, to address the Rohingya's rights claims, its management of conflict in Rakhine state and perceptions the administration pandered to extreme Buddhist nationalists.[30]

Words as Weapons

Myanmar was a latecomer to the internet revolution. Before 2012, mobile phone ownership levels were so low that, per capita, only North Korea had fewer mobile phones.[31] Policy changes early in Thein Sein's tenure saw mobile phone SIM cards reducing in price from thousands of dollars to as little as one dollar. In a country where the gross domestic product (GDP) per capita scarcely exceeded US$1,000, mobile phone technology was previously a luxury well beyond the reach of the average person.[32] When the mobile phone market was opened to international carriers and prices fell, there was a huge growth in mobile phone penetration. From a very low base, mobile phone penetration rates grew quickly to more than fifty per cent by 2015, passed eighty per cent in the 2015/16 financial year and were estimated to have topped ninety per cent by the end of 2016.[33] There are now more active SIM cards in Myanmar than people.[34] This made the internet readily available to the majority of Myanmar's around fifty-one million residents for the first time and overnight changed the way they communicated with each other. Media reforms ensured that for Myanmar's majority, their first experience of internet technology was on a cheap Chinese smartphone, using Facebook, rather than on a desktop computer using a more established search engine like Google or Yahoo. As a regular visitor to Myanmar in the period of these changes, I witnessed the impact of the internet's arrival on the country, and became concerned about the way people frequently seemed to uncritically consume 'news' posted to Facebook, and the likely political consequences of this.

Until pre-publication press censorship ended in 2012 Myanmar had one of the world's most restrictive news media environments.[35] In the military-controlled era, reporting of issues deemed sensitive by the authorities was heavily censored. Generations in Myanmar grew up without having experienced a free domestic press. In President Thein Sein's term in office this situation rapidly changed with pre-publication censorship formally ended, and the country becoming awash with smartphones. The internet's arrival in Myanmar had some sudden and negative political consequences, aided by the way people increasingly consumed news using online social media, or free messaging applications like Viber or WhatsApp. Viber produced Myanmar-specific sticker graphics allowing users to share patriotic images representing Aung San Suu Kyi, and the company's cartoon mascot 'LegCat' participating in Buddhist religious activities and visiting the Shwedagon Pagoda. People commonly had their social media accounts set up for them by mobile phone shop staff, and it was not unusual to find Myanmar mobile phone users who did not understand that the internet existed beyond what was available to them through preloaded social media applications. Political and media freedoms provided chances for divisive voices to foment ethnic and religious conflict that in the past would have been suppressed by the military-led government, nervous that any public political expression might ultimately threaten their own rule.

Nationalist Buddhist groups, including the staunchly anti-Muslim 969 Movement and the Association for the Protection of Race and Religion, known by its Burmese-language acronym Ma Ba Tha, used new media and political freedoms to pursue anti-ethnic minority and anti-Muslim political agendas, including advocating policy changes that aimed to severely curtail the rights of ethnic and religious minorities. Nationalist leaders often used provocative and extreme language to make their political case. Buddhist monk and prominent Ma Ba Tha leader Wirathu, who had previously been sentenced to a 25-year prison sentence by the country's military-led government for inciting religious hatred – only to be released in an amnesty for political prisoners in 2012 – said, 'In every town, there is a crude and savage Muslim majority' and he warned about Muslims who 'target innocent young Burmese girls and rape them'.[36] Wirathu said that, 'Muslims are like the African carp. They breed quickly, and they are very violent and they eat their own kind. Even though they are minorities here, we are suffering under the burden they bring us.'[37] In 2013, Wirathu was labelled in a 2013 *TIME* cover story as the 'Face of Buddhist Terror' and human rights groups accused his rhetoric of inciting anti-Muslim violence and contributing to the exclusion of Muslims from the political mainstream.[38]

Wirathu has been a rigorous user of social media, especially Facebook and YouTube, regularly making inflammatory posts to his more than 500,000 followers, and on a number of occasions his posts have been removed or his accounts frozen by Facebook. It was reported he was permanently removed from Facebook in early 2018. In 2016, I reported to Facebook an anti-Muslim post by Wirathu that I believed unquestionably breached Facebook's Community Standards. It took weeks and numerous other complaints before this post was removed by Facebook's monitors, by which time it had been shared across Myanmar tens of thousands of times. Journalists in Myanmar frequently told me their concerns about the unchecked power of social media, particularly Facebook, and opportunities this had provided nationalists to foment anti-foreigner and particularly anti-Muslim attitudes that had contributed to violence.

In 2012, as new communication technologies were still establishing themselves in Myanmar, nationalists used the new political freedoms to hold public meetings and circulate printed anti-Muslim tracts and DVDs with sermons by nationalist monks. Their aim was to elevate anti-Muslim attitudes and actions to the level of a religious duty – violence was portrayed as a Buddhist religious necessity. This manipulation of identities, which laid the foundations for violence, was explored in detail in Francis Wade's *Myanmar's Enemy Within*, which documented how during 2012, in Rakhine state, violence between Buddhist and Muslim communities occurred following weeks of rising sectarian tensions that were variously ignored or encouraged by the authorities.[39] Amid rising tensions that were obviously stoked by nationalist groups, Buddhists and Muslims told Human

Rights Watch that the 'authorities provided no protection and did not appear to have taken any special measures to pre-empt the violence'.[40]

The proximate spark for widespread violence in 2012 was the rape and murder of a young Buddhist woman by three Muslim men, and the retaliatory murders of ten Muslims and one Buddhist mistaken as Muslim, who were dragged from a Yangon-bound bus by a Rakhine Buddhist mob. Human Rights Watch summarized the violence, describing how, in June 2012, 'Arakan [Rakhine] and Rohingya mobs attacked homes, shops, and houses of worship. Witnesses recalled mobs from both populations storming neighbourhoods, pillaging and setting fire to homes and other buildings, and beating those they found with crude weapons, such as swords, bamboo sticks, metal bars, and poles.'[41] Witnesses also recalled Myanmar's security forces disarming Muslim communities before retreating and not intervening as armed Buddhist mobs attacked the defenceless Muslims.[42] There were reports too of security forces themselves committing abuses, including arbitrary arrests and unlawfully using force against Rohingya communities, and working in concert with ethnic Rakhine mobs to target Rohingya.

At least 5,000 buildings, overwhelmingly homes in Muslim areas of Sittwe like the Nasi Quarter, were razed to the ground, leading to the large-scale displacement of Rohingya residents. Entire Muslim neighbourhoods of Sittwe were laid waste. The violence also involved acts of heritage destruction like the ransacking of the historic Jama Mosque, a previously prominent feature of Sittwe's main commercial street. Built in the mid-nineteenth century, in Arabesque style, Jama Mosque's age and location close to the Rakhine State Parliament and other official buildings, like the Rakhine State Museum, made it a key and symbolic representation of the long-term and legitimate presence of Rohingya. The sacking of Jama Mosque and its closure since 2012 was raised frequently by Rohingya as representing a symbolic attack on their group's historical legitimacy in Rakhine state.[43]

Outbreaks of violence involving Rakhine Buddhist and Rohingya Muslim communities between May and October 2012 resulted in around 200 deaths, injuries to 265 and the displacement of 140,000.[44] Most of the dead and the overwhelming majority of those displaced were Muslims from the Rohingya community. Accusations followed that Myanmar's authorities had instigated key violent episodes by disarming Rohingya villagers before encouraging Buddhist mobs to attack the now defenceless Muslims, yet the authorities treated the violence as a communal dispute between Buddhist Rakhine and Muslim Rohingya communities.[45] The government's strategy to prevent further conflict

Figure 5 Sittwe's concentration camps, opened in 2012, were supposed to be temporary. More than 100,000 Rohingya remained confined to these camps in 2020.

was to physically separate these groups. The Rohingya community bore the brunt of this approach, with officials taking the opportunity to further restrict their rights. Displaced Rohingya were prevented from returning to their former neighbourhoods to rebuild their destroyed homes and tens of thousands were incarcerated in concentration camps with no indication of when, if ever, they would be allowed to leave.[46] Today, more than 120,000 of those Rohingya first displaced in 2012 remain confined to Myanmar's domestic camps.[47]

The long-term confinement of more than 120,000 Rohingya in camps within Rakhine state, and of thousands more locked down in their communities, prompted me to consider the appropriate labels for those places. The locations to which tens of thousands of Rohingya have been confined within Myanmar since 2012 are frequently described as internally displaced person (IDP) camps and this is the term the UN uses. While these are certainly sites where internally displaced persons reside, the IDP label does not accurately reflect the true nature of these camps. Camp residents cannot freely leave and are prevented from returning to their former homes by armed guards, although they have not been arrested. This situation potentially aligns with legal scholar David Lowry's definition of internment – 'an extrajudicial deprivation of liberty by executive action. The essence of internment lies in incarceration without charge or trial.'[48]

Myanmar's Rohingya camp system operates in a context where the Rohingya's rights have been restricted for decades.[49] The motivations underpinning Myanmar's decision to incarcerate Rohingya in squalid camps with no indication of when they might ever be released seems far beyond the scope of Lowry's internment label.

Euphemistic labels only serve to protect Myanmar's authorities from legitimate criticism about their discriminatory policies and mistreatment of the Rohingya community. The true nature of these camps ought to be acknowledged in their labelling. Normal life cannot continue in these places – educational opportunities are scarce, medical facilities are limited and there is little hope of work. Life there is bleak and allows for the barest of opportunities. These camps are unquestionably a part of the authorities' decades-long strategy of Rohingya persecution. Dan Stone's *Concentration Camps* presented a basic working definition as, '*an isolated, circumscribed site with fixed structures designed to incarcerate civilians*' (emphasis in original).[50] Andrea Pitzer's study of concentration camps, *One Long Night,* examined the history of camps worldwide and described a concentration camp as 'a place to which an unlimited number of people could be sent without legal recourse.'[51] Pitzer visited the Rakhine state camps to which Rohingya are confined and readily labelled them concentration camps. I agree with this label, and so use the term concentration camps, rather than alternative euphemisms that can serve to obscure the camps' true nature and purpose.

The violence that led to such large-scale Rohingya displacement had been encouraged by Myanmar's nascent internet presence and by public meetings, printed flyers and DVDs. In the years following, internet penetration would substantially increase, and Myanmar's majority would gain access to an internet that provided them with a steady diet of anti-Rohingya and anti-Muslim propaganda. In that environment it was surely only a matter of time before there was another catastrophe on a scale rivalling the violence of 2012.

One of the journalists I spoke to about Myanmar's media changes (whose ongoing work in the region necessitates their anonymity) told me in 2015 that in the new media and telecommunications environment, Myanmar's population had found the Rohingya were 'somebody to direct their anger at – before it was the military government. Now people have another target. Anti-Muslim attitudes did exist before, but it seems they weren't as prominent.' They expressed a concern too that in the short time the internet had been readily available in Myanmar, millions, possibly tens of millions, of Myanmar's residents were already accustomed to using social media platforms, particularly Facebook, as their sole source of news. They suggested that since Myanmar's telecommunications sector had been liberalized social media had become,

> ...incredibly influential. Some people use it as their primary news source. In fact, a lot of people use it as their primary news source now. You speak to a lot of people and they say they don't know what the internet is, they just know Facebook. And so, everything that they learn about what's going on in the country is coming from Facebook. Obviously, a lot of people still do read newspapers, but Facebook is the primary source of information for a lot of people now. Which is terrible because a lot of what's going on on Facebook is wrong and rumour ridden, particularly the posts that are shared by Wirathu and Ma Ba Tha.

Facebook has been criticized internationally for providing a platform for politically motivated false information. The promotion of 'fake news' on social media platforms is regarded as contributing to unexpected victories for Donald Trump in the US, and the 'Brexit' leave campaign in the UK, yet in late 2015, the term 'fake news' was not widely used in Myanmar. That soon changed. Myanmar's Muslim community was often a target of false and inflammatory social media posts and at times this has had devastating consequences. A false 2014 report that a Muslim tea shop owner in Mandalay raped a Buddhist employee led to violent disturbances lasting several days that left one person dead and more than a dozen injured.[52]

Facebook's efforts to prevent its platform being used to promote extreme views were anaemic at best, prompting my journalist colleague to recount how, 'Facebook's done one thing, which is to allow you to report things as hate speech. But in my experience, that hasn't really worked. I've tried to report people on Facebook that have been spreading rumours or defaming Muslims. And it comes back with "this wasn't sufficiently racist". Not advocating a return to the censorship familiar in Myanmar in days past, they went on to suggest that Facebook set the bar unreasonably high in terms of defending freedom of speech rather than placing limits on how the platform can be used to promote hate speech or to incite violence. They prophetically noted that, 'It seems like Myanmar is going in a very dangerous direction with social media.'

Positive media portrayals of Muslims became extremely rare in Myanmar and were to be found usually only in the country's foreign language media. With little chance to respond to widespread criticisms, the Rohingya were increasingly scapegoated in both mainstream and social media. The concerns about the impact of social media would be repeated by senior UN officials in the aftermath of the 2017 Rohingya crisis. The UN Special Rapporteur for Human Rights in Myanmar, Yanghee Lee, blamed Facebook for, 'inciting a lot of violence and a lot of hatred against the Rohingya and other ethnic minorities.'[53] The chairman of the UN Human Rights Council's Independent Fact-Finding Mission on Myanmar (UN Fact-Finding Mission), Marzuki Darusman, said social media had played a 'determining role' in Myanmar, describing how it 'substantively contributed to the level of acrimony and dissension and conflict, if you will, within the public. Hate speech is certainly of course a part of that. As far as the Myanmar situation is concerned, social media is Facebook, and Facebook is social media.'[54] Facebook's feeble response to complaints about inappropriate content in Myanmar were raised by US lawmakers when the company's Chief Executive Officer (CEO), Mark Zuckerberg, appeared before the US Senate's Commerce and Judiciary Committees in 2018.[55] Since then, Facebook has created an oversight committee of international experts to decide which content should be removed from the platform. Whether this will meaningfully curtail hate speech in places like Myanmar will largely depend on whether the company now devotes the necessary resources to identify and remove hateful posts in a timely manner.

This is what genocide looks like

Sittwe was by 2015 a town divided. Barbed wire, sandbags and armed guards separated the Buddhist communities of 'Free Sittwe' from restricted Muslim areas. The physical separation that was a key part of the authorities' strategy to prevent a repeat of the violence of 2012 came at a terrible price for the state's Muslims, who found themselves confined to their villages or trapped in camps or urban Sittwe's Aung Mingalar ghetto. In an area no bigger than a couple of square kilometres, around 4,000 Rohingya Muslims had been confined since 2012. Trapped just a few blocks from the main town market, the hospital and other services, Muslims in Aung Mingalar quarter were not free to visit those places. When I visited Aung Mingalar in November 2015, residents told me doctors visited just twice weekly and emergency hospital visits required official approval, a process that was invariably slow and usually involved the payment of a bribe to corrupt Bamar or Rakhine officials. Residents in need of medical care and without the financial resources to pay the necessary bribe were forced to rely on home remedies. These Rohingya lived with the constant fear the authorities could, if they chose, easily cut off all access to medicine or to food and water.

Aung Mingalar's residents relied for their survival on diaspora remittances and support from Rohingya camps on the outskirts of Sittwe, which they could occasionally access. In Aung Mingalar a ghetto of the worst possible variety had been created.

Myanmar's authorities spent decades making the conditions of life for the Rohingya so arduous that for many, escape, even if this meant a dangerous boat journey in the hands of a human trafficker, became preferable to life in Myanmar. During the 2000s, these maritime journeys were undertaken by tens of thousands of Rohingya annually and were frequently relied upon by the families of young men expected to find work and return desperately needed remittances. In 2015 Thailand's authorities shut down the most popular trafficking routes. The US' 2015 *Trafficking in Persons Report* downgraded Thailand (where a 2014 military *coup d'état* had recently ousted the elected government of Yingluck Shinawatra) to the 'Tier 3' list of the world's worst human trafficking offenders alongside Myanmar, Haiti, Iran, North Korea, Syria and South Sudan.[56] The perception of a national security failure was embarrassing for Thailand's new military government and they responded quickly, closing informal migration routes used by Rohingya, and refusing migrant boats permission to land in Thailand.

Almost immediately, Rohingya already at sea were caught in a nautical limbo, unable to land or return home. A dramatic standoff followed off the coasts of Thailand and Malaysia, with desperate migrants fast running out of supplies, yet unable to land. A regional summit sought a solution – as if to deliberately highlight the underlying causes of the Rohingya's migration, Myanmar's representatives objected to delegates using the name Rohingya.[57] After protracted negotiations, Indonesia and Malaysia agreed to provide migrants already at sea with a haven, although the long-term consequence was the effective closure of maritime escape routes for Rohingya; the causes of the migration were not addressed. This created a pool of young men in northern Rakhine state whose long-term plans had been stymied by the authorities. After the events of 2015, young Rohingya men expected to spend the remainder of their lives confined to Rakhine state. A 2016 International Crisis Group (ICG) report, *Myanmar: A New Muslim Insurgency in Rakhine State*, suggested that by stopping their migration and confining these young men to Myanmar, further limiting their life chances, the authorities 'closed a vital escape valve' and the associated 'increasing sense of despair has driven more people to consider a violent response'.[58] That the Rohingya did not embrace militancy sooner can be traced in part to the existence of opportunities for young men to escape, and the importance to their families of the remittances they would send home. The

Rohingya's migration situation was changed markedly from mid-2015, and when I visited Rohingya concentration camps near Sittwe in November 2015 the absence of routes of escape for young men was regularly mentioned.

A clear lack of rights improvements during Myanmar's first term of quasi-civilian government led to increased calls from the Rohingya community, human rights groups, scholars and UN Special Rapporteurs for a greater emphasis on the Rohingya's human rights situation. In 2015, academics Penny Green, Thomas MacManus and Alicia de la Cour Venning identified the Rohingya's circumstances as so dire as to be considered genocide.[59] Their International State Crime Initiative (ISCI) report, *Countdown to Annihilation: Genocide in Myanmar*, raised an alert that the Rohingya were in imminent danger of becoming victims of mass killing and needed urgent international protection. Making a pressing call too was Azeem Ibrahim in *The Rohingyas: Inside Myanmar's Hidden Genocide*, which was sympathetic to the Rohingya's political claims and asserted, 'the reality facing the Rohingyas . . . is the threat of genocide'.[60] This mirrored Maung Zarni and Alice Cowley's description of the Rohingya as facing a 'slow-burning genocide'.[61] A Yale University student law clinic report used data provided by human rights group Fortify Rights, finding 'persuasive evidence that the crime of genocide has been committed against Rohingya Muslims'.[62]

ISCI's scholars assessed the Rohingya's persecution in places like the Aung Mingalar ghetto and the camps against the stages of genocide outlined by Daniel Feierstein in his seminal work *Genocide as Social Practice*.[63] Feierstein's work depicted genocide as involving interrelated and overlapping processes that he categorized into six steps: stigmatization or the construction of 'negative otherness', harassment, isolation, policies of systematic weakening, extermination and symbolic enactment that involves removing the victim group from the collective history. ISCI's team concluded that the Rohingya were already victims of four of the six stages of genocide outlined by Feierstein and were at serious risk of becoming victims of the two final stages: extermination and symbolic enactment. ISCI's researchers explained that:

> . . . detailed research found ample evidence that the Rohingya have been subjected to systematic and widespread violations of human rights, including killings, torture, rape and arbitrary detention; destruction of their homes and villages; land confiscation; forced labour; denial of citizenship; denial of the right to identify themselves as Rohingya; denial of access to healthcare, education and employment; restrictions on freedom of movement, and State-sanctioned

campaigns of religious hatred. It also found compelling evidence of State-led policies, laws and strategies of genocidal persecution stretching back over 30 years, and of the Myanmar State coordinating with Rakhine ultra-nationalists, racist monks and its own security forces in a genocidal process against the Rohingya.[64]

This research portrayed how the Rohingya were victims of a 'systematic weakening process that has accompanied the dehumanisation, violence and segregation [that] has been so successful that the Rohingya in Myanmar can be described as a people whose agency has been effectively destroyed. Those who can, flee, while those who remain endure the barest of lives.'[65] Such loss of social vitality was characterized by Claudia Card as 'social death', which she argued is a serious and distinctive harm of genocide.[66] So complete was the Rohingya's loss of social vitality that ISCI asserted, 'Now, the Rohingya potentially face the final two stages of genocide – mass annihilation and erasure of the group from Myanmar's history.'[67] Having witnessed the Aung Mingalar ghetto and spent time travelling through northern Rakhine state, including visiting Rohingya camps, I find it impossible to disagree with the ISCI's conclusion that genocide was certainly underway against the Rohingya in Myanmar by 2015 (and that genocide against the Rohingya had likely already been underway for years). Sadly, ISCI's more disturbing predictions have already come to pass.

The Rohingya's mistreatment by Myanmar's authorities demonstrated a pattern of policies and practices designed to weaken and ultimately destroy the group. Narratives of history that labelled the Rohingya as 'Bengali', a pejorative designed to portray them as recent foreign interlopers and a threat to Myanmar's Buddhist culture and character, have served to harden domestic attitudes against the Rohingya and retarded their rights claims. Myanmar's authorities have frequently adopted practices with the effect of 'othering' the Rohingya, separating the group from society – forcing them into concentration camps, or confining them to isolated villages with restricted access or to tightly policed urban ghettos. Official restrictions on the Rohingya's human rights, including their ability to earn a living, marry, have children, travel, access education and healthcare, have been well documented by human rights groups including Amnesty International,[68] Fortify Rights,[69] Human Rights Watch,[70] Médecins Sans Frontières (MSF),[71] and Physicians for Human Rights.[72] The threat of violence hangs constantly over the Rohingya and they are frequent victims of corrupt Myanmar officials, and have their everyday activities restricted by police and soldiers. The Rohingya's collective situation has not improved during Myanmar's recent years of quasi-civilian government, whether these administrations have been headed by ex-general Thein Sein or former icon of the democracy movement Aung San Suu Kyi. ISCI researcher Alicia de la Cour Venning ominously declared: 'This is what genocide looks like, just prior to the mass killing phase.'[73] Tragically for the Rohingya, the mass killing would soon follow.

As academics were increasingly labelling Myanmar's mistreatment of the Rohingya as genocide and Tatmadaw crimes against the Rohingya were news worldwide, the UN never formally applied the genocide label. This was despite dozens of reports from UN Special Rapporteurs highlighting egregious human rights violations against the Rohingya, assertions from the UN's High Commissioner for Human Rights that practices of ethnic cleansing were underway against the Rohingya, and clear statements from the UN Fact-Finding Mission that genocide crimes had been committed by the Tatmadaw. Having conducted their research throughout 2017 and 2018, the UN Fact-Finding Mission had little difficulty characterizing the Tatmadaw's 2017 campaign in northern Rakhine state as involving genocide crimes, crimes against humanity and war crimes.[74] They reported that 'The crimes in Rakhine State, and the manner in which they were perpetrated, are similar in nature, gravity and scope to those that have allowed genocidal intent to be established in other contexts', and identified 'Factors pointing at such intent include the broader oppressive context and hate rhetoric; specific utterances of commanders and direct perpetrators; exclusionary policies, including to alter the demographic composition of Rakhine State; the level of organization indicating a plan for destruction; and the extreme scale and brutality of the violence.'[75]

Had the UN, at any time, labelled Myanmar's crimes against the Rohingya as genocide, this would have compelled international action to prevent further crimes and to punish the perpetrators. A genocide declaration could have safeguarded the human rights of Rohingya civilians, saved lives and perhaps prevented the devastating 2017 forced deportation. Prevention should be a crucial part of the UN's approach to atrocity crimes and genocide. In practice the UN's response to ongoing genocides has been weak. High-level UN reluctance to take action that could have protected the Rohingya was sadly not an isolated failure, as previous inaction in Bosnia and Herzegovina and Rwanda illustrate.[76]

The narrow legal definition of genocide within the *Convention on the Prevention and Punishment of the Crime of Genocide* (*Genocide Convention*) may well have contributed to the UN's reluctance to acknowledge that the egregious human rights violations against the Rohingya amounted to genocide. Based on the work of Raphael Lemkin, who first developed the term genocide by creating a new word by amalgamating the Greek word *genos* (tribe or race) with the Latin word *cide* (killing), the *Genocide Convention* defines the crime as,

> ... any of the following acts committed with intent to destroy, in whole or in part, a national, ethnical, racial or religious group, as such: (a) Killing members of the group; (b) Causing serious bodily or mental harm to members of the group; (c) Deliberately inflicting on the group conditions of life calculated to bring about its physical destruction in whole or in part; (d) Imposing measures intended to prevent births within the group; (e) Forcibly transferring children of the group to another group.[77]

There is strong evidence the Rohingya are victims of criminal acts identified by the *Genocide Convention*. However, the question of whether Myanmar's authorities or Tatmadaw perpetrators demonstrated an 'intent' to destroy the Rohingya presented the UN with a ready excuse for inaction. The genocidal intent of Myanmar's authorities seems obvious and has been noted by human rights groups, scholars, and of course the Rohingya themselves, but this has not been the case among Myanmar's allies at the UN Security Council (UNSC) – China and Russia – and others reluctant to intervene unless their own national interests are directly threatened.

Establishing incontrovertible legal evidence of genocidal intent can take years and provide perpetrators with more than enough time to complete genocide crimes before they face an international response. As had been the case in other instances, tragically in Rwanda, debate and uncertainty about whether legal intent could be established and thus the genocide threshold had been reached contributed to high-level UN inaction and the impunity of perpetrators as they continued to commit atrocity crimes. In the Rwandan case, there was evidence too that governments avoided using the genocide label as it would have compelled them to act.[78] US President Bill Clinton's administration for instance, which used the word genocide privately and was aware of a 'final solution to eliminate all Tutsis', avoided using the word genocide publicly while the massacres in Rwanda were ongoing for fear this might legally oblige US intervention.[79]

The *Genocide Convention* certainly creates unintended challenges that limit the chances of real-time action to prevent genocide crimes, although for some scholars another key issue is that the heinous nature of genocide may inadvertently discourage action to address what are frequently treated as 'lesser' crimes, such as war crimes or crimes against humanity.[80] The *Genocide Convention* creates a double bind whereby action to prevent other atrocity crimes may be unintentionally discouraged (as key actors wait for clear evidence of genocide), as action to prevent genocide then becomes unlikely because of the high threshold required to adequately determine genocidal intent. The *Genocide Convention* certainly failed the Rohingya, just as it has frequently failed as a tool to prevent imminent genocide crimes in other contexts, including Bosnia and Herzegovina and Rwanda. The UN's 'Responsibility to Protect' (R2P) principles have been a similarly ineffective tool to prevent imminent mass atrocity crimes against vulnerable groups like the Rohingya. Within the R2P framework, the use of force to protect civilians remains the prerogative of the UN Security Council, is subject to potential veto by permanent members, and as such acts as a handbrake on action to prevent imminent atrocity crimes.

The international community must urgently consider what additional means of preventing imminent atrocity crimes might be available to it. Frustration with the *Genocide Convention* led the UK's Lord Alton to propose a *Genocide Determination Bill* to limit political interference in genocide determinations by removing these decisions from politicians and vesting them with the courts.[81] Lord Alton's proposals would be a useful addition to the genocide prevention arsenal and could provide a model for other jurisdictions. Yet without the political will to act, national governments are always likely to find excuses for their inaction in the face of genocide, especially if they perceive that their national interests are not directly impacted, or if there is a lack of domestic political support for intervention. The *Genocide Convention* might be useful for identifying and labelling genocides after they have occurred (such as with modern genocides in Bosnia and Herzegovina and Rwanda) and Rohingya would certainly welcome the UN's application of the genocide label, but its traditional application has been largely unhelpful to the Rohingya.

Hope the *Genocide Convention* might be used to curtail ongoing genocide crimes has been offered through an innovative strategy pursued by The Gambia, however. The Gambia began a formal legal dispute with Myanmar over its failure to protect the Rohingya from genocide. The Gambia's action through the ICJ was based on both countries being signatories to the *Genocide Convention*, which Gambia alleged Myanmar had breached.[82] Myanmar's initial defence was led by Aung San Suu Kyi, who attended the ICJ's courtroom in The Hague, and characterized her role as defending Myanmar from attack by the international community – a political pitch that played well domestically among Myanmar's Bamar majority. The legal defence Aung San Suu Kyi laid out was less well received. She admitted war crimes and other crimes against humanity may have been committed against the Rohingya but asserted that the atrocities stopped short of genocide. The ICJ is likely to spend years hearing the case before it makes any definitive determination about whether genocide might have been committed against the Rohingya, yet did agree, in January 2020, to The Gambia's request for Provisional Measures, akin to an emergency ruling, which required Myanmar to take steps to prevent genocide (including by the military), ensure evidence of crimes are not destroyed and to regularly report to the court about this. For the Rohingya, the ICJ's order of Provisional Measures, which are enforceable under international law (ultimately by the UNSC), represented the group's first taste of justice since Burma's military coup in the 1960s.

A politician not an icon

In the five years between Myanmar's first and second elections of the quasi-civilian era, Aung San Suu Kyi's political fortunes changed markedly for the better and the Rohingya's situation deteriorated further. Aung San Suu Kyi had spent the 2010 election under house arrest and could not participate in an election that elected Rohingya MPs. When Myanmar's next general election was held in November 2015, this situation was reversed – Aung San Suu Kyi's NLD participated and overwhelmingly won, and the Rohingya were barred from the

Figure 6 Having been disenfranchised, Rohingya in Maungdaw avoided public spaces on polling day 2015.

election, having been collectively disenfranchised by administrative fiat eight months before. The March 2015 cancellation of all 'White Card' identity documents by Thein Sein's government disenfranchised hundreds of thousands of Rohingya and an estimated 100,000 other Myanmar residents, including ethnic Chinese and people living in conflict zones and unable to access other citizenship documents.[83] The electoral roll in Rohingya MP Shwe Maung's Buthidaung constituency shrank to include the names of just ten Rohingya voters.[84] Virtually all Rohingya had been made ineligible to vote, let alone stand for election. The UEC further diminished Rohingya electoral participation by ruling that previously elected Rohingya law makers, including Shwe Maung – by then no longer associated with the USDP and seeking election as an independent candidate – could not recontest their seats.[85] This change in fortunes of the Rohingya Muslims and Aung San Suu Kyi's NLD between 2010 and 2015 provided a stark contrast that pointedly illustrates the Rohingya's increasing domestic political weakness throughout that time, the NLD's growing strength and the ambiguous nature of Myanmar's claimed transition to democracy.

In northern Rakhine state Muslim-majority communities like Buthidaung and Maungdaw, the Rohingya's political isolation was obvious by their invisibility at polling places. The streets of Buthidaung and Maungdaw, where I spent the 2015 election, ranged from subdued to deserted. On election day I saw long queues of ethnic Rakhine waiting to vote, boisterous members of the small local Hindu community determined to participate, and noticed the ethnic Chin voters that were entitled to elect a member of their own ethnicity to the Rakhine state *Hluttaw*. Maungdaw, with a roughly ninety per cent Rohingya population, resembled a ghost town: shops were shuttered, people were not on the streets and there was little traffic. With no chance to vote, Maungdaw's Rohingya avoided public spaces. This was a sad situation on a day election observation teams, which had been allowed for the 2015 poll, were reporting high voter attendances nationwide.[86] The UEC would claim a nationwide turnout of sixty-nine per cent.[87]

When I had visited Myanmar for the 2010 election, I did not imagine how the fortunes of the Rohingya and the NLD would diverge in the single parliamentary term that followed. Aung San Suu Kyi would be released from house arrest, and the NLD would be registered as an official political party and win a landslide election victory. The NLD would, after the 2015 election, form Myanmar's government, making Aung San Suu Kyi the country's State Counsellor, the de facto Prime Minister. Despite decades of discrimination and rights restrictions imposed on them by the authorities, the Rohingya had participated in the 2010 poll. They elected Rohingya MPs, which then gave Rohingya community leaders cause for cautious optimism about their group's future during the early years of Myanmar's new quasi-civilian administration. This situation had changed markedly by 2015, by which time the Rohingya's right to vote had been removed and more than 140,000 Rohingya in Rakhine state had spent the previous three years interred in squalid concentration camps.[88] In these circumstances, with the Rohingya's links to Myanmar's democratic processes severed and the Rohingya victims of mass incarceration, it surprised me that the Rohingya's mainstream political leadership remained implacably opposed to political violence and commonly retained hope that Aung San Suu Kyi's new government might help them. Sadly, they were wrong.

Aung San Suu Kyi came to power in 2016 as a global icon whose fight for democracy in Myanmar saw her placed under house arrest for fifteen years. She was prevented from seeing her children or gravely ill husband; Briton Michael Aris died of cancer in 1999 having not been allowed to visit Myanmar or see his wife for the previous four years.[89] Aung San Suu Kyi's civilian government has consistently failed to prioritize domestic human rights concerns. There have been strong international criticisms of her administration's failure to adequately address issues in Rakhine state and particularly for acquiescing to continued Tatmadaw rights abuses against the Rohingya. These criticisms have come from human rights activists, political leaders, other Nobel Peace Prize Laureates and, significantly, the UN's Fact-Finding Mission.[90] The UN Fact-Finding Mission, noting that Myanmar's civilian authorities lack the constitutional ability to directly control the actions of the military, found that, 'through their acts and omissions, the civilian authorities have contributed to the commission of atrocity crimes.'[91] Its 2018 report strongly criticized the country's civilian leader, asserting, 'The State Counsellor, Daw Aung San Suu Kyi, has not used her de facto position as Head of Government, nor her moral authority, to stem or prevent the unfolding events in Rakhine State.'[92]

I share this perspective and believe Aung San Suu Kyi's actions and public statements about the 2017 Rohingya refugee crisis helped to shield the Tatmadaw from legitimate domestic and international criticism, contributing to Tatmadaw impunity and encouraging brutality towards civilians in Rakhine state and elsewhere in Myanmar.[93] Myanmar's civilian government acquiesced to the Tatmadaw's 2017 'clearance operation' and for four crucial weeks – when almost half a million Rohingya were violently deported to Bangladesh – Aung San Suu Kyi was mute about the crisis. When she finally broke her silence, she delivered a speech in English – clearly targeting an international audience – in which she said her government did not 'fear international scrutiny' over how it handled the crisis in Rakhine state.[94] In an extraordinary display that indicated either breathtaking ignorance of events in Rakhine state or callous indifference, Aung San Suu Kyi expressed surprise that Muslims were fleeing Myanmar: 'We are concerned to hear that numbers of Muslims are fleeing across the border to Bangladesh' and 'We want to find out why this exodus is happening. We want to talk to those who have fled as well as those who have stayed.'[95] These attitudes reflected prevailing political opinion within Myanmar, where many believed Tatmadaw accounts in state media that a widespread Rohingya insurgency was underway and urgently needed to be put down. That Aung San Suu Kyi leaned towards narratives like this ought not have come as a surprise. In 2011, Aung San Suu Kyi told visiting US Secretary of State Hillary Clinton that she would rather be seen as a politician than as an icon, indicating she would likely be guided more by public opinion than a commitment to high-minded political principles.[96]

This was not the only time Aung San Suu Kyi cast doubt on Rohingya accounts of atrocities committed by the Tatmadaw. Perhaps most shockingly, she dismissed accounts of Tatmadaw sexual violence, using the capitalized two-word label 'FAKE RAPE' on her official Facebook page and the official State Counsellor website.[97] In December 2016, Aung San Suu Kyi or someone representing her posted this label alongside photos of Rohingya women who alleged they were raped by Myanmar soldiers (these posts remained on sites controlled by Aung San Suu Kyi years later). For decades, human rights groups have documented Tatmadaw use of rape as a weapon of war against Myanmar's ethnic and religious minorities.[98] Aung San Suu Kyi's indifference to Rohingya victims reflects her government's indifference to rights violations against the Rohingya generally, and contributes to Tatmadaw impunity for atrocity crimes like these committed against the Rohingya and other minorities in Myanmar.

There have been strong criticisms of Aung San Suu Kyi's actions by former high-profile international supporters. More than a dozen other Nobel Peace Laureates, including Desmond Tutu, Malala Yousafzai and Muhammad Yunus, accused her of acquiescing to continued rights abuses against the Rohingya.[99] From 2017, international criticism of Aung San Suu Kyi became more widespread, with cities and institutions that previously lauded her role as a champion of democracy reversing these decisions. The city of Oxford, where Aung San Suu Kyi was famously a student, revoked her 'freedom of the city', her *alma mater* St Hugh's College removed her portrait from public display and Canada's government revoked her honourary citizenship.[100] Musician, anti-poverty activist and Band Aid charity founder Bob Geldof characterized Aung San Suu

Kyi as 'a murderer', suggesting 'perhaps she should appear at the Hague tribunal' and he returned his own freedom of the City of Dublin (an honour Aung San Suu Kyi also held) as a protest, because 'I do not wish to be associated in any way with an individual currently engaged in the mass ethnic cleansing of the Rohingya people of north-west Burma.'[101] City honours bestowed on Aung San Suu Kyi from London, Dublin, Glasgow and Paris were revoked, and Amnesty International withdrew its highest honour, the Ambassador of Conscience Award, 'in light of the Myanmar leader's shameful betrayal of the values she once stood for'.[102] The US Holocaust Memorial Museum revoked the Elie Wiesel Award, pointing out how the NLD under Aung San Suu Kyi's leadership had 'refused to cooperate with UN investigators, promulgated hateful rhetoric against the Rohingya community, and denied access to and cracked down on journalists trying to uncover the scope of the crimes in Rakhine State'.[103]

Increasingly, Aung San Suu Kyi is seen internationally as embodying the worst characteristics of a politician, yet her standing within Myanmar remains high, especially among the ethnic Bamar majority. A 2019 poll by Myanmar's People's Alliance for Credible Elections indicated that Aung San Suu Kyi was the most popular public figure in the country by a wide margin, with a net positive (confidence) rating of sixty per cent nationwide and in excess of seventy per cent confidence in Bamar-majority areas.[104] By comparison, public confidence in religious leaders was just thirty-four per cent, institutions like the UN fared worse with twenty-one per cent confidence, and the courts had a negative five per cent rating.

While symbolic actions like revoking Aung San Suu Kyi's awards and honours reflect concerns she and her civilian administration have not done enough in recent times to address the Rohingya's appalling circumstances, humanitarian and human rights organizations have been raising concerns about the Rohingya's mistreatment for decades. Since the 1970s there have been a range of research reports addressing the persecution and dire circumstances of Muslims in Rakhine state. Key among these has been research by Amnesty International, Fortify Rights, Human Rights Watch, Physicians for Human Rights, Refugees International and frequent public statements by groups including *Action Contre la Faim*, Concern, MSF, Oxfam, the Red Cross and Save the Children.[105] Amnesty International described how the Rohingya have been subject to 'decades of severe persecution' and that before the 2017 'clearance operation' Myanmar's security forces subjected the Rohingya to mistreatment that may 'constitute crimes against humanity'.[106] This echoed Human Rights Watch's conclusions in the aftermath of the 2012 violence, that the Rohingya (and Kaman Muslims) had been subject to 'crimes against humanity carried out as part of a campaign of ethnic cleansing'.[107] Despite this, and the common use of political violence by ethnic minority groups Myanmar-wide, mainstream Rohingya political opinion for decades rejected a strategy of political violence. By late 2016 this attitude appeared to have changed for some Rohingya with the emergence of the Arakan Rohingya Salvation Army (ARSA) militant group, which claimed to represent the interests of the Rohingya community.

A new insurgency

Strategies of political violence have been adopted by Myanmar's ethnic minority groups since the country's independence. Yet after suffering decades of discrimination by Myanmar's authorities since the 1960s, mainstream Rohingya opinion had not commonly advocated a strategy of political violence. A post-independence Rohingya *Mujahid* insurgency had mostly ended by the 1960s and by the 1970s Rohingya militancy was almost entirely defunct. The Rohingya can legitimately be regarded as a Muslim group that suffered decades of mistreatment by Myanmar's authorities though did not radicalize.[108] However, there is now evidence that since the Rakhine state violence of 2012 and subsequent mass incarceration of Rohingya, some Muslims in northern Rakhine state became sympathetic to political violence and engaged with the ARSA group.

Co-ordinated attacks by ARSA militants on three internal border posts on 9 October 2016 indicated efforts were being made within the Rohingya community to adopt a more militant approach. Responsibility for the attacks, which killed nine security officials, was quickly claimed by ARSA, sparking fears of a possible return to the Rohingya's *Mujahid* militancy of the 1950s, or the emergence of an Islamic State in Iraq and Syria (ISIS)-style insurgency aiming for exclusive Muslim control of territory in Rakhine state. ARSA is allegedly substantially foreign funded, with its leader Ata Ullah having been a long-time Saudi Arabian resident, but the group has consistently denied transnational jihadi links. In response to media reports that an ARSA member planned to attack Myanmar's Malaysian Embassy, ARSA issued a prompt refutation via Twitter: 'It is, once again, reassured that #ARSA only legitimately and objectively operates as an #ETHNO-NATIONALIST movement within its ancestral homeland (Arakan) in #Burma & its activities had not & will not transcend beyond its country.'[109] The Tatmadaw's response to ARSA's October 2016 attacks was immediate, aggressive and prolonged. Subsequent ARSA attacks in August 2017 provided the Tatmadaw with the licence they needed to undertake a more widespread and brutal clearance operation than that of the year before. As will be outlined in the following chapters, mainstream Rohingya leaders have focused on peaceful political strategies in recent decades, although the involvement of local Rohingya with the October 2016 and August 2017 attacks indicated attitudes towards non-violent political action had certainly changed for some.

The brutality of the Tatmadaw's response to ARSA's 2016 and 2017 actions has since given those who might have been attracted to ARSA serious cause to reconsider the utility of an armed Rohingya insurgency. The relative success of the ethnonationalist Rakhine Arakan Army (AA) militants against Tatmadaw targets should not be underestimated as a potential motivator and model for future ARSA activity within Rakhine state if ARSA manages to regroup there. ARSA's 2019 report *Reviving the Courageous Hearts* indicated the group intended to do precisely that and remained, 'determined to continue its struggle and fight to end the genocide'.[110] Since Myanmar's authorities have made little effort to address the grievances underpinning ARSA's emergence, this may well be a long and bloody fight – a point not lost on ARSA's leadership, who ended their 2019 report by ominously stating, 'ARSA will not give up until the last breath or until all its demands are fulfilled'.[111] Yet, political violence remains a minority strategy among the Rohingya community, whose mainstream leadership holds to strategies of peaceful political engagement. This peaceful approach is jeopardized by the continued abuse of Rohingya civilians by Myanmar government policies, Tatmadaw violence and deteriorating conditions for Rohingya refugees in Bangladesh.

Rohingya in northern Rakhine state reported that, in 2016 and 2017, Myanmar's authorities did not support or protect moderate village leaders or those who spoke against political violence when ARSA was first organizing within their communities. Scores of moderate Rohingya village leaders and those who spoke against ARSA were alleged to have been killed by ARSA in northern Rakhine state during that time (although there were likely also killings by crime gangs and others using ARSA as a cover to settle old scores).[112] Myanmar's authorities refused to intervene when Rohingya communities asked for help. Unlike their regulation and control of virtually every other aspect of Rohingya lives, Myanmar's authorities treated these security concerns as internal Rohingya community matters and refused to provide help. This official inaction was counter-productive, cost the lives of moderate Rohingya village leaders, contributed to ARSA's unchecked growth as alternative community voices were silenced by fear or death, and ultimately enabled ARSA's 2016 and 2017 attacks. Worryingly, there have been signs that Bangladesh's authorities might adopt similarly counter-productive approaches to security in Rohingya refugee camp communities. Instead of ensuring Rohingya have peaceful outlets to express their political views and are included in camp decision-making, in 2019 and 2020 Bangladesh's authorities restricted the rights of Rohingya refugee camp communities, erecting barbed wire fences around camps, confiscating mobile phones and SIM cards from refugees, and strictly enforcing a dusk-to-dawn curfew inside the camps.

After the removal of pre-press censorship and the speedy proliferation of smartphones, internet access and social media, Myanmar's authorities retained a range of methods to limit publication about topics deemed sensitive. By 2017 the media freedoms of the previous five years were once again under serious pressure from Myanmar's authorities. Topping the list of sensitive topics include criticisms of the Tatmadaw and mention of the Rohingya's citizenship and human rights situation. As my journalist colleague explained, by 2015, the authorities, in the absence of pre-publication censorship, had devised other means to limit discussion of sensitive topics. There were frequent arrests and prosecutions of journalists for critical reporting of the civilian government or Tatmadaw. The highest profile of these were the December 2017 arrests of Kyaw Soe Oo and Wa Lone, two young Reuters reporters investigating allegations soldiers murdered Rohingya men and disposed of their bodies in a mass grave at the northern Rakhine state village of Inn Din.[113] The arrest of these journalists drew international attention to the pressures Myanmar's authorities place on the media to portray official actions in a positive light, even when these actions have included appalling human rights violations against groups like the Rohingya.[114] Charged using the country's *Official Secrets Act*, a little used colonial remnant, a farcical trial followed. The allegedly secret information was shown to be publicly available, yet Kyaw Soe Oo and Wa Lone were found guilty and sentenced to seven years in jail.[115]

Under intense international pressure, the Tatmadaw reluctantly undertook an investigation into the actions of its troops at Inn Din. Senior General Min Aung Hlaing's office later issued a statement on Facebook (in Myanmar, Facebook has been the preferred platform for official announcements), admitting to the existence of the mass grave and declaring that the Rohingya victims were 'Bengali terrorist' prisoners who were executed by Tatmadaw troops.[116] The clear implication from the Tatmadaw's top brass was that the Rohingya victims deserved their fate. A later Tatmadaw Facebook post confirmed that seven soldiers were sentenced to '10 years in prison with hard labor in a remote area' for participating in the murders.[117] This was the first Tatmadaw admission of extra-judicial killings in the 2017 clearance operation, and came only after Reuters published incontrovertible evidence that Tatmadaw troops had committed the atrocity and reporters had been jailed – no doubt to send a warning to others who might report on Tatmadaw crimes.[118]

Reuters' work on the Rohingya's expulsion from Myanmar was recognized with a 2019 Pulitzer Prize that noted the contribution of Kyaw Soe Oo and Wa Lone.[119] The shockingly harsh treatment meted out to Kyaw Soe Oo and Wa Lone for working to uncover evidence of Tatmadaw crimes, when compared with the Tatmadaw's reluctance to investigate and admit wrongdoing, further contributed to an environment of Tatmadaw impunity. This episode marked a key inflection point in the decline of press freedom in Myanmar, with the reaction of Aung San Suu Kyi, the State Counsellor, representing a chilling reminder of the pressures faced by Myanmar's journalists.[120] Foreign diplomats recalled how Aung San Suu Kyi reacted angrily to suggestions she ought to intervene to ensure the reporters' release and they subsequently spent more than 500 days in jail before obtaining a presidential pardon, necessary because the biased judicial process had ordered them jailed. Worryingly, the UN issued a statement suggesting the eventual release of Kyaw Soe Oo and Wa Lone represented evidence that Myanmar's authorities remained committed to a democratic transition.[121] These brave young journalists' jailing surely represented the opposite – a strong indication Myanmar's authorities, whether civilian or military, rejected fundamental democratic pillars like press freedom and justice, and will not soon change their attitude or discriminatory policies towards ethnic and religious minorities like the Rohingya.

A political problem with a political solution

The 2019 optimism of Myanmar's UN leadership about the country's progress towards democracy reflected a longer-term approach by the UN in Myanmar that had prioritized maintaining friendly relations with the country's leadership above human rights concerns. Myanmar's UN office has been accused of ignoring clear early warning signs that violence against the Rohingya was escalating and widespread atrocity crimes were likely to occur, with an internal UN memo from April 2017 describing the UN's Myanmar operation as 'glaringly dysfunctional'.[122] The UN's Myanmar resident co-ordinator between 2014 and 2017, Renata Lok-

Dessallien, a career UN staffer, certainly muted domestic UN criticisms of the Myanmar authorities' mistreatment of the Rohingya during her time in charge. This approach did not lead to any useful policy change by Myanmar's authorities, and the UN's failure to call out systematic rights violations was blamed for giving licence to the Myanmar authorities' continued mass incarceration of Rohingya civilians in Rakhine state, and to discriminatory practices against the Rohingya.[123]

Frustration with the UN's engagement in Rakhine state was frequently raised with me by humanitarian workers, human rights advocates and UN staffers, yet some foreign officials were far from pessimistic. One foreign official with expert knowledge of the Rohingya's situation and the specifics of Lok-Dessallien's approach spoke optimistically to me in late 2015 about the role the UN could play. Their ongoing work in Rakhine state required anonymity and so they are identified here as 'John'. John argued the UN could provide frameworks that would be useful for both development and humanitarian progress in Rakhine state, but in so doing identified a UN strategy that would, in the years following, be criticized for having acquiesced to the Myanmar authorities' discrimination against the Rohingya.

Central to the approach outlined to me by John, particularly after the controversial expulsion of INGOs from Rakhine state in 2014, was the provision of development assistance to ethnic Rakhine communities that matched the UN funding for humanitarian aid being provided to Rohingya communities. A key motivation for this approach was the hope that demonstrating to ethnic Rakhine that their community, along with the Rohingya, were beneficiaries of UN funds might temper ethnic Rakhine anger towards the UN's humanitarian role in Rakhine state, reducing perceptions that Rohingya were benefiting more from foreign assistance, and so diffuse tensions between Buddhist and Muslim communities. UN funds were spent to achieve a political outcome – the political support of ethnic Rakhine – rather than on the basis of community need.

Rakhine perceptions that the Rohingya were unfairly receiving international assistance that the Rakhine were denied were considered by key UN figures to have fuelled anti-Rohingya and anti-foreigner attitudes that contributed to a fraught environment for the UN and humanitarian INGOs in Rakhine state. John suggested of this,

> The United Nations has an opportunity to do two very significant roles, firstly to provide that global development and humanitarian framework processes. The UN brings to Rakhine a series of skill sets that will be very important for development. Secondly, perhaps even more importantly, it has a moral and

political authority that no NGO can match, and it can speak on behalf of humanity. The UN is a sort of honest broker. Even though it's been accused by Rakhine nationalists as being pro-Muslims, pro-Rohingya. It has moral authority to speak out on behalf of issues. The Union government and particularly Aung San Suu Kyi will listen to the UN.

The outcomes for the Rohingya did not live up to this optimistic perspective. The UN's direction in Myanmar was understandably criticized by human rights groups and former senior UN Myanmar officials for failing to adequately press the authorities to improve the Rohingya's humanitarian situation (including by closing the concentration camps to which the Rohingya had by then been confined for years) and grant speedy access to citizenship.[124] The separation of Rakhine state's Buddhist and Muslim communities, which involved confining Rohingya to concentration camps, was argued by human rights advocates as entrenching discrimination against the Rohingya.[125] Despite human rights led criticisms the UN has continued to support Myanmar's concentration camp system, cooperating with Myanmar's authorities to provide food aid and basic medical care for the more than 100,000 incarcerated Rohingya civilians.

The UN's Rakhine state strategy, from John's perspective, was based on using development funds to help progress towards a peaceful resolution of the crisis rather than seeking the immediate repatriation of Rohingya from camps. The UN in Myanmar appeared to have assumed that stability and infrastructure development in Rakhine state would lead to economic progress and then eventually to peace. There was little apparent push from the UN's highest-level staff for improved rights for the Rohingya, or for a formal dialogue that would allow the Rakhine and the Rohingya to share, negotiate and address their grievances. The Rohingya's residency and human rights situation remained mostly stagnant for years after the 2012 violence. This contributed to criticisms of the UN's Myanmar leadership for failing to demonstrate appropriate concern about the Rohingya's ongoing humanitarian situation and their mass incarceration. While John characterized the outcome of the 2015 general election as representing a demand for 'change' and 'a clear message to everyone that the status quo was not acceptable', the UN's approach nonetheless actively contributed to a discriminatory status quo. John still spoke enthusiastically about the potential for Rohingya to return to their home communities: 'The government agreed last year, the Union government, through the Rakhine state government, to have people returned, other than those in the urban Sittwe camps, to return to their original homes.' These promised repatriations were desperately slow to occur and ensured that more than 100,000 Rohingya languished in concentration camps for years. Human rights groups expressed concerns that the UN in Myanmar, by failing to more vocally assert the Rohingya's right to return to their home communities, was acceding to the continuation of discriminatory policies towards the group and their continued displacement.[126]

Likely motivating the UN's Myanmar leadership focus on development progress in Rakhine state rather than prioritizing human rights was the belief the Rakhine state economy had suffered badly because of inter-communal violence and the subsequent long-term separation of Buddhist and Muslim communities. John told me that,

> It's hugely affected the economy. Firstly, on a day-to-day basis, there has been a strong economic relationship between Rakhine and Muslims for generations. Muslims were largely fishermen in Rakhine, they were the agricultural labourers, they helped harvest the rice crop here and many of the traders in Sittwe and other towns were Muslim. Now the contribution of those individuals is tiny because they are locked up in camps or they are unable to move. I frequently hear from Rakhine communities that I talk with and individuals lamenting the fact that they can't have Muslim workers, that tradesman are unavailable, that the cost of getting things repaired has come up enormously because there is only half the tradesmen to do it, so there is a practical cost to this separation of communities. On a larger level, Western countries certainly will be very reluctant to invest here through private companies or through the provision of development aid unless the situation of human rights issues is resolved. So, for the state itself, it's got chronic development issues in infrastructure, transport, health services and so on. To get real assistance has been restricted by the perceptions of human rights abuses, instability, insecurity for internationals to come here. So, at the grassroots and the macro level there has been a considerable cost to this conflict in Rakhine.

This was not incorrect – Rakhine state's economy had previously been acknowledged as Myanmar's second worst performing after Chin state, although following the violence of 2012, the World Bank released data indicating Rakhine state had become Myanmar's poorest, with a poverty rate of seventy-eight per cent.[127] The perilous state of the local economy was consistently borne out by my research, with ethnic Rakhine and Rohingya regularly raising with me their concerns about the destruction of local economies in the aftermath of the 2012 violence and the forced separation of their communities. This separation, and particularly the isolation of

Muslim communities, was widely acknowledged to have badly affected the economy, and the ongoing rights violations against the Rohingya limited the enthusiasm of potential investors.[128] As John explained, 'There are huge development issues here – for international investment to take place, for people to have confidence to invest in Rakhine and to support the state government there will have to be a resolution of human rights issues, freedom of movement and so on.'

Rakhine state was badly in need of development and this was a concern frequently raised with me by ethnic Rakhine and Rohingya. However, development progress in a context of widespread discrimination against the Rohingya would not improve the economy equally for all, and instead reinforce the Rohingya's relative disadvantage. As it turned out, from 2012 there would be little development progress to the benefit of ordinary ethnic Rakhine either. Instead, the bulk of investment in Rakhine state, notably in the oil and gas sector, would be to the benefit of the central authorities, the Tatmadaw, cronies, a small cohort of local elites and of course international investors.

By late 2017, as a Tatmadaw clearance operation forcibly deported hundreds of thousands of Rohingya, John's perspective would prove to have been unrealistically optimistic, and the UN's role in Rakhine state would be increasingly scrutinized and criticized. In October 2017, the UN's most senior figure in Myanmar, Lok-Dessallien, was removed. This was interpreted by many as a rebuke of her approach to Rakhine state issues generally, and particularly the perception she had deprioritized addressing the Rohingya's humanitarian situation and instead pursued a strategy prioritizing development progress. Throughout my research, divergent opinions within the UN about the appropriate strategy to adopt in Rakhine state became clear. The Lok-Dessallien approach was not universally admired, and other UN staffers working in Myanmar focused as much as possible on human rights and the urgent need to address the Rohingya's appalling humanitarian situation.

A senior Myanmar UN official whom I spoke with in Yangon in early 2016 presented a much less optimistic picture of the UN's engagement. Their ongoing work in Myanmar likewise necessitated anonymity so they are identified here as Mark. Unlike John, he suggested the urgent need to address the Rohingya's dire humanitarian circumstances and was sceptical that a development-focused approach would improve the humanitarian situation in Rakhine state. Characterizing the Rakhine state crisis as a political rather than economic problem, Mark told me the Rohingya's situation was, 'A political problem with a political solution that cannot be resolved by humanitarian or development actors.' They illustrated the hazards of the UN's focus on development aid, saying,

'Development of Rakhine state will help with any solution, but it is not a solution in itself.'

Mark expressed disappointment that the international response to the 2015 migration crisis focused on human trafficking rather than the underlying causes of the Rohingya's migration – their lack of citizenship and the appalling human rights abuses they suffered in Myanmar. He said, 'One of my big disappointments last year was the boat crisis. The response regionally, and of the international community, was really focusing on the trafficking. And there was talk initially about dealing with the root causes of this whole crisis, and the root causes are lack of freedom of moment and a lack of rights.' Mark believed Myanmar's authorities did not want to resolve the Rohingya's displacement problem and did not want to resettle Rohingya outside of the Rakhine state camps. He cited the speedy resettlement in permanent accommodation of Buddhists displaced by a 2015 conflict between the Tatmadaw and the AA, explaining that, 'As humanitarians we are used to working in countries where the government can't do response, and here it's not that at all, it's something very different.' Unlike the Rohingya, displaced Buddhists were not expected to languish in camps indefinitely. Describing the authorities' biased approach to displaced Buddhist and Muslim communities, Mark said, 'when they want to resolve a displaced community, they can.'

This points to both the disingenuous approach of Myanmar's authorities and clear failings in the strategy adopted by the UN's Myanmar leadership during the period between Rakhine state's 2012 violence and the 2017 crisis. The removal of Lok-Dessallien from her post as UN Myanmar resident co-ordinator in late 2017 seemed to suggest that the UN's New York hierarchy also considered her strategy had failed. Since Lok-Dessallien's removal, there has not been a major realignment of the UN's Myanmar strategy. This indicated that Lok-Dessallien's position had become politically untenable following the Rohingya's 2017 forced migration rather than her approach being rejected by the UN hierarchy. The evidence certainly bears this out – the UN has continued to be involved with the mass incarceration of Rohingya in concentration camps, and Lok-Dessallien's replacement Knut Ostby has pursued a development-led approach, similar to that which has so obviously failed the Rohingya in the past.

Not all UN agencies were wilfully blind to Myanmar's mistreatment of the Rohingya and to Myanmar's failed democratic transition. Since beginning its work in March 2017, the UN Fact-Finding Mission had consistently voiced concerns about human rights violations by Myanmar's authorities against the Rohingya and the mistreatment of other minorities, including the Kachin and Shan. The Fact-Finding Mission portrayed Tatmadaw actions in northern

Rakhine state as having included genocide, crimes against humanity and war crimes.[129] It called for the prosecution of senior Myanmar military figures by either a referral to the International Criminal Court (ICC) or the creation of an *ad hoc* international criminal tribunal. These accusations and recommendations ensured that the Rohingya's situation was at least considered by the UNSC, although any discussion of the Rohingya's situation happened over the objections of key Myanmar allies, China and Russia. In October 2018, UN Fact-Finding Mission chair Marzuki Darusman told the UNSC that,

> Our report characterizes the recent events in Rakhine state as a human rights catastrophe that was foreseeable and planned. It will have a severe impact for many generations to come, if not forever. The report describes in detail the Tatmadaw's so-called clearance operations in six villages, marked by large-scale massacres and other killings of civilians, including women, children and the elderly, as well as mass gang rape, burning and looting.[130]

Darusman alerted the UNSC that an ongoing genocide was taking place and described how Rohingya who remained in Rakhine state were 'at grave risk', while steps to return those Rohingya who fled were 'tantamount to condemning them to life as subhumans and further mass killing'.[131] He concluded with a blunt rebuttal of the UNSC's frequent excuse for inaction on atrocity crimes – national sovereignty – by stating that, 'National sovereignty is not a license to commit crimes against humanity or genocide.' Darusman's compelling testimony did not convince Myanmar's UNSC allies to change their approach. China's UN Ambassador Ma Zhaoxu told the council, 'it should not get involved in country-specific human rights issues' and that the briefing would 'not help to resolve the issue of Rakhine state but will rather further complicate it'.[132] China and Russia failed to stop the UNSC discussing the Rohingya's situation, yet as permanent members with veto power they have proved an effective roadblock to any UNSC action to prevent further atrocities in Myanmar, to hold perpetrators to account and to a referral to the ICC.[133]

Frustration with the lack of action from the UNSC led the UN Human Rights Council to establish an Independent Investigative Mechanism for Myanmar.[134] This body's role was to gather evidence that could be used to facilitate future criminal proceedings against the perpetrators of atrocity crimes – a step welcomed by the UN General Assembly. Calls to hold perpetrators accountable were heeded too by the ICC's Chief Prosecutor, Fatou Bensouda. As a veteran of the International Criminal Tribunal for Rwanda, established to judge people responsible for the genocide against the Tutsi in the 1990s, the Gambian prosecutor had played a key role in the first international tribunal to recognize rape as a strategy of genocide.[135] This would be useful experience for the Myanmar case, where human rights groups have long argued that sexual violence was a key Tatmadaw strategy unleashed against Myanmar's ethnic and religious minorities. The UN Population Fund documented 'horrific' accounts of rape and sexual assault against Rohingya women and girls fleeing the Tatmadaw's 2017 'clearance operation' and suggested this might be 'just the tip of the iceberg'.[136]

The absence of an UNSC referral created challenges for the ICC to establish jurisdiction. Matters for the ICC were further complicated because its jurisdiction in South and Southeast Asia has long been patchy. Myanmar had a lengthy history of refusing to cooperate with international human rights investigations and steadfastly refused to sign the *Rome Statute* that established the ICC.[137] This contributed to the Tatmadaw's sense of impunity – Tatmadaw perpetrators of atrocity crimes in Myanmar were above the law domestically, and avoided international law. Significantly, in 2010 Bangladesh's government ratified the *Rome Statute* and so Bensouda considered whether the Rohingya's forced deportation to an ICC member state might provide the court with jurisdiction and the ability to undertake prosecutions for crimes against the Rohingya.[138] She portrayed the Rohingya's forced deportation as akin to 'a cross-border shooting' where the crime 'is not completed until the bullet [fired in one state] strikes and kills the victim [standing in another state].'[139] By arguing that an 'essential element' of the crime of deportation involved the Rohingya's forced migration to the territory of a *Rome Statute* signatory, Bensouda maintained that this presented the ICC with clear grounds to assert its jurisdiction.[140] Judges from an ICC Pre-Trial Chamber agreed, and the ICC has subsequently begun to investigate whether the Tatmadaw and others committed crimes against humanity (and potentially other crimes including genocide) during the 2017 deportation of the Rohingya.[141] ICC justice moves slowly, and it may be decades before perpetrators of atrocity crimes against Rohingya victims of the 2017 forced deportation are brought to trial, if at all. In the absence of concrete action from the UNSC, and with Myanmar's civilian authorities reluctant to address Tatmadaw criminality, Rohingya are increasingly putting their hopes for justice in the hands of international legal processes available through bodies like the ICC and the ICJ.

5

Conflicting Historical Narratives

Any reasonable judgement of history would conclude that the Rohingya were indigenous to Myanmar and entitled to citizenship rights there. However, since the 1960s, governments and the Tatmadaw have rejected Rohingya citizenship claims with devastating human rights consequences. In this chapter, I briefly summarize how Rohingya historical perspectives clash with official beliefs. I describe how this has contributed to the ongoing denial of Rohingya citizenship, which the authorities use to enable human rights abuses against them. Addressing common disagreements over the Rohingya's heritage is important because it explains their circumstances during military rule, why the recent policy liberalizations – lauded by Western governments – have not included granting citizenship rights to the Rohingya, and why certain historical narratives remain so deeply entrenched. This will help to contextualize the contemporary Rohingya perspectives presented in the chapters that follow.

History continues to be central to how Myanmar's political actors frame their assertions to legitimacy and present their grievances. This has especially been the case for ethnic minority groups who describe how official narratives (including school textbooks) minimize their visibility to undermine their legitimacy. While this book has focused on the Rohingya's use of history to claim Myanmar citizenship and rights, other ethnic minority grievances and claims are just as frequently grounded in history and met with hostility from Myanmar's authorities. Even Rakhine assertions about history have been aggressively rejected. Prominent Rakhine nationalist political figure Dr Aye Maung (a former state MP and leader of the Rakhine nationalist Arakan National Party, or ANP) was arrested following his speech at a January 2018 protest marking the anniversary of the 1784 Burmese conquest of Arakan's Mrauk-U kingdom.[1] He was subsequently charged under the Unlawful Associations Act and sections of the Penal Code relating to 'high treason' and incitement. Media reports indicated that official fears that his speech 'could cause disunity among the majority Bamar and Rakhine communities' motivated his arrest.[2] In 2019, Aye Maung received a twenty-year prison sentence.[3] Tatmadaw leaders have also drawn heavily on history to frame their own legitimacy, portraying themselves as continuing a warrior king tradition associated with revered Burmese dynastic rulers.

The use of history in post-independence constitutions and the *Burma Citizenship Act (1982)* meant the collective right to citizenship as a *taingyintha* has accrued to ethnic groups resident in Myanmar prior to the British colonial period. Understandably, contemporary Rohingya leaders have sought to show how Rohingya meet this criterion by pointing to their group's lengthy residency in Myanmar (and the jurisdictions that preceded it). Multiple factors account for the Muslim population in historic Arakan. Until its 1784 invasion by Burma, the Arakan kingdom's internal development had been generally independent of the Buddhist kingdoms east of the Arakan Yoma mountains. Being bordered by populous Muslim lands helps to clarify how Arakan could develop with a majority Buddhist population and a substantial Muslim minority, in contrast to its overwhelmingly Buddhist eastern neighbours. Throughout the last millennium, freedom of movement between Arakan and the Muslim lands to its west has been the rule rather than the exception. Substantial Muslim settlement in pre-colonial Arakan was documented over a long period of time by visitors to the kingdom, who noted the influence of Muslim-dominated maritime trade. The visibility of Islam in Arakan was evidenced too by Arakanese rulers' use of Muslim courtesy titles and the minting of trilingual coins bearing Arakanese, Bengali and Persian language inscriptions and commonly including the *Kalima*. Frequently unacknowledged by Myanmar's authorities, the Tatmadaw, nationalists *and* Rohingya leaders is the involuntary transportation to Arakan of slaves (Hindus and Muslims) taken from Bengal. This was, for centuries, a key element of Arakan's economic strategy and accounted for Bengali and Muslim settlement in Arakan prior to British colonial rule.

Rohingya historians, organizations like the Arakan Rohingya National Organisation, the Arakan Rohingya Union and those contemporary Rohingya leaders regarded as particularly knowledgeable about the group's history, including Kyaw Hla Aung, Nurul Islam and Wakar Uddin (whose perspectives are examined in detail in Chapters Six and Seven), regard evidence of a Muslim population in the former Arakan kingdom as evidence of a historic Rohingya population there. Prominent Rohingya figures like Abu Tahay, Htay Lwin Oo, Kyaw Hla Aung and Nurul Islam frequently rely on the published writings of Francis Buchanan as evidence for the presence of the Rooinga (Rohingya) in pre-colonial Arakan. They describe evidence of Muslim settlement in Arakan dating back centuries to constitute proof that settlers represented the forebears of the modern-day Rohingya, and they argue that the Rohingya must consequently be recognized as a *taingyintha* and so granted Myanmar citizenship. The perceived strength of the Rohingya's historical claims has contributed to the widespread belief among contemporary Rohingya leaders that their people would be accepted as Myanmar citizens if only Myanmar's decision-makers acknowledged the evidence backing their claim and could be sufficiently motivated to deliver for the Rohingya the rights to which they are legally entitled.

Mainstream Rohingya leaders commonly assert that Muslims began to arrive in Arakan from the eighth century, with the first arrivals by sea (including from shipwrecks along Arakan's coast). This perspective of how Islam came to Arakan and Rohingya identity developed from the eighth century has dominated international media representations of what the Rohingya themselves believe to be their history. Recurring themes throughout my research were the Rohingya's strong identification with the Rohingya name, and their centuries of connection with the Rakhine state area. Rohingya leaders generally present one of two accounts for the origins of the Rohingya name – either that it derived from the name of the land, Rohang, an old name for Arakan, or that it derived from the word *rahma*, which they usually identified as an Arabic word for mercy that had been used by shipwrecked Arab sailors. Both *rahma* and Rohang were understood to have evolved, over time, to Rohingya.

Among the more influential historians of the Rohingya have been Tahir Ba Tha and Muhammad Yunus. Tahir Ba Tha's 1963 Burmese language history *Rohingyas and Kamans* was translated to English by A.F.K. Jilani as *A Short History of Rohingyas and Kamans of Burma*. Jilani's historical knowledge became influential among the Rohingya too. Tahir Ba Tha's book was frequently referred to by Rohingya and has been described by the Bangladesh-based, Rohingya-run Kaladan Press Network as a 'landmark in the history of Rohingya people'[4] Tahir Ba Tha understood Islam had first come to Arakan before Arakan's Vesali dynasty was established in 788, and that Rohingya had lived in Arakan since 'time immemorial'.[5] He described the Mrauk-U kingdom as an Islamic Sultanate (like the neighbouring Bengal Sultanate) where there was Buddhist and Muslim concord, and he blamed British colonial rulers for creating animosities and conflict between Arakan's confessional groups. Tahir Ba Tha presented multiple explanations for how the name Rohingya came to be used by Arakan's Muslims – some of these explanations have been accepted by contemporary Rohingya leaders; for instance, that the Rohingya name derived from an old Arakan label for Muslims – Rohai or Roshangee. These he indicated were probably a corruption of the Arabic word for blessing – *Raham*. Perhaps the more compelling explanation was Tahir Ba Tha's claim that the name Rohingya might have derived from Arakan's old name, Rohang. Muhammad Yunus generally followed Tahir Ba Tha's lead, describing the origins of the Rohingya name in similar terms, claiming Arakan as a one-time Islamic Sultanate and believing its founder Min Saw Mon/Narameikhla to have been a Muslim convert.[6] For Yunus, evidence for this was strengthened by Arakan's official use of the Persian language until the mid-nineteenth century. Although Tahir Ba Tha did not present evidence for the use of Persian by Arakan's court, he was correct about this. Persian was a diplomatic *lingua franca* for Bay of Bengal polities until the nineteenth century and was certainly used by Arakan's rulers throughout that time.

Documentary evidence of Arakan's links with the wider world have unfortunately often been beyond the ready reach of scholars from that region. The Burmese conquest saw the wholesale destruction of Arakan's government records, and a consequence of Britain's later role as a colonial power is that substantial manuscript collections relating to Arakan are held by the British Library and British Museum in London, around 10,000 kilometres from Rakhine state. However, the recent resurgence in interest in Arakan's history will likely contribute to a more thorough examination of these and other foreign-held collections (such as the VOC archive) in the coming years, and this will likely bring forward further evidence of Islam's long-term influence in Arakan and of the kingdom's historic links with regional and world trade networks.

One palm leaf manuscript, held by the British Museum, demonstrates how in 1728, Arakan's King Sandawizaya provided a Persian-language trade permit to an Armenian merchant based in Chennaipattana (Chennai), named Khwaja Georgin.[7] I have found archival evidence in the British Library's collections that Arakan's government was using Persian during the reign of its last king, Maha Thammada. He wrote in Persian to Warren Hastings, Britain's Governor-General at Calcutta, in May 1783. Maha Thammada's poetic missive told Hastings: 'Whirlwinds, fog, cloud, smoke and the gloom of the night, these five principles of darkness I dispel, and restore the day, and as the sun illuminates the whole horizon in like manner do I diffuse light around me. I am adorned from head to foot with virtues and excellencies. I am Master of the Country . . . called by us Rukking.'[8] An indication of the then calamitous internal state of the Arakan kingdom, Maha Thammada demanded that the British capture and return his enemies, who he alleged had fled to British-controlled territory. Otherwise, he threatened, 'I will ravage your country, and carry them away with me.' Hastings did not immediately respond (a not infrequent approach in such cases) and the Burmese invasion of Arakan that followed shortly after ended any potential that

Maha Thammada's troops might 'ravage' British territory. Ironically, Burma's post-conquest government in Arakan made a similar request of the British, seeking the arrest and return of leaders of Maha Thammada's fleeing Arakan government (Buddhists and Muslims). Britain's reluctance to acquiesce to this Burmese demand was a factor contributing the first Anglo-Burmese War.

The use of Persian as a court language may not necessarily indicate that the rulers themselves were Muslim, but it is evidence of strong Islamic influence in pre-colonial Arakan and suggests far-reaching links with trade and political networks. Unsurprisingly, few contemporary Buddhist nationalists admit Persian was an Arakanese court language and that at Arakan's political and economic peak, its leaders routinely governed using a Middle Eastern language commonly associated with Islam. The historic use of Persian in Arakan may be significant to contemporary claims for the origin of the Rohingya name. Authors of Rohingya history after Tahir Ba Tha and Muhammad Yunus commonly relied heavily on their works – this contributed to agreement over elements of Rohingya history. Tahir Ba Tha, Nurul Islam, Habib Siddiqui and Muhammad Yunus believed the Rohingya name derived from an old Arabic name for Arakan – *Rohang* (likely from Mrauk-U/Mrohaung). By doing so, they claimed for the Rohingya an identity that was both Islamic and connected to the land of Arakan, on which they claim to have lived since 'time immemorial'. Other writing, including by Abid Bahar, Htay Lwin Oo and Habib Siddiqui, presented differing accounts.[9] They relied on the shipwreck story and their belief Muslim Arabic-speaking mariners' pleas for mercy, *rahma*, accounted for the origins of the Rohingya name.[10]

These explanations have not been without their critics. A common criticism has been that the reliance on the use of Arabic seems a too convenient link with Islam's origins to be credible. However, this argument is seriously weakened by evidence that Arakan's commercial and maritime history did bring Arabic speakers there, and that Persian was an official language of the kingdom. Similarities between aspects of the spoken forms of each language might well have led historians to assume Arabic when Persian – a language certainly understood and used by Arakan's officials – could have been spoken. Authors of Rohingya history might understandably have been keen to ascribe a link between the Rohingya name and Arabic speakers as evidence for a long-term Muslim connection with Arakan, yet perhaps links with Persian speakers provide stronger evidence of the long-term Islamic influence in Arakan.

Contemporary scholarship, including by Azeem Ibrahim, Maung Zarni and Alice Cowley, has suggested the name Rohingya was a descriptor of Arakan's

Muslims from pre-colonial times.[11] Relying on Buchanan's publications, they assert the Rohingya (Rooinga) name was certainly known and used before 1823. My examination of Buchanan's writing strengthens claims the Rohingya were present in pre-colonial Arakan and that use of the Rooinga name (a word derived from the Bengali name for Arakan) was widespread. However, Rohingya leaders generally (although not always) avoided linking Buchanan's Rooinga with Bengal's language, culture or population. This reluctance was likely because of modern sensitivities that any indication of Rohingya connections with Bengal would be deliberately misrepresented by Myanmar's authorities to indicate that the group's heritage derived from Bengal rather than Arakan. This contributed to a frequent focus on the claimed Arabic origins of the Rohang name. Some Rohingya leaders referred to Buchanan's Rooinga and explained that the modern Rohingya name derived from an old name for Arakan. By claiming the Rohingya name derived from an old name for Arakan, Tahir Ba Tha, Nurul Islam and Habib Siddiqui traced a potentially longer Rohingya history in Arakan that preceded any eighth century shipwreck. Claiming ancient origins for Arakan's Rohingya implies the Rohingya were already well established in Arakan before the arrival there of the ethnic Rakhine's antecedents in the ninth and tenth centuries.

Buchanan's writing has often been used solely to prove the pre-colonial use of the Rooinga name – it unquestionably does. Buchanan also provided useful evidence that the Rooinga group was indigenous (and was noted in other British colonial records too). This is important and more can be made of this by Rohingya advocates. A focus on the aspect of Buchanan's account that indicates the fact of a Muslim group (of whatever name, and separate to the Kaman) resident in Arakan in 1795, rather than an exclusive focus on his use of the Rooinga name, would further strengthen Rohingya assertions that there was a Muslim population, long-settled in Arakan, that qualifies as a *taingyintha* – and that this population represent the Rohingya's ancestors. Prioritizing clarity about the group's rightful claim to *taingyintha* status would be aided by an increased focus on how Rakhine state's largest Muslim group were acknowledged as citizens by the country's democratic post-independence governments.

Colonial-era migration continues to be a sensitive and politically charged topic in Myanmar. Myanmar's laws privilege pre-colonial ancestry, guaranteeing the centrality of colonial migration to present-day citizenship and rights claims. Rohingya historians have been reluctant to tackle questions of colonial migration directly, underplaying its role. Siddiqui and Bahar for instance suggested some colonial migration was the return of refugees who fled the 1784 Burmese invasion (a point made by Abu Tahay and Htay Lwin Oo), while Islam skirted the issue, claiming that in the post-independence period only 200 refugees came to Burma because of the Bangladesh War of Independence.[12] Colonial migration has continued to be central to nationalist narratives of Islam's threat to Myanmar's Buddhist identity.

There was certainly considerable migration into Burma throughout the British colonial period, but British census data support important aspects of Rohingya perspectives about its characteristics. Data from Burma's 1931 census, undertaken one century after the British gained control of Arakan, indicated that the proportion of Muslims living in Arakan had seemingly not increased from the thirty per cent noted by British Sub-Commissioner of Arakan Charles Paton in his 1826 report.[13] The 1931 census recorded 192,647 Indian Muslims (as the Rohingya were identified by Britain's enumerators, who used a racial classification in census reports from the late nineteenth century) resident in Arakan, which then had a population of 1,008,535.[14] Since the proportion of Muslims in Rakhine state in modern times is similar to the proportion reported by early British colonial researchers, Rohingya historians have dismissed the contribution of colonial and post-independence migration to Rakhine state's contemporary demographic makeup. Instead they have asserted that the modern Rohingya's ancestors were already long-term residents of Arakan when British rule began.

As was outlined in Chapter Three, colonial-era migration need not weaken contemporary Rohingya assertions that they should be a *taingyintha*. A criticism of Rohingya claims from some scholars is that colonial-era migrants swamped a pre-colonial Muslim group in Arakan. The descendants of these migrants have been argued to be the contemporary Rohingya, whom it is suggested co-opted the identity of the pre-colonial Muslim population and now seek acknowledgement as a *taingyintha*.[15] However, this position rests heavily on manipulating the available data – disregarding evidence of a substantial Muslim population in Arakan by the early 1820s, ignoring the influx of Buddhists into Arakan in the first half century of British rule (which diluted the proportion of Muslims in the local population), and then pointing to an increase in Muslim migration between 1880 and the 1940s (again disregarding its legal and predominantly male character). All colonial-era arrivals were legal migrants, and considering the length of time that has passed and the limited marriage opportunities outside the Muslim community in Arakan/Rakhine, there must by now be few descendants of Muslim colonial-era migrants who are not linked to an indigenous ancestor. Those Rohingya outside this category must be few and decreasing with each generation born to an indigenous-linked, Muslim parent.

Post-independence census data similarly strengthen Rohingya views that their population is overwhelmingly indigenous. If there was to be migration from Bangladesh into Rakhine state, it would surely have happened in the 1970s, a period of extreme political instability in Bangladesh, which endured a civil war and serious natural disasters. This has frequently been identified as a time of Bangladeshi migration into Burma, yet the evidence indicates this was not the case: there was no notable increase in Arakan's population between the censuses of 1973 and 1983, indicating little if any permanent migration from Bangladesh during the 1970s.[16] This population clearly meets all of Myanmar's legal thresholds to be granted citizenship, which indicates that the Myanmar authorities' attempts to separate pre-1823 Muslim residents and their descendants from post-1823 Muslim arrivals and their descendants are little more than a strategy to try and further stall the acknowledgement of the Rohingya's legitimate citizenship. With most Rohingya, likely the vast majority, tracing ancestry to before the colonial period (and frequently able to provide documentary evidence from the post-independence democratic period), this shows why Myanmar's authorities have so aggressively sought to remove documentary evidence of their legitimate residency and citizenship from Rohingya.

Rakhine state's history has been interpreted very differently by opponents of the Rohingya's aspirations. Myanmar's military leadership, the modern civilian government and nationalists reject assertions about a well-established and substantially sized pre-colonial Muslim population and commonly disregard the legal nature of colonial-era migration. These groups describe Rohingya identity as a post-Second World War creation and assert that there were few Muslim settlers in Arakan prior to the British colonial period. They routinely dismiss Rohingya *taingyintha* claims because of scant British-era references to the specific Rohingya name – which they can assert only by ignoring documentary evidence like Buchanan's Rooinga references and the British use of anglicized names to identify Arakan's Muslims.

The authorities and nationalists regard the forebears of Rakhine state's Muslim population to be overwhelmingly colonial and post-independence immigrants. They divide this population between descendants of colonial-era migrants, post-independence arrivals and the small Kaman group, which is acknowledged as a *taingyintha* and is the only Muslim group recognized as having a pre-1823 heritage in Myanmar (although the relatively small Kaman group is also commonly subject to human rights abuses). Matters have been complicated by inconsistent and at times contradictory use of identity labels. Myanmar's authorities portray the Rohingya's identity as a post-independence creation and so treat those adopting it as post-independence immigrants (who do not have a legitimate right to residency, let alone citizenship). They label colonial-era migrants as 'Bengalis', although they occasionally lump these two groups together under the 'Bengali' label (as Myanmar's general public and media also commonly do).[17] Despite colonial-era migrants having entered Burma legally and their descendants certainly qualifying for citizenship based on residency (according to the 1982 citizenship law), popular opinion opposes even citizenship rights for Muslim descendants of this group. While Myanmar's laws ensure that pre-independence migrants from Bengal are entitled to citizenship rights, the lived experience of Rakhine state's Muslims is that access to these rights is routinely denied. In a 2012 interview, President Thein Sein explained that from his perspective, 'Before 1948, the British brought Bengalis to work on the farms, and since there were ample opportunities to make a living here compared to where they came from, they didn't leave ... According to our laws, those descended from [the Bengalis] who came to Burma before 1948, the "Third Generation", can be considered Burmese citizens.'[18] Thein Sein's comments highlight the confusion caused by the inconsistent use of identity labels by various actors in Myanmar, and by disputes over the heritage of Rakhine state's Muslims. Thein Sein noted two distinct Muslim groups in Rakhine state – those who arrived before independence and those arriving after. From his perspective, the Rohingya name is applied to post-independence migrants. He claimed that, 'In Rakhine state now, there are two distinct generation groups. The first group is those born from the pre-1948 Bengalis. Another generation group, under the name Rohingya, came to Burma later.'[19]

Thein Sein might have followed the letter of the citizenship law by identifying British-era Muslim migrants as legal arrivals and so entitled to citizenship rights. However, his insistence on labelling them as 'Bengali' would have diminished their legitimacy in the eyes of the Myanmar public. Post-independence arrivals he labelled Rohingya, and their migration he believed illegal. The 'Bengali' label used by Thein Sein to describe pre-1948 migrants is understandably rejected by Rohingya, who consider it a slur designed to portray them as foreigners. Thein Sein ignored the historical evidence for a substantial Muslim population in Arakan prior to 1823. As I outlined in Chapters One and Two, there is considerable evidence for a well-established and substantially sized Muslim group in Arakan well before the British colonial era, which identified itself using the Rooinga label.

Myanmar's nationalists reject citizenship rights for Muslims in Rakhine state out of hand, believing they should have no claim to stay despite what the law may mandate. Nationalists and prominent ANP and USDP political figures disagree with Thein Sein's perspective of legal colonial-era Muslim migration. These groups have aggressively rejected Rohingya assertions of indigeneity and regard virtually all Muslim migration into the country as illegitimate (whether the arrivals came in the British colonial era or post independence). That Rakhine state's Muslims should be labelled as 'Bengalis' and have no claim to Myanmar citizenship rights has often been advocated by ethnic Rakhine writers and reflected in Myanmar's Burmese-language media. Aye Chan and Maung Tha Hla have argued that because Rakhine state's largest Muslim group claims an identity (Rohingya) for which they believe there is insufficient evidence of long-term residency, then members of the group must be recent arrivals and cannot be indigenous.[20] Even the use of the Rohingya name is treated as evidence of recent, and hence illegal, immigration. The Rohingya have found that their name has been misapplied and subsequently weaponized by Myanmar's authorities and nationalists to deny them the citizenship rights they ought to be entitled to.

A key impediment to Rohingya citizenship is that Myanmar's civilian and military authorities, have actively resisted it. Since the Ne Win era, citizenship laws have been manipulated to prevent the Rohingya from accessing rights they should clearly be granted. However, even if the authorities continue to refuse acknowledgement of the Rohingya as a *taingyintha*, most of those who today claim the Rohingya identity would likely qualify as citizens within Myanmar's current citizenship framework based on individual assessments of ancestral citizenship and residency – if the country's laws were applied fairly. Such processes require the applicant to put aside the Rohingya name, however, and could only be for claims for Associate or Naturalized citizenship, on an individual basis. The overwhelming majority of Rohingya have resisted applying for this form of citizenship because it denies them recognition as Rohingya and because these processes require them to relinquish their documentary evidence of citizenship.

The Rohingya's collective experience has been that once relinquished to Myanmar's government, documentary proof of their citizenship entitlement will never be returned. The 2015 cancellation of the 'White Cards' given to hundreds of thousands of Rohingya when their other identity documents were removed for scrutiny (yet never returned) underscores this point. Associate or Naturalized citizens are vulnerable to being collectively stripped of their citizenship by the government at any time. Yet, even with the tenuous nature of these citizenships, those few Rohingya who were prepared to make such applications have nonetheless found Myanmar's bureaucracy painfully slow and reluctant to formally assess their residency and citizenship.[21] The Myanmar Council of State's ability to 'revoke the citizenship or associate citizenship or naturalized citizenship of any person except a citizen by birth' means any Rohingya who might manage to acquire Associate or Naturalized citizenship remains vulnerable to the future revocation of those rights at the government's whim.[22] Considering the Rohingya's collective experience of discrimination and human rights violations, the prospect of putting aside their Rohingya name and claim to indigeneity to potentially gain a form of citizenship that could be arbitrarily and easily revoked is far from an inviting prospect. This surely contributed to Rohingya resistance in 2019 and 2020 to Myanmar's citizenship verification processes being applied to the refugees in the Bangladesh camps as a condition for their return to Myanmar. For Rohingya leaders, the only citizenship they believe likely to provide any future certainty of their rights is collective recognition as a *taingyintha*.

Demonstrating the strength of the Rohingya's case for recognition as a *taingyintha* is important, because it illustrates clearly how the group has been unfairly denied rights to which they are legally entitled. In the current context, when there are more Rohingya living in camps in Bangladesh than remain in Myanmar, and where repatriation of camp residents is high on the Bangladesh, China, Myanmar and UN political agendas, recognition of the Rohingya's rightful claim to be a *taingyintha* should have a crucial influence on the repatriation arrangements ultimately agreed by these actors (noting that Rohingya representatives have been routinely excluded from repatriation discussions involving the UN and governments of Bangladesh and Myanmar). However, highlighting the strength of their citizenship claims has not gained the Rohingya the legal recognition that they desire and deserve – Myanmar's authorities currently stand firmly in the way of this. Sadly, neither have international actors, like the government of Bangladesh or the UN, been prepared to make citizenship guarantees a precondition of Rohingya returns to Myanmar. Repatriation arrangements involving Bangladesh, Myanmar and the UN do not guarantee the citizenship rights of any returnee and there are understandable concerns by Rohingya refugees that they would be forced to return to Myanmar to face the same discrimination, human rights violations and violence that they fled.[23]

6

People Would Like to Demolish Our History

Jama Mosque's muezzin no longer calls the faithful to prayer. Its Arabesque minarets are silent, its gate is locked and Myanmar's authorities bar entry to visitors – armed guards are ready to move on those who try to enter, who loiter too long outside or take photographs showing the damage done when it was ransacked in 2012. Built in the mid-nineteenth century and one of the oldest buildings in Sittwe, Jama Mosque was once a powerful symbol of the long-term and legitimate residency of Muslims in Rakhine state's capital. This significance was underscored by Dr Anita Schug, a prominent Switzerland-based Rohingya activist and spokesperson for the European Rohingya Council, who told me how Jama Mosque,

> ... carries the importance of our faith of our Rohingya people in the past and present. Its physical presence in Arakan proves our existence and belonging to Arakan. It holds the key to our unity. Its physical presence stands as a historical witness that practising Islam once was acceptable and didn't threaten others. The mosque is the proof of our past that Rohingya did coexist with other religions peacefully. Jama Mosque [is] now witness that Rohingya and their faith are under attack. Demolishing the mosques is erasing our history of being natives of Arakan. [Myanmar's] Military is not only killing us physically but also spiritually. Protecting the mosque is protecting our identity, our faith and our history and our heritage.[1]

The shuttering of Jama Mosque accompanied the mass incarceration of more than 140,000 Rohingya in Rakhine state concentration camps. These events provide a stark reminder of how Myanmar's authorities have actively rewritten the country's history to erase the long-term and legitimate presence of its Rohingya population.

Jama Mosque was far from the sole representation of Sittwe's well-established Rohingya community. Until relatively recently, there had been Rohingya businesses in Sittwe's main commercial areas. Once their Rohingya owners and

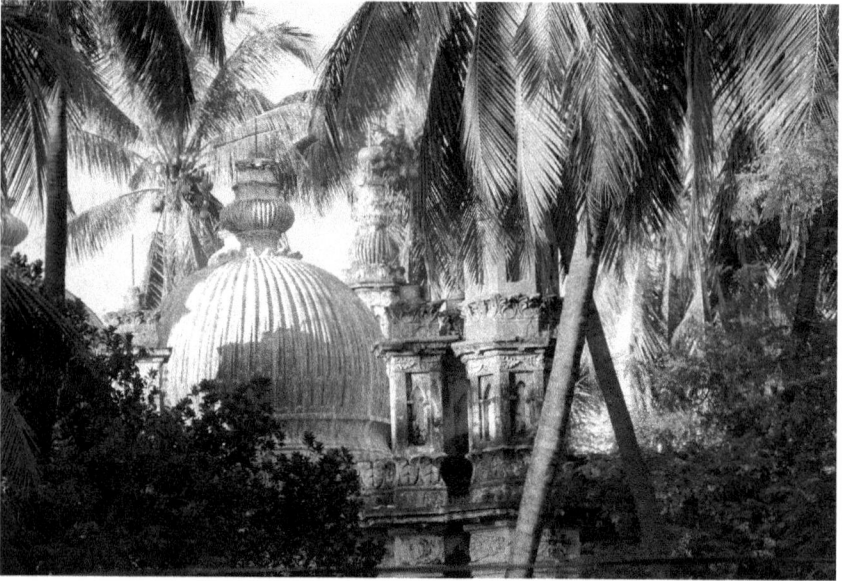

Figure 7 Sittwe's Jama Mosque, built in the nineteenth century, is a powerful symbol of long-term and legitimate Rohingya residency, but access has been blocked by the authorities since 2012.

workers were banned from Sittwe's public spaces in 2012, these stores were either taken over by Buddhists or shut. Empty former Rohingya stores were defaced with anti-Rohingya graffiti, reminiscent of Nazi vandalism of Jewish businesses. Reminiscent too of Nazi atrocity crimes, just a couple of hundred metres away from Sittwe's main commercial district, a Rohingya ghetto was created in the Aung Mingalar quarter. Having survived the 2012 burning of Sittwe's Rohingya homes, Aung Mingalar's 4,000 Rohingya residents were permanently confined by armed guards. While they remained in their own homes rather than having been herded to Sittwe's concentration camps, there were few work opportunities, and their access to education and healthcare was severely restricted. Unsurprisingly, Aung Mingalar's Rohingya residents commonly described themselves as victims of an ongoing genocide.

That the Rohingya were victims of genocide and other atrocity crimes at the hands of Myanmar's authorities was commonly raised with me by Rohingya. My focus in this chapter is on the perspectives of Rohingya I interviewed in Myanmar and from the diaspora between 2015 and early 2017. This research happened in a fast-changing political environment, so presenting the interviews chronologically helps contextualize interviewee's statements and experiences. My aim is to provide a platform to a broad cross-section of the

Figure 8 In Sittwe, a few hundred metres from the Rohingya ghetto, empty former Rohingya stores were defaced with anti-Rohingya graffiti, reminiscent of Nazi vandalism of Jewish businesses.

Rohingya's mainstream leadership – from Rakhine state, Yangon and among the diaspora – to explain, in their own words, Rohingya history and what they ask of Myanmar. Engagement with the international community has been central to the Rohingya's political approach, and English was Burma's official language until independence, so unsurprisingly many Rohingya leaders are capable English speakers. Foreign language skills have become rarer among northern Rakhine state's Rohingya because of education restrictions in recent decades. Consequently, the interviews in this chapter were undertaken primarily in English, while those with newly arrived residents of the Bangladesh camps presented in Chapter Seven were in Rohingya language and assisted by a local translator.

Most Rohingya I spoke with asserted their group's right to be identified using the name they choose, rather than a designation forced upon them by Myanmar's authorities, the Tatmadaw or by Buddhist nationalists. A number specifically referenced the UN's *Declaration on the Rights of Persons Belonging to National or Ethnic, Religious and Linguistic Minorities*, which asserts that members of such groups 'have the right to enjoy their own culture, to profess and practise their own religion, and to use their own language, in private and in public, freely and without interference or any form of discrimination.'[2] They often asserted their right to be identified as Rohingya for the practical reason that it *is* their group's name. They considered that the coerced use of any other name represented an attempt to erase their people's legitimate name and identity. Importantly, frequently missing from my interviews was an acknowledgement of the role domestic political discourse in Myanmar (especially attitudes towards the Rohingya among the voting public) might have on the Rohingya's citizenship and rights claims.

Recurring themes in my interviews included the group's centuries of connection to the Rakhine state area, their hope the international community might come to the group's aid and the negative consequences of the *Burma Citizenship Law (1982)*. With few exceptions, Rohingya leaders explained the strength of their claim to Myanmar citizenship by outlining their people's history. They set out how the Rohingya were long-term residents of Myanmar and according to the country's laws ought to be regarded as a *taingyintha*, identified by the Rohingya label. Rohingya leaders generally presented one of two accounts for the origins of the Rohingya name, suggesting it was either derived from the name of the land, *Rohang*, a claimed Arabic name for Arakan, or derived from a word *rahma*, usually identified as an Arabic word for mercy used by shipwrecked Arab sailors, which evolved to the word Rohingya. Each account portrayed the Rohingya as indigenous and so entitled to citizenship within Myanmar's legal framework. Some Rohingya asserted that their group's citizenship rights had been acknowledged by the civilian-era authorities after independence and later incrementally stripped away by the military.

> '**The government are trying to reduce our number . . . It's a kind of genocide.**'
> Myo Win, Aung Mingalar Quarter, Sittwe, November 2015

Sittwe's Aung Mingalar quarter can be eerily quiet. In contrast to the cacophonous streets nearby there is no industry, little commerce and vehicles of any kind, motorized or otherwise, are rare. Entry to Sittwe's Rohingya ghetto requires foreigners to gain permission from Myanmar's authorities and invariably further negotiation with the armed guards who confine the thousands of Rohingya residents. I visited Aung Mingalar quarter to meet with Myo Win in late 2015 and received strict police instructions to leave before sunset. The consequences of overstaying were implied, and I understood this would likely involve creating problems with the authorities for anyone I had met in the quarter, so I heeded the warning and departed before dark. I heard Myo Win's passionate assertions about the Rohingya's heritage and rights claims, which mirror the views of other Rohingya I have spoken with in Rakhine state.

Myo Win is smart, works hard and speaks good English. This helped him find work with an international humanitarian organization and made him a leading voice for his community. He could not freely leave the Aung Mingalar quarter,

Figure 9 Security checkpoint at Sittwe's Aung Mingalar ghetto. 2015.

but his humanitarian work allowed him to travel to and from the Rohingya camp on the outskirts of Sittwe, which crucially gave him access to a small income and to market supplies. Illustrating how movement restrictions enforced on the Rohingya have artificially separated communities that previously interacted, Myo Win recalled how before 2012, 'I have many Rakhine and Burmese friends. Most of the friends are Rakhines.'

For decades during the military dictatorship, much of Rakhine state was closed to outsiders. Information about the rights abuses faced by the Rohingya were difficult to access, although this began to change when President Thein Sein's quasi-civilian administration came to power. The new government's policies briefly encouraged tourism and allowed more access to international media and scholars than had been the case in the previous decades. For some Rohingya, these new freedoms brought an optimism that once the international community became aware of what was happening to them in Myanmar, international political pressure could lead to improved rights and the return of Rohingya citizenship. Seeking international support for their cause became a key political strategy for the Rohingya, and Myo Win expressed gratitude for a chance to bring the group's plight to any international audience. High priorities for Myo Win were the Rohingya's citizenship claims and their right to self-identify. He believed that as a Rohingya, he was already a citizen of Myanmar and that the *Burma Citizenship Law (1982)* had been unfairly used by the authorities to restrict Rohingya citizenship rights. He outlined how the authorities further limited Rohingya rights by confiscating 'White Card' identity documents to pressure Rohingya to participate in a discriminatory and biased citizenship assessment process: 'They just take it. And then they issue a slip. Because the people do not want to apply 1982 citizenship law, then you can have citizenship card. We are opposing this law … We have to apply again, that would be nonsense for us, because we are already citizens of Myanmar. So why we have to apply again?'

A key concern for Myo Win in 2015 was the ability to be accepted as Rohingya, rather than identified with a different label. Difficulties achieving this he blamed on the country's military dictatorship: 'Of course we are Rohingya Muslims, we know that, but we can't express because of the military. We have right to say something. If it's a real democratic country, everybody should have rights to say our identity.' Myo Win's sentiments were frequently echoed by Rohingya throughout my research. They outlined how, having once been respected as citizens, the authorities unfairly applied Myanmar's citizenship laws to block Rohingya citizenship claims. It was hardly surprising Myo Win considered the authorities' motivations disingenuous where citizenship law was concerned. Referring to the citizenship verification processes then underway in Myebon, south-east of Sittwe, which prevented applicants being identified as Rohingya on official identity documents, Myo Win said, 'That is why [Rohingya] people don't apply.' Despite frequent Rohingya objections to such processes (only a few thousand of the more than a million Rohingya would ever take part), Myanmar officials would continue to insist that for Rohingya to have any hope of being acknowledged as citizens, they must undergo a citizenship verification process in which they cannot identify as Rohingya. Mandatory participation in this citizenship verification process has been presented by Myanmar officials as a prerequisite for the repatriation of Rohingya refugees from Bangladesh. Myanmar's officials, visiting the Rohingya's Bangladesh camps in 2019, distributed brochures to the refugees outlining a process where Rohingya would give to Myanmar documentary evidence of their legitimate citizenship and residency claims in exchange for a National Verification Card that would not provide the holder with any proof of citizenship. Rohingya refugees, understandably nervous that Myanmar's aim was to erase evidence of their legitimate citizenship claims, refused to participate in the process.

Myo Win regarded the authorities' attempts to pressure the Rohingya to change their name as part of a broader strategy to portray them as foreign and undermine their legitimacy, which he could not accept. Myo Win did indicate that he might – reluctantly – accept a flexible approach to the label applied to his group, so long as this resulted in improved rights and did not involve applying the 'Bengali' label. Similar attitudes were expressed by other Rohingya I met in Rakhine state – that while they identified as Rohingya, their more pressing concern had become mitigating the appalling human rights violations they faced. The case was different among the Rohingya outside of Rakhine state – they expressed far less flexibility about the group's name. It would be easy to characterize this situation as being due to their having less personally at stake and so being less pressured towards compromise, yet this was not necessarily the case. For Rohingya, their group's claim to rights was often based on the strength of their citizenship claim, and this hinged on their being accepted as a *taingyintha* – making acceptance of the Rohingya identity and label integral to their rights claims. From that perspective, any movement away from the Rohingya label threatened to weaken the group's rights claims.

Prominent Rohingya figures in Yangon (including Abdul Rasheed, Abu Tahay and Kyaw Min, whose interviews are presented below) and among the diaspora (including Malaysia-based Muhammad Noor, UK-based Nurul Islam and US-based Wakar Uddin) asserted that the only appropriate identity label for Rakhine state's major Muslim group was Rohingya, although Myo Win nonetheless pointed to the fact of debate about this within the Rohingya community at the time we spoke. He noted that some, weary from rights abuses and aggressive official rejections of the Rohingya name, might, out of desperation due to their appalling circumstances, consider accepting alternative names for the group. However, Myo Win noted that the authorities rejected every name that suggested indigeneity: 'They just would like to name us Bengali.' He argued the group was better off sticking with the name that was grounded in their history – Rohingya. The Rohingya being forced to choose between their legitimate identity label and their human rights highlighted the precarious situation they faced in Rakhine state. This ought to have led to international pressure on Myanmar's government to change its approach, as Myo Win hoped. Sadly, those international actors that readily claimed to promote human rights – Western governments like Myanmar's former colonial power Britain, the European Union and US – were more interested in the economic opportunities that appeared likely once Aung San Suu Kyi's new NLD administration took power.

'We lose everything there, our property, and our house and mosque were destroyed by government bulldozer. Why government bulldoze mosque? Mosque was bulldozed. Since independence, not a single government do such thing, so this Thein Sein government did it.'

Kyaw Hla Aung, Sittwe camp, November 2015

The Aung Mingalar quarter was not the only Muslim area of Sittwe where access had been tightly restricted since 2012. Entering the Thet Key Pyin camp on the outskirts of Sittwe required me to pass through two security checkpoints staffed mostly by men who looked much too young to be soldiers or police, yet likely were. One of the armed young men who checked my credentials wore a Glasgow Celtic Football Club jersey rather than military fatigues or police uniform. His gun and his colleagues determined who could and who could not enter or leave the concentration camp. It was difficult to see these young men as more than a crudely organized armed mob, but they nonetheless played a key role in the lives of camp residents like Hyaw Hla Aung. Hyaw Hla Aung is an articulate Rohingya community leader whose legal background, professional history and advancing age (when we first spoke he was in his late 70s) had not prevented his confinement to a home attached to the Thet Key Pyin concentration camp and severe limits on his freedom of movement.

Hyaw Hla Aung endured appalling mistreatment by the authorities yet still regarded himself loyal to Myanmar and did not want to leave Rakhine state. Sittwe had long been his home and he wanted to stay. Asked about this, he said,

> I want to be here on this land. We born here, and we want to die here. So, we want to improve our country. This government alleging us that we are illegal immigrants from Bangladesh. Who will come in this land, suffering like animals? You will consider – they have so many guards, navy and army and police, Na Sa Ka [a border and immigration inter-agency force], so how can these people come? Who will come here? So, before 1970, when East Pakistan was there, this government didn't call us Pakistani, or Indian, they call us Rohingya or Rakhine Muslim. I have many documents but after 1971, when Bangladesh was independent, they named their country Bangladesh, so they [Myanmar's authorities] call us 'Bengali'.

This was an unfair and inaccurate label in Kyaw Hla Aung's view, and he stated emphatically that they ought to be recognized by the Rohingya name. He traced the origins of the Rohingya name to an old name for Arakan – Rohang. He outlined the recent history of the group's use of the Rohingya name by saying,

> Rohang was the previous name of this land. Rohang, after that Arakan, then Rakhine. First our land was Rohang so the people who lived in Rohang, they Rohingya. But then [ethnic] Rakhine they name them Rakhine. After that we called Arakanese Muslim, Rakhine Muslim like this. So, then the government dislike it to call Rakhine Muslims to call Arakanese Muslim so that we collect our name, the first name.

He suggested the name Rohang was used, 'Since Rohang [Arakan] was started. Even my foremothers name was Rohanti, great grandmother from Mrauk-U.' This was likely a reference to the same origins for the Rohingya name as Buchanan noted when he identified Rovingaw as a Bengali-language name for Arakan. Despite this strong claim to indigeneity, the Rohingya's situation in Myanmar was so grim that Kyaw Hla Aung, like Myo Win, had come to regard human rights concerns as the immediate priority. In light of this, and since Myanmar's authorities were so opposed to the Rohingya label, I asked him whether he might be prepared to tolerate an alternative designation for the group, were the authorities prepared to compromise and guarantee the group's access to citizenship and the rights that should accompany it. From Kyaw Hla Aung's perspective, any alternative label that indicates indigeneity or a legitimate connection to Rakhine state will be rejected by Myanmar's authorities. He pointed to past failed attempts to reach such a compromise, asking,

> Why they didn't accept Rakhine Muslim? If government accept Rakhine Muslim, we can organize the people to accept. Previously I have some document, Rakhine Muslim, even in my fathers . . . They mention Rakhine Muslims. Arakan Muslims, we use it up to a few years. Up to the coup of Ne Win, Rakhine Muslim . . . Rakhine Muslims' Association, Rakhine Muslim Students' Association, Burmese Muslims' Association and Arakan Muslim Association, the secretary is still alive in Canada . . . When the government denied call themselves Rakhine Muslims, so people go to call themselves Rohingya. But the word is the same. Rohingya, Arakan Muslim and Rakhine Muslim . . .

While there was a widespread perception among Buddhist nationalists, Myanmar's political elites and the Tatmadaw that the country's Muslims harboured plans to dominate territory in Rakhine state, that was certainly not Kyaw Hla Aung's desire – 'No, no, we never tell this. But we want to live together peacefully.' He did not advocate for a separate Rohingya state, but firmly believed the Rohingya's heritage in Myanmar predated the arrival of the British and entitled the group to be a *taingyintha*. As was common among Rohingya I spoke with, he referred to the published work of Francis Buchanan. This claimed indigeneity was key to Kyaw Hla Aung's belief that Rohingya like him were legally entitled to be citizens. When asked whether he was a citizen of Myanmar, Kyaw Hla Aung replied with a confident 'Yes.' He was unhappy as he described the inconsistent and seemingly arbitrary way Myanmar's authorities had doled out identity documents, saying,

Yes, we have National Registration Card. Not 'White Card'. Also, two daughters have a 'White Card', but now they are alleging these 'White Card' holders are from Bangladesh. And one of my daughters in Yangon, she got 'Pink Card'. Even I cannot get 'Pink Card'. [You could not vote?] No, but I can stand for parliament member with the NRC, National Registration Card. National Registration Card was issued in 1959 to me, then it was lost, then I apply, and it was also issued in 1963, and also the Prime Minister U Nu held this National Registration Card. They don't want to give our right because living together since decades ago.

There was a consistency to the views of Kyaw Hla Aung and Myo Win. Both strongly asserted their right to be identified as Rohingya and recognized as legal citizens of Myanmar. Both spoke of a time in the recent past when local Buddhist and Muslim communities were much more integrated and lived together peacefully. They retained optimism about the Rohingya's future. In 2015 and 2016, it was not uncommon for Rohingya, even after their then recent disenfranchisement, to express the hope that a new Aung San Suu Kyi-led government would quickly improve their situation. As 2016 ended, that optimism was frequently replaced by frustration and, for many, pessimism. Aung San Suu Kyi's election had not resulted in positive change for the Rohingya, and the likelihood of future positive change seemed more remote than ever.

> **'I don't know why they reject us. We have been in Rakhine state for many, many centuries. Our language is not like Bengali. Our culture is not like Bengali.'**
> Kyaw Min, President of Democracy and Human Rights Party, Yangon, 2015

Muslims in Yangon have not found themselves subject to the same restrictions as those in Rakhine state. Yangon's Indo-Aryan Muslims have been frequently acknowledged as citizens, although only on an individual rather than collective basis – they have not been recognized as part of a *taingyintha*. Members of Yangon's small Rohingya community can integrate among the broader Indo-Aryan Muslim population there. In Yangon, there has been less scrutiny of Muslims than in Rakhine state and the same rights restrictions have not applied, yet this has not stopped Myanmar's authorities from targeting Rohingya activists living there.

A former school principal, Kyaw Min was politically active in the 8888 Uprising. He spoke with me in his capacity as a senior Yangon-based Rohingya political leader. Born in Buthidaung township, Kyaw Min was formerly chair of the Mayu 'Democracy Fighting Committee' and was an executive member of the 'Arakan State Peace Committee', where he served alongside Arakan's chief Buddhist monk. In 1988, this multi-ethnic and multi-religious group had taken responsibility for maintaining peace within the state when the central authorities' control collapsed amid the uprising. He was elected to represent a Buthidaung constituency in the 1990 elections, the outcome of which Myanmar's military junta refused to acknowledge. Kyaw Min's political background and activism mark him as a loyal Myanmar citizen committed to community service, although it was his activism in support of the human rights and citizenship claims of Myanmar's Rohingya that led him to be sentenced to forty-seven years in prison. Released as part of a 2012 amnesty, along with members of his family who had been similarly prosecuted (including his daughter Wai Wai Nu whose comments are below), by 2015 Kyaw Min lived in Yangon and, when he spoke with me, was president of the Democracy and Human Rights Party (DHRP). The DHRP was then probably the highest profile Rohingya political party and it managed to symbolically nominate a number of Myanmar citizens under its banner to contest an election from which Rohingya were excluded.[3]

We met at the DHRP's offices in downtown Yangon, and Kyaw Min spoke at length about the Rohingya's history in Arakan. Like Myo Win and Kyaw Hla Aung, Kyaw Min strongly rejected the 'Bengali' label and asserted that the Rohingya were previously accepted by the authorities as citizens of Myanmar. He explained how this had changed over time,

> I don't know why they reject us. We have been in Rakhine state for many, many centuries. Our language is not like Bengali. Our culture is not like Bengali ... [After independence] We thought things would be easy like British time, since independence we are under their grasp, exploited, marginalized, we didn't enjoy much rights. The former government, parliamentary period, military period, Ne Win's early period, they did not deny us our citizenship ...

For Kyaw Min, further evidence that Rohingya uncontroversially possessed identity documents and were acknowledged as legitimate citizens was the long-term presence of Rohingya traders in downtown Sittwe. He told me, 'In the downtown, if you own a plot, a shop, a place for industry you need official documents, registrations, without registration, without documents how can you own all these things? But they say these are illegal immigrants.'

Kyaw Min expressed his unhappiness with the NLD's decision not to field any Muslim candidates at the 2015 general election. Insightfully, he suggested that the NLD had by then already adopted similar policy positions to the USDP administration on important questions of ethnicity and religion. He argued, 'They [are] on the same page now. Now the NLD, opposition party. Their political assertion, explanation concerning Rohingya is the same.' In this context he feared Myanmar's ASEAN neighbours were likely to follow the lead of the new NLD administration, and while he believed regional support for the Rohingya's cause was important, he pinned his hopes on Western support. He said, 'So finally, what we need, international community, Western countries . . . So Western countries, we give some hopes in Western countries.' The expectation Western countries would render assistance once they learned of the Rohingya's plight was repeated frequently by Rohingya I spoke with.

Seeking foreign support by bringing the Rohingya's case to international attention had become a key strategy for the group and was reminiscent of Aung San Suu Kyi's approach in the decades following the 8888 Uprising. The Rohingya's leadership have undoubtedly brought the group's plight to the attention of an international audience and made their situation a key policy concern for numerous countries' engagement with Myanmar. Wildly differing domestic attitudes towards Aung San Suu Kyi and the Rohingya help account for how a strategy of seeking international support might have been useful to the former, yet detrimental to the latter.

Myanmar's history of colonialism has contributed to enduring anti-foreigner attitudes and particularly to sensitivities about foreign domestic influence and political control. By encouraging international actors to pressure Myanmar's authorities to accept the Rohingya's citizenship and rights claims, the Rohingya were criticized domestically for inappropriately advocating foreign interference in Myanmar's internal affairs. In the past, the Tatmadaw made similar criticisms of Aung San Suu Kyi, portraying her as a foreign puppet because of her marriage to a foreigner, long-term foreign residence, and her advocacy of international support for the political opposition.[4] Widespread domestic support for Aung San Suu Kyi's political aspirations helped shield her and the opposition from Tatmadaw criticisms. Aung San Suu Kyi's status as the daughter of independence hero General Aung San helped to maintain her domestic popularity. Domestic attitudes towards the Rohingya's political aspirations are different. Rohingya are commonly regarded as foreigners and so their encouragement of foreign powers' involvement with Myanmar's domestic politics has largely been viewed in negative terms. This has undermined the Rohingya's domestic rights claims among ordinary residents and voters to a greater extent than the Rohingya's contemporary leaders have collectively acknowledged.

Rohingya calls for international support may have inadvertently contributed to greater public acceptance of nationalist claims that Rohingya have links to foreign militants and that Myanmar faces what nationalist agitator Wirathu characterized as a 'serious threat from jihadist groups'.[5] Perceptions of Rohingya militancy serve to further diminish the Rohingya's already limited domestic support. This has no doubt been frustrating for Rohingya leaders, including Kyaw Min, because the Rohingya's mainstream leadership, unlike that of other ethnic minorities in Myanmar, for decades rejected strategies of political violence. Yet Rohingya have found their citizenship and rights claims undermined because of perceptions they *might* embrace political violence and receive foreign support to do so.

'Firstly, recognize Rohingya as an ethnic group and restore their citizenship.'
Abu Tahay, Chairman of Union Nationals Development Party, Yangon, 2016

Abu Tahay was another knowledgeable and prominent Yangon-based Rohingya politician prevented from contesting the 2015 election because of his ethnic identity. An engineer by training and in his early fifties, Abu Tahay was chairman of the Union Nationals Development Party, which claimed a membership of more than 50,000. Myanmar's authorities, determined to prevent Rohingya electoral participation, had already taken three and a half years to assess the party's registration, and when the election was held this was still pending. The insults of Myanmar's electoral bureaucracy did not end there. Abu Tahay was himself prevented from contesting the election on the grounds his parents were deemed not to be citizens of Myanmar at the time of his birth, despite him presenting documents to the authorities that showed they were. For Abu Tahay, these represented more of a long list of arbitrary government actions to exclude the Rohingya from Myanmar's political life.

Like Kyaw Hla Aung and Myo Win, Abu Tahay recalled fondly the time when Rohingya and ethnic Rakhine lived together peacefully: 'Before 2012 these two communities, Rakhine and Rohingya, are living peacefully together, they are cooperating with each other's communities, they are studying in one classroom, working in one company, travelling together, but after 2012 these people [are] hating each other. Not allowed to live peacefully together again for the time being.' He believed the sectarian conflict in Rakhine state that occurred in 2012 stemmed from decades of national policies of Burmanization. His solution involved addressing both the proximate causes of recent sectarian conflict and the longer-term discriminatory national policy framework. He said, 'When we look into the long-term solutions, we have to look at two issues: Burman issues and sectarian issues. We need to work and to bring together these two issues, Burman and sectarian issues together concurrently.' Abu Tahay exclusively blamed the national government for instituting Burmanization policies, and he downplayed the role domestic politics – the attitudes of Myanmar's Bamar majority – might have played in encouraging the authorities to persist with Burmanization. This perspective was not dissimilar to the views of Kyaw Hla Aung, Kyaw Min and Myo Win.

The solution, from Abu Tahay's perspective, must involve government steps to 'recognize Rohingya as an ethnic group and restore their citizenship'. While he firmly asserted the Rohingya's right to be recognized as a *taingyintha*, he was nonetheless critical of the country's citizenship framework. He outlined how Myanmar's use of ethnic and religious identity to determine citizenship rights, which had been especially problematic for the Rohingya, contributed to ongoing conflicts between Myanmar's authorities and other ethnic minority groups. The country, Abu Tahay argued, would be better off with 'one national identity', with all citizenship rights determined without reference to ethnicity or religion.

Like most Rohingya community leaders, Abu Tahay strongly rejected arguments that the Rohingya's ancestors are mostly colonial-era migrants, although he did acknowledge domestic controversy about the Rohingya name. 'This is a big argument' he said, and claimed, 'Today, some of the radical [Buddhist nationalist] groups are trying to brand Rohingya as "Bengali".' For Abu Tahay, the contention Rohingya were really 'Bengali' was incorrect, and like many Rohingya he backs this by presenting evidence of long-term Muslim heritage in Myanmar, which included publications by Francis Buchanan (and other publications that cited Buchanan's work). He attributed much of the British-era Muslim migration to Arakan to those who fled the Burmese invasion returning to their former homes: 'These people return to their old homes, they had fled in 1784.' Abu Tahay believed there was archaeological evidence of mosques built in Rakhine state as long ago as the eighth century and that this was clear evidence of a well-established Muslim community before the colonial period. He believed too that if Myanmar's laws were fairly applied this history would entitle the Rohingya to be collectively recognized as citizens as a *taingyintha*.

Keen to address a common criticism of Rohingya *taingyintha* claims, Abu Tahay pointed out how the seeming lack of colonial-era records specifically referencing the group did not mean their identity was a recent creation. He instead outlined how the Rohingya name was used widely prior to the British occupation and how the British recorded the Rohingya using alternative English language labels: 'During the British time … they use Arakanese Muslim and sometimes they use Musselman.' As I outlined in Chapter Two, there is strong documentary evidence to support Abu Tahay's case. Abu Tahay, like other Rohingya leaders, noted a similar absence of colonial-era documentary evidence of the ethnic Rakhine. Of British administration census reports, he said, 'One point is the ethnic identification – this report never used Rakhine, they used Magh. Similar they used Musselman, never use Rohingya,' plus, 'There is no appearance of Rohingyas, same time there is no appearance of Rakhine. In 1872 this census used Arakanese Muslim, same time they use Arakanese, but they never use Rohingya or Rakhine.' From Abu Tahay's point of view, if it is plausible to suggest that the absence of specific Rohingya references in British colonial records indicated an absence of a Rohingya population, then the absence of British references using the Rakhine label must then mean 'There is no Rakhine people living in Rakhine state.' Abu Tahay made clear that this was of course ridiculous, and he acknowledged of the Rohingya and Rakhine that, 'both are recorded under indigenous' in British-era records, although using different labels to those identifying their populations today.

Abu Tahay's rights claims could not have been more reasonable. He did not make separatist claims, and he advocated political action through peaceful, democratic means. For him, the Rohingya's aspirations did not involve a separate Rohingya state: 'No, no,' he said, 'We are looking for equal rights, equal rights meaning based on citizenship rights.' Abu Tahay asked for the historical truth of long-term Rohingya residency to be acknowledged and for the group to be granted the rights that this ought to bring according to Myanmar's citizenship law.

'Rohingya is ancient name of Arakan.'
Abdul Rasheed, Chairman of the Rohingya Foundation, Yangon, 2015

The violence of 2012 refocused Abdul Rasheed's politics. A Yangon-based activist in his fifties, he had previously supported the NLD, but when we spoke in 2015 his focus was on working to restore the Rohingya's human and citizenship rights as vice president of the DHRP. He was additionally an adviser to human rights advocacy group Fortify Rights, and chairman of the Rohingya Foundation charity. He was keen to outline the Rohingya's heritage and lengthy history and said, 'Actually, Rohingya is ancient name of Arakan. Sometime Arakan be called Rohang. So, for Rohang, Arakan people being called Rohingya … We have nothing to do with the "Bengalis". We are quite different. So, the Muslim existed in Arakan, before the Rakhine and Burmese exist. The main thing is this.' During my research, Rohang was frequently identified as an old name for Arakan's former dynasty and capital, Mrohaung (modern Mrauk-U). It was frequently claimed the word Rohang corrupted to the Bengali language Rovingaw and Rooinga names noted in Buchanan's journal, and later evolved into the modern Rohingya name.

Abdul pointed to Arakan's frequently under-examined pre-eighth century Hindu culture, which predated the arrival of Buddhism and Islam. He outlined how Islam came to Arakan by two principal ways: overland from Arakan's western neighbours and by Arab sailors. He believed that the Rohingya's forebears were unquestionably present in Arakan prior to the start of the British colonial era and they were thus entitled to be citizens according to Myanmar law:

> Before seventh or eighth centuries most of the people in Arakan they believe in Hinduism, not believe in Buddhism. There was two parts enter Islam in Arakan. Is one part from Mughal culture rulers and another is Arab sailors. So, there is two ways Islam came to Arakan. So, at first Muslim started, [people] become Islam there, converted to Islam. Seventh to tenth centuries. That time called Arakan. Maybe Arakan is a word given from Arabian, Arabic, because you can use this word, you can take it from Persian as well. Arakan is also a word of Persian and a word of Arabic. But it is probably Persian people given the name Arakan. Akyab is also Persian word. A-ab, one water. So Muslim history is going down and down and their history is coming up and up. I am Myanmar citizen. There is an undeniable fact, we are citizen of this country. According to Myanmar Citizenship Law 1982 all Rohingya who are issued National Registration Certificate. Actually, this is National Registration Certificate. We are holding the same card the president hold. We are holding the same card a Supreme Court Justice hold. We are holding the same card that army general hold. So, we are undeniable citizen. So whatever exercise they are doing here is not according to law. It is according to policy. It is a misusing of power. I reject 1982 citizenship law which made us stateless.

Abdul suggested that he, like other Rohingya, had been previously acknowledged as a Myanmar citizen yet was made legally stateless by the provisions of the 1982 citizenship law. He noted how the 1962 military coup represented a turning point for the Rohingya, explaining, 'We got independent in 1948 until 1962. In this country our people enjoyed full democracy. People are very happy. Rohingya community themselves are part of the country, they are citizen, they are recognized as ethnic of Myanmar by the U Nu government. We have full citizenship at that time before the military coup. We did not find any discrimination at that time.' In Abdul's opinion, it was Ne Win's military administration that first introduced practices responsible for generating Myanmar's modern-day anti-Muslim attitudes:

> Military coup in Myanmar in 1962, this in itself military coup was on the basis of revenge on Muslims. Actually, Ne Win came into power with the one kind of

anger, because when he saw his people here in Myanmar, because there is a lot of dominated in business by Muslims, that time Burmese people have less access to business opportunities. He was disappointed with that, and suddenly after he come into power he imposed nationalized policy and then that stop all Muslims owning properties, business and many people from India they have to leave by boat to their country, back. So, since that time there is gradually growing up anti-Muslim sentiment in Myanmar.

Acknowledging the importance of public attitudes and opinions, Abdul Rasheed – like other mainstream Rohingya leaders – mostly directed his advocacy and his claims about Rohingya history towards Myanmar's authorities and the international community rather than a mainstream domestic audience.

Belief the 1982 law stripped Rohingya of their citizenship has led Rohingya leaders to align their advocacy with the provisions of this law by demonstrating their strong historical links with Arakan. As I outlined in Chapter Three, not only the provisions of the 1982 law have been problematic for the Rohingya: the law's interpretation and enforcement have had seriously negative consequences too, and strongly indicate that Myanmar's authorities use the law as a convenient cover to deny what they know are legitimate rights claims by groups like the Rohingya. In these circumstances, strategies focused on demonstrating how Rohingya meet the criteria of the 1982 law are unlikely to be successful. This suggests that advocating political change – either of the country's leadership or the attitudes of the voting public – ought to become Rohingya priorities.

> **'The solution is abolishing all discriminatory policies and promoting the rule of law. Everyone under the law, everyone should be equal.'**
> Wai Wai Nu, Yangon, Director, Women Peace Network Arakan,
> Yangon, 2015

Wai Wai Nu is a Myanmar community leader in her early thirties. Her father's (Kyaw Min) political activism led Myanmar's military regime to arrest her entire family. With Kyaw Min sentenced to forty-seven years in jail, the eighteen-year-old Wai Wai Nu received a seventeen-year sentence and was sent to Yangon's infamous Insein Prison, a colonial relic known for its inhumane conditions. Released as part of a political prisoner amnesty, she has since completed a law degree, and in response to the Rakhine state violence of 2012 she set up the Women's Peace Network Arakan, an NGO that arranged trainings and workshops aimed at promoting understanding between members of different religious and ethnic groups, particularly among young people. In late 2017, I joined Wai Wai Nu on a panel organized by Australian Catholic University's Institute for

Religion, Politics and Society, which considered Australia's obligations towards Myanmar's Rohingya, and just as when I first interviewed her in Myanmar two years before, for safety, to avoid angering Myanmar's authorities and risking further incarceration she chose her words carefully and focused her comments on her peace-building work.

Like all prominent Rohingya figures I spoke with, Wai Wai Nu believed the Rohingya have a lengthy history in Rakhine state, certainly predating the arrival of the colonial British, and while she too blamed decisions taken by Ne Win for diminishing the Rohingya's rights, it was the 1982 Citizenship Law and the government's accompanying list of indigenous groups that she considered mostly to blame for the Rohingya's ongoing statelessness. She believed claims that the Rohingya are mostly illegal 'Bengali' immigrants became widespread only relatively recently:

> So, the steps and the legislation, those show that for us we can calculate that this is General Ne Win's idea and policy to deny and strip off the rights of the Rohingya and exclude the Rohingya from politics, from social politics of this country ... Degrading citizenship status, when you are degraded citizenship status you became unequal in the society ... Before 1990s there were no illegal immigrant, we never heard of that story and we never heard of 'Bengali', the term 'Bengali'. The term 'Bengali' was imposed after 1990s by this military government ... Before 1990s, no one called the Rohingya as 'Bengali'. Whether they may call Muslims, or kalar, or if they don't want to call Rohingya but they never call 'Bengali'. But the term 'Bengali' became popular after 1990s and now it's become very hot.

Wai Wai Nu described herself as 'an activist working on promotion of human rights and democratic ideas, liberal democracy among the young people' and she talked proudly about the 'My Friend' campaign she started, where young people are encouraged to take selfies with friends of different religions and ethnicities and share these on social media. Her proposed solutions to the Rohingya's plight included changes to the law and Myanmar-wide peace-building activities. She said,

> The solution is abolishing all discriminatory policies and promoting the rule of law. Everyone under the law, everyone should be equal ... But the second thing they have to do is reforming citizenship law or granting, restoring Rohingya's full citizenship rights should be the solution ... And also, if you think the community are divided [and] they hate each other, the government say 'This is very popular. Oh, they hate each other, we cannot do anything.' If you think so you can, take some affirmative effort that creating programmes of reconciliations by the TV, radio and so allowing people, civil society, to create peace in the country. But by blocking everything you cannot accuse people they hate each other.

Wai Wai Nu perhaps more than any other Rohingya leader I spoke with demonstrated an understanding of the power of domestic political discourse in Myanmar and the influence of both public opinion and new telecommunications technologies, and the importance for the Rohingya of tailoring strategies to take account of these.

As other leaders focused their political claims almost exclusively on assertions about the Rohingya's history, Wai Wai Nu looked beyond this approach. Her acknowledgement of the need for active peace-building strategies that were inclusive of Myanmar's Bamar population made her exceptional among the Rohingya leadership. This was perhaps because she was younger than most prominent Rohingya figures, and so was less invested in pre-existing strategies. Living in Yangon she had been readily able to access new communications technologies as they were introduced to Myanmar. Throughout my research, I was impressed by a number of the younger Rohingya activists, especially Wai Wai Nu and those among the diaspora in Australia, Canada and Ireland, whose approach to seeking rights improvements seemed more in tune with the realities faced by the group than the approaches of more established Rohingya leaders. Wai Wai Nu was also one of the few prominent female Rohingya leaders. It was difficult to overlook this as a factor contributing to her focus on strategies to improve the Rohingya's situation that were less invested in the approach of the more established, frequently older, male Rohingya leadership.

> '1982 citizenship law is oppressive, and it was enacted in contradiction of international law. We had this citizenship, we are still citizens.'
>
> Nurul Islam, President, Arakan Rohingya National Organisation,
> London, 2016.

Living in London were prominent Rohingya activists Nurul Islam, Tun Khin and Ronnie. Nurul Islam was the long-time President of the Arakan Rohingya National Organisation, which he formed from former militant Rohingya groups in the 1990s, and he has been active in Rohingya advocacy and politics for decades. Younger and more recent arrivals to Rohingya activism are Tun Khin, the President of the Burmese Rohingya Organisation UK (BROUK), and Ronnie, a regular UK spokesperson for the European Rohingya Council (ERC). Being London based has had advantages for these activists, providing them with ready access to major international media outlets, political leaders and UK-based human rights organizations focused on Myanmar.

In the global Rohingya community, Nurul Islam has long been an influential elder statesman whose name was regularly raised with me by other Rohingya activists as a trusted and knowledgeable source of information about the Rohingya's history. In 2015, we spoke at length, and Nurul Islam told me the Rohingya had previously been acknowledged by the authorities as citizens of Myanmar. He outlined how citizenship rights acknowledged in the democratic period had been incrementally curtailed by the military dictatorship, with devastating human rights consequences. He said,

> The Burmese authorities who came to power, ruled the country in various forms, manifestations, all these people have respected the Rohingya's right to some extent … during parliamentary government, we enjoyed a sort of rights and freedom, although discrimination existed, and during Ne Win time he started curtailing, to curtail our rights, one by one, freedom of movement … education, it becomes now worse under this government, the reform government … It is very obvious because now we have been reduced to nothing, we are not human beings.

Nurul Islam was incensed by the suggestion that the Rohingya lacked a legitimate claim to Myanmar citizenship rights. He believed the group's culture, which was drawn from both South Asia and Southeast Asia, had been unfairly manipulated to denote the Rohingya as foreign. He was also unhappy about Myanmar officialdom's opposition to the Rohingya name, which he considered had a legitimate basis in Myanmar's history. He outlined how,

> [In] Arakan we are the borderline people. Definitely we are from two cultures. Arakan grew uninterrupted for 100 years … One hundred years Bengal, part of Bengal, particularly the Chittagong region. The most important governor was in Chittagong city, the governor at Chittagong is either son of the king or brother of the king, and then Arakan was under the influence and under the rule of Bengal for more than 200 years, vassal state … Then Anglo-Burmese War, 1824–26 and Arakan becomes part of Bengal, it was that time ruled from Calcutta … for 120 years … We have very much extensive, very extensive relationship, in all field, political, social, cultural, religious [with Chittagong]. So that historians used to call Chittagong greater Arakan, or extended Arakan, extended Chittagong …

On the question of whether the Rohingya wanted recognition as a distinct Myanmar *taingyintha*, Nurul Islam provided an emphatic 'Yes', and again said 'Yes' when asked whether they ought to have the right to be called Rohingya. The etymological origins of the Rohingya name were, in his view, traceable to Bengali language speakers in the region and there were historic records that attest to this. He said, 'These Bengali, Arakan is known to them as Rohang, one of the names

. . . So, we call those who were living in Rohang, Rohingya, but there are historical records that we people, the Muslim people, are known as Rohingya, the people living in Arakan.' Islam indicated he understood Rohang to be a Bengali word rather than Arabic, as others have claimed (although as I outlined in Chapter Five, Persian rather than Arabic was the more likely Middle Eastern language used in old Arakan). All are of course possible – Rohang may have been used concurrently by Arabic/Persian and Bengali speakers among the Muslim population, before evolving into the Bengali dialect name Rooinga identified by Buchanan.

Nurul Islam, like Abu Tahay, Htay Lwin Oo and Kyaw Hla Aung, referred to Buchanan's publications to establish the long-term historical legitimacy of the Rohingya identity. He recounted how the widespread modern use of the Rohingya name arose partly because of a rejection by ethnic Rakhine of Muslim's use of identity labels that included specific reference to Arakan. He explained that since references to Arakan or Rakhine had been sources of conflict, Muslims widely adopted the Rohingya name in the expectation that this would be more acceptable:

> We are very peaceful. Peace loving and peaceful living. We tried to develop an integrated policy, our forefathers, our elders, on the basis of Arakan nationalism, whether you are Buddhist or whether you are Muslim, no problem, we are Arakanese. Let us develop Arakanese on the basis of Arakanese-ness . . . [In the] Burmese set up, individual rights are not guaranteed, rights and privileges are given on the basis of collective rights. In the case of Burma, on an ethnic basis you are given rights . . . When we tried to develop a policy jointly, Rakhine said, 'No, how can you be Arakanese? We can't accept you as Arakanese.' We tried to embrace them, they always deny us. We tried to develop our integrated policy together with the Rakhine, but they disown us. They disown us, saying 'You can't be Arakanese.' So, we have to go take on our own as Rohingya. Rohingya as an ethnic group – that should be acceptable.

From Nurul Islam's perspective the Rohingya have already compromised on the question of their group's name, so any suggestion there might be a further change was unacceptable to him. Noting that the authorities had previously accepted the Rohingya name, he said,

> No, I say no. This name has already been accepted by the government . . . Why should we change this name? We can't change this name because we call each other Rohingya, we know each other as Rohingya. Indivisible Arakan, we are not going to divide Arakan. We are with our brothers the Rakhine people. We live

together. We lived together. We are living, and we have to live until doomsday. But the ball is in their court. They were not against this name once while it was recognized. They did not raise any objections while it was recognized by the U Nu government. This is the policy of the Burmese government, military … they're encouraging this to make it unstable. Only because they don't want to share power with us. If two brothers cannot live together, still we have to try separately.

The desire for exclusive Rohingya territorial control of territory was not a claim I regularly heard. Rohingya leaders, including the Myanmar-based Abu Tahay, Kyaw Hla Aung and Kyaw Min, were clear that they wanted the Rohingya to be acknowledged as citizens of Myanmar and to have their human rights acknowledged, yet they did not seek separate Rohingya territory. Nurul Islam's support for Rohingya territorial control demonstrated that this was not true of all prominent Rohingya figures. This added credibility to nationalist fears that the Rohingya project, particularly the aspects associated with militancy, might be about more than regaining lost rights and include a claim for territorial control. Nurul Islam believed the Rohingya ought to be entitled to their own state – a claim that would be aggressively opposed by nationalists, the Tatmadaw and likely a majority of Myanmar's residents. He wanted the Rohingya acknowledged as a key indigenous *taingyintha* like the eight groups specifically named in the 1982 citizenship law (Bamar, Chin, Kachin, Karen, Kayah, Mon, Rakhine and Shan). He spoke passionately about this, telling me,

> We are a people. From the concept of international law, we are a people. We have all the ingredients, qualities of a people. As a people we have a right to self-determination. But of course, the self-determination we are talking about is international self-determination. We exercise this, we want to live together with our Rakhine brothers. By exercising our right to self-determination, we want to be one. If they cannot accept us, with the federation we will be separate. If they cannot accept us or they deny us, the way they are now treating us, they have to change their attitude. We should have our own state within the federation of Burma like other ethnic nationalities of the country.

These claims would be deeply unpopular with the ethnic Rakhine community, and would certainly be rejected by Myanmar's government and aggressively opposed by the Tatmadaw.

The claims of other London-based Rohingya leaders were less controversial. In 2016, Ronnie, a regular spokesperson for the ERC, was pessimistic about the likelihood of international actors like the UN coming to the Rohingya's aid.

Ronnie's analysis of the situation was more nuanced than many. He marked a clear distinction between Western actors whose Myanmar priorities included trade while encouraging progress towards democracy, and powerful nations like China, India and Russia whose interests in Myanmar were more pragmatic. In the years after we spoke, Myanmar's UN delegation frequently relied on the support of China and Russia to shield it from Security Council action, oftentimes preventing discussion of the Rohingya's situation.[6] Ronnie also believed the desire of countries like China and India to access Rakhine state's natural resources had contributed to the outbreak of the 2012 violence. He said,

> The causes of 2012 violence, the riots, raise important issues: there was some international policy changes which has a direct effect to the situation. The Chinese policy itself. It has a policy of expansion and creating a geopolitical strategy for themselves, creating a road and control of the sea. And then the Indians has the same ambition and those both are linked up in Arakan. The finance investment that is done by the Chinese and the Indians which is billions of dollars, and billions more to come. And thirdly, Rakhine, which is the most poor state now, will become the richest state if everything goes according to their plan. The problem is what's behind the move – the collective rights of the people. They want to destroy the collective rights of the people. Burmese democracy can never be complete without giving rights to the Rohingya. The compromise shouldn't always be on our own back, on the Rohingya's back. He will ask for collective rights. They needed a shield to protect them. This should be the Lady.

Like many Rohingya I spoke with, Ronnie did not limit his call for improved human rights to the Rohingya community. He understood that human rights abuses were widespread in Myanmar, believed Aung San Suu Kyi had a responsibility to safeguard the human rights of every Myanmar resident, and was frustrated that she had failed to do this. In light of the appalling rights abuses faced by the Rohingya, Ronnie said he might be prepared to consider a citizenship process that assessed applicants individually rather than conferred group citizenship rights – if human rights improvements would quickly follow and if the process did not come at the cost of the right to identify as Rohingya. Asked about citizenship assessments without the Rohingya label, Ronnie gave a firm no: 'For the Rohingya, this is our identity. I don't think anybody would accept that.' Nurul Islam had been blunter, rejecting the very premise of the question, 'I don't agree with one point – your question – 1982 citizenship law is oppressive, and it was enacted in contradiction of international law. We had this citizenship. We are still citizens.' This was a point regularly made by Rohingya leaders – that the Rohingya were acknowledged as citizens by the country's authorities and so, according to the law, remain citizens today – even if their rights are not acknowledged by Myanmar's government. This, of course, has not been the view of Myanmar's authorities.

In 2016, I spoke as well with Tun Khin, the BROUK President. He told me bluntly, 'I'm not that optimistic. Not optimistic, and I worry that most probably there will be only focus [on the Rohingya's situation] for a while maybe few years ... I don't think they [Myanmar's authorities] will discuss full citizenship issues and ethnic rights at all.' Tun Khin was particularly frustrated with the failure of Aung San Suu Kyi to speak up in defence of the Rohingya. He recalled, 'We campaigned for Aung San Suu Kyi's release, as Rohingya organizations. They were speaking up when she was in house arrest ... but she never spoke for Rohingya. She dismisses ethnic cleansing and she never visited Arakan state.' Rohingya criticisms of Aung San Suu Kyi would become increasingly frequent as the NLD's time in office lengthened and frustrations with her lack of support for the Rohingya's aspirations grew.

In circumstances where the Rohingya were denied access to their human rights, had been disenfranchised and were now finding their optimism about Aung San Suu Kyi to have been misplaced, it was surely only a matter of time before members of the group advocated alternatives to the peaceful strategies long pursued by mainstream Rohingya leaders. It was in the months following my interviews with Nurul Islam, Ronnie and Tun Khin that Rohingya militancy re-emerged in the form of the ARSA group. Despite Rohingya figures indicating their opposition to political violence, there was emerging evidence that some Rohingya in Rakhine state had come to favour an alternative approach.

In Myanmar, political violence has been a commonly adopted strategy of ethnic minorities – many among Myanmar's dozens of ethnic armed groups are acknowledged as legitimate participants in the country's political life.[7] Mainstream Rohingya opinion has opposed political violence for decades, although it is important to acknowledge that for a number I spoke with – notably older Rohingya figures – that was not always the case. During the 1980s Nurul Islam had been involved with the Arakan Rohingya Islamic Front, before becoming a key figure in the Arakan Rohingya National Organisation and adopting non-violent strategies, and Maung Kyaw Nu had been involved with 8888 Uprising fighters, an approach he characterized (below) as part of the campaign to return the country's lost democracy.[8] Unfortunately, Rohingya militancy is viewed in very different terms to the militancy of other ethnic minorities.

Rohingya who advocate political violence are likely to be branded terrorists rather than legitimate political actors. This has limited the political options of mainstream Rohingya leaders – confining them to non-violent strategies because any advocacy or threat of violence would likely be counter-productive to their cause. While mainstream Rohingya leaders have long advocated non-violent political solutions, Myanmar nationalists and the Tatmadaw brand Rohingya as likely terrorist threats.[9] The ARSA group germinated in the aftermath of the 2012 Rakhine state violence, which Myanmar's authorities had described as 'communal' violence. ARSA believed the Rohingya faced 'genocide and crimes against humanity' – a clear indication ARSA intended to take decisive action.[10]

In 2015, I had heard talk of a militant group organizing in northern Rakhine state, although it was not until their 2016 attacks on security posts there that the ability of the group to actually mobilize supporters became clear. ARSA's October 2016 and August 2017 attacks, and the brutal Tatmadaw crackdowns that followed, influenced much of the remainder of my research for this book. From late 2016 onwards, Rohingya leaders frequently expressed opinions about the utility or otherwise of political violence. The perceived consequences of ARSA's actions – precipitating brutal Tatmadaw crackdowns and subsequent forced deportations were raised too. Mostly it was the impact ARSA might have on official attitudes and actions (of the civilian authorities and the Tatmadaw) towards the Rohingya, rather than its influence on public opinion, that was the focus of most commentary.

> **'In Saudi Arabia a lot of people are ready to die for Saudi Arabia, unfortunately, but they are not ready to die for Arakan.'**
> Muhammad Noor, Rohingya Vision TV, Kuala Lumpur, 2016

When I interviewed Muhammad Noor in February 2016, ARSA's emergence as a fighting force was still months away, but the fact ARSA was already organizing in Rakhine state adds new context to a number of his comments. Muhammad was a high-profile, Malaysia-based Rohingya leader, headed the satellite television channel Rohingya Vision TV, and served as chairman of the Kuala Lumpur-based Rohingya football club. He had previously lived in Pakistan and Saudi Arabia, and we met in Ampang, a Kuala Lumpur district hosting a substantial refugee population, including numerous Rohingya.

While Rohingya leaders more commonly identified the 1962 coup or the 1982 citizenship law as the pivotal factors contributing to their loss of rights, Muhammad traced the roots of the Rohingya's dire circumstances to unresolved Second World War violence. A major front had opened in Arakan, and the area's major confessional groups aligned with different combatants – the Muslim community generally backed the British, while Buddhists supported the Japanese. British retreat and the collapse of state authority contributed to widespread inter-religious violence, left potentially tens of thousands dead and permanently reshaped Arakan's demographics by separating Buddhist and Muslim populations.

Muhammad characterized the violence as a massacre of Muslims, saying, 'This massacre happened under the supervision of the Burmese entity and the British government. Somebody has to be responsible for this, of killing about 100,000 people.' The extent of the killing is difficult to know with certainty, although an indication of its scale can be ascertained by its influence on Arakan's demographics, with most Muslims then moving to the north, while Buddhists moved to the south. This remained an accurate reflection of Rakhine state's demographics more than seventy years later when I spoke with Muhammad. While Muhammad portrayed Arakan's Second World War violence as a massacre of Rohingya, this conflict (unlike the violence of 2012) was far from one-sided. Ethnic Rakhine accounts of this period, such as those by Buddhist nationalist Khin Maung Saw, identify the Rakhine as the victims of a massacre at the hands of the Muslim community.[11]

Rohingya Vision television regularly reported instances of abuse, discrimination and violence towards Rohingya by Myanmar's authorities, so Muhammad of course characterized the Rohingya's contemporary circumstances in Rakhine state as grim. He recounted how Rohingya were excluded little by little from Myanmar's political mainstream, saying, 'This entire race [the Rohingya], we used to be a nation, from a nation they made us into a minority of the country, from a minority we become stateless of that country. From stateless we become homeless, from homeless we become the floating people. The people of 'No.' Everywhere we are going by boat. We are like the pandas of China. We are fading out of the entire world.' Muhammad also outlined the Rohingya's collective loss of official identity documentation: 'Rohingya used to have National ID card, and it has changed from NRC to "White Card", which is called a Temporary Card. From the Temporary Card, they are now giving them verification process, lower than the temporary card itself.' He was understandably frustrated by this mistreatment and was firm in his belief there should be no compromise about the Rohingya name. However, aspects of the language Muhammad used in our interview might cause unease among those fearing the re-emergence of Rohingya militancy:

> Why don't we accept as a Burmese Muslim? It is not that we are negotiating Rohingya new word. It has been there for the last consecutive decades, four governments, four governments have recognized the word. From 1948, from

independence until 1982 Rohingya was an ethnic minority in Arakan. It is an established fact ... Now during 1982 when they wrote the citizenship laws. From here until today they are talking about changing the word. We are not ready even to change the spelling of it. R.O.H.I.N.G.Y.A. If they put the Y before the G we cannot put that. We are talking about the ownership of the land, that land is our ancestral land ... there is our roots. Every other race has been allowed to have their own title except us. It is not ethically fair, it is not ethically right, it is not morally right, it is not even to international standard. I should keep my own name. Nobody should tell me by force to change my name, unless it is my willingness. So, we are not willing to discuss the name at all under any cost. Because that is the name we are going to fight for. These people who have fought and died for that name we are dishonouring them.

Explaining the motivation for his Rohingya Vision television network, Muhammad again used language that might cause unease for some. He said,

> In Saudi Arabia a lot of people are ready to die for Saudi Arabia, unfortunately but they are not ready to die for Arakan. So now somebody has to come with a plan. How can we preserve our culture, our nation? If I don't do it, my soul cannot be at rest. Because we know this is going on. We cannot blindfold, we cannot sit back. If they're pushing hard, we got to push harder back. We will all die fighting. We need political solution, we need humanitarian solution, we need media solution. So, I am totally focusing on the media.

Considering the subsequent ARSA attacks, Muhammad's choice of language was unfortunate because he had frequently expressed his support for non-violent political approaches. He acknowledged as well that the consequences of Rohingya militancy would be likely devastating for the group. In 2017, he told media, 'Picking up arms is like giving the (Myanmar) military a licence to kill us ... We cannot achieve anything through violence; we are not going to win a war. And being Muslims, if we support an insurgency like other Myanmar ethnic groups, (governments) will look for links to outside terrorist groups.'[12] Muhammad's statements reflected the frustration of the Rohingya, whose 2015 disenfranchisement removed their last direct influence on Myanmar's domestic political processes. This, the closure of migratory routes of escape for young men, combined with the perception that Aung San Suu Kyi and the NLD had abandoned the Rohingya, undoubtedly strengthened ARSA's hand, making recruitment in northern Rakhine state easier.

'We are Rakhine? No, we are Burmese.'
Htay Lwin Oo, Rohingya history specialist, Bangkok, 2016

The US-based Htay Lwin Oo, whom I interviewed in a Bangkok café in 2016, has been recognized in the Rohingya community as a historian of the group. He expressed frustration at Myanmar government pressure for the Rohingya to accept the 'Bengali' label, which he believed incorrectly portrayed them as foreigners. His belief about the origin of the Rohingya name was that it was a corruption of the Arabic word *rahma*, meaning 'mercy', rather than being derived from the *Rohang* name as other Rohingya figures indicated. Outlining the group's indigeneity, he told me, 'We are there [in Arakan] in seventh century.' Htay Lwin Oo believed there was documentary evidence the Rohingya were present in Arakan by the eighteenth century, a clear reference to Buchanan's work, although he pointed me to an 1815 German publication by Johann Severin Vater (which cited Buchanan), as evidence for 'the name Rohingya in 1799'. He also directly referenced Buchanan's work, saying 'in 17-something appears Rooinga, but according to 1982 law, they mention that before 1823, who settled down in Burma, their ancestors settled down in Burma, their ancestors would be directly national of Burma.' He argued that the evidence meant Rohingya should, according to Myanmar's laws, be acknowledged as a *taingyintha* on equal terms with groups like the Bamar and Rakhine (rather than as a Rakhine subgroup); he asked, 'We are Rakhine? No, we are Burmese.'

The claim for the Rohingya to have the same rights and to be treated on equal terms with groups specifically named in the 1982 citizenship law came with an implied political assertion. A common perception in Myanmar is that ethnic groups named in the law have a right to territorial control of a state, which they will politically dominate. This meant Htay Lwin Oo's claim for the Rohingya to have similar rights to such groups would be considered a political claim in Myanmar asserting the right for Rohingya territorial control. Unsurprisingly, the historical basis of Htay Lwin Oo's claim has been rejected by Myanmar's authorities, who deny the Rohingya's pre-colonial residency. Htay Lwin Oo was dismissive of the Myanmar authorities' approach and said, 'They don't know about their history.'

Htay Lwin Oo was reluctant to discuss the potential of renewed Rohingya militancy and changed the subject quickly when I raised it. The political action he advocated was peaceful – believing a return of international economic sanctions might help the Rohingya's cause. He was hesitant to discuss the potential that colonial-era migration might have contributed to the Rohingya's population in Arakan. He said, 'They come back to their home,' echoing the opinion of Abu Tahay that Muslim arrivals to Arakan in the British colonial period were overwhelmingly returnees, displaced by Burma's 1784 invasion.

Reluctance to discuss British colonial-era migration was understandable in a context where the Rohingya have been so unfairly portrayed by Myanmar's authorities as recent arrivals from Bangladesh. Any admission to heritage from Bengal was a potential problem for the group that risked undermining their citizenship and rights claims. Htay Lwin Oo was keen to represent the contemporary Rohingya as a group distinct from anyone who might have origins in the land that forms modern-day Bangladesh.

Addressing more recent history, Htay Lwin Oo described how the Rohingya were already a clearly defined ethnic group prior to the Second World War,

> ...already in 1933, the Rohingya people is Rakhine Muslims, and later the Rakhine people say, 'You are not Rakhine, you come from Bangladesh.' Then in 2008, they gave the name 'Bengali', 'You accept the Bengali name, we give you equal rights.' I want to know why they fight the name Rohingya? Rohingya people, they have their history for centuries, and they have the right to claim themselves as Rohingya, and actually Burmese government, and Burmese people know that they are Rohingya, but they knowingly deny the name.

Htay Lwin Oo, like Abdul Rasheed, Muhammad Noor, Nurul Islam and Wai Wai Nu, asserted that the Rohingya's situation changed for the worse in the Ne Win era, when the authorities increasingly restricted the Rohingya's rights, including by limiting their ability to self-identify. When we spoke, the Rohingya's rights situation had deteriorated so much that Htay Lwin Oo believed Myanmar's authorities unquestionably 'commit genocide'.

'I love my country, I always dreamed that I would go back to Myanmar one day, or tomorrow. I am waiting for tomorrow for over thirty years' time.'
Maung Kyaw Nu, President, Burmese Rohingya Association in Thailand,
Bangkok, 2016

Maung Kyaw Nu became politically active as part of the 8888 Uprising's student movement, and more recently was president of Thailand's Burmese Rohingya Association. We spoke in June 2016, by which time Aung San Suu Kyi's NLD administration had been in power for close to three months. Like many 88 Generation activists, Maung Kyaw Nu fled in the aftermath of the 8888 Uprising and lived for years in the Karen Hills and later in Bangkok. Maung Kyaw Nu did not describe his thirty years living outside of Myanmar as a migration, instead considering his time abroad as exile: 'I don't like to go further from my country. I love my country, I always dreamed that I would go back to Myanmar one day, or tomorrow. I am waiting for tomorrow for over thirty years' time.'

Reflecting his background as an 88 Generation activist, Maung Kyaw Nu focused less than others on the Rohingya's group history and more on their contemporary situation and Myanmar's political future. He did not limit his concerns about lost rights to the Rohingya, expressing sympathy for others suffering rights abuses by Myanmar's authorities: 'All the people in Myanmar have the problem. Whether they are Bamar, Karen, Kachin or Rohingya, but the Rohingya are in the worst.' Maung Kyaw Nu was unusual among the Rohingya figures I spoke with because he positioned his political activism firmly within a domestic framework and, like Wai Wai Nu, he understood the importance of engagement with people throughout Myanmar. His long-term desire was to, 'make Burma a democratic country within ASEAN' but he was growing disappointed with Aung San Suu Kyi, although not supporting her came reluctantly to him:

> We have a lot of respect for Daw Aung San Suu Kyi. But after she got elected this
> time people who elected her blindly, for change, for change. After she got power
> most of the activists don't like her ... I'm not just talking about Rohingya. So, I
> can't support her, especially as a Rohingya, I cannot support her. She is a toothless
> lion. She cannot do anything.

For Maung Kyaw Nu, the group should of course be entitled to self-identity as Rohingya. He considered Aung San Suu Kyi's 2016 request to avoid using the 'Bengali' label to have been a win of sorts, yet he believed alternative names for the Rohingya that emphasized their religious complexion (like Rakhine Muslim) would be unhelpful. He said, 'I am very happy. This is one kind of success ... Muslim is not an ethnic name, Muslim cannot be an ethnic name, this cannot be an ethnic name, putting another name to us is not acceptable. We don't like this sort of thing. "Bengali" is not our name. Imposing a lot of names on us is not acceptable.'

Maung Kyaw Nu said he wanted to remind Aung San Suu Kyi about the numerous activists, including Rohingya, who helped her on her political journey and who now appeared to have been forgotten. He would tell her, 'You are not a student, but you became a leader due to the 88 Generation.' That Aung San Suu Kyi had forgotten, or was choosing to ignore, the contribution to her political success of other 8888 Uprising leaders has been increasingly noted by high-profile 88 Generation activists in recent years.[13] The sense of abandonment by Aung San Suu Kyi must have been more acutely felt by those like Maung Kyaw Nu – 88 Generation and Rohingya.

Frustration about the Rohingya's lost rights was amplified because of the belief that the Rohingya ask very little of Myanmar – merely that the authorities return the rights the Rohingya formerly enjoyed and which were stripped away, 'slowly, slowly', by the military dictatorship. Maung Kyaw Nu said,

> We don't want anything. We only like to regain our lost [rights]. It means we used to have every right . . . Our rights to equality, need to have. Many types of rights, our National Registration Card, NLC, our own language, we used to have even the minister. They took from us our voting rights 2015 election. We don't like to ask for anything from them, but we'd like to ask to return our rights.

He believed the process of diminishing Rohingya access to rights had continued under the country's quasi-civilian administrations, and that the Rohingya's group identity and history continued to be targeted: 'People would like to demolish our history.' He was 'pessimistic' too about the prospect of the Kofi Annan-led Advisory Commission on Rakhine State leading to positive change. A prescient perspective – while the Commission made dozens of recommendations that, if implemented, would improve the Rohingya's situation, Myanmar's authorities have been painfully slow to implement them. The Commission's key recommendation about decoupling the link between ethnicity and Myanmar citizenship has been ignored by Aung San Suu Kyi's government.

While mostly addressing the Rohingya's contemporary rights situation, Maung Kyaw Nu did explain that the Rohingya are made up of a mix of peoples, and unlike most Rohingya I spoke with, he was prepared to acknowledge that legal, colonial-era migration had contributed to the Rohingya's population. His Myanmar nationalism led him to become an 88 Generation activist and to fight a military dictatorship whose actions he equated with terrorism. By October 2016, a few months after we spoke, it would become clear that not all Rohingya rejected militancy as a political tactic and that frustrations with the decades of official rights abuses had led some to support the newly emerged ARSA militant group. Maung Kyaw Nu did not endorse militancy, telling me, 'I am not a terrorist. I took the gun to fight against the terrorism. In Myanmar, every community and group indigenous has armed group now . . . The Rohingya used to have before . . . I don't like any result come through a gun barrel, I use the pen like you. I would like to use the pen for my community.'

Maung Kyaw Nu was clearly proud of both his Myanmar and Rohingya identities. He presented a Rohingya identity that included a Myanmar nationalism that was wildly at odds with the way Myanmar's authorities have portrayed the Rohingya. He was unusual too among the Rohingya figures I spoke with because he acknowledged and desired a place for the Rohingya among the Myanmar mainstream – an acknowledgement of their rights in Rakhine state and their rights and obligation to participate fully in Myanmar's national life. Even while enduring appalling rights abuses, mainstream Rohingya leaders have rejected the kind of political violence that has been routine for other ethnic minority groups in Myanmar. As the interviews presented in this chapter illustrated, political violence (including its advocacy) has not been a key Rohingya political strategy in recent decades. The Rohingya's modern leadership commonly believed violence would run contrary to their group's interests and likely invite an aggressive military response while potentially hardening nationwide public opinion against them. These have, with just a few exceptions, been the approaches of mainstream Rohingya leaders since the early 1960s, when Arakan's *Mujahid* insurgents surrendered to the central authorities.

A few months after speaking with Maung Kyaw Nu, it became clear that numbers of Rohingya had run out of patience with peaceful strategies and embraced militancy, directed by the ARSA group. ARSA's first significant action in October 2016 prompted an aggressive Tatmadaw crackdown and tens of thousands of Rohingya civilians fled to Bangladesh.[14] ARSA's next major operation, in 2017, precipitated a larger-scale Tatmadaw 'clearance operation' that resulted in the forced deportation of most Rohingya from Myanmar. This sadly proved the case made by Maung Kyaw Nu and others that renewed Rohingya militancy was not in the group's interests.

Aside from non-violence, mainstream Rohingya leaders have overwhelmingly focused on seeking international support for their claims to Myanmar citizenship. They frequently expressed the hope that international pressure from the UN, foreign governments and human rights groups might cause Myanmar's authorities to acknowledge the legitimacy of their citizenship and rights claims. This focus on international support has been widely perceived in Myanmar as an attempt to undermine the country's sovereignty, allowing nationalists to portray Rohingya as disloyal to Myanmar and further eroding the Rohingya's domestic support. Sadly, many Rohingya leaders I spoke with also indicated that the chances Rohingya circumstances might soon improve had decreased in recent times. While nationalists and the Tatmadaw had been expected to continue rejecting the Rohingya's aspirations, Rohingya had commonly hoped their situation would improve with Aung San Suu Kyi's ascension to political power. Instead, the Rohingya's circumstances worsened considerably during her tenure. Consequently, by 2016, the already disenfranchised Rohingya would have rightly believed their group had no influential domestic political allies. Rohingya would have felt their political options had become limited to hoping for international help, or taking up arms themselves – a perspective that, as has been shown, was not the preferred position of mainstream Rohingya leaders. Lack of domestic support has had dire consequences for the Rohingya, who have been denied citizenship and subjected to discriminatory government policies and gross human rights violations. The lack of domestic sympathy for Rohingya claims allowed the Tatmadaw to forcibly deport more than 700,000 Rohingya to Bangladesh in late 2017 and early 2018 without meaningful public or political opposition. Recent militancy has not worked for the Rohingya, and neither have elements of the peaceful approaches preferred by the Rohingya's mainstream leadership.

We are Rohingya

Since the early years of independence, Myanmar's ethnic minorities have embraced political violence as a strategy to place their demands on the national political agenda. Today, among Myanmar's dozens of armed insurgencies are well-resourced armies from among the Kachin, Karen, Shan and Rakhine communities. Remarkably, considering the conditions the Rohingya were subjected to, their mainstream leadership had held fast to mostly peaceful political approaches since the 1960s. The violence of 2012, the mass incarceration of Rohingya that followed, and the Rohingya's 2015 disenfranchisement and exclusion from democratic life prompted a rethink about the utility of peaceful strategies for some Rohingya. This chapter's focus is on Rohingya experiences after the re-emergence of militancy.

In October 2016, a newly emerged Rohingya militant group launched a series of attacks on northern Rakhine state security posts, killing nine security personnel and looting weapons and ammunition. Known originally by the Arabic name *Harakah al-Yaqin* (Faith Movement), the group has come to be more commonly referred to as the Arakan Rohingya Salvation Army or simply referenced by the acronym ARSA. The Tatmadaw's response, a 'clearance operation' claimed as a search for ARSA militants, employed aggressive tactics that Amnesty International said involved the 'collective punishment' of the civilian Rohingya population.[1] This prompted around 90,000 Rohingya to flee their homes in northern Rakhine state for Bangladesh. John McKissick, the head of the UNHCR agency in Cox's Bazar, close to Bangladesh's Myanmar frontier, criticized the Tatmadaw as having, 'engaged in collective punishment of the Rohingya minority' and described 'their ultimate goal of ethnic cleansing of the Muslim minority in Myanmar'.[2] The brutality of the Tatmadaw's reaction and their clear targeting of Rohingya civilians ought to have placed international actors like the UN on high alert that, given an excuse, the Tatmadaw would undertake more widespread atrocities against Rohingya civilians. As it had for decades, the UN in Myanmar instead worked to mitigate the worst humanitarian

Figure 10 Kutupalong and nearby refugee camps, close to Cox's Bazar, Bangladesh, are now home to more than one million Rohingya refugees.

consequences for mistreated Rohingya civilians without taking meaningful political steps to pre-empt and prevent more Tatmadaw atrocities. Further contributing to the military's sense of impunity was the absence of a UN Security Council condemnation of the Tatmadaw's targeting of Rohingya civilians.

ARSA's October 2016 attacks had surprised Myanmar's security forces, and Tatmadaw leaders were determined not to be caught out again. As the 2017 wet season was drawing to an end, battle-hardened troops from the 33rd and 99th light infantry divisions, known for their aggressive counter-insurgency campaigns against ethnic minorities, were deployed to Rakhine state.[3] The arrival of Tatmadaw units with well-known histories of human rights violations against ethnic minorities in other parts of Myanmar was guaranteed to stoke fear and tensions among the Rohingya. By late August 2017, Rohingya communities in northern Rakhine were locked down and food and medicine supplies were blocked – many legitimately feared a repeat of the one-sided violence of 2012, or potentially a massacre by the recently arrived Tatmadaw troops. In a febrile environment, ARSA claimed the need to strike first as a necessity to defend Rohingya civilians. On August 25, the group tweeted a statement:

> Rohingya Community in Rathedaung has been under a Burmese government sponsored atrocities and blockade for more than 2 weeks which is starving them

(the Rohingya people) to death. Over the last 2 days, Burmese security forces along with some Rakhine extremists killed over a dozen people in the township.

As they prepared to do the same in Maungdaw; and conducted raids and committed atrocities in some Rohingya villages in the township last night (August 24 night), we had to eventually step up in order to drive the Burmese colonizing forces away.

Currently, we have been taking our defensive actions against the Burmese marauding forces in more than 25 different places across the region.[4]

ARSA's attacks of course prompted another, and this time much more brutal and widespread, Tatmadaw crackdown. Again, Myanmar's military supposedly searching for militants made little distinction between civilians and potential insurgents. Tatmadaw troops terrorized Rohingya communities in northern Rakhine state, arbitrarily arresting, murdering, assaulting, raping and torturing Rohingya they encountered.

Myanmar's Rohingya, who had already endured decades of creeping rights limitations, now suddenly experienced violent genocidal crimes that prompted forced migration on a massive scale. Hundreds of thousands of Rohingya fled their homes and villages. Within three weeks, more than 409,000 Rohingya fled to Bangladesh – within ten weeks this number had reached 620,000, and by year's end more than 650,000 had left Myanmar.[5] Satellite images obtained by Human Rights Watch highlighted the scorched earth tactics employed by the Tatmadaw – the military partially or totally razed at least 300 Rohingya villages (by 2020, the number of Rohingya villages destroyed had increased to at least 400).[6] Human Rights Watch considered the military's actions amounted to 'crimes against humanity'.[7] Amnesty International described the situation as a 'human rights and humanitarian catastrophe'.[8] The UN's High Commissioner for Human Rights, Zeid Ra'ad Al Hussein, believed it was 'A textbook example of ethnic cleansing'.[9]

The brutality of the Tatmadaw's actions and the subsequent forced migration crisis at last drew world attention to Myanmar's mistreatment of the Rohingya, led to discussion at the UN Security Council, and prompted the US government to investigate whether the atrocities committed by Myanmar's military met the legal definition of genocide.[10] A UN Human Rights Council team identified widespread human rights violations by the Tatmadaw, and recommended 'investigation and prosecution of Myanmar's Commander-in-Chief, Senior General Min Aung Hlaing, and his top military leaders for genocide, crimes against humanity and war crimes'.[11] The UN Security Council did discuss the Rohingya's situation, yet did nothing more and there was no resolution to demand that Myanmar cease its brutal mistreatment of Rohingya civilians.

Myanmar is the site of the world's longest running civil war. Since independence, every ethnic minority has been a target of Tatmadaw violence. Conflict between the government and armed groups representing ethnic and religious minorities (including *Mujahid* fighters and the Rakhine), communists, and at times the remnants of the Republican Chinese *Kuomintang* contributed to the decision of the military to launch a *coup d'état* in 1962, which ushered in five decades of brutal military dictatorship yet did not end the nation's internal conflicts. These groups' motivations and political claims varied greatly, although a common political claim among ethnic minority groups has been for the devolution of political power from the Bamar-dominated centre, along the lines of the federation many believe was central to the 1947 *Panglong Agreement*. Negotiated between ethnic minority leadership and the Burmese government headed by Aung San immediately prior to independence, the *Panglong Agreement* provided for full autonomy in the administration of frontier areas, as the country's fringe territories were then known.[12] Myanmar's government and military reject ethnic minority claims for increased political control, but it is noteworthy that these groups have rarely made separatist or independence claims.

In Arakan, the *Mujahid* insurgency operated after the Second World War, when political instability meant Burma's authorities effectively controlled little more than the major population centres. Arakan's hinterlands were in the hands of various militants, including the *Mujahids*, two separate communist armies and ethnic Rakhine nationalist forces.[13] *Mujahid* militancy was far from homogenous. A minority supported the incorporation of Muslim communities into the recently independent Pakistan, while most Muslims in Arakan aimed for increased Muslim political influence within Burma amid fears that promised statehood would result in local Buddhist political dominance of the Muslim population. The MFA's creation in 1961 took political impetus away from the *Mujahid* militants, who would never again be a serious force. The MFA's subsequent scrapping became a key motivation for small numbers of Rohingya to maintain a commitment to political violence. This was not the approach embraced by the mainstream Rohingya leadership in recent decades: their focus has been on advocating for improved access to human rights and acknowledgement of collective Rohingya citizenship rights. Nevertheless, Myanmar's authorities have pointed to the existence of the small Rohingya groups who maintained a commitment to political violence throughout the 1970s, 1980s and beyond.

Armed groups claiming to represent the Rohingya certainly existed after the demise of *Mujahid* militancy. These groups are widely acknowledged to have had small memberships (commonly in the dozens) and very limited capacity. Martin Smith, who has written extensively about Myanmar's ethnic armed groups (EAG), identified two such groups as the Rohingya Solidarity Organisation (RSO) and the Arakan Rohingya Islamic Front (ARIF). Smith pointed out that while at one time in the mid-1990s an alliance between the ARIF and RSO created a group known as the Rohingya Solidarity Alliance, which may have had the support of up to 500 men under arms, these militant groups were commonly 'extremely limited and factionalised', and this contributed to alliances being short-lived and their capacity for military action limited, frequently involving small arms fire or grenades. These were hardly markers of a popularly supported and well-resourced insurgency.[14] Tracing the history of Muslim militancy in Myanmar, international security scholar Andrew Selth characterized Rohingya militants as highly factionalized and with extremely limited military capacity between the 1960s and 1990s.[15] Selth identified the RSO as a precursor to the ARIF, believing both groups derived from the Rohingya Independence Force (RIF), a group that objected to Burma's military coup of 1962 and the subsequent banning of Rohingya organizations. Selth acknowledged that Muslim militancy has been at times exaggerated or deliberately misrepresented, and did not link Rohingya militants with trans-national jihadi groups, instead indicating that one Rohingya militant group, the Rohingya Patriotic Front (another off-shoot of the RIF) was inspired rather than resourced by 1970s worldwide pan-Islamic movements and did advocate Muslim separatism. Rohingya militant groups were never large, and by the 1990s were generally defunct. The International Crisis Group noted that the RSO label became something of a militant brand that could be used by anyone regardless of their connection to the original group.[16] That the RSO was blamed by Myanmar's authorities for a 2014 attack on Border Guard Police while armed criminal gangs were known to operate in the area was likely a reflection of this, as was Myanmar's initial labelling of ARSA's 2016 attacks as the responsibility of the RSO despite a lack of evidence that this could have been the case.

Rohingya militancy was functionally extinct by the 2000s and mainstream Rohingya leaders advocated a non-violent approach to politics. Ongoing human rights violations, the denial of citizenship, Rakhine state's violence of 2012 and the Myanmar authorities' subsequent mass incarceration of Rohingya strained the credibility of this approach. One consequence of media liberalizations by Myanmar's first quasi-civilian administration was that the plight of Rohingya victims of the 2012 violence received far more international media attention than had Rohingya victims of rights violations in the preceding decades. The

Rohingya's situation became a *cause célèbre* within the *ummah* (worldwide community of Islam), motivating some among the Rohingya diaspora to promote militancy as a viable political strategy, and leading to the formation of the ARSA group.

With the communist insurgencies ended, EAGs in Myanmar now generally represent ethnic minorities comprised of Buddhists or Christians. By the time Myanmar's military handed elements of government power to a notionally civilian administration in 2011, there were dozens of active EAGs, and in a number of instances they controlled territory. The country's peace process, which brings together representatives of ethnic minorities for negotiation with the central government and Tatmadaw, has arguably become as influential in Myanmar's political life as the country's parliament. Until ARSA's emergence, Muslim groups had not for decades embraced political violence, so they had not been party to any of the negotiations associated with the nationwide peace process. In recent years, civil war conflict in Myanmar has generally involved the Tatmadaw and EAGs from groups in Kachin, Karen and Shan states. By 2020 the AA, a Rakhine Buddhist group, was increasingly active in Rakhine state and adjacent parts of Chin state. The escalation of this conflict and the potential it might lead to full-scale war in Rakhine state was evidenced by an AA report that during 2019 its fighters had engaged in almost 700 clashes with the Tatmadaw. The scale of AA violence dwarfs that of ARSA, and while it has been met with a strong Tatmadaw response, this has not had the ferocity of the 2017 anti-Rohingya clearance operation.[17]

ARSA's 2016 emergence as a military presence sparked fears of a possible return to the *Mujahid* militancy of the 1950s, or the emergence of an ISIS-style insurgency seeking exclusive Muslim control of territory. ARSA has consistently presented itself as an ethno-nationalist group rather than having trans-national jihadi motivations. The group has maintained an online presence using YouTube, Twitter and, until banned from the platform in 2017, Facebook. ARSA's 2019 report *Reviving the Courageous Hearts* depicted the group as reluctantly embracing political violence to protect Rohingya from a 'slow-burning or hidden Genocide'.[18] ARSA claimed it was motivated to embrace political violence because,

> As the existence and human rights of the Rohingya people were not protected in the country, as a last resort, [ARSA] stood up against the Burmese genocidal tyrants in response to the genocidal violence. ARSA will continue its resistance to defend the people from the genocidal military in line with the right to self-defence under International Law; until all the legitimate rights of the Rohingya people and their native ethnic status are restored in Burma.[19]

While ARSA's public messaging has portrayed the group as soldiers defending vulnerable Rohingya civilians, there is evidence that the motives of some among ARSA's leadership are less pure. Rohingya told me in 2016 and 2017 about moderate village leaders murdered in northern Rakhine state that were understood to have been killed on ARSA's orders. In 2019 and 2020, similar practices and violence against the small Rohingya Christian community have been identified in the Rohingya's refugee camps. Amnesty International has made claims about ARSA crimes, including the 2017 murders of around 100 Hindus in northern Maungdaw township.[20] Hostility towards Christians and Hindus suggests a number of key ARSA figures consider a strict interpretation of political Islam as a key characteristic of Rohingya identity and are prepared to violently enforce their perspective.

ARSA's 2016 attacks precipitated the kind of brutal crackdown from Myanmar's military that mainstream Rohingya leaders had feared would be the consequence of renewed Rohingya militancy. Further ARSA attacks in 2017 occurred in the context of a major Tatmadaw troop build-up in northern Rakhine state in the weeks before Kofi Annan launched the final report of the Advisory Commission on Rakhine State. The troop build-up contributed to fears that Tatmadaw attacks on Rohingya civilians were imminent regardless of ARSA's actions. Aung San Suu Kyi had previously committed the government to implementing the Kofi Annan Commission's recommendations in full – an approach that would have made senior Tatmadaw figures uneasy.[21] Having spent a year studying the situation in Rakhine state, the Commission was charged with finding solutions that could lead to peace there. A key recommendation was removing the link between citizenship and ethnicity – an approach likely to improve Muslim citizenship prospects that was strongly opposed by the Tatmadaw.[22] However, just hours after Kofi Annan delivered his Commission's findings to the government on 23 August, ARSA launched a series of attacks on security posts in northern Rakhine state that precipitated an immediate, evidently well planned and brutal Tatmadaw response.

The Tatmadaw, who had long desired to rid Myanmar of the Rohingya and facing the prospect that the country's laws might be altered to improve Rohingya citizenship prospects, took the opportunity to violently deport virtually all of northern Rakhine state's Rohingya population. This significantly altered the political landscape, shifting Myanmar's and international actor's focus away from the Kofi Annan Commission's recommendations and towards northern Rakhine state's humanitarian and security situation. The Commission's recommendations were soon mostly forgotten by Myanmar's key political actors.

Regardless of whether the 2017 violence was initiated by the ARSA or instigated by the Tatmadaw, the outcome for ordinary Rohingya was dreadful, and certainly a vindication of the mainstream Rohingya leadership's long-term strategy of non-violence.

'We Rohingya, activists and leaders were completely shocked by what has happened.'

Dr Anita Schug, Spokesperson, European Rohingya Council,
Switzerland, 2017

A prominent Switzerland-based Rohingya activist and a spokesperson for the European Rohingya Council, Dr Anita Schug met with me a number of times throughout my research, we communicated regularly online, and spoke at length in early 2017. A couple of months after ARSA's October 2016 attacks, Dr Schug told me, 'We Rohingya activists and leaders were completely shocked by what has happened.' This shock can only have been at the fact of ARSA's attacks rather than a militant group's existence in northern Rakhine state. Rumours had been circulating for the previous year about a new, non-state armed group recruiting in Rohingya communities, although those rumours were usually accompanied by the caveat that the group was incapable of action. ARSA had proved its capacity to act, yet confusion remained about precisely who the group was, and why they considered political violence was a shrewd strategy for the Rohingya when the government had recently announced that Kofi Annan would head a commission of inquiry to seek solutions to Rakhine state's conflict.

Dr Schug expressed confusion about the identity of the attackers and suggested of ARSA's attacks, 'This attack, who were they? Till today we don't know really what's the truth. We are completely dismayed from this incident ... Why the thing happened after Kofi Annan commission announced? We don't know who is that person who has attacked. We do see that there is some Rohingya people, kids, involved but we don't know.' There was similar confusion within the diplomatic corps, media, among scholars and, for a time, Myanmar's government.

In the aftermath of the violence, Myanmar's authorities moved quickly, and with seemingly little or no evidence to link the group with previous Rohingya militant outfits confidently identified the attackers as being from the long dormant (and potentially defunct) RSO.[23] After evidence of ARSA's involvement was clear, Myanmar's authorities then claimed the group was connected with Al Qaeda and ISIS, and officially designated ARSA an 'extremist terrorist' group.[24] ARSA has also been identified as a terrorist group by other influential regional actors, including the governments of Bangladesh, China and India. ARSA consistently rejected claims of links with trans-national jihadi groups and tweeted about this, telling its online followers: 'It is, once again, reassured that #ARSA only legitimately and objectively operates as an #ETHNO-NATIONALIST movement within its ancestral homeland (Arakan) in #Burma & its activities had not & will not transcend beyond its country.'[25] The International Crisis Group believed ARSA was financed by a committee of supporters in Mecca and Medina, and that its leader Ata Ullah (also known as Ataullah abu Ammar Jununi) was a Pakistan-born Rohingya who had lived for much of his life in Saudi Arabia.[26] This added credibility to claims about ARSA's international links.

Even with ARSA's emergence, Dr Schug held fast to a belief that the Rohingya were better off continuing a peaceful political strategy, but did concede that by relinquishing all military capacity, they may have become an easier target for government oppression. It was likely that ARSA's recruitment strategy involved making a similar point. This highlighted a dilemma faced by the Rohingya. Taking up arms had likely strengthened the hand of other ethnic minority groups whom the Myanmar authorities could not so easily isolate from mainstream life as they had the Rohingya. Dr Schug told me,

> The tragedy is because we are very optimistic throughout and very non-violent throughout – this was the reason for extermination. If you look at the Shan, if you look at the Kachin, they fought . . . they're fighting back . . . It was so easy for the military government. We were easy prey because it was the cheapest, there was no resistance from our side. We did not have any army who would protect us or fight against the government. We were cheap for the military.

Dr Schug might well have been correct – conditions for the Rohingya would likely have been better had they not been so easy a target for Myanmar's government and military. As I outlined in Chapter Three, when the military dictatorship was expelling Chinese and Indian populations from the country, they did not simultaneously target Arakan's Rohingya population where *Mujahid* fighters had only then recently surrendered and would have reorganized in response to sudden rights abuses.

Rights violations against the Rohingya began in earnest once the capacity for Rohingya militancy was effectively extinguished. While other ethnic minorities, including those with armed insurgencies, have certainly suffered appalling rights abuses (including similar tactics to those used by the Tatmadaw against the Rohingya) they have not been isolated from mainstream Myanmar life as the Rohingya have. Myanmar's Rohingya have been disenfranchized, effectively banned from public space and confined to Rakhine state, where they suffer mass incarceration and face arrest if they seek to escape.[27] The few Rohingya in Yangon and elsewhere can live there only by avoiding scrutiny of their identity documents or by bribing corrupt officials to turn a blind eye to their status. The Rohingya have been made invisible to the remainder of Myanmar's population and routinely labelled by the government, military and domestic media as 'Bengali' and hence foreign. The political context of the ARSA's emergence had changed markedly from when the Rohingya last had a meaningful military capacity more than fifty years ago. In that changed context, re-emerged Rohingya militancy was sure to be aggressively resisted and this had no doubt strongly encouraged mainstream Rohingya leaders to avoid it.

Despite the Rohingya's long-term mistreatment, isolation and history of forced migration, Dr Schug also raised concerns for the well-being of Myanmar's other minorities. Like Maung Kyaw Nu, she believed they faced similar mistreatment to the Rohingya once the authorities considered they had adequately diminished Myanmar's Rohingya population. Dr Schug pointed out that,

> If the government is successful at pushing us completely out of Burma, then things will start with Shans and Kachins. Kachins are Christians and they have English script and they will be targeted. Because we are the cheap person, they want to get rid of us and then slowly they start with the other ethnicities until everyone says they are Burmans. All borders are man-made borders. So, it evolves from time to time and changes from time to time. They are very exclusive in their policies – Burma is the land of Burmans, Myanmar is the land of Buddhists.

Dr Schug's criticism of Myanmar's Burmanization policies highlighted the shared experience of discrimination by Rohingya and other minorities at the hands of the Bamar-dominated government and Tatmadaw. This, and the risk other minorities will be targeted with more serious discrimination in the future, may provide opportunities for Rohingya leaders to make common cause with the country's other ethnic minority groups. Dr Schug echoed the perspectives of Abu Tahay, Habiburahman (see below), Kyaw Hla Aung and Myo Win that Myanmar's authorities, particularly the military, used religion and religious difference as a means of 'othering' the Rohingya. Dr Schug believed the Rohingya's isolation from Myanmar's Buddhist majority allowed the authorities to blame them collectively for the militancy of a small minority. She said,

> I think how the military over decades of oppressing the people and maintaining their position, their politics or ruling the country, it has used religion and

ethnicity, it has poisoned the public's mentality . . . we are not seeing years ago so strongly and now recently with the involvement of the monks, the military, pre-planned stuff, even the public suddenly started seeing [the Rohingya] as the common enemy. . . They directly calling kalar . . . This was there but not to such a degree . . . There are some terrorist groups who describe themselves as Muslims. We Rohingya suffered out of it. So, I think also because of the rise of nationalism. I'm very, very pessimistic about the future of the Rohingya . . . But I do have a hope if there is a strong support from the international community . . . for our ethnicity, for our minority . . .

Like many Rohingya, Dr Schug was proud of her Myanmar heritage. Her criticisms were not of Myanmar – instead she criticized the discriminatory policies that she believed had been detrimental to Rohingya and to Myanmar as a whole. While pessimistic about the Rohingya's future there, Dr Schug would like to return to her home and contribute her skills as a medical doctor to help Myanmar:

If my country accepts me right now, I will go back to Burma. I have the challenge to serve my community if they allow me – Europe does not need my qualities, they do not need my advice. My community needs me, not only my community, the whole of Burma. All are willing to go back to Burma if we are allowed. We are not economic migrants, our land is very fertile, we are very hard working. If we are allowed to go back to our original land, our land of our ancestors, we will make out of nothing gold there. Everyone is willing to go back because in your country you are a king or a queen. You will always remain a foreigner outside so in your land you have everything. People abroad, in exile, we all are willing to go back . . .

Clearly, Dr Schug can offer a lot to Myanmar – medical skills are desperately needed in the country – yet when we spoke the already unlikely prospect of Rohingya expatriates being allowed to return was about to become an impossibility. Seven months later, ARSA again attacked government security posts in northern Rakhine state and the Tatmadaw responded with a 'clearance operation' that precipitated the forced migration that would quickly become a dominant feature of my research and is sure to affect the Rohingya community for generations to come.

'Muslim people are like the salt between the chickpea. We will be eaten by both sides.'
Habiburahman (Habib), Australian Burmese Rohingya Organization,
Melbourne, 2016

Melbourne-based Rohingya community leader Habiburahman (also known as Habib) was far from optimistic about the Rohingya's future in Myanmar when we spoke in late 2016. By his mid-thirties, Habiburahman had a lengthy experience of rights violations in Myanmar and elsewhere, including having spent thirty-two months in Australian immigration detention before arriving in Melbourne. Journalist Melinda Trouhu described how, 'At the age of 35, Habiburahman has already experienced torture, raids, human trafficking, humiliation, exploitation as a clandestine worker, and detention. Still, his greatest woe is being stateless.' Habiburahman has written an award-winning book (with Sophie Ansel) about his experiences, *First, They Erased Our Name*, and has been a regular speaker about the Rohingya's situation at Melbourne community events and in the media.

The continued denial of Rohingya citizenship rights frustrated Habiburahman, who considered Rohingya indigenous to Myanmar. He told me,

> [The Rohingya] belong to the Arakan state, also called Rakhine state. Historically our people are from there. Our people are not migrated from anywhere. We are originally from there. [Rohingya are a] stock of different groups. Often the religion has been migrated into that region . . . various religion has been migrated into that region. Our people has been converted into Islam, Muslim and majority accepted Muslim and formed as the Rohingya and that's why today Rohingya are facial appearance and language much similar to India, and also the stock also mixed from the Bengal and some Middle East, seafarer and also native of Arakan. So, we are not migrant, it is very clear, and we have also evidence that we have been living there for centuries. So, the people are not migrated, but religion is migrated. We are from there, we come from a mix of different type of stock. We are born in there, we grow up in there and we speak the language.

With regard to the origins of the Rohingya name and identity, Habiburahman used the shipwreck narrative, while indicating that the group's name might be associated with 'In Rakhine language – old village tiger.'

Habiburahman argued that the Rohingya are not granted equal rights because they are crushed between the political and economic power of Myanmar's majority Bamar Buddhists and Rakhine state's Buddhist majority: 'Muslim people are like the salt between the chickpea. We will be eaten by both sides.' This situation created circumstances where Rohingya had been leaving Myanmar in large numbers, 'It is the nature, they will love where is less oppressed, where is more freedom. So, they will try to move. If they treat everyone equal, everyone will want to stay at home.'

He was frustrated too with the new Aung San Suu Kyi administration and had been particularly disappointed with the NLD's failure to stand even a single Muslim candidate at the 2015 election. He said,

So, what Suu Kyi said – 'rule of law' – equal rule of law that should be available to everyone and that should be restored. Now we have no representative for Rohingya, we have no even representative for Muslim, even like in central Burma or anywhere, even Muslim people religion is the second biggest in Burma, after Buddhism, so Suu Kyi has kicked out or cleared, all the Muslim members of her party. We need the government and the constitution. First, they have to change the constitution. Rohingya needs to be full rights as others. We want equal justice and equal rights available to everyone.

While frustrated with the group's political exclusion, Habiburahman still advocated a non-violent path forward for the Rohingya. Of ARSA's 2016 attacks and the Myanmar military's response, he said,

We as the Rohingya community we condemn whatever attack. We condemn both sides. The government is not taking steps to find solutions. They just started taking retaliations steps. Targeting the entire Rohingya community and killing unarmed civilians and killing women and children under the title of insurgency. They are targeting civilians, they just attacking civilians. The operation [2016] should be like Aung San Suu Kyi says, everything should be fair and then Suu Kyi has also said not to compete by force, but her army, the military, her very army has been attacking civilians, it is not similar to what Aung San Suu Kyi is given in the press statement. So, law and rule of law should be there even in the war, when the other side has been surrendered, they cannot kill them, they have to give them space, so now why they targeting civilians and attacking unarmed civilian populations?

Habiburahman believed Myanmar's authorities had a vested interest in prolonging the Rohingya crisis and he suggested it would continue until stopped by international involvement. Myanmar's authorities, he argued, 'keep that matter alive forever. I don't trust they will find solutions, or they will cease the crisis until the international community interfere in this region.' Habiburahman's analysis suggested much of the problem could be traced to deliberate government strategies designed to drive a wedge between the Rohingya and the Rakhine. Like Abu Tahay and Nurul Islam, Habiburahman focused mostly on conflict between Rakhine and Rohingya. When we spoke, he ignored the possibility that Bamar attitudes and nationwide political discourse might play an influential role in the Rohingya's circumstances. Habiburahman expressed little optimism about the possibility for future cooperation between ethnic Rakhine and Rohingya, suggesting the Rakhine's poverty made them easy to manipulate by Myanmar's authorities, who used the Rakhine to oppress the Rohingya. Referencing the same Second World War atrocities as Muhammad Noor, Habiburahman expressed how this made him uncomfortable with any situation where the Rohingya might find themselves politically dominated by their numerically larger Buddhist neighbours. Acknowledging the central authorities' anti-Rohingya attitudes and actions, he nonetheless suggested (in 2016) it might be better for Rohingya communities to be administered similarly to the MFA rather than by a Rakhine-dominated state government.

During the 1950s, Myanmar's central authorities were widely regarded by Arakan's Muslims as being more sympathetic to their political aspirations than the ethnic Rakhine, who were expected to use their numerical superiority to their group's advantage in any future Arakan state. This perspective led Rohingya politicians in the pre-1962 democratic period to call for the creation of the MFA, and for some to oppose the creation of an Arakan state – contrary to ethnic Rakhine aspirations. Habiburahman explained, 'Rohingya have already had experience how they have been treated under the Rakhine so they feel more safer living under central rulers than Rakhine [a reference to Second World War violence] ... the Rakhine has history of always waging war against us.'

Similar perspectives had motivated Rohingya in the 1950s to advocate for the creation of the MFA, although this is not a position that is often argued by Rohingya leaders today. Of those I interviewed, only Habiburahman and the London-based Nurul Islam directly advocated for separate Rohingya territory, and then only because other options had failed the group. In the absence of alternative strategies Habiburahman fell back upon past policies that he considered to have worked in the Rohingya's interest. Central government administration was suggested as the alternative to a likely worse, Rakhine-dominated administration – this indicated that Habiburahman's main concern was to prevent ethnic Rakhine political domination of Rohingya communities.

Central to disputes between the national authorities and Myanmar's ethnic minorities have been disagreements about minority rights to territorial control. Kachin and Shan groups already effectively control territory. Surprisingly, exclusive territorial control has not been central to mainstream Rohingya political thinking, which has – in recent decades – focused on the group's human rights claims. In not making a claim for exclusive territorial control, the Rohingya have been out of step with the strategies of other ethnic minorities in Myanmar. Habiburahman's suggestion, while an unusual position for a Rohingya leader, would more closely align the Rohingya's political strategy with that of other Myanmar ethnic minorities. Habiburahman believed the Rohingya would be better off by making a territorial claim, and stated his long-term vision that,

They [the authorities] have to give us the opportunity to build our own state . . . Own territory, like autonomous state, like Mayu [Frontier Administration]. Local autonomy, it is better we have our own and live separate, part of Myanmar. International community – they have to recognize the plight of the Rohingya, grant them special region. We need to protect this community from attack. So, we need a place to put them. They have to find a safe place in that region or keep under United Nations authorization to keep safe from the attacks.

While Habiburahman's perspective about territorial control has not been central to mainstream Rohingya political thinking for decades, elements of his views may well become more widespread among the Rohingya community in the aftermath of the 2017 forced deportation crisis. The scale of this forced displacement will surely prompt a rethink within the Rohingya community about whether autonomous Rohingya territory within Myanmar might be safer for the group. The Tatmadaw's 2017 'clearance operation' may well have created a political demand among the Rohingya that was not widespread before – a desire for territorial control.

Another Melbourne-based Rohingya leader I spoke with was Shawfikul Islam. Shawfikul has become a key Rohingya community organizer, working with the National Union of Workers, which represents Rohingya agricultural workers and labourers. Originally from Maungdaw, when Shawfikul was eight years old his family managed to escape Rakhine state for Yangon. It was once possible for middle-class Rohingya families to live relatively safely in Yangon (although this involved frequent bribes to corrupt Myanmar officials). The journey from Rakhine state to Yangon was then, as now, a difficult one for Rohingya because of tightly enforced travel restrictions. The young Shawfikul travelled disguised as a Buddhist by wearing thanaka paste make-up (made from ground bark and worn by women and children for its cosmetic and sun protection properties) and pretending to be the child of a Buddhist family friend.[28] In Yangon, Shawfikul managed to continue his education, completed high school and attended university, yet his reluctance to accept the racial slurs and discrimination commonly meted out to Myanmar's Muslims led him to seek asylum outside of Myanmar.

Shawfikul told me he was offended that Myanmar's authorities treated the Rohingya as 'intruders' on their own ancestral lands. He identified big differences between official treatment of the Rohingya and Buddhist communities, and highlighted how people were enticed to convert to Buddhism with the promise of basic rights like the freedom to travel from one village to another. He said, 'If you say [you are] Buddhist then everything is there for you – travelling – now they are targeting non-Buddhism communities, when you say, "Buddhism from today" then everything has been solved.' In 2016, with Aung San Suu Kyi's civilian administration in power for a little more than six months, Shawfikul maintained a more optimistic outlook than Habiburahman about the prospects of the new NLD administration delivering improved outcomes for the Rohingya:

> Compared to the past ruler, Aung San Suu Kyi is the best person for the country ... she is a Nobel Laureate, so we think she will do something, even she will not let attacking of Rohingya, even right on citizenship can be given later, but still she would be the best person. In Burma the whole politician, the whole figure, there we don't find anyone trusted apart from her. So, she is still the right person ... she is still the best person. All the Rohingya leaders expect of Aung San Suu Kyi trust. At least some of the country is in peace, their hope has been materialized, so maybe slowly group after group so maybe ten years for the Rohingya. But we have to change the constitution, military drafted constitution. We have to remove the military from power, that military has been taking three key positions, so we have to remove them so maybe slowly there can be a shift. Aung San Suu Kyi is quite good at listening, international community or UN or other government, she is listening good compared to the last government that is denying and denying, at last she is paying more attention.

Much of Shawfikul's faith in Aung San Suu Kyi was because he perceived she might be influenced by the international community to support the Rohingya's citizenship and rights claims. This again highlighted the common Rohingya strategy of hoping international pressure would force domestic political change. By late 2016 the utility of this strategy was increasingly questionable and some Rohingya in northern Rakhine state had already concluded that a strategy of political violence would serve the group better.

> **'Rohingya people want to be integrated, reintegrated as they were in 1940s, 50s and 60s, integrated into the mainstream of society as part of Myanmar population.'**
>
> Dr Wakar Uddin, Director General of the Arakan Rohingya Union,
> Pennsylvania, 2017

The immediate consequences of the Tatmadaw's 2016 'clearance operation' were dominating international media reporting about Myanmar when I spoke with the US-based Dr Wakar Uddin, the Director General of the Arakan Rohingya Union. News reports focused on the scale of the forced displacement and the manner with which the Tatmadaw had seemingly targeted civilians as a 'collective punishment' for ARSA's attacks. Despite this mistreatment by Myanmar's military, Dr Uddin told me that the Rohingya ought not desire a separate state within Myanmar and nor should they harbour a desire for Rohingya-majority communities in northern Rakhine to become part of another nation-state like Bangladesh. Dr Uddin, while reiterating his view that the Rohingya want to be part of Myanmar, did ponder whether this had been the best approach for the group:

> ...that's what Rohingya people want – to be part of Myanmar like other ethnic minorities. And to underscore this they have no interest in separate state, or autonomous region. Because there was apparently after independence, during the partitioning of Myanmar, Burma in 1948, Rohingya people choose to go along with Myanmar government rather than going with India at that time. Rohingya leadership choose at that time to go along with Myanmar. Looking back, we don't know if that was a mistake or not...We still hope that it wasn't a mistake that the Rohingya people choose to go along with Myanmar rather than go somewhere else.

While Dr Uddin likely overstated the influence of Muslim leaders on the negotiations that led to Burma's independence, his point was that the forebears of the Rohingya did not agitate in a significant way for inclusion in the newly created state of Pakistan and were instead content to be part of independent Burma. That reflected his own position, and when asked whether the Rohingya desired to exclusively control territory, he said, 'We are not interested. We want to be part [of Myanmar], we want to be integrated.' While never a majority opinion, Muslims had agitated for territorial autonomy following the Second World War, and amid the chaos of post-war Arakan Muslim *Mujahid* militants for a time did control territory.

Government concerns that insurgency could result in territorial loss to the then recently independent Pakistan likely contributed to the decision to establish the MFA. In recent decades Rohingya calls for autonomous territory have been rare, and Dr Uddin was correct to suggest the mainstream Rohingya leadership had not agitated for territorial control. Like other Rohingya leaders I spoke with, Dr Uddin suggested the Rohingya wanted to be part of mainstream Myanmar society rather than separate from it, and he was concerned that ongoing violence and rights violations against them made this more difficult while simultaneously damaging Myanmar's international reputation.

Dr Uddin expressed disappointment (like Habiburahman, Maung Kyaw Nu and Tun Khin) with Aung San Suu Kyi and her government, noting:

Because of turbulence, the violence, discrimination, genocide taking place in Rakhine state, this is becoming a stumbling block for the democratic transition in Burma. It is becoming an issue, international criticism. Now support for the country is dwindling. Aung San Suu Kyi has been criticized by Nobel Laureate fellows … there is no true democracy, they say 'democracy', but military is holding the power, tremendous amount of power, and holding the ministry. So, Aung San Suu Kyi has little say.

Dr Uddin told me the Rohingya were resident in Arakan before the 1784 Burmese conquest and so ought to be considered indigenous:

The fact that they are the indigenous population of that region of Myanmar, Arakan. They are an indigenous population of Rakhine state. They have historically lived there for many centuries, not even one century, two centuries, way back. They are natives of that region. Rohingya, indigenous population was there in that region before the country of Myanmar came into existence. Because that region Arakan/Rakhine was a kingdom at that time. Burmese came, conquered Rakhine. So, Rohingya people were predating the history of Myanmar in Rakhine state. They have an indigenous population with all cultural attributes, their language, their cultures, their religious beliefs, all other cultural traditions the Rohingya holds. But because they are part of Asia, one would expect maybe some similarities, religious similarities, cultural similarities, linguistic similarities with different countries on that Asian region, start from the Middle East, Persia, Pakistan, India, to Bangladesh and some Burmese became part of Rohingya culture. Predominantly Rohingya are culturally, linguistically, religiously, they are connected to the Middle East and South Asia … And they have been in Myanmar prior to independence during British Colonial period, and … They have been citizens of the country every time citizenship is traditionalized. Rohingya have been counted as nationals.

Agreeing with the explanation provided by Francis Buchanan that the Rohingya name derived from the name of the land, Dr Uddin set out how,

It's like English, England-ish … Rohingya, the word Rohingya comes from Rohang, the region … The northern Arakan state, nearly half of that is densely populated by Rohingya …So that region, northern Rakhine state, its original name is Rohang … People from that region is known as Rohingya, Roanga – Rohingya, R.O.H.A.N.G. The name … Gya – is like Malaysia – Malaysian, England-English, the suffix … People from Rohang is Rohingya … So that is a big problem for some of the people from Myanmar/Burma because they do not want that identity to be existed, because that identity goes to a region, so they want to eliminate the name Rohang, Rohingya, [by] falsely claiming this Rohang, the region Rohingya, would be aiming at separate state. It is a simple fact, inhabitants, indigenous population of the region, Rohang is Rohingya.

This was certainly a claim to indigeneity that would be aggressively rejected by nationalists. Dr Uddin's explanation for the origins of the Rohingya name was a variation of that provided by other Rohingya I spoke with, yet certainly traced similar roots. He claimed the group were long-term residents of Arakan/Rakhine, indigenous, and so should, according to all three of the country's post-independence constitutions and the 1982 citizenship law, be entitled to collective citizenship rights.

Like Kyaw Hla Aung and Nurul Islam, Dr Uddin argued that the Rohingya had been officially acknowledged as citizens in the years following Burma's independence, and since then their citizenship rights had been removed and government efforts made to delegitimize the Rohingya's rights claims (including their claim to be identified by their actual name). Dr Uddin rejected any citizenship verification process that involved relinquishing their right to be identified as Rohingya. He regarded such processes as part of a deliberate strategy to mislabel the Rohingya as interlopers in Rakhine state so that the authorities could limit their rights. Dr Uddin explained that according to the,

1947 Constitution, Rohingya were citizens of Myanmar and before that during colonial period, and then Rohingya people successfully served various governments as parliamentarians, all forms of leadership, civil servant, military officers. Until 1963 even Rohingya people served in the parliament as parliamentarians during the military dictatorship. There were five Rohingya in USDP [2011 to 2016] government, three of them were in the central government, national parliament, and two of them state legislature. So, all along Rohingya were citizens like any other ethnic group. Now, the recent election the military has disqualified, I should say, the Rohingya from voting, banned Rohingya from voting. Those Rohingya who has voted for military party, USDP, in 2015 elections, they were deprived of their rights. Not only right to vote but also right to contest the election. They were not allowed to contest the election. Complete shutdown, 180-degree turnaround from citizenship to no voting rights. Particularly in recent years, calling the Rohingya illegal immigrants. The Rohingya – the government of Myanmar has given NRC card. A long time they held NRC card ... They are trying to define from Rohingya to 'Bengali'. So why they want to use 'Bengali'? Because to delegitimize the identity of Rohingya. To effectively make them illegal immigrants, interlopers from neighbouring countries. Rohingya people categorically deny those terminology used by Myanmar government. And now Myanmar government has set up a process called verification process, verifying what? Who are you nationalizing? People who have been holding the citizenship of the country from the very beginning, prior to independence. Now are redefining them. You are trying to nationalize them who are already citizens of the country. So Rohingya people reject that process, they are not going to cooperate, they are not going to call themselves 'Bengali'. They are not going to be nationalized because they are already the citizen ... A lot of them could end up in camps permanently. In camps, without any facilities, a lifetime in camps.

Dr Uddin's frustration reflected attitudes I heard frequently from Rohingya, but his opinions about the nature of colonial-era migration, and his description of claims to the Rohingya identity from people in eastern Bangladesh, did not.

Colonial-era migration has long been controversial in Myanmar, and Rohingya leaders have often been reluctant to address it. As I outlined in Chapter Two, there was significant British-era migration from the subcontinent. While those arrivals were generally seasonal labourers who returned home annually, others might have permanently settled in Burma. Residents of colonial Rangoon, for instance, would have experienced high levels of migration so that by the early 1930s Rangoon had an Indian majority. Dr Uddin was prepared to address the claim that ancestors of the contemporary Rohingya first settled in the country in the colonial era. He accepted there was immigration from the Indian subcontinent throughout the colonial period, but he argued this was mostly migration to Burma proper and not to Arakan. His explanation was that there was little economic incentive for migrants coming to Arakan to permanently settle there, in contrast with urban centres like Mandalay or Rangoon (Yangon) where migration would likely have been permanent:

There are a lot of immigrants during the British colonial period came from the Indian subcontinent, to Burma, economic migrants. They are still there, Indian, Pakistani, and Bengalis in proper Burma, they are business people and a lot of them came during the British trade. A lot of them stayed there. Some of the Burmese extremists try to link the Rohingya with them, saying they also came from East Pakistan, now Bangladesh, a part of India, during British era ... Rohingya do not come from East Pakistan or India. Because there is no economic incentive, Rakhine state was not developed, there is no business there. Only Indian people come to Burma for trade, business ... You see today Rakhine is remote, underdeveloped ... You can imagine during the British era how underdeveloped it would be ... people did not emigrate [to Arakan] from anywhere during the British colonial period, like Indians. Indians, Pakistanis and Bangladeshis emigrated to Burma for business reasons ... There are two very different things ... Burmese extremists try to lump us and Indians and Pakistanis and Bangladeshis who came to Burma during the British time for economic reasons ... There is nothing attractive. Have you seen anything in Rakhine state that would attract anything from other countries? People are leaving ... Economy is so depressed and so underdeveloped, people left ... In forties and fifties, during British colonial time Rohingya people left ... This is a very critical matter that Myanmar people are making that up that's not true ... Emigration from India to Burma, during British time for economic reasons, has nothing to do with Rohingya ... Rohingya were already in Rakhine state for many, many, many, many centuries there even before Indians emigrated to Myanmar ... There are two things to be quite separated because historically that are facts ... British did not try to develop Arakan, only what they did was made some small-scale roads for military transportation ... The British did not really develop Rakhine state unless it has a specific location, it has a military interest, strategic and then they build some roads, tunnels ... Government has shut down their future, people cannot advance ... That's a strategic tool to shut down the population's future ... Nothing can be worse for the future of a population ...

Dr Uddin took care to avoid portraying the Rohingya's origins as north of the Naf River. This was an understandable response to the claim the Rohingya regularly face – that their ancestors are relatively recent arrivals to Myanmar from Bangladesh and so should not be entitled to citizenship rights. In that context, any admission of ancestry from north or west of the Naf River (no matter how long ago) risked undermining the group's collective claim to citizenship and rights in Myanmar. Dr Uddin's assertions about the nature of colonial-era migration may have been motivated by a desire to fit the Rohingya's history within Myanmar's citizenship framework, yet he was not incorrect to identify that most colonial migration was to urban centres in Burma proper rather than to Arakan. Colonial-era migration from the Indian subcontinent into Burma was legal migration, meaning any Rohingya who do trace their ancestral origins to colonial movement are resident in Myanmar legally and have a right to citizenship. While this should not undermine the Rohingya's legal claims, Myanmar's authorities have commonly conflated illegally arrived post-Second World War migrants from Pakistan/ Bangladesh with legal colonial-era migrants from those same areas, and they have used this to excuse limiting the Rohingya's access to citizenship and other rights.

Disputes about history have been central to the Rohingya's appalling human rights situation. Myanmar's authorities have frequently argued that the Rohingya are foreigners and have used this to justify denying the group access to their human rights. In these circumstances it cannot be surprising that Rohingya advocates like Dr Uddin aimed to present the group in the best possible light by minimising references to historical facts that might weaken their claim to citizenship and rights. Dr Uddin focused, as did other Rohingya leaders, on assertions about the group's history that strengthen Rohingya claims to Myanmar citizenship and rights within the country's legal citizenship framework.

'We didn't have any different name, only we have the name Rohingya.'
Saifullah Muhammad (Saiful Rohin), Rohingya Youth Activist, Kitchener,
Canada, 2017

Increasingly, younger diaspora activists have been playing crucial roles as international advocates for their people, urging their new countries' governments to pressure Myanmar's authorities to end anti-Rohingya discrimination and violence. Muhammad Saifullah (Saiful Rohin) is a Rohingya community leader, aged in his early thirties, living in Canada. He modestly described himself as a 'Rohingya youth activist'. He is a good one and is part of a team that has helped capitalise on Canada's renowned sense of compassion to place the plight of the Rohingya high on the Canadian domestic political agenda. The 'Rohingya Youth Voice Canada' group, of which Saifullah is a key member, has more than 33,000 Facebook followers. When Canada's government announced it would match private donations to those local charities working to assist Rohingya victims of the 2017 military crackdown, C$12.5 million was quickly raised through private donations, bringing Canada's contribution to C$50 million by December 2017.[29]

Canadian Rohingya activists have worked to promote their people's cause and have engaged with figures across the political spectrum with a high degree of success. Canada's Liberal Party Prime Minister Justin Trudeau was among the first international leaders to call out Aung San Suu Kyi for her silence and inaction in the face of the Rohingya's obvious mistreatment by both the Tatmadaw and the civilian authorities. Trudeau spoke with Aung San Suu Kyi while both attended the 2017 APEC (Asia-Pacific Economic Cooperation) summit, a conversation recounted using diplomatic language as 'very direct'.[30] In 2018, Trudeau's government led international calls for a UN referral of the crisis to the International Criminal Court, citing the Myanmar government's failure to investigate mass atrocities.[31] The UNSC did not refer accusations of atrocity crimes committed by Myanmar's authorities to the ICC, although in 2018 the ICC's Chief Prosecutor Fatou Bensouda did begin investigating these crimes. Trudeau appointed high-profile former Ontario province premier and ex-national Liberal Party leader Bob Rae as Canada's special envoy to Myanmar, with a remit to 'reinforce the urgent need to resolve the humanitarian and security crisis in Myanmar and to address the situation affecting vulnerable populations' and to advise Canada's prime minister 'on how Canada can best support efforts to respond to the needs of those affected and displaced by the recent violence'.[32] Rae's involvement and the activism of Rohingya like Saifullah have kept the Rohingya's plight on Canada's political agenda. Support for the Rohingya spans the ideological spectrum, with many having addressed Canada's parliament about the Rohingya's situation, including former New Democratic Party leader Tom Mulcair and the Conservative Garnett Genius, who has been a prominent and consistent voice in support of Rohingya human rights claims.[33] This no doubt contributed to the Canadian government's 2019 decision to support The Gambia's case against Myanmar before the ICJ. All are signatories to the *Convention on the Prevention and Punishment of the Crime of Genocide*, which The Gambia alleged Myanmar breached by mistreating the Rohingya and demanded Myanmar make good on its responsibilities under the Convention by stopping all genocidal crimes, bringing perpetrators to justice, ensuring a safe return for displaced Rohingya and not repeating the original crimes.[34]

Canada's roughly 400 Rohingya live mostly near to the city of Kitchener, Ontario, about an hour's drive from Toronto, and like Saifullah, they are overwhelmingly resettled refugees. Saifullah was born in Rathedaung and came to Canada in 2016. After being exiled from his home and the Rohingyas' decades of rights violations in Rakhine state, he argued the case for peaceful coexistence between Rohingya and Rakhine communities. Like many Rohingya I spoke with, Saifullah foregrounded the group's relationship with the Rakhine while ignoring the influence of Myanmar political discourse outside of Rakhine state. He told me, 'Rohingya never want separate country or separate state or anything. Rohingya want citizenship back, like a sister community with the Rakhine people … to share everything with the Rakhine people.' Saifullah was all too aware that Myanmar's authorities have been successful at driving a wedge between the Rohingya and their 'sister community'. He feared Myanmar's authorities will turn their attention to persecuting the Rakhine once the Rohingya have been driven away from Myanmar and that creating a moral panic about the Rohingya's perceived political aspirations (associated with the group's use of the Rohingya name and potential links with militant Islam) was a key part of that strategy. He outlined how, 'For me, the name Rohingya is not being used because two, three reasons – they are trying to drive out the Rohingya, using the Rakhine as middle men because they are saying, as Rohingya are going out, "everything is yours"... The military government they are using them as a friend but ... once Rohingya is all destroyed they will destroy their [Rakhine] community as well.'

Saifullah was convinced the Rohingya were victims of an official strategy designed to destroy the group. While he did not use the word genocide when we spoke, his belief that the Rohingya were victims of genocidal actions by Myanmar's authorities was clear. There was little doubt Saifullah believed the Rohingya had a long history in Myanmar, and that the group had been known as Rohingya for generations and that this was previously acknowledged by the national authorities. He said, 'Even my grandparents have some papers written to Rohingya as an ethnicity.' Saifullah's story that his grandparents possessed Burmese government documents that recorded the name Rohingya is far from unusual – I heard this often. In 2017, refugees in the Bangladesh camps showed me old Burmese government identity documents that used the Rohingya name. This was clear evidence previous governments did acknowledge the legitimacy of their identity and the legality of their residency.

Saifullah's frustration – that the Rohingya are no longer acknowledged as a distinct ethnic group – was mirrored by his displeasure over the authorities similarly now regarding the Rohingya name as illegitimate. Saifullah recalled his mother singing him a nursery rhyme as a child that used the Rohingya name and noted, 'We didn't have any different name, only we have the name Rohingya.' Asked why, if this was the case, the Rohingya name was not more widely known to outsiders, Saifullah suggested the reason was because there was no need to use it since the two main communities in Rakhine were 'very close', so there was no need to identify as anything other than from Burma and from Rakhine. He said, 'We were called Rohingya and there is a problem. But more people don't use that name because we didn't need to use that name. Because the Rakhine people, they never use their name as Rakhine ... So, and then Rohingya people they didn't use their name, because they didn't use two. They didn't need to use that name because they didn't use two.' Saifullah's belief, shared by the overwhelming majority of Rohingya I spoke with, was that the group's heritage meant they should be recognized as a *taingyintha* and entitled to collective citizenship rights.

In Canada, Saifullah has been a shrewd political activist working to harness public support for the Rohingya's cause, yet he did not factor into his political strategy the increasingly influential role of domestic discourse in Myanmar – which stands mostly in opposition to the Rohingya's aspirations. Instead, he prioritized international pressure on Myanmar's authorities to help the group achieve the citizenship and rights they claimed. Were this an isolated example it would be easy to dismiss criticisms of this approach by suggesting that diaspora activists like Saifullah believed they were unable to influence public opinion in Myanmar yet could influence their adopted national governments. Strategies based on using international pressure to seek domestic policy change in Myanmar are frequently employed by Rohingya activists both outside and inside Myanmar, so Saifullah's approach cannot be regarded as simply a consequence of his location. Instead it ought to be understood as reflecting a much more common Rohingya strategy, which I argue underestimates the importance and potential of Myanmar's domestic politics.

'Who will take care of us?'

Sayad Ullah, Melaka, Malaysia, 2017

Another young activist, Sayad Ullah, like Kyaw Hla Aung and Wakar Uddin, believed the Rohingya name was derived from the name of the land, Arakan. He told me, 'Rohingya comes from Arakan, Arakan country' and portrayed the group as clearly indigenous to the Rakhine state area. Sayad Ullah was an active Rohingya community member in his twenties. He spoke with me at the October 2017 'International Flotilla 2 Arakan' meeting in his adopted home of Melaka, a Malaysian city of around half a million people south of Kuala Lumpur. Like Rohingya Vision's Muhammad Noor, he traced the beginnings of the Rohingya's decades of mistreatment to Second World War massacres of Muslims in Arakan. He told me how, 'My grandfather explained, in colonial rule in 1942, more than one million people have been dead' and he linked the events of 1942 with those of 1978, when more than 200,000 Rohingya fled the Tatmadaw's *Nagamin* operation. Sayad Ullah depicted the authorities' mistreatment of the Rohingya as involving frequent violence, denying the group access to education and inaccurately labelling them as 'Bengalis'. He said,

> 1942, 1977/78 ... Unforgettable tortures. They attack on Rohingya very brutally. On this attack [1977/78] more than 200,000 people have been displaced to neighbouring Bangladesh ... In 1982, Bangladesh and Myanmar together with an agreement to return to their own country to their own homeland ... We have in 1962 the citizenship of Myanmar government, of Myanmar country, of Myanmar citizenship law ... I feel very sad for my land. The Myanmar government is planning from 1962 to date. Their planning is very devilish. They are depriving us from the education. My cousin was in class nine but he have no chance to complete matriculation [secondary school matriculation in Myanmar is at grade ten]. Our nation have no education. It is true that education is back bone of a nation but our nation have no education. I have achieved my education

secretly – I told I was Bengali to achieve my education, but I am not Bengali. Rohingya was in British colonial rule. There was a country named Arakan between Bangladesh and Myanmar. We are Arakan, which is named now Rakhine state, this is Arakan.

Sayad Ullah believed Rohingya were acknowledged as citizens of Burma until at least 1962 when the Ne Win administration singled them out for persecution because of their religion. He told me, '1960 the Rohingya were citizens ... After 1962, in 1962 Myanmar government have been start attacking Rohingya people because Rohingya are Muslim minority in Myanmar.'

A further concern of Sayad Ullah was that a consequence of the Rohingya's mistreatment by the authorities in Myanmar was their forced migration to countries like Malaysia, where their lives continued to be precarious. Rohingya in Malaysia are generally undocumented, and Sayad Ullah told me of around 1,000 Rohingya living in Melaka who were not formally registered with the UN and of numerous others in Malaysia in a similar position. Malaysia is not a signatory state to the *Convention Relating to the Status of Refugees* or the 1967 *Protocol Relating to the Status of Refugees*. Consequently, the UN's role with refugees in Malaysia is limited, and irregular migrants generally do not receive documentation from the UN.[35] The UNHCR estimates there are more than 100,000 Rohingya living in Malaysia, of whom around half are undocumented.[36] I heard similar concerns from other Rohingya figures in Malaysia, who worried that refugees, including young children, were denied access to education and healthcare, with the Malaysian government expecting them to pay for private medical treatment and schooling – which were well beyond the means of undocumented workers who usually earn less than the local minimum wage. Sayad Ullah highlighted the precarity of life for Rohingya migrants to Malaysia by pointing to the tragedy of a recent landslide in Penang that killed eleven people, mostly undocumented foreign construction workers – including Rohingya.[37] The poor safety conditions of undocumented Rohingya workers were widely believed to have contributed to the high death toll. He asked, 'Who will take care of us?'

Sayad Ullah's views were unsurprising for a Rohingya migrant to Malaysia. He believed the Rohingya were entitled to citizenship rights in Myanmar as a *taingyintha* and that there was a long history of official mistreatment of the group within Myanmar. His concerns about the well-being of Rohingya migrants in Malaysia pointed to the emergence of a new Rohingya claim for their rights to be acknowledged and respected in their adopted countries. By late 2017, there were more Rohingya living outside of Myanmar than in it, and while Rohingya diaspora were not collectively subject to the same violence as the Tatmadaw would subject Myanmar's Rohingya communities, their circumstances were frequently far from ideal. A claim for Rohingya diaspora rights represents an acknowledgement of the permanent nature of much Rohingya migration – those who leave Myanmar and the Rohingya refugee camps in Bangladesh very rarely return. This was a demonstration too of a growing confidence among the Rohingya diaspora, who considered that the human rights they sought in Myanmar ought to be available to them in other countries as well. In the case of Malaysia, where there was public sympathy and mainstream political support for the Rohingya, the 2017 crisis may well have contributed to a renewed push for improved rights for Rohingya migrants there.

'We want democracy in Myanmar. We want our ethnic name. And democracy in our country.'

Ziaur Rahman, Kuala Lumpur, November 2017

In Malaysia, Ziaur Rahman became prominent as a young Rohingya leader because of his activism on behalf of the migrant community. We communicated online throughout my research and met in Kuala Lumpur in November 2017. Like Sayad Ullah, Ziaur Rahman highlighted the difficulties faced by Rohingya in Malaysia, where their undocumented status limited access to government services and prevented long-term refugees opening bank accounts, creating ongoing challenges accessing housing and employment. He pointed out how preventing children of Rohingya migrants (including those born in Malaysia) from accessing education and health services created inter-generational precarity and poverty. Ziaur Rahman wanted to see this situation change and lobbied Malaysia's authorities, including government ministers, to improve the conditions of Malaysia's undocumented Rohingya migrants.

While young Malaysia-based Rohingya activists like Sayad Ullah and Ziaur Rahman were concerned about the welfare of the Rohingya migrant community, this did not mean they were less concerned about the mistreatment of Rohingya in Myanmar. Ziaur Rahman's family had been victims of a 1990s Tatmadaw deportation from Rakhine state; he spent his first twenty-one years in Bangladesh refugee camps and was all too familiar with the consequences of Myanmar's mistreatment of the Rohingya community. He considered Myanmar's treatment of the Rohingya to unquestionably be a genocide and he set out both the group's long history in Myanmar and his frustration with their lack of Myanmar citizenship by saying,

The history of the Rohingya is not new for me and for my mother. Is happening more than many decades already passed by. Myanmar government is killing and harassing and raping and destroying them … We are stay in Arakan state, my mother, and my grandfather they have National Identity Card. Why now they are confiscating National Identity Card? Why they are giving the 'White Card' to Rohingya? Why? Because you are replacing the Rohingya in Arakan state. You are doing the genocide. You are killing people. Even you are not allowing the international media.

Ziaur Rahman wanted the Rohingya to return to a democratic Myanmar where their rights, including their right to be known as Rohingya, would be acknowledged. He expressed how, 'We want democracy in Myanmar. We want our ethnic name, and democracy in our country. This is our country. Arakan state. This is our land. We have our language … people want to go back with the rights of human.'

> **'When Rohingya go back [they] must have security, the right of freedom of religion. We need a UN peacekeeping.'**
> Zafar Ahmad bin Abdul Ghani (Zafar), President, Myanmar Ethnic
> Rohingya Human Rights Organization Malaysia, Melaka, 2017

While the younger Rohingya activists I spoke with in Malaysia (Sayad Ullah and Ziaur Rahman) had been concerned about both the circumstances of Rohingya in Myanmar and those who are forced to seek refuge in other countries, the more established Zafar Ahmad bin Abdul Ghani, commonly known as Zafar, focused squarely on the Rohingya's status in Rakhine state. He was President of the Myanmar Ethnic Rohingya Human Rights Organization Malaysia and like others among the Rohingya community in Myanmar and abroad, central to Zafar's solutions for the Rohingya was the involvement of international actors. He recounted to me that the solution was for the 'Burmese government to accept [the] citizenship of Rohingya'. He made clear his belief that the Rohingya are indigenous to Arakan state:

Rohingya is the indigenous people in Arakan state. Arakan is a Muslim name … General Than Shwe, and General Ne Win they changed Arakan name. The Arakan state the land is Muslim land, also our money, Muslim writing, Arabic writing on money. Also have king of Muslim. First, they are called Rohang. Rohang become Rohingya … Before part of independence we had received our citizenship, our language, our newspaper, our language, radio station. 1962 we had recognized, we are accepted. Rohingya is the one race is indigenous. We ask our rights.

While Zafar desired international involvement, he went further than others by demanding the involvement of UN peacekeepers. Referring to the potential repatriation of those who fled Rakhine state in 2017, Zafar demanded that,

> When Rohingya go back [they] must have security, the right of freedom of religion. We need a UN peacekeeping. When the Rohingya go back must have together UN peacekeeping have the monitor see what happening. Who killing who? Why they killing? They can monitor. We are demanded UN peacekeeping. We also go to UN office. Every country we go we demanded. Please open your heart. We need your protection. We are human.

Zafar's demand for UN peacekeepers went beyond the type of international involvement advocated by most Rohingya I spoke with, whose focus was on using international actors like national governments and the UN to pressure Myanmar's authorities to deliver improved conditions for the Rohingya. Zafar's suggestion was far from an outlandish demand in a context where the UN Security Council in 2017 formally discussed the situation in Myanmar for the first time since 1999.[38] The Security Council called on Myanmar to end excessive military force and intercommunal violence in Rakhine state issuing a statement that expressed,

> ... grave concern over reports of human rights violations and abuses in Rakhine State, including by the Myanmar security forces, in particular against persons belonging to the Rohingya community, including those involving the systematic use of force and intimidation, killing of men, women, and children, sexual violence, and including the destruction and burning of homes and property ... The Security Council calls upon the Government of Myanmar to ensure no further excessive use of military force in Rakhine State, to restore civilian administration and apply the rule of law, and to take immediate steps in accordance with their obligations and commitments to respect human rights, including the human rights of women, children, and persons belonging to vulnerable groups, without discrimination and regardless of ethnicity, religion, or citizenship status.[39]

Any potential for foreign military to enter Myanmar, even endorsed UN peacekeepers as part of a temporary 'Responsibility to Protect' obligation, would be aggressively resisted by Myanmar's authorities and likely by Myanmar's majority too. Perceived infringements of Myanmar's sovereignty would be aggressively resisted by the Tatmadaw and would provide nationalists with a further chance to claim Rohingya disloyalty to the nation, further undermining the Rohingya's domestic standing. Zafar's calls for UN peacekeepers were a logical consequence of a Rohingya strategy that privileged international pressure above building domestic political support. Within this framework, the appalling violence and forced displacement of 2017 demanded such calls from Rohingya activists. Yet if there were countries prepared to push for direct UN intervention, while Myanmar retained the support of permanent UN Security Council members China and Russia such proposals would always be blocked.

This highlighted a major flaw with an approach based on seeking international support for the Rohingya's cause – it risked inflaming domestic anti-Rohingya feeling, while demands for international military action were unlikely to ever be successful. The hollowness of hoping for international military protection was vividly demonstrated throughout the 2017 crisis, when the largest forced migration in the region since the Second World War resulted in an UNSC briefing and discussion that was not followed by a binding resolution or any indication that the UNSC might ever be inclined to intervene to protect Rohingya civilians.

A genocidal military campaign

During 2017, the security crackdown on northern Rakhine's Rohingya communities, prompted by ARSA's August attacks, resulted in a massive forced migration. Within just eight monsoon season weeks, a staggering 600,000 people fled Myanmar on foot. By early 2018 this figure had risen to more than 700,000 people. New refugee camp arrivals joined hundreds of thousands already forced to live in Bangladeshi camps – victims of previous intensive Myanmar military operations like *Nagamin* and *Ye The Ha*. Yet, if there was anything positive about the sprawling Rohingya refugee camps near Cox's Bazar, it was that the residents – despite their appalling experiences and obvious deprivation – were at least safe there from the Tatmadaw.

When I visited the Rohingya's refugee camps near Bangladesh's city of Cox's Bazar in 2017 the exodus was still ongoing, and there were new camp arrivals by the hour. The scale of the forced migration was truly horrifying. In the space of a little more than ten square kilometres, almost one million Rohingya refugees were crowded. Every available space was used to provide basic accommodation of blue UN tarpaulins stretched over bamboo frames. Camp residents had to contend not only with the trauma of their deportation and the Tatmadaw crimes that preceded it, but with a relief effort that struggled to keep pace with the scale of the catastrophe, monsoonal weather conditions and even rampaging elephants whose traditional roaming paths had been disturbed by the new camps. I spoke with dozens of camp residents and their stories were heartbreaking. They were often ordinary Rohingya rather than leaders of their communities – community leaders had frequently already either been arrested, arbitrarily detained or killed by Myanmar's security forces.

The 2017 crisis occurred within a domestic political context where new political and media freedoms had allowed online nationalist and anti-Rohingya rhetoric to proliferate. Liberalizations to Myanmar's communication and media environment have been widely identified as contributing to anti-Muslim and anti-Rohingya attitudes within Myanmar. Mainstream and social media representations of the Rohingya might not have been universally negative, but Rohingya frequently described how positive media representations of Muslims have become rarer and how the Rohingya were increasingly scapegoated in mainstream and social media. The role of social media was greatly scrutinized in the aftermath of the 2017 Rohingya forced migration crisis and Facebook was singled out for special criticism by the UN's Fact-Finding Mission.[40]

The key role played by the Tatmadaw in promoting anti-Rohingya attitudes through social media has recently emerged. A staff of 700 military operatives were claimed to be involved in a social media propaganda campaign targeting the Rohingya that utilized incendiary posts, false names, sham accounts and trolls to spread anti-Rohingya material.[41] This was, and likely continues to be, a sophisticated and well-resourced content manipulation campaign by the Tatmadaw aimed at domestic social media users, to influence domestic attitudes. It also indicates that domestic anti-Rohingya and pro-Tatmadaw attitudes might not be as deeply ingrained in the Myanmar population as was earlier believed, and that elements of prevailing public opinion might have been a consequence of psychological warfare tactics by the Tatmadaw. Just how much anti-Rohingya attitudes are deeply ingrained in the community and how much is the result of propaganda and so might be shallow and changeable remains unclear. The fact the Tatmadaw felt the need to devote such staggeringly large resources to an anti-Rohingya campaign suggests senior Tatmadaw figures considered that influencing public opinion was both a priority and would require significant resources. This provides hope that attitudes in Myanmar can change in the future, to be less opposed to Rohingya aspirations.

Anti-Rohingya attitudes had been actively encouraged by state media, too. State media dominate Myanmar's broadcast sector, and most television channels and radio stations are state owned. When the 2017 crisis began, reporting from Rakhine state was already highly securitized and headlines frequently adopted

sensationalist tones when describing alleged Muslim insurgents – the example
of the state-owned *Global New Light of Myanmar* (GNLM) newspaper provides
a telling example. Published by the Myanmar Ministry of Information, the
GNLM, an English-language daily, is the country's longest-running newspaper
(it has been in print in various forms since 1914, and was nationalized by the
military-led government in the 1960s when it was published as the *Working
People's Daily*). GNLM reporting in August 2017 routinely portrayed Myanmar
as under siege by Muslim terrorists, publishing headlines including: 'Terrorists
Trying to Destroy Maungtaw', 'Let Us Eradicate Extremist Terrorists, Destructive
Elements Together!', 'Extremist Terrorism on the Rise!', 'Issuing Notification of
Acknowledging and Urging the People Not to Encourage, Support and Abet
Extremist Terrorists', and 'Warning in Relation With Extremist Terrorists.' State
media's sensationalized approach contributed to a domestic political context
that encouraged nationalist hate speech, particularly against the Rohingya,
helping to provide licence and encouragement for Myanmar's military campaigns
against the Rohingya. The consequences for Rohingya communities were
devastating.

The brutality of the 2017 'clearance operation' was neither opposed nor
criticized by Aung San Suu Kyi's civilian administration, causing understandable
consternation among international actors – particularly Western governments.
Aung San Suu Kyi's stance ought not have been surprising. Prior to the 2015
election, her NLD party had already demonstrated an unwillingness to risk
alienating nationalists – the NLD bowed to nationalist pressure and did not field
a single Muslim among its 1,151 candidates nationwide. Since taking office,
Aung San Suu Kyi's administration had similarly avoided confrontation with
nationalists by choosing not to revoke the 'race and religion' laws (which
discriminate on the basis of religion and sex), and had again, in late 2016, avoided
being on the wrong side of nationalist opinion (risking a potential confrontation
with the Tatmadaw) by endorsing the military's approach in northern Rakhine
state. The Tatmadaw's previous 'clearance operation' in 2016 ought to have been
a strong warning of what was to come. Researchers at the ISCI identified the
Tatmadaw's 2016 'clearance operation' as an attempt by the military to test the
reaction of Myanmar's public and international actors.[42] Citing genocide scholar
Gregory Stanton's work, they identified how during the 'preparation' stages of
genocide, prior to large-scale killings, 'trial massacres' can occur to test the
response from the local and international community. ISCI asserted, 'Impunity
for these preparatory forms of violence signal a green light to continue mass
killings.'[43] Finding Myanmar's public generally supportive (or at least not

opposing) of their 2016 'clearance operation', and with little meaningful response from international actors, the Tatmadaw proceeded with the larger-scale operation of 2017, confident this too would be supported by the public. Brutal Tatmadaw actions against the Rohingya took place with the support of the government and popular opinion. Had either the government or the public taken a different view about the merits of the 2017 'clearance operation' its scale and brutality would likely have been considerably diminished. The Tatmadaw knew they had the support of Myanmar's civilian government and that nationwide public opinion was also on their side – sadly, there were few domestic calls to rein them it.

Camp residents had recently experienced the violent consequences of the Rohingya's political isolation and lack of citizenship and rights. Their longer-term experience was of a cruel apartheid system in Myanmar. Kutupalong camp is the largest refugee camp in the world and is at the centre of a camp network that houses more than one million Rohingya refugees. Parts of Kutupalong are designated as 'new' or 'old' depending on whether the residents arrived because of the 2017 crisis or had been victims of earlier forced deportations from Myanmar – there were already more than 200,000 Rohingya refugee victims of the 1991–1992 deportation resident in Bangladesh camps. Camp resident's accounts, unlike those of Rohingya who were not directly affected by the 2017 forced migration, understandably focused much more on the more proximate causes of this migration than on questions of group history. Nevertheless, new camp arrivals I spoke with asserted the Rohingya's claims to be a group with a long history in Myanmar, the right to be regarded by the citizenship law as indigenous and identified as Rohingya, and frequently noted that members of their group have been previously acknowledged as citizens by Myanmar's authorities. There have been high-profile examples of victimization by Myanmar's authorities of those who have spoken out about their mistreatment by the Tatmadaw or government: this has included journalists who have reported these crimes. Consequently, the contributions of camp residents presented here are partially anonymized to minimize the risks to them were they to return to Myanmar. While their prospects of return remain slim, many nonetheless expressed a desire to return to Myanmar in the future if their rights and safety could be guaranteed.

One of the first camp residents to speak with me was an old man, a farmer from Buthidaung. We took shelter from the baking eastern Bangladesh sun beneath a UN-supplied tarpaulin. He quickly became understandably emotional when he told me about his recent experience:

I lost my two sons, and two daughters. At midnight the military come in my house and burnt the house but first they raped my two daughters and they shot my two daughters in front of me. I have no words to express how it was for me to suffer, to look at daughters being raped and killed in front of me. Also, my two sons were killed by government. I was not able to get the dead bodies of my daughters, it is a great sorrow for me . . . It was not sufferable, the persecution was very dangerous, we are falsely come here, not to live long, we want to back again, so if you Sir has anything to back us from here to our own country please say . . . If you have anything to do for them, please try to do as soon as possible.

Another elderly man, Faisal, who had recently arrived in the Kutupalong new camp, explained to me that among his family, his son and a daughter were killed by the military. Faisal recounted sorrowfully that one of his daughters was raped by soldiers who burned down the family's house. He outlined how the military arrested young people, and that ten men were arrested in his village and their families had not heard from them since. He said the military tricked residents by calling them to religious work but then told his village's residents to leave. He said, 'The military led us to prayer and some kind of religious work, and they openly told us to go to Bangladesh – otherwise you will be killed.' Camp residents routinely recalled how their home villages had not been involved with militancy, but that this had not mattered to Myanmar's security forces who they considered acted as though any young Rohingya men were likely violent militants. A middle-aged man, Abdul, characterized his village as 'friendly', 'quiet' and not involved with militants, but that this had not saved them from the violence of Myanmar's military. He told me, 'We were living there, very friendly. At midnight we heard the sound of bullets, we went outside to see what is happening. I think they behaved like this – arresting, torturing, shooting, hitting – because we are Rohingya and Muslim. We're not at fault, we are really innocent.' Abdul, like Faisal, explained how this was the experience of his village too. He said,

> . . . some military, another group of military come to the village, and arrested young people from my village, only men. The military arrest fifteen young boys from my village, between twenty and thirty years old, there are some old men among them . . . They were very innocent people, but the Myanmar government came in. I think they did this kind of behaviour with us like arresting, torturing, shooting, hitting because we are Rohingya and Muslim. There is not any fault with us, we are really innocent. Not in my family were killed but some near my home were killed.

Another man I spoke with, Mohamed, recalled the military coming to his village accompanied by armed ethnic Rakhine Buddhists. He said the military came to the village and indiscriminately fired guns, 'There were old men, children they were not considered. They were firing. All the villagers ran away to Bangladesh. As far as I know twenty people are dead, I saw with my own eyes ten people.' Rofik, a young garage mechanic from near Maungdaw, depicted how decades of discrimination within Myanmar recently culminated in mass killings and other atrocities. He said, 'The Myanmar doesn't let us to go to one village to another village, they deprive us from education. At last shoot us, and they burn some houses, and arrest us and that's why we come here.' For Rohingya, the 2017 crisis seemed to represent a cataclysmic, yet somehow logical, progression of the discrimination they had endured within Myanmar for decades. Myanmar's authorities had for decades claimed the Rohingya were 'Bengali' and restricted their ability to freely move around Myanmar – now they violently deported them to Bangladesh. While Myanmar's authorities had restricted the Rohingya's ability to access education, in 2017 the military targeted educated Rohingya to be murdered.

UN investigators documented how the Tatmadaw systematically targeted educated Rohingya and young men. A September 2017 report by the UN Office of the High Commissioner of Human Rights outlined how, 'Information received also indicates that the Myanmar security forces targeted teachers, the cultural and religious leadership, and other people of influence in the Rohingya community in an effort to diminish Rohingya history, culture and knowledge.'[44] The targeting of educated Rohingya for arrest or killing was considered by ISCI researcher Thomas MacManus to be a genocide crime, and part of the Myanmar authorities' strategy of weakening the Rohingya by destroying their culture and history. In 2018, he told media, 'The objective appears to be to destroy the Rohingya, and one way to do that is to destroy their culture and remove their history. It's part of the genocide tactic.'[45]

Aged in his late twenties and a former schoolteacher, Sadik was lucky to escape the Tatmadaw's drive to eliminate educated Rohingya. Sadik expressed frustration that as an educated man he had been prevented from working in Myanmar – pointing to the apartheid system that Myanmar's authorities had long operated in Rakhine state. He also recounted how the military came to his village, bringing violence and killing many, before razing the village with fire. He said,

> After midnight, after coming there they [Myanmar security forces] showed their gun ... We come out from our houses and villagers went to the land, and when we come out from our house, they burnt our houses ... We lost everything, brother, sister, relatives and assets, we came here but we forced to come here, not willingly we come here, we don't want to leave Maungdaw. If Myanmar government accept us with our right as an ethnic who are living in Myanmar like Burman, Rakhine we want to go with our right, we want to live with them friendly, that will be better for us.

Even after the violence Sadik and his family had endured, he had only reluctantly left his home in Maungdaw township and would return if allowed to live in Myanmar with guaranteed rights and safety.

Almost everyone I spoke with in the camps had a desperately sad story to tell. A 60-year-old man from Buthidaung, Maung, was very emotional when he expressed how his village was burnt, showing me a large bandage on his leg he said was from a bullet wound. He had come to Bangladesh by foot, and because of his badly wounded leg the journey had taken him eleven days of walking. He bluntly outlined why his village's residents all fled for Bangladesh:

> Among my four sons, one was killed by the military in front of me, and one arrested, and one of my daughters, adult daughter arrested but I don't know where she is ... Myanmar military came in our village, there were about 3,000 people in my village, only 1,500 were able to reach Bangladesh, other person were died, my village also were burned, there is nothing else, all things were burned.

He was very emotional as he recalled this, and my translator whispered to me, 'He is crying for his daughter, he doesn't know where she is.' The clear implication being that she was in the hands of Myanmar's security forces and was not expected to be seen alive by her family again.

An articulate young man from Maungdaw, Zahid proudly told me how he had successfully graduated secondary school, and felt he was lucky to escape his village with his life. He witnessed his grandfather being shot dead by Myanmar's security forces, and the rapes of women in his village. He told me how the military had asked for educated people to identify themselves:

> My grandfather is dead from a bullet in front of me, he was eighty years old. There are seven women in one house, some military group came there and raped all seven. The military went there one by one and raped them. Seven women are dead by rape. Three hundred military raped seven women. The Myanmar government called to the educated person to come and said to them 'we are

calling you only to discuss how we improve your fate in Rakhine' but they arrested them. From my village, seven person, among the seven person there are four women. Near my village another village. The military officer said to the village, 'villagers, due to nothing to worry about, you may stay in peace, we will do nothing with you' but after some days the military came to the village and were shooting, many people were dead in the village.

The accounts told to UN Human Rights Council investigators reflected the trauma inflicted on Rohingya communities by Tatmadaw troops. Having conducted hundreds of interviews with survivors and witnesses of Tatmadaw sexual violence, the UN documented how troops used sexual violence to punish ethnic minorities like the Rohingya: 'Soldiers from Myanmar's armed forces, the Tatmadaw, routinely and systematically employed rape, gang rape and other forms of sexual violence in blatant violation of international law. Survivors have included women, girls, boys, men and transgender people.'[46] Tatmadaw sex crimes were identified as ongoing against minorities in Kachin and Shan states too, but the severity of the sexual violence unleashed against Rohingya communities led investigators to assert it was 'a factor indicating the Myanmar military's genocidal intent to destroy the Rohingya population in whole or in part'.[47] So severe and deliberate was the Tatmadaw's campaign of sexual violence in Rohingya communities that investigators concluded that genocidal intent against the Rohingya population could be inferred through the Tatmadaw's 'widespread and systematic killing of women and girls, the systematic selection of women and girls of reproductive age for rape, attacks on pregnant women and on babies, the mutilation and other injures to their reproductive organs'.[48] Investigators found too that the Tatmadaw physically branded female victims 'by bite marks on their cheeks, neck, breast and thigh' and that victims' injuries were so severe 'that they may be unable to have sexual intercourse with their husbands or conceive'.[49] Tatmadaw sexual violence is a key part of The Gambia's case before the ICJ that Myanmar has breached its obligations under the Genocide Convention.

Shocking Tatmadaw brutality was a recurring theme throughout my research in the refugee camps. I was frequently told how military helicopters had been used to raze Rohingya villages by fire. The wholesale destruction of Rohingya villages has been documented by Human Rights Watch, who used satellite images to show how around 400 Rohingya villages have been utterly destroyed – Myanmar's authorities have since taken steps to remodel these places to erase evidence of previous Rohingya residency there. Kyaw recounted what happened when the military came to his village, saying, 'On Friday morning the military shoot from the helicopter, the machine gun to burn our houses and also some military shot with gun.' Those who 'died by bullet the military take the dead body to the camp where the military were'. He explained:

> The villagers ran away, there were some dead bodies and injured seriously laid on the ground, the military also shoot them and burned them using the petrol oil, and the burned body were awashed in the river, and they [villagers] take some dead body from the river and they graved them ... When our village was burned we move to another village, and they [Myanmar military] come to burn that village, and we move another village, and when they come to burn that village we move, and that's how we come here at last...They use the helicopter to burn the villages. Three helicopters, one red colour and another two, military colour [khaki] ... There were some pregnant, eight months pregnancy, unable to move and they were attacked by the military, and there were some little children and they throw them on the fire.

Witnesses recalled how entire Rohingya villages were burned by the Tatmadaw. Amnesty International identified a military land grab of former Rohingya villages once those villages had been razed and their residents expelled.[50] A young man in his 20s, Khin, told me how Myanmar's security forces brought violence to his village, explaining that once villagers fled, the military razed the village:

Figure 11 Humanitarian groups struggled to deal with the scale of the displacement of Rohingya from Myanmar during 2017.

There is a police station in my village, and at midnight I heard some bullets shooting, and the same night the military were rushing around the village ... After we are leaving our village, the village was burned ... When we were at the top of the hill we were able to see our village was burned ... When our village was burned, we moved to another village, and then they came to burn that village, and we moved another village, and when they came to burn that village and we moved, and that's how we came here at last. They used the helicopter to burn the villages ... We were suffering from hunger, two days, also had to walk. From my village, eight were injured by bullet and the villagers were trying to take them here, and four persons were dead on the way.

Significant numbers of refugees arriving at the Bangladesh camps recounted how the Tatmadaw set fire to Rohingya homes and even mosques, spreading fires using devices similar to flame throwers and helicopters. Unsurprisingly, the Tatmadaw rejected accusations of wrongdoing – their claims of innocence did not tally with the evidence. The Tatmadaw's protestations were seriously undermined when journalists on a media tour of northern Rakhine state witnessed buildings being set alight by Buddhist residents pretending to be Rohingya.[51] Journalists witnessed and documented villages in areas controlled by the Tatmadaw burning days after the Rohingya residents had fled.[52] UN investigators described the burnings as,

> systematic, deliberate and targeted destruction, mainly by fire, of Rohingya-populated areas across the three townships. At least 392 villages (40 per cent of all settlements in northern Rakhine) were partially or totally destroyed, encompassing at least 37,700 individual structures. Approximately 80 per cent were burned in the initial three weeks of the operations, a significant portion of which after the Government's official end date of the 'clearance operations'. More than 70 per cent of the villages destroyed were in Maungdaw, where the majority of Rohingya lived. Most destroyed structures were homes. Schools, marketplaces and mosques were also burned. Rohingya-populated areas were specifically targeted, with adjacent or nearby Rakhine settlements left unscathed.[53]

Satellite images strengthened claims that Tatmadaw troops had targeted Rohingya communities with precision – they showed destroyed Rohingya villages while adjacent Buddhist homes were undamaged by fire.[54] Satellite images demonstrated the deliberate remodelling of Rohingya villages to erase evidence of Rohingya connections with their former homes, showing how heavy machinery had been used to clear all structures from at least fifty villages.[55]

Amnesty International noted how at least one military base had been brazenly constructed over the ashes of a burned Rohingya village.[56]

Stories of appalling mistreatment by Myanmar's security forces were common among those I spoke with, yet still Rohingya expressed a desire to return home to Myanmar, so long as their rights and safety there would be guaranteed. Their home was Myanmar, they felt a strong connection to its land and had a loyalty to the nation despite the mistreatment they had suffered. Camp residents told me their ancestors had lived in Myanmar for hundreds of years and so they ought to be recognized as a *taingyintha*. Kyaw told me, 'It is humble request to the world community that we want to [go] back [to] our community again and we would like to live there as other people can [as citizens].' Another young man, Anif, told me,

> We don't want to stay here any more, we don't want to stay in Bangladesh, we want to go back to our home country with our rights, education, as Myanmar citizenship because we have been living there ... We are Rohingya, but the Myanmar government call us Bengali but the Rohingya people humbly request to the world to give us the solution to go back to our country as soon as possible ... The Myanmar deprived us from education, and anyhow after learning the education we are unable to get any job anywhere. Humbly request to you that, we want to be a human, live as a human, the Myanmar behaves with us as animals. We want to go back there as a human.

Like many Rohingya, Faisal maintained that his family had been previously acknowledged as citizens of Myanmar. He showed me official Burmese identity documents originally belonging to his long-dead grandmother, which acknowledged her as a citizen of Burma and recorded her ethnicity as Rohingya (the documents were from the 1950s). He struggled to understand why Myanmar's authorities would not now acknowledge him as a citizen the way they had previously acknowledged his family members as citizens. He concluded it was because the Rohingya were Muslim and so did not fit within the government's official narrative that Myanmar was primarily a Buddhist state. Another older Rohingya man, Husein, who showed me old identity documents indicating how his family members had been acknowledged as Burmese citizens, told me that the Rohingya's situation began to change after 1962. He explained that his family had been acknowledged as Burmese citizens before the coup: 'I have old documents like passport of grandfather.' He showed me those documents, which he had carefully protected inside plastic bags for the difficult journey to the camp; included among them were a 1953 Burma identity card and a 1961 Burma passport. These experiences were emblematic of the challenges Rohingya have faced since 1962 with Myanmar's authorities refusing to recognize their legitimate – and often previously recognized – citizenship claims. Since the 1962 coup, the Rohingya population has been alienated from mainstream Myanmar life, disenfranchised and made effectively stateless. The country's military have routinely brutalized the Rohingya population and created a series of large-scale forced migrations to Bangladesh.

The Tatmadaw's 2017 'clearance operation' represented a key event in Rohingya history. It was the largest single migration of Rohingya refugees and resulted in a majority of the Rohingya population living in Bangladesh refugee camps rather than their native Myanmar. The effects of this forced migration will likely be felt by the Rohingya population forever. The scale of the catastrophe will likely lead the Rohingya's leadership to reassess the utility of their political strategies. Not likely to be reassessed is the group's commitment to their Rohingya identity. This point was highlighted by Jafar. He felt lucky to have escaped Myanmar with his life and was incredulous at the mistreatment of his family by Myanmar's security forces – he told me eleven of his family members were murdered, including his father and mother, both of whom were in their nineties. Despite this, Jafar felt a strong connection with his ancestral home in Rakhine state and was proudly Rohingya. He said, 'My grandfather was born there, my father was born there, I was born there. After all, the Myanmar government call us "Bengali", but we are not "Bengali", we are Rohingya. When we demand we are Rohingya.'

The Mother of humanity

In the aftermath of the 2017 forced deportation, there was an outpouring of sympathy from Bangladesh's residents for the mistreated Rohingya. Memories of Bangladesh's own national struggles and lived experience of forced migration made concerns about genocide crimes against the Rohingya particularly resonant for many Bangladeshis. Bangladesh's Prime Minister Sheikh Hasina, aware that a national election would soon be held, adopted a humanitarian approach embracing the Rohingya's cause. Hasina's Awami League political party labelled her the 'mother of humanity' – a fact they advertised widely on billboards and posters. Bangladesh's government subsequently created a national 'Mother of Humanity' award in Hasina's honour, to recognize exceptional contributions to humanitarian work.[57] Bangladesh's 170 million people are overwhelmingly ethnically Bengali and around ninety per cent are Muslim. Their sympathy for the displaced Rohingya and Hasina's support for the refugees provided the

Awami League with a useful campaign issue. Initially, Bangladesh's authorities treated the Rohingya as victims, but by acknowledging them as Myanmar nationals, made clear the expectation was for a future Rohingya repatriation to Myanmar.

For the 'Mother of Humanity' the Rohingya were not to be long-term Bangladesh residents, and as was the case in the 1990s the governments of Bangladesh and Myanmar soon began negotiations for their repatriation. However, in 2020, conditions for Rohingya within Myanmar remained so perilous that only the extremely brave or extremely foolish would dare return voluntarily. Hundreds of Rohingya villages have been razed by fire, erasing much physical evidence of long-term Rohingya residency in Rakhine state, and more than 120,000 Rohingya civilians were imprisoned in concentration camps there.[58] The apartheid conditions that contributed to decades of appalling human rights abuses against the Rohingya continued to be firmly enforced by Myanmar's authorities. Despite this, there has been little meaningful international pressure or sanction for Myanmar's government, its leaders or military for crimes committed against the Rohingya, although an ICC investigation has begun, there are some limited travel bans on senior military figures and a handful of military-connected social media accounts have been shut down.[59] These hardly represented penalties likely to prevent future crimes against humanity within Myanmar or deter similar criminality elsewhere. With little meaningful international pressure on Myanmar's government or the Tatmadaw to change their approach towards the Rohingya, human rights violations within Myanmar have continued, making Rohingya refugees extremely reluctant to voluntarily return.

Bangladesh's frustrations with this situation were understandable: the large temporary Rohingya refugee population living in its territory increasingly appeared to be becoming semi-permanent because their former homes in Myanmar were unsafe for them to return to; there was little meaningful international pressure for Myanmar to change its approach; and the UN's Joint Response Plan to cover the costs of food, water, shelter, sanitation and medical care for Rohingya refugees was significantly underfunded.[60]

By 2020, changes in the attitudes of Bangladesh's residents were discernible too. While Bangladesh had seen economic growth and rising living standards in recent years, it remains far from a rich country. Once the region's poorest, a decade of annual economic growth above six per cent had seen Bangladesh's GDP per capita rise to $1,698, eclipsing that of Pakistan ($1,472.90) and Myanmar ($1,326) but still lagging well behind India ($2,015.60) and Western nations like the UK ($42,491.40) and US ($62,641).[61] Key welfare indicators – infant mortality, school enrolment and life expectancy – had also improved, although life for many Bangladeshis remained economically marginal, with poverty a reality for roughly forty million people, half of whom lived in extreme poverty, getting by with less than $1.90 every day.[62] In this context, the presence of a large population of foreign nationals receiving government assistance and foreign aid was likely to soon undermine sympathy for the refugees. As the Rohingya's stay in Bangladesh appeared more and more permanent, attitudes towards the Rohingya in the popular consciousness slowly morphed for some, from victims in need of help to burdensome foreign interlopers. Having overwhelmingly won the December 2018 general election, Hasina's Awami League government throughout 2019 adopted a less humanitarian approach towards the Rohingya refugees, which indicated an increased willingness to accept Myanmar's official assurances that the time was right to repatriate the Rohingya.[63]

The Rohingya refugee population was frustrated too. They collectively refused efforts by Bangladeshi authorities for a repatriation to Myanmar until their safety there was guaranteed. Bangladesh had scheduled the first group to be returned in August 2019 but no refugees volunteered to go home to Myanmar, where they expected to face genocidal conditions.[64] Rohingya have similarly been reluctant to be moved from their refugee camps close to the Myanmar frontier to other locations within Bangladesh. Bangladesh's plan to move 100,000 refugees to Bhashan Char, a recently emerged silt island, far off the coast and more than 100 kilometres from Myanmar, was vigorously resisted by the Rohingya population. Without a regular ferry service (it takes three hours to travel by boat from Bhashan Char to the mainland), no economy and prison-like accommodation, Bhashan Char has been described by Human Rights Watch as an 'island prison'.[65] Even in land-poor Bangladesh, Bhashan Char had not attracted permanent settlement with fears of its vulnerability to flood and being easily cut off by poor weather. The international media was made aware of the Rohingya's concerns during August 2019 when 200,000 Rohingya gathered at Kutupalong refugee camp, the world's largest, for a peaceful rally to commemorate the second anniversary of the 2017 forced exodus.[66]

This event represented peaceful yet assertive Rohingya politics – letting the global community know that they want a future that is safe, with an end to the practices of genocide that have been perpetrated against them for decades, and with their Myanmar citizenship rights acknowledged. Concerns were also raised about the potential relocation to Bhashan Char and lack of access to educational opportunities within the refugee camps. During early 2020, Bangladesh took steps to address this, easing thirty-year-old restrictions on Rohingya access to education within the refugee camps and allowing camp schools to teach the Myanmar curriculum. However, host countries do not always look fondly on politically assertive refugees, and Bangladesh's government responded by sacking the official that approved the gathering and imposing restrictions on Rohingya access to telecommunications.[67] There was soon an effective communications blackout throughout the camps, with police confiscating phones and SIM cards, severing a vital refugee link with family members, humanitarian actors and the outside world. On the pretext of keeping out traffickers, the Bangladesh authorities also erected barbed wire fencing around some camps.[68] These actions sent a strong signal to the refugee community that future public gatherings and assertive rights claims are unlikely to be welcomed and might well come with the risk of collective punishment. There is now strong implied pressure from Bangladesh's government for Rohingya to be more compliant with government demands, including for their transport to Bhashan Char, and to potentially accept an unsafe repatriation to Myanmar.

Bangladesh's newfound hard-line approach is both unhelpful and misguided because it assumes responsibility for the Rohingya's residence in Bangladesh lies with the Rohingya themselves. The fault lies with the Tatmadaw who forcibly deported the Rohingya, and with Myanmar's civilian authorities, led by Aung San Suu Kyi, which continue to allow apartheid conditions to exist within Rakhine state. Pressure to change ought to be applied to Myanmar's civilian and military authorities rather than the refugee community. Limiting refugees' rights and their ability to express themselves politically is a poor policy that risks pushing desperate people towards strategies of political violence that they have previously resisted. Deeply troubling is that it seems out of their frustration with official Myanmar's recalcitrance, the government of Bangladesh has turned its attention towards the Rohingya refugees themselves. Blaming the Rohingya for their situation allows Myanmar to continue mistreating ethnic and religious minorities without consequence. This sends a strong message to other countries who might similarly abuse their minority populations that it is possible to deflect blame onto the minorities themselves.

The Indian government's 2019 citizenship registration process in Assam state, which also shares a border with Bangladesh, has been criticized by human rights groups for creating a stateless population there of close to two million people. The question of what India's government intends for those now regarded as non-citizen residents is unclear, but the construction of ten new detention camps indicated that mass incarceration of civilians, which already occurs to Rohingya in Myanmar, might be on the cards.[69] The sectarian nature of policies championed by Narendra Modi's Hindu nationalist Bharatiya Janata Party (BJP) administration was highlighted by the 2019 *Citizenship Amendment Act*.[70] This changed India's *Citizenship Act (1955)* so the government could provide a pathway to citizenship for members of certain religious groups who might have entered India illegally – although not Muslims. When the BJP-led government announced plans for a register of citizens (similar to Assam's register) to be undertaken nationwide, this stoked fears that the government aimed to revoke citizenship rights from many among the country's Muslim population while ensuring others accused of being non-citizens (Hindus, Sikhs, Buddhists, Jains, Parsi and Christian migrants from Afghanistan, Bangladesh and Pakistan) retained a path to citizenship.[71] Understandably, during late 2019, large protests began in India demanding the government revoke the *Citizenship Amendment Act*, which was justifiably claimed to discriminate against Muslims and to threaten India's secular founding principles.[72] This presents disturbing evidence that other regional actors have taken note of how Myanmar mistreated and forcibly deported its Rohingya minority without any meaningful international consequences or sanction. The failure of the international community to take steps to safeguard Rohingya rights may well have consequences for other groups far beyond Myanmar's borders.

8

Seeking Common Ground

The international community can do much more to assist the Rohingya, but the origins of their woeful circumstances are domestic, and the solutions are largely domestic too. Myanmar's laws have been weaponized, denying Rohingya citizenship and other rights, to enable genocide. If the Myanmar state applied laws fairly the Rohingya would be recognized as a *taingyintha*, and as citizens with their human rights safeguarded. But for decades, the authorities have treated the law and how laws are enforced as opportunities to further political ends, with devastating human rights consequences. These practices are often seen in authoritarian states, but Penny Green and Tony Ward have noted the prevalence of state crimes – 'state organisational deviance involving the violation of human rights' – in democracies too.[1] It is a situation that is unlikely to alter without significant domestic political change, so in this chapter, I suggest a realignment of the Rohingya's campaigning focus to prioritize engagement with Myanmar's domestic politics. Acknowledging their extremely challenging circumstances, I will outline some (admittedly limited) political opportunities that might help contribute to improvements in the Rohingya's situation over the long term. By working with other mistreated groups, including ethnic minority victims of Burmanization policies and youth activists, the Rohingya leadership might prioritize two long-term domestic goals: removing the link between ethnicity and citizenship, and working to curtail the Tatmadaw's unchecked power.

A renewed domestic focus

Myanmar's colonial history has been an important contributor to the Rohingya's circumstances, where animosity remains towards those perceived to be foreign or to have benefited from colonial rule. The constitution and the citizenship law, with their focus on indigeneity for pre-1823 groups, are built upon a rejection of colonial-era migration. These factors mean international engagement with Myanmar, especially if it is perceived to support colonial-era migration or groups considered to not be indigenous, comes with a high risk of being interpreted as unwelcome foreign interference, even if this engagement is to provide humanitarian assistance. This has been the experience of aid groups in Rakhine state, where nationalist protests demanded their removal, and there were similar objections to the involvement in Myanmar of UN agencies, and even Kofi Annan's advisory commission – Aung San Suu Kyi's decision to refuse visas for UN Human Rights Council investigators was popularly received. A major consequence of limited domestic political support and sympathy is that not only are the Rohingya denied citizenship rights and routinely subject to gross human rights violations, but that these practices continue without strong domestic political opposition.

This has understandably encouraged Rohingya leaders to focus their demands on the international community, which they believe to be more receptive to their human rights and citizenship claims. However, Rohingya efforts to seek international support for their cause regularly backfire domestically, because without domestic support they are interpreted as a call for foreign interference. This approach has been unintentionally perceived by some in Myanmar as an attempt to undermine the country's sovereignty, which has led to Rohingya being unfairly portrayed as disloyal to Myanmar, and indeed as an external group, foreign to the body politic. Such accusations further erode the Rohingya's already limited domestic support. This was how Aung San Suu Kyi framed her defence of Myanmar at the ICJ – as standing up for Myanmar's national interests and protecting the country's reputation from unfair foreign attack.

A serious consequence of the Rohingya's political isolation is limited public opposition to Myanmar's security forces' violence towards Rohingya civilians, although it does not necessarily need to be like this. Mainstream Rohingya leaders have not sufficiently focused on the role of Myanmar's domestic discourse and public opinion in determining the group's access to citizenship and other rights in recent times. Those Rohingya who did consider the group's Myanmar relationships as important focused almost exclusively on the relationship between the Rohingya and their near neighbours, the Buddhist Rakhine. Yet while the relationship with the Rakhine is certainly important, other ethnic minorities have suffered under the central authorities' Burmanization policies. This presents opportunities for Rohingya advocates to forge a common cause with them on issues of shared concern, pointing to a way forward for the Rohingya through domestic political engagement.

In the past, Rohingya leaders have often found other Myanmar minorities reluctant to cooperate with them. However, there are emerging indications of increased willingness to acknowledge a common experience of mistreatment by Myanmar's authorities and particularly by the military. Widespread reporting of the 2017 'clearance operation' has given credibility to long-running Rohingya claims of official repression. The decision of the ICC to examine 'alleged coercive acts having resulted in the forced displacement of the Rohingya people, including deprivation of fundamental rights, killing, sexual violence, enforced disappearance, destruction and looting' gave credibility to Rohingya assertions that atrocity crimes were committed against their population – just as they so frequently have been against other minorities.[2] Many in Myanmar are aware of or have themselves experienced Tatmadaw brutality, and unlike previous violations of Rohingya rights, which were characterized by administrative discrimination or by lower-level violence that received limited media focus, the recent violence drew significant media attention and contributed to both domestic and international criticisms of the military.

The Tatmadaw has been responsible for atrocity crimes against other non-Bamar ethnic groups. Christians among the Chin, Kachin and Karen populations have been victims of Burmanization policies, as have Rakhine Buddhists, although the Rohingya have been a particularly targeted group. Long-term Tatmadaw mistreatment of ethnic minorities has been regularly documented by academics, human rights groups and the media. These experiences are reflected in a marked difference in attitudes towards the military between Myanmar's Bamar and ethnic minority communities. People's Alliance for Credible Elections 2019 polling demonstrated this, with the military receiving a confidence rating of just over thirty per cent in Myanmar's Bamar-majority regions, yet in the states with larger ethnic minority populations the outcome was a net negative 0.9 per cent.[3]

Central to explanations for the authorities' approach are conceptions by key Tatmadaw and government figures that the Myanmar state ought to be Bamar dominated and to privilege the Buddhist religion. Since the 1960s the country's civilian and military authorities have been dominated by Bamar Buddhists. Myanmar's authorities have been frequently accused of undertaking a nationwide campaign of Burmanization, with the aim of homogenizing the country's ethnic, religious and cultural minorities into a hegemonic Bamar state. The logic of Burmanization means groups like the Rohingya must either be assimilated or removed from the national fabric. The deportation of the Rohingya from the country has been an approach commonly adopted by governments and military, who have undertaken processes to limit Rohingya rights since the 1960s, and through travel restrictions have prevented interaction between Rohingya and others, making it easier to portray the Rohingya as outsiders. For many in Myanmar, especially those living beyond Rakhine state, the Rohingya must by now seem genuinely foreign. For ethnic Rakhine, who until recently did routinely mix with Rohingya, their interactions since 2012 have become increasingly rare because of the forced separation of Buddhist and Muslim communities and mass incarceration of Rohingya in concentration camps. In that context, the 2017 'clearance operation' represented another active measure by Myanmar officialdom to further exclude the Rohingya from Myanmar's national fabric.

Similar brutal tactics to those employed in anti-Rohingya 'clearance operations' have been used against other ethnic minorities, but there have been differences in their scale. A likely motivation for the targeting of Muslims is the nationalist trope that Islam represents an existential threat to Buddhism and Myanmar's Buddhist character, and that the conversion to Islam of previously Buddhist-dominated communities in what are now Indonesia and Malaysia illustrates this danger. Christian groups in Myanmar have undoubtedly been victims of Burmanization policies and endured aggressive military actions against them (including the destruction of Christian places of worship), yet similar arguments over the conversion of nearby, previously Buddhist countries to Christianity cannot be made. This suggests a key reason why Christian groups might be more easily tolerated by the Buddhist and Bamar-dominated authorities, military and nationalists and so have not suffered permanent deportations of a similar magnitude to the Rohingya. The Rohingya are not the only community to have suffered large-scale forced deportation at the Tatmadaw's hands – the displacement of Karen to Thailand has been well documented, as has the displacement of Kachin to China.[4] However, the permanence of Rohingya deportation, its massive scale and appalling violence serve as a warning to others that their own situation could always be made worse if they continue to resist Burmanization. This is a way that Burmanization is forced on others – with the implied threat of suffering the same fate as the Rohingya for those who resist their incorporation into a Burmanized Myanmar.

Mistreatment of the Rohingya serves a dual Burmanization purpose. It removes an indigenous Muslim population from the country and issues a stern warning to others who might resist Burmanization, for instance among the Chin, Kachin, Karen, Shan or even the Rakhine, that their resistance comes with the implied risk of similar treatment to that visited upon the Rohingya. Ongoing rejections of legitimate Rohingya claims to citizenship are about political will, not an ignorance of history. Rohingya historians and leaders did not suggest Myanmar's authorities were unaware of their history and the strength of their citizenship claims. Instead, the Rohingya's contemporary circumstances were portrayed as being a consequence of decisions by Myanmar's government and military, which are now commonly supported by public opinion, to deny the group citizenship and other rights despite the strength of Rohingya claims. As was outlined in the book's early chapters, the Rohingya clearly meet the criteria to be *taingyintha*, and their collective ancestry in pre-Second World War Burma means most would also qualify for citizenship because of their long-term residency in the country. Rohingya citizenship was uncontroversially acknowledged by the authorities during the period of civilian government following independence. Myanmar's authorities are well aware of the strength of Rohingya citizenship claims, yet for decades rejected them. This has more to do with who the authorities consider *ought* to be a *taingyintha* than whether the Rohingya *are* legitimately part of this category according to Myanmar's laws. Debate about who ought to be part of the Myanmar nation points to a conflict that will not be resolved solely by demonstrating the strength of the Rohingya's citizenship entitlement. Achieving recognition of the Rohingya's rights requires more than proving the group's case, it requires political actors – the civilian and military authorities – agreeing to respect those rights.

There are two major challenges faced by Rohingya citizenship claimants – the nature of *taingyintha* claims, and the reluctance of the authorities to respect legitimate Rohingya claims. However, this points towards an opportunity for the group. Rohingya claims to *taingyintha* status are routinely rejected by official Myanmar, but theirs is not the only group to have suffered because of the government and Tatmadaw's focus on this kind of citizenship. The burden of policies of Burmanization have often fallen upon the country's minorities. *Taingyintha* discourse represents a citizenship and identity ideal that Myanmar's residents are hesitant to apply collectively to a predominantly Muslim group. Acknowledgement that the *taingyintha* discourse itself is central to the Rohingya's statelessness, and has been used to undermine other groups as well, provides a clear indication that contemporary Rohingya leaders ought to vigorously oppose its continuation. The nature of the *taingyintha* citizenship being sought by the Rohingya is a serious impediment to their achieving citizenship rights. Ending the Myanmar citizenship system based on concepts like *taingyintha* and replacing it with a system where ethnicity, race or religion are not part of the citizenship processes ought to be a priority for Rohingya leaders and advocates.

The problematic nature of Myanmar's current citizenship framework was noted too in the final report of Kofi Annan's Advisory Commission on Rakhine State, which sensibly recommended a reassessment of Myanmar's link of citizenship with ethnicity.[5] Aung San Suu Kyi had indicated the government would implement the recommendations of Kofi Annan's Commission, which gave hope there could be future support from the civilian government to remove race and religion from the citizenship process. To help progress this, Rohingya leaders could well find common cause with other ethnic groups, including among the Chin, Kachin, Karen, Rakhine and Shan, who have suffered because of the authorities' policies of Burmanization. Whether these groups choose to cooperate directly with the Rohingya on this would be less important than whether they themselves advocated the removal of *taingyintha* concepts from the central role they currently occupy in Myanmar's citizenship regime. This would be a campaign that could be supported by international actors, whose encouragement of ethnic minorities to seek changes to the system of citizenship might minimize the expected backlash against the Rohingya if they were to be the sole proponents of this. Of course, this would be a long-term strategy rather than one likely to lead to immediate improvements in citizenship practices.

There are also opportunities to build solidarity with civil society groups among the Bamar population, particularly among those unhappy with Tatmadaw actions and their domination of the political process. While there were public rallies in Yangon in 2018 supporting the Tatmadaw's approach in Rakhine state, there have been examples of individuals and groups publicly indicating their opposition to those actions. The Myanmar rights and advocacy organization Progressive Voice has described the Rohingya's situation in Myanmar as 'apartheid' and an 'ongoing genocide'.[6] In August 2018, Tin Maung Kyi, a central committee member of the Movement for Democracy Current Forces, was arrested when he organized an anti-military protest outside Yangon City Hall, unfurling a banner that read, 'UN and ICC – come quick and arrest Myanmar's murderous generals'.[7] Anti-Tatmadaw protesters would be aware they risk almost certain arrest and incarceration because of their participation in anti-military political activities. This suggests there may be others in Myanmar who are unhappy with the Tatmadaw's actions but are not yet prepared to publicly demonstrate and risk arrest. This is another group (albeit a minority) with which Rohingya might find a common cause. A key impediment of Rohingya access to citizenship and human rights in Myanmar has been the desire of the military to limit Rohingya rights. The Tatmadaw's unrestrained power has been a disaster for the Rohingya, and other groups in the country too, and so bringing the military under the control of democratically elected civilian authorities must be a campaigning priority for the group domestically and in its international advocacy.

The defining feature of modern Myanmar politics has been the 8888 Uprising, yet more than seventy per cent of Myanmar's population was not born when it occurred. Myanmar's young people are, for the time being, far from political influence and power. However, this will change, which means there is hope that a more humanitarian approach towards the Rohingya could be a consequence of generational change in the country's politics. This points to domestic youth activists as another key group with which the Rohingya leadership should actively seek common political ground. Young inter-faith activists like Thet Swe Win, and activists from the Generation Wave group like Moe Thway, have also been vocal in their support for human rights for all in Myanmar, including the Rohingya, and they are strongly critical of the military's continued political influence.[8]

Young political activists, especially those from ethnic minority groups, have grown increasingly frustrated with restrictions on freedom of expression and public expressions of racism. The 'Don't call me Kalar' social campaign is a powerful example of this. In modern Myanmar, virtually any criticism of the military or civilian government, whether in the media or through political activism, risks prosecution and incarceration. By 2020, despite Aung San Suu Kyi's NLD having held political power for years, human rights defenders, environmental and political activists, and even poets critical of the authorities are routinely subject to intimidation, arrest and imprisonment. In a Myanmar where there are still hundreds of political prisoners, Amnesty International has criticized the military and the civilian administration for the continued harassment of activists and government critics. Even good faith media reporting risks jail. In May 2020, the editor of a Karen state media outlet was given a two-year prison sentence because his publication reported a coronavirus-related death in eastern Myanmar, close to the Thai border from where 16,000 migrant workers had recently returned. This conflicted with the official narrative of zero coronavirus-related deaths in the state at that time (achieved through extremely limited testing), and points to the authorities' hyper-sensitivity to criticism. Official pre-publication censorship of news media might have ended during Thein Sein's presidency, but Aung San Suu Kyi's administration maintains a modern version whereby journalists and editors risk arrest and incarceration for even minor government criticisms. Another way the authorities minimize criticism and scrutiny involves using internet blackouts. Shutting down internet access has become a common Tatmadaw tactic in conflict zones, but increasingly blackouts are spread much further than the sites of conflict and continue indefinitely. An internet blackout in northern Rakhine state and adjacent parts of Chin state where there was Tatmadaw conflict with the Arakan Army has been described by Human Rights Watch as 'the world's longest government-enforced internet shutdown.'[9] Even the coronavirus pandemic of 2020 did not lead to a ceasefire or the lifting of this internet blackout.

Myanmar's telecommunication liberalizations have been frequently weaponized with anti-Muslim and anti-Rohingya hate speech, but these tools can nonetheless provide the Rohingya with opportunities to communicate with people outside of conflict zones. While traditional media outlets resist even using the Rohingya name, social media provide the group with opportunities to bypass this censorship and more easily communicate with a domestic audience. Ironically, this would involve greater use by the Rohingya and their allies of the same social media platforms that have so often been used against them in recent years. Reaching out to ethnic minorities and youth activists and then communicating common messages onto the national political stage can help leverage the Rohingya's domestic position and reduce the ability of the state to externalize them. A renewed focus on domestic discourse, particularly by using the available social media platforms and engaging with the country's other ethnic minorities who frequently share an experience of military brutality, and with young people, might provide opportunities to influence Myanmar's future politics and contribute to future rights improvements for the Rohingya.

The Tatmadaw's 'unfinished job'

The Rohingya's situation has been further undermined by constitutional arrangements guaranteeing military independence from civilian government oversight. Armed forces Commander-in-Chief Min Aung Hlaing does not consider the Rohingya to be an indigenous group, saying bluntly in 2018 that the Rohingya, 'do not have any characteristics or culture in common with the ethnicities of Myanmar'. He outlined his belief that tensions in Rakhine state were 'fuelled because the Bengalis demanded citizenship'.[10] Ominously, Min Aung Hlaing indicated the genocidal intentions of the military by characterizing the 2017 'clearance operations' in Rohingya communities as an 'unfinished job' from the Second World War, posting to Facebook, 'The Bengali problem is a long-standing one which has become an unfinished job despite the efforts of the previous governments to solve it.'[11]

If the civilian authorities' approach to Rohingya citizenship claims has frequently been characterized by inaction, the military's approach has been characterized by aggressive action. 'Clearance operations' in Rohingya communities during 2016 and 2017 were described by UN Human Rights Council investigators as including genocide, crimes against humanity and war crimes that warrant the prosecution of Senior General Min Aung Hlaing and other military commanders.[12] Min Aung Hlaing's comments that the forced deportation of hundreds of thousands of Rohingya was an 'unfinished job' were noted by The Gambia's legal team at the ICJ in December 2019 as indicating the clear genocidal intent of the Tatmadaw and its leaders.[13] Genocidal intent has certainly been evident in actions throughout the decades of military rule, and the origin of rights violations against the Rohingya trace to the 1960s when the country came to be controlled by the military. There were military-led pogroms against Rohingya communities in 1978 and 1991–1992, which involved violent atrocities committed against civilians, the widespread destruction and looting of property, and large-scale forced deportations to Bangladesh.[14]

Myanmar's majority might not be intent on violent genocidal destruction of the Rohingya community, but many nonetheless share Tatmadaw attitudes that Rohingya ought to be labelled 'Bengali' and denied citizenship rights. These views have come to be echoed by Myanmar's largest political parties, who have been steadfast in their opposition to Rohingya citizenship.[15] This was likely a key motivation for the NLD's decision to field no Muslims among the 1,151 candidates it put forward to contest the 2015 elections.[16] In 2017, Aung San Suu Kyi made it clear that her attitudes towards the Rohingya's rights claims were closer to those of the Tatmadaw than Rohingya had hoped when the NLD came to power. Aung San Suu Kyi's public statements in the aftermath of the 2017 'clearance operation' were strongly supportive of the military's aggressive approach and played down accusations of atrocities, which she labelled as 'a huge iceberg of misinformation'.[17] Despite obvious evidence of military crimes against civilians, Aung San Suu Kyi has not softened her stance. In December 2019 she presented Myanmar's case to the ICJ, defending the Tatmadaw against accusations of genocidal acts. Central to Myanmar's rejection of The Gambia's request for the ICJ to order 'Provisional Measures' to protect the Rohingya from further genocidal harm was the assertion the Tatmadaw might have committed war crimes or crimes against humanity rather than genocide, arguing that this placed military atrocities beyond the court's remit.

Sadly, in recent years, differences of opinion between the NLD administration, its parliamentary opponents in the USDP and ANP, and the Tatmadaw over the Rohingya's rights claims have become rare. Aung San Suu Kyi's support of the military's approach has led to international criticism, notably by the UN Fact-Finding Mission, which found that 'The State Counsellor, Daw Aung San Suu Kyi, has not used her de facto position as Head of Government, nor her moral authority, to stem or prevent the unfolding events in Rakhine State.'[18] The UN Fact-Finding Mission further criticized her civilian administration and asserted that, 'through their acts and omissions, the civilian authorities have contributed to the commission of atrocity crimes.'[19] With few influential domestic political supporters, Rohingya leaders have understandably regularly looked to the international community for help.

The alignment of public opinion and views of the NLD administration with the perspective of the Tatmadaw represents a major change in Myanmar's domestic politics. Accord between these groups indicates a noteworthy political realignment that will have long-term consequences for individuals and groups beyond the boundaries of Rakhine state. For decades since the 8888 Uprising, a major domestic political cleavage has been between the military and opposition groups, including Aung San Suu Kyi's NLD, who rejected military rule and called for a return to democracy. Recent events suggest the NLD's mostly Bamar and Buddhist legislators have been co-opted to support Tatmadaw actions and the perspectives of nationalists, and that this has occurred with popular domestic support. Throughout the dictatorship, the Tatmadaw was often depicted as failing to convince the country's majority that it acted in their interests. This contributed to a strong opposition movement among the majority Bamar that frequently cooperated with ethnic minority groups, including their armed wings. However, by their mistreatment of the Rohingya, military leaders have seemingly found a way to demonstrate to Myanmar's Bamar and Buddhist majority that they are defenders of the interests of Myanmar's majority and the country's sovereignty against perceived interlopers. In the aftermath of the Rohingya's recent deportation, public opinion in Myanmar, especially in Bamar majority areas, was no longer as reflexively anti-Tatmadaw as in the decades prior.

Increased public support for the military ought to be concerning to Myanmar's democrats, regardless of their attitude to the Rohingya's aspirations. The Tatmadaw has undertaken coups in the past, and enforced decades of dictatorship. Some scholars (notably Taeko Hiroi and Sawa Omori) have argued coups are more common in hybrid regimes like Myanmar, rather than autocracies or democracies, and are likely to be sparked by factors including societal instability, regime transition and economic crisis. They believe a key requirement for a successful *coup d'état* is public support.[20] This makes resurgent military popularity among Myanmar's Bamar majority deeply concerning. Myanmar's transition towards anything more than a procedural democracy appears unlikely while the armed forces can veto constitutional change. Although with the military increasingly receiving civilian government support, they can progress their own objectives without meaningful scrutiny from the country's civilian leaders. Of course, this situation could quickly change were there to be societal instability to an extent that Tatmadaw leaders warranted it required direct intervention. With Myanmar's track record of economic crisis, multiple ongoing domestic armed conflicts and the country's extreme vulnerability to climate change – the *Global Climate Risk Index 2020* labelled Myanmar as having the world's second greatest vulnerability to extreme weather events – such possibilities in the near future cannot be discounted.[21]

This points to a significant political realignment in Myanmar and suggests domestic political actors, including the NLD, are increasingly comfortable with how far along the path to democracy the country has now travelled. There are implications for domestic and international actors. It may lead to a more assertive Tatmadaw in the coming years that directs its focus towards other non-Buddhist and non-Bamar groups that it considers to not be sufficiently supportive of its national project or qualify as fully indigenous. Ethnic Kachin communities in northern Myanmar suffered Tatmadaw attacks soon after the Rohingya's 2017 deportation. The Rakhine have similarly suffered at the hands of the more assertive Tatmadaw. Since 2017, the Tatmadaw engaged a series of 'clearance operations' against perceived Arakan Army supporters that have devastated Rakhine communities and displaced tens of thousands. Myanmar's domestic political realignment will impact the nationwide peace process too, as calls from ethnic minority groups for a federation with devolution of government power are now less likely to be met with the necessary support from NLD lawmakers. This represents a reaffirmation of the political power Tatmadaw leaders wielded during the military dictatorship. One consequence may be that ethnic minority voters blame the civilian government and the NLD for this change in fortunes and switch their future political allegiance to favour ethnic minority parties. This would inject increased instability into Myanmar's politics, further reducing the ability of the parliament and the quasi-civilian administration to take decisive action against the military in the future.

The unrestrained Tatmadaw has worked to normalize Burmanization practices, routinely mistreating ethnic minorities and aggressively pursuing the anti-Rohingya agenda it began in the 1960s. By silencing criticisms and alternative voices through detention, fear and violence, the Tatmadaw has also limited civilian government impulses to rein them in. Myanmar's constitutional arrangements mean the military is both a driver of Bamar chauvinism and a roadblock to the political action that might restrain it. In practice, the Tatmadaw continues to be above the law, which serves to curtail the Rohingya rights improvements that might be achieved were future civilian governments freer to act. Problematically, the Tatmadaw has an effective veto on constitutional change, which can only come about with the agreement of military bosses. However, the situation is not hopeless. The Rohingya are far from the sole domestic victims of unrestrained military power, and as the 8888 Uprising demonstrated, there have been times when popular revolt has come close to wrestling power away from the Tatmadaw.

Pushing for further constitutional change to ensure civilian oversight of the military ought to be on the agenda of Rohingya leaders, who may find common cause with other ethnic minority groups about this. However, Aung San Suu Kyi's 2015 election victory has made any prospect of revolutionary change in Myanmar remote – major change is more likely to be achieved by military leaders concluding that their long-term interests are best served by themselves managing further constitutional amendments. Unfortunately, at present, the likelihood of even this is remote, yet there are opportunities to pressure the military leadership so that they rethink the utility of fighting to retain Myanmar's unusual constitutional arrangements, where the military are completely independent of elected political leaders. Change may come if the military leadership can be convinced that the long-term cost to them of fighting to retain existing constitutional arrangements is higher than the cost of changing them. Domestically, political pressure can be applied by ethnic minorities and by democrats and youth activists among the Bamar majority, but the international community can play an important role by targeting the Tatmadaw financially and refusing to trade with its business interests and those associated with them.

A broken system

Not only has Myanmar's political system failed the Rohingya, the international system has failed them too. In 2017, when most Rohingya were violently deported to Bangladesh, the UNSC lacked the political will to formally criticize egregious human rights violations, let alone take action to prevent them. The failure to protect Rohingya civilians, clearly victims of atrocity crimes, points to an international system that not only failed but is fundamentally broken. The *Genocide Convention*, while useful to The Gambia's ongoing ICJ dispute with Myanmar, did not lead to any meaningful action that might have prevented or curtailed the appalling crimes associated with the 2017 'clearance operation', or crimes committed by the Myanmar state during the preceding decades. The Responsibility to Protect framework was similarly unhelpful and allowed Myanmar to violently deport more than 700,000 of its residents without response. If violent forced deportation on such a massive scale, widespread destruction of Rohingya villages and a documented Tatmadaw campaign of sexual violence as a military tactic could not lead to an immediate international response, the question is surely – what would?

Inaction by the international community was short-sighted. It is likely that Myanmar's approach towards the Rohingya will be reproduced by others who desire to persecute and deport their own country's ethnic or religious minorities and are now certain they can do so without the UNSC or others stopping them. The consequences of this are likely to be long-lasting. For example, there are already disturbing signs that the government of Myanmar's neighbour, India, is adopting similar policies towards its Muslim population – with aggressive citizenship verifications and the potential of mass incarceration or deportation for those residents Modi's Hindu nationalist government determines are not legitimate citizens. A forced deportation of members of India's Muslim community could inflame tensions between India and its neighbours, especially Bangladesh and Pakistan. However, by changing the way they engage with Myanmar, international actors concerned about human rights can still play a useful role that might contribute to improvements in the Rohingya's humanitarian circumstances and serve as a warning to other would-be human rights abusers that their crimes come with international consequences. If we are to avoid Myanmar's mistreatment of the Rohingya being seen worldwide as a template for despots and human rights abusers, then at the very least the UN must accurately label the Rohingya's appalling mistreatment as genocide and demand these crimes stop.

Governments, particularly Western powers, and the UN, who have expressed a desire to encourage Myanmar's fuller transition to democracy, ought to reassess both their objectives and their strategy for engagement with Myanmar. Any movement Myanmar had been making towards democracy must now surely be regarded as ceased. Aung San Suu Kyi's high-profile support of the military's anti-Rohingya 'clearance operation' underscored this point, as did her refusal (as Foreign Minister) to grant visas to UN Human Rights Council investigators, further shielding the armed forces from international scrutiny. As it currently stands, the military-drafted constitution has taken the country as close to democracy and genuine civilian government as it is ever likely to. The closeness of Aung San Suu Kyi's NLD administration's perspectives to those of the Tatmadaw surely requires Western actors like the European Union (EU), UK and US, who have long publicly pressed Myanmar on human rights and democracy, to re-examine their engagement and consider whether objectives that include helping the country along a democratic path remain feasible without a significant change to their approach.

Those international actors who claim to be hungry for solutions to the Rohingya's situation should press Myanmar towards constitutional change that normalizes government–military relations. Racism and prejudice have stood in the way of recognition of the Rohingya's rights claims. Encouraging international actors to prioritize the removal of ethnicity from politics and increase civilian oversight of the Tatmadaw ought to be key priorities for Rohingya advocates and an important focus of their domestic and international advocacy. Those external to Myanmar cannot themselves change the citizenship laws or alter the constitution, although they can exert much greater influence than they have on the Myanmar authorities to do this. Movement towards democracy is important but removing ethnicity from politics and bringing the military under civilian authority ought to be key priorities as well. While ethnicity remains central to Myanmar citizenship law and to politics, and the Tatmadaw remains beyond civilian oversight, further progress towards democracy is unlikely.

Flaws with the UN's method of engagement within Myanmar have become increasingly clear in recent years. A stated goal of the UN and others has been to achieve progress on human rights, the rule of law and democracy, yet the nature of the engagement – within a restrictive framework determined by Myanmar's authorities – cannot realistically have been expected to achieve meaningful progress towards these goals.[22] This indicates that other motivations, such as the desire to promote economic development and trade or to benefit from Myanmar's natural resources and strategic position on the Bay of Bengal, were more likely motivations for the engagement of most international actors. It has been obvious for decades that the Rohingya and other groups are routinely discriminated against by official Myanmar and particularly by the military. In these circumstances, continuing to prioritize high-level political engagement in the hope this might lead Myanmar's civilian authorities and the Tatmadaw to change their long-standing practices of persecuting groups, including the Rohingya, seems foolish, and risks overlooking other more productive approaches.

The UN in Myanmar has been deeply divided over how best to address the Rohingya's situation. During the last half-decade, an alternative approach by the UN might have more readily improved the Rohingya's access to human rights. A report by Fieldview Solutions (a business that helps organizations deploy staff into conflict zones and areas of human rights abuse), which focused heavily on the role of the UN in Myanmar, described, 'years of secrecy, self-censorship and silent compliance with government policies of abuse' and called on 'all actors to engage in more forthright reporting and advocacy, confronting government harassment more boldly'.[23] Similar concerns were raised by UN Human Rights Council investigators, who called for, 'As a matter of urgency, a comprehensive, independent inquiry into the United Nation's involvement in Myanmar since 2011, with a view to establishing whether everything possible to prevent or mitigate the unfolding crises was done'.[24] The Human Rights Council's report suggested that, 'The United Nations should urgently adopt a common strategy to ensure that all engagement with Myanmar takes into account, and addresses, human rights concerns, in line with the Human Rights Up Front Action Plan. This should guide all UN engagement in Myanmar, particularly in relation to Rakhine State'.[25] An immediate change the UN should urgently make is to stop supporting the mass incarceration of Rohingya in concentration camps. The UN's involvement with this gives credibility to Myanmar's official position that those places are benign IDP camps rather than tools of genocide. So long as the UN supports these tools of genocide, the camps' existence will be prolonged and Rohingya denied the right to return to their former communities.

As has been shown throughout this book, much international engagement with the authorities of Myanmar has served to reinforce a status quo where Rohingya rights are routinely violated – UN support for the concentration camp system is just one serious example of this. There are also significant practical and symbolic issues with the engagement of foreign governments with Myanmar, and clear examples of their human rights rhetoric failing to be matched by appropriate action. For example, the duplicity of the EU's approach is illustrated by its decision to rent, at great expense, its official ambassador's residence from the family of dictator Ne Win. Despite EU claims to the contrary, this is often interpreted in Myanmar as implied support for Ne Win's centre-piece policies – an exclusionary citizenship system, Bamar-hegemony and an unrestrained Tatmadaw.

The approach of the EU, like that of many Western governments, to sanctions has been equally problematic, commonly providing loopholes that make their imposition ineffective. In the case of the EU's ban on arms sales to Myanmar, exemptions that allow for the purchase of non-military *matériel* that can easily be refitted and then used for military purposes not only diminish the utility of this strategy but embolden the Tatmadaw – who regard the West's lack of desire to reign in their criminality as tacit support. 'Dual use' exemptions that allow Western businesses to trade with a genocidal military, as Western political leaders virtue signal their support for human rights to the electorate, diminish the strength of calls for further more effective action in the West and serve to strengthen the Tatmadaw's hand at home. Similarly ineffective is the targeting of a small handful of senior military figures for personal sanctions and travel bans. The UK's 2020 approach highlights this – imposing sanctions on military chief Min Aung Hlaing and his deputy Soe Win while allowing UK companies to continue doing business with the Myanmar military. The solution is not to stop sanctioning Myanmar's military criminals but rather to impose sanctions that are more likely to be effective.

Sanctions are, of course, imperfect tools, imposed from outside with domestic political aims. In the past, the Tatmadaw has demonstrated a willingness to ignore Western sanctions, regarding them as a necessary cost to maintain their domestic political control.[26] However, sanctions present a more useful tool to influence domestic Myanmar politics today than they did in the 1990s, when Aung San Suu Kyi was actively demanding them. During the military dictatorship, Western sanctions were often regarded as having limited utility, particularly since Myanmar's ASEAN neighbours and China continued to engage economically with Myanmar. This contributed to a heavy economic and political reliance on China that Myanmar's military leaders came to be uncomfortable with and sought to rebalance. In more recent times, this rebalancing and Myanmar's economic liberalizations mean that military-connected business cronies have expanded their economic footprint beyond the borders of Myanmar. Tatmadaw businesses now have a much greater interest in access to Western finance and markets. In the contemporary economic and political environment, genuine economic sanctions that target the military and businesses associated with them might well prompt cronies to pressure the Tatmadaw leadership towards further constitutional change. For sanctions to be effective they need to be more than symbolic. Sanctions and travel bans must aggressively target businesses associated with the military and the individuals involved with them, not just a few senior military leaders. Ordinary people can help with this by demanding their own governments formally recognize the genocide that is taking place and institute meaningful penalties for companies that do business with the Tatmadaw.

Foreign governments have an important role to play as well when it comes to addressing social media hate speech that has normalized and excused abuse of human rights in Myanmar. The role of social media companies, like Facebook, in countries like Myanmar ought to be understood as a digital colonialism that is just as economically and socially exploitative and damaging to the national fabric as many practices of the country's colonial-era rulers or the East India Company. The *laissez-faire* approach of most social media companies in Myanmar, where few resources are devoted to addressing inappropriate use of their platforms, needs to end. In Myanmar's case, the social media platforms used to promote anti-Rohingya hate speech are not domestic – they are foreign owned, employ few (regularly no) domestic staff and generate profit for shareholders living far from the devastating consequences of their business practices. It is a disturbingly similar business model to that of the East India Company. Ironically, arguments that social media have brought benefits to Myanmar, despite the obvious consequences for groups like the Rohingya, mirror the arguments made by defenders of colonial economic practices – that they introduced modern technology and so promoted economic development. It is time for stronger regulation of social media platforms, especially of anonymous social media accounts – all that prevents this is the desire to maximize profit. Social media companies have not been lacking in options to better regulate improper use of their platforms (for instance by limiting the shareability of anonymous posts) yet they have been reluctant to take action that might affect their profitability. While social media companies can prioritize profit ahead of responsibility for the outcomes of the hate speech their platforms support, little will change. Considering the profitability of large social media platforms, there can be no excuse for failing to urgently address this or for providing Myanmar with a lesser standard of regulation than would be acceptable in the West.

Future hopes

Years after their forced deportation from Myanmar, the circumstances of Rohingya living in Bangladesh's refugee camps remain far from rosy. Rohingya are largely excluded from decisions about their collective future and live with the constant threat of further forced migration to the Bhashan Char mud island in the Bay of Bengal. Bangladesh's authorities have addressed concerns about camp security by imposing stringent curfews, blacking out internet access and erecting fences. Bangladesh's securitization of Rohingya refugee camps is counter-productive. Limiting refugees' contact with the outside world only serves to empower criminal elements, including the regrouping remnants of ARSA. Despite public statements to the contrary, these are signs Bangladesh, Myanmar and the UN regard these refugees as likely to be long-term – possibly lifelong or inter-generational – camp residents.

This book's examination of the Rohingya's history, identity and politics demonstrated strong evidence for the Rohingya's indigeneity and their collective right to Myanmar citizenship. Through the published and unpublished work of Francis Buchanan and other colonial-era records I have outlined evidence that an indigenous Rooinga group was resident in pre-colonial Burma and that its existence was documented at that time – the British regarded this Muslim population as indigenous. By examining Myanmar's various post-independence citizenship frameworks, I have also shown how Rohingya were acknowledged as indigenous and as citizens during the post-independence democratic period. The Rohingya's circumstances changed markedly from the time of the 1962 military coup and in the decades of military dictatorship following it. Many Rohingya I spoke with in the Bangladesh refugee camps said that despite these decades of mistreatment in Myanmar, they would return home if their rights there were guaranteed. In the foreseeable future, there seems to be little prospect of this.

Myanmar's authorities have taken no steps to improve the Rohingya's rights situation and strongly reject Rohingya claims to indigeneity. Appallingly, the UN has (as with previous repatriations) not made recognition of Rohingya citizenship rights a precondition for UN involvement with their return to Myanmar. Neither has the UN insisted on Rohingya involvement with decisions about any future repatriation – signalling to Myanmar's authorities that they do not regard Rohingya rights claims as legitimate. Sadly, the risks of atrocities at the hands of Tatmadaw soldiers in Myanmar have potentially increased. The hundreds of thousands of Rohingya who remain living in Rakhine state are subject to severe rights restrictions, including limits on their ability to travel or access education and healthcare, and face arrest if they try to escape to Yangon or leave the country. Around 120,000 Rohingya civilians are subject to mass incarceration in Myanmar's concentration camps, with little prospect of release or escape. The UN Fact-Finding Mission claimed Rohingya in Myanmar are at as much risk of genocide as ever, concluding that, 'the evidence that infers genocidal intent on the part of the State ... has strengthened, that there is a serious risk that genocidal actions may occur or recur.'[27] However, mistreatment by Myanmar's authorities does not detract from the fact of Rohingya indigeneity.

Rohingya consistently described their group as indigenous to Myanmar – with a history there that certainly pre-dates the colonial period and likely also pre-dates the arrival in the Arakan/Rakhine area of the ethic Rakhine Buddhist population. As an indigenous group, Myanmar's Rohingya feel an understandable connection to their ancestral lands and want to live there with their rights respected. The Myanmar government and Tatmadaw have made this impossible. This means the Rohingya's prospects are only likely to significantly improve if there is domestic political change within Myanmar. Sadly, the Rohingya's journey towards official acknowledgement of their Myanmar citizenship and the rights that should accompany it will be lengthy, and there are frustrations ahead for the group – but they are determined to fight for their rights. As Jafar told me in the Kutupalong refugee camp, days after his forced deportation from his Myanmar home, 'My grandfather was born there, my father was born there, I was born there ... we are Rohingya.' The Rohingya are proud of their heritage. They hope and want to be part of a Myanmar that acknowledges their citizenship and respects their human rights and Rohingya identity. They deserve no less.

Acknowledgements

'History . . . is a nightmare from which I am trying to awake.'
Stephen Dedalus, from *Ulysses* by James Joyce, 1922[1]

James Joyce's *Ulysses*, like Homer's *Odyssey*, is about a journey and an eventual return home. Joyce's Dedalus seeks to escape from a history that pushes too many people towards nativism and prejudice, and he is described as rejecting the 'too-easy answers of xenophobia, racism, and sentimental nationalism'.[2] Sadly, many Rohingya today find themselves too far from home and rejected by a Myanmar that struggles to break free of the chains of colonialism, military domination and racism.

This book is the product of a research project that I dearly wish did not need to be undertaken. The Rohingya have been badly mistreated by their country, they have suffered terrible human rights abuses, their history is often denied and they deserve better than the circumstances that they have found themselves in. I hope that this work can contribute in some way to making a better world for them.

I am immensely grateful to those from the Rohingya community who participated in this work – in Myanmar, Bangladesh and further afield. The assistance and efforts of Yahiya Khan during my time researching in Bangladesh deserve special note. Thank you all so much for generously giving your time and your views. This book is for you and for your community and I have done my best to represent your perspectives faithfully and hope you have found that reflected in these pages.

Research like this can be challenging to undertake and I am lucky to have had the support of many people, including my parents, Sean and Mary Lee, who understand the migrant experience and encouraged me in this work from its earliest days. I could not be luckier with the support of my wonderful partner, Kate, whose thoughtfulness and care have made such a difference during this oftentimes challenging research. Your advice and enthusiasm about grammar has been indispensable.

Professor Penny Green, Dr Thomas MacManus and Dr Alicia de la Cour Venning from Queen Mary University of London's International State Crime Initiative warrant special recognition: their ground-breaking work on the Rohingya and genocide was essential to my research.

This book would not have been possible without the team at I.B. Tauris, especially Tomasz Hoskins and Nayiri Kendir, and the work of Selena Class and Merv Honeywood. My grateful thanks also go to those who have so generously provided advice or assistance throughout this project, including my thesis supervisor Associate Professor Anthony Ware, Dr Frank Leader, Dr Virginie Andre, Dr David Kelly, Professor Michael Charney, Pat Connolly, Steve Brown, Dr Azeem Ibrahim, Sean Gleeson, Kayleigh Long, Poppy McPherson, Saw Closay, Dr José Antonio González Zarandona, Dr Gerhard Hoffstaedter, Dr Derina Johnson, Paul Greening, Mo Hasan, Kyaw Win, Greg Constantine, Chris Lewa, Fatima Kanji, Knowles-Mofford, Laura Disley and Miles Jury.

Since our interview during 2016, Maung Kyaw Nu sadly died. He was an impressive advocate for his people, but as a Rohingya, his talents were a loss to Myanmar many years before he passed away. Maung Kyaw Nu knew far too well the pain of exile from Myanmar and he told me, 'I love my country, I always dreamed that I would go back to Myanmar one day, or tomorrow. I am waiting for tomorrow for over thirty years' time.' Too many Rohingya accounts in this book are stories of unwelcome migration, and of the longing to return to Myanmar with acknowledgements of their citizenship and human rights. I hope the Rohingya's Myanmar citizenship rights can be acknowledged soon, and they can return home and live their lives in peace.

Bibliographical Survey

This is a selection of articles, books and reports most likely to be useful to students and a general audience wishing to find out more about Myanmar's Rohingya genocide and the themes addressed throughout this book.

Books

Allchin, J. (2019), *Many Rivers One Sea: Bangladesh and the Challenge of Islamist Militancy*. London: Hurst.

Callahan, M. (2003), *Making Enemies: War and State Building in Burma*. Ithaca: Cornell University Press.

Collis, M. (1943), *The Land of the Great Image: Being Experiences of Friar Manrique in Arakan*. London: Faber & Faber.

Cockett, R. (2015), *Blood, Dreams and Gold: The Changing Face of Burma*. New Haven & London: Yale University Press, 53.

Dallaire, R. (2004), *Shake Hands With The Devil: The Failure of Humanity in Rwanda*. London: Arrow Books.

Feierstein, D. (2014), *Genocide as Social Practice: Reorganising Society under the Nazis and Argentina's Military Juntas*. New Brunswick: Rutgers University Press.

Fink, C. (2009), *Living Silence in Burma: Surviving Under Military Rule*. London: Zed Books.

Green, P. and Ward, T. (2004), *State Crime: Governments, Violence and Corruption*. London: Pluto Press.

Habiburahman and Ansel, S. (2019), *First, They Erased Our Name: A Rohingya speaks*. Brunswick, Victoria: Scribe.

Ibrahim, A. (2018), *The Rohingyas: Inside Myanmar's Hidden Genocide*. London: Hurst

Keane, F. (1996), *Season of Blood: A Rwandan Journey*. London: Penguin Books.

LeBor, A. (2006), *"Complicity with Evil": The United Nations in the Age of Modern Genocide*. New Haven: Yale University Press.

Manrique, S. (1927), *Travels of Fray Sebastian Manrique 1629–1643*. Oxford: The Hakluyt Society.

Pitzer, A. (2017), *One Long Night: A Global History of Concentration Camps*. New York: Little, Brown and Company.

Rogers, B. (2012), *Burma: A Nation at the Crossroads*. London: Rider & Co.

Sadan, M. (2013), *Being and Becoming Kachin: Histories Beyond the State in the Borderworlds of Burma*. Oxford: Oxford University Press and the British Academy.

Sands, P. (2016), *East West Street: On the Origins of Genocide and Crimes Against Humanity*. London: Weidenfeld & Nicolson.

Sardiña Galache, C. (2020), *The Burmese Labyrinth: A History of the Rohingya Tragedy*. London: Verso.

Sherwood, M. (2007), *After Abolition: Britain and the Slave Trade Since 1807*. London: I.B. Tauris.

Skidmore, M. (2004), *Karaoke Fascism: Burma and the Politics of Fear*. Philadelphia: University of Pennsylvania Press.

Smith, M. (1991), *Burma: Insurgency and Politics of Ethnicity*. London: Zed Books.

Smith, S. (2011), *Creolization and Diaspora in the Portuguese Indies: The Social World of Ayutthaya 1640–1720*. Leiden: Brill.

South, A. (2008), *Ethnic Politics in Burma: States of Conflict*. London: Routledge.

Steinberg, D. (2010), *Burma/Myanmar: What Everyone Needs to Know*. Oxford: Oxford University Press.

Stone, D. (2017), *Concentration Camps: A Short History*. Oxford: Oxford University Press.

Thant Myint-U. (2019), *The Hidden History of Burma: Race, Capitalism, and the Crisis of Democracy in the 21st Century*. New York: W. W. Norton & Company.

Wade, F. (2017), *Myanmar's Enemy Within: Buddhist Violence and the Making of a Muslim 'Other'*. London: Zed Books.

Articles and reports

Amnesty International (2017), *Caged Without a Roof: Apartheid in Myanmar's Rakhine State*. London: Amnesty International.

Buchanan, F. (1799), 'A Comparative Vocabulary of Some of the Languages Spoken in the Burma Empire'. *Asiatic Researches* 5(1799): 219–240.

Green, P., MacManus, T. and de la Cour Venning, A. (2015), *Countdown to Annihilation: Genocide in Myanmar*. London: International State Crime Initiative.

Green, P., MacManus, T. and de la Cour Venning, A. (2018), *Genocide Achieved, Genocide Continues: Myanmar's Annihilation of the Rohingya*. London: International State Crime Initiative.

Human Rights Watch (2012), 'The Government Could Have Stopped This'. Available online www.hrw.org/reports/2012/07/31/government-could-have-stopped

Human Rights Watch (2013), '"All You Can Do Is Pray": Crimes Against Humanity and Ethnic Cleansing of Rohingya Muslims in Burma's Arakan State'. Available online www.hrw.org/sites/default/files/reports/burma0413webwcover_0.pdf

Notes

Introduction

1   UN Human Rights Council (2018), 'Myanmar: UN Fact-Finding Mission releases its full account of massive violations by military in Rakhine, Kachin and Shan States'. Available online www.ohchr.org/EN/HRBodies/HRC/Pages/NewsDetail. aspx?NewsID=23575&LangID=E

2   UN News (2017), 'Rohingya refugee crisis a "human rights nightmare," UN chief tells Security Council'. *UN News*, 28 September. Available online https://news.un.org/ en/story/2017/09/567402-rohingya-refugee-crisis-human-rights-nightmare-un-chief-tells-security-council

3   Cheesman, N. (2017), 'How in Myanmar "National Races" Came to Surpass Citizenship and Exclude Rohingya', *Journal of Contemporary Asia*, 47 (3): 461–483.

4   Gearan, A. (2013), 'Burma's Thein Sein Says Military "Will Always Have a Special Place" in Government', *The Washington Post*, 20 May. Available online www. washingtonpost.com/world/national-security/burmas-thein-sein-says-military-will-always-have-a-special-place-in-government/2013/05/19/253c300e-c0d4-11e2-8bd8-2788030e6b44_story.html

5   Birsel, R. and Wa Lone (2017), 'Myanmar army chief says Rohingya Muslims "not natives", numbers fleeing exaggerated'. *Reuters*, 12 October. Available online https:// uk.reuters.com/article/uk-myanmar-rohingya/myanmar-army-chief-says-rohingya-muslims-not-natives-numbers-fleeing-exaggerated-idUKKBN1CH0HG

6   Frontier (2019), 'Twitter suspends Tatmadaw chief's account, says newspaper'. *Frontier Myanmar*, 16 May. Available online https://frontiermyanmar.net/en/ twitter-suspends-tatmadaw-chiefs-account-says-newspaper

7   Al Jazeera (2016), 'Myanmar bans officials from saying "Rohingya"'. *Al Jazeera*, 22 June. Available online www.aljazeera.com/news/2016/06/myanmar-bans-officials-rohingya-160621131628167.html

8   Gerin, R. (2016), 'Aung San Suu Kyi, John Kerry Discuss Myanmar's Rohingya Issue And Sanctions'. *Radio Free Asia*, 23 May. Available online www.rfa.org/english/news/ myanmar/aung-san-suu-kyi-john-kerry-discuss-myanmars-rohingya-issue-and-sanctions-05232016162223.html

9   Al Jazeera (2014), 'Myanmar asks for shunning "Rohingya" name'. *Al Jazeera*, 20 August. Available online www.aljazeera.com/news/asia/2014/08/myanmar-asks-shunning-rohingya-name-201482085741256557.html

10 World Bank (2016), 'World Data Bank: World Development Indicators'. Available online http://databank.worldbank.org/data/reports.aspx?source=2&country=MMR

11 Burma Campaign UK (2014), 'UNFPA, DFID & Other Donors Should Withdraw Burma Census Support'. Available online https://burmacampaign.org.uk/unfpa-dfid-other-donors-should-withdraw-burma-census-support

12 Myanmar Information Management Unit (2016), 'The 2014 Myanmar Population and Housing Census'. Available online www.themimu.info/census-data

13 UNHCR (2018), 'Global Trends Forced Displacement in 2017'. Available online www.unhcr.org/5b27be547.pdf

14 Al Jazeera (2018), 'Who are the Rohingya?' *Al Jazeera*, 18 April. Available online www.aljazeera.com/indepth/features/2017/08/rohingya-muslims-170831065142812.html

15 United Nations Office for the Coordination of Humanitarian Affairs (2019), 'Rohingya Refugee Crisis'. Available online www.unocha.org/rohingya-refugee-crisis

16 UN General Assembly (1951), 'Convention Relating to the Status of Refugees'. *United Nations Treaty Series*. (189): 137; UN General Assembly (1967), 'Protocol Relating to the Status of Refugees'. *United Nations Treaty Series*. (606): 267.

17 UNCHR (2011), *States of Denial: A Review of UNHCR's Response to the Protracted Situation of Stateless Rohingya Refugees in Bangladesh*. Geneva: UNHCR Policy Development and Evaluation Service; UNHCR (2015), 'Bangladesh Factsheet'. Available online www.unhcr.org/50001ae09.pdf; UNHCR (2016), 'Global Focus Malaysia 2016 Report: People of Concern'. Available online http://reporting.unhcr.org/node/2532?y=2016#year

18 UNCHR (2011), *States of Denial: A Review of UNHCR's Response to the Protracted Situation of Stateless Rohingya Refugees in Bangladesh*. Geneva: UNHCR Policy Development and Evaluation Service.

19 BBC (2020), 'Myanmar Rohingya: what you need to know about the crisis'. *BBC News*, 23 January. Available online www.bbc.co.uk/news/world-asia-41566561

20 Ministry of Home Affairs (2015), 'Displacement of Rohingya Tribes'. *Government of India*, 22 July. Available online https://pib.gov.in/newsite/PrintRelease.aspx?relid=123478; Hussain, Z. (2019), 'India deports second Rohingya group to Myanmar, more expulsions likely'. *Reuters*, 3 January. Available online https://uk.reuters.com/article/uk-myanmar-rohingya-india/india-deports-second-rohingya-group-to-myanmar-more-expulsions-likely-idUKKCN1OX0FK

21 Files, E. (2019), 'Milwaukee Likely Has Largest Rohingya Refugee Community in US'. *WUWM*, 4 January. Available online www.wuwm.com/post/milwaukee-likely-has-largest-rohingya-refugee-community-us

22 UNHCR (2015), 'UNHCR report shows sharp increase in sea crossings in Bay of Bengal'. Available online www.unhcr.org/news/briefing/2015/5/554c8adf9/unhcr-report-shows-sharp-increase-sea-crossings-bay-bengal.html

23 Tay, A.K., Islam, R., Riley, A., Welton-Mitchell, C., Duchesne, B., Waters, V., Varner, A., Silove, D. and Ventevogel, P. (2018), *Culture, Context and Mental Health of Rohingya Refugees: A Review for Staff in Mental Health and Psychosocial Support Programmes for Rohingya Refugees*. Geneva: United Nations High Commissioner for Refugees.

24 Su Myat Mon (2018), 'The Kaman: Citizens who suffer'. *Frontier Myanmar*, 28 May. Available online https://frontiermyanmar.net/en/the-kaman-citizens-who-suffer

25 Yegar, M. (1972), *The Muslims of Burma: A Study of a Minority Group*. Weisbaden: Otto Harrassowitz.

26 Thant Myint-U. (2007), *The River of Lost Footsteps*. London: Faber & Faber.

27 MacGregor, F. (2016), 'Why were Kaman Muslim deaths ignored?' *Myanmar Times*, 6 May. Available online www.mmtimes.com/opinion/20164-why-were-kaman-muslim-deaths-ignored.html

28 Department of Population (2017), *Overview of the Result of the 2014 Population and Housing Census*. Naypyitaw: Ministry of Labour, Immigration and Population.

29 Department of Population (2015), *The 2014 Myanmar Population and Housing Census Rakhine State Census Report Volume 3-K*. Naypyitaw: Ministry of Labour, Immigration and Population.

30 Walton, M. (2013), 'The "Wages of Burman-ness:" Ethnicity and Burman Privilege in Contemporary Myanmar', *Journal of Contemporary Asia*, 43 (1): 1–27.

31 Rogers, B. (2012), *Burma: A Nation at the Crossroads*. London: Rider & Co.

32 Steinberg, D. (2010), *Burma/Myanmar: What Everyone Needs to Know*. Oxford: Oxford University Press.

33 Callahan, M. (2012), 'The Opening in Burma: The Generals Loosen Their Grip', *Journal of Democracy*, 23 (4): 120–131; The Economist (2016), 'Should you say Myanmar or Burma?'. *The Economist*, 20 December. Available online www.economist.com/blogs/economist-explains/2016/12/economist-explains-19

34 McQuillan, L. (2012), 'Suu Kyi: it's Burma, not Myanmar'. *Sydney Morning Herald*, 23 November. Available online www.smh.com.au/world/suu-kyi-its-burma-not-myanmar-20121122-29wlh.html

35 UN News (2016), 'Myanmar's first civilian leader to address Assembly in 50 years cites UN as inspiration'. Available online https://news.un.org/en/story/2016/09/539882-myanmars-first-civilian-leader-address-assembly-50-years-cites-un-inspiration

36 Irish Independent (2016), 'Aung San Suu Kyi: You can call my country Myanmar or Burma'. *Irish Independent*, 22 April. Available online www.independent.ie/world-news/asia-pacific/aung-san-suu-kyi-you-can-call-my-country-myanmar-or-burma-34651556.html

37 Australian Government Department of Foreign Affairs and Trade (2019), 'Myanmar'. Available online https://dfat.gov.au/geo/myanmar/Pages/myanmar.aspx

38 The White House (2014), 'The President's Trip to China, Burma and Australia'. Available online https://obamawhitehouse.archives.gov/issues/foreign-policy/asia-trip-2014

39 US Department of State (2018), 'U.S. Relations With Burma'. Available online www.state.gov/u-s-relations-with-burma/

Chapter 1

1 Galache, C. (2017), 'Arakan Divided'. *New Left Review*, 104: 151–159; Harvey, G. E. (1967), *History of Burma: From the Earliest Times to 10 March 1824, The Beginning of the English Conquest*. London: Frank Cass & Co.

2 Charney, M. (1998), 'Crisis and Reformation in a Maritime Kingdom of Southeast Asia: Forces of Instability and Political Disintegration in Western Burma (Arakan), 1603–1701'. *Journal of the Economic and Social History of the Orient*, 41 (2): 185–219; Eaton, R.M. (1993), *The Rise of Islam and the Bengal Frontier, 1204–1760*. Berkeley: University of California Press; Hall, D.G.E. (1950), *Burma*. London: Hutchinson's University Library.

3 Bengali, S. (2017), 'Myanmar's long-suffering Rohingya Muslims hoped that Aung San Suu Kyi would make them full citizens. They were wrong'. *Los Angeles Times*, 9 April. Available online www.latimes.com/world/la-fg-myanmar-rohingya-2017-story.html; Winn, P. (2013), 'Do "rapidly breeding" Rohingya Muslims really threaten Myanmar's Buddhist identity?'. *Public Radio International*, 14 October. Available online www.pri.org/stories/2013-10-14/do-rapidly-breeding-rohingya-muslims-really-threaten-myanmars-buddhist-identity; Wong, M. (2016), 'Myanmar nationalists stage protest, insisting Rohingyas be called "Bengalis"'. *Channel News Asia*, 10 July. Available online www.channelnewsasia.com/news/asiapacific/myanmar-nationalists-stage-protest-insisting-rohingyas-be-called-7939236

4 Gutman, P. (1976), *Ancient Arakan* (Doctoral dissertation). Canberra: Australian National University.

5 Ibid.

6 Lee, A. (2013), 'Roman Warfare with Sasanian Persia', in B. Campbell and L. Tritle (eds), *The Oxford Handbook of Warfare in the Classical World*, 708–725, Oxford: Oxford University Press.

7 Johnson, E. (1944), 'Some Sanskrit Inscriptions of Arakan', *Bulletin of the School of Oriental and African Studies*, 11 (2): 357–385.

8 Gutman, P. (1976), 63.

9 Gutman, P. (1976).

10 Hudson, B. (2005), *Ancient geography and recent archaeology: Dhanyawadi, Vesali and Mrauk-u*. In: "The Forgotten Kingdom of Arakan" History Workshop, November 2005, Chulalongkorn University.

11 Dien, A. (2007), *Six Dynasties Civilization*. New Haven: Yale University Press.

12 Pew Research Center (2015), 'The Future of World Religions: Population Growth Projections, 2010–2050: Buddhists'. Available online www.pewforum.org/2015/04/02/buddhists

13 Dien, A. (2007).

14 Ibid.

15 Hoyland, R. (2015). *In God's Path: The Arab Conquests and the Creation of an Islamic Empire*. Oxford: Oxford University Press.

16 Fa-Hsien (2013), *A Record of Buddhistic Kingdoms*. (J. Legge, trans.). Available online www.gutenberg.org/files/2124/2124-h/2124-h.htm

17 Lalitha, V. (1991), 'The Silk Route'. *Proceedings of the Indian History Congress*, 52 (1991): 894–902; Silk Road Foundation (1997), 'Han Emperor Wu-ti's Interest in Central Asia and Chang Chien's Expeditions'. Available online www.silkroadfoundation.org/artl/wuti.shtml

18 Gutman, P. (1976).

19 Lalitha, V. (1991).

20 Ray, H.P. (2006), 'The Archaeology of Bengal: Trading Networks, Cultural Identities', *Journal of the Economic and Social History of the Orient*, 49 (1): 68–95.

21 Wicks, R. (1992). *Money, Markets, and Trade in Early Southeast Asia*. Ithaca: Cornell University Press.

22 Ibid.

23 Gutman, P. (1978), 'The Ancient Coinage of Southeast Asia', *Journal of the Siam Society*, 66 (1): 8–21.

24 Wicks, R. (1992).

25 Wicks, R. (1980), 'Bull/trisula coin issues of the firth to eighth century from Arakan, Assam and Bengal: A revised typology and chronology', *American Numismatic Society Museum Notes*, 25 (1980): 109–131.

26 Ibid.

27 Hall, K. (1985), *Maritime Trade and State Development in Early Southeast Asia*. Honolulu: University of Hawai'i Press.

28 Strabo (1917), *The Geography of Strabo*. (H. Jones, trans.). London: Will Heinemann.

29 Hall, K. (1985).

30 Ibid.

31 Houston, G. (1988), 'Ports in Perspective: Some Comparative Materials on Roman Merchant Ships and Ports'. *American Journal of Archaeology*, 92 (4): 553–564.

32 Hall, K. (1985), 30.

33 Schoff, W. (1917), 'Navigation to the Far East under the Roman Empire'. *Journal of the American Oriental Society*, 37 (1917): 240–249.

34 Hall, K. (1985).

35 Silk Road Seattle (1985), *The Voyage around the Erythraean Sea*, (L. Jenott, trans.). Available online http://depts.washington.edu/silkroad/texts/periplus/periplus.html

36 Josephus, F. (c. 94), *The Antiquities of the Jews*, (W. Whiston, trans.). Available online https://lexundria.com/j_aj/8.176-8.211/wst, 176.

37 Tibbetts, G. (1956), 'Pre-Islamic Arabia and South-East Asia'. *Journal of the Malayan Branch of the Royal Asiatic Society*, 29 (3): 182–208.

38 Schoff, W. (1917).

39 Cowell, E. (ed.) (1901), *The Jataka, Vol IV* (W. Rouse, trans). Available online www.sacred-texts.com/bud/j4/index.htm, 10.

40 Manguin, P.-Y., Mani, A. and Wade, G. (2011), *Early Interactions Between South and Southeast Asia: Reflections on Cross-Cultural Exchange*. Singapore: Institute of Southeast Asian Studies.

41 Chelliah, J. (1985), *Pattaputtu: Ten Tamil Idylls (Tamil Verses with English Translation)*. Thanjavur: Tamil University.

42 Tahir Ba Tha (2007), 'A Short History of Rohingya and Kamans of Burma', (A.F.K. Jilani, trans.). *Kaladan Press Network*, 13 September. Available online www.kaladanpress.org/index.php/scholar-column-mainmenu-36/arakan/872-a-short-history-of-rohingya-and-kamas-of-burma.html

43 Harvey, G.E. (1967), *History of Burma: From the Earliest Times to 10 March 1824, The Beginning of the English Conquest*. London: Frank Cass & Co.

44 Ferrand, G. ([1913] 2015), *Relations de Voyages et Textes Géographiques Arabes, Persans et Turks Relatifs à l'Extrême-Orient du VIIIᵉ au XVIIIᵉ Siècles*. Cambridge: Cambridge University Press.

45 Keown, D. (2004), *A Dictionary of Buddhism*. Oxford: Oxford University Press.

46 Schober, J. (1997), 'In the Presence of the Buddha: ritual veneration of the Burmese Mahāmuni Image', in J. Schober (ed.), *Sacred Biography in the Buddhist Traditions of South and Southeast Asia*. Honolulu: University of Hawai'i Press, 260.

47 Ibid.

48 Ibid.

49 Keown, D. (2004).

50 San Tha Aung (1979), *The Buddhist Art of Ancient Arakan*. Rangoon: Ministry of Education, 108.

51 San Tha Aung (1979), 110.

52 Prasse-Freeman, E. and Mausert, K. (2020), 'Two Sides of the Same Arakanese Coin: "Rakhine," "Rohingya," and Ethnogenesis as Schismogenesis', in E. Prasse-Freeman, P. Chachavalpongpun and P. Strefford (eds), *Unraveling Myanmar: Critical Hurdles to Myanmar's Opening Up Process*. Kyoto: Kyoto University Press, 6.

53 Ibid.

54 Gutman, P. (1976), i.

55 Sonn, T. (2016), *Islam: History, Religion, and Politics*. Chichester: John Wiley & Sons.

56 Parthasarathi, P.T. (2016), 'Cheraman Perumal between Legend and History: A Search of His Existence in Kerala History'. *Journal of Multidisciplinary Studies in Archaeology*, 4 (2016): 446–453.

57 Ray, A. (1994), 'The State Formation in Sultanate of Bengal'. *Proceedings of the Indian History Congress*, 55: 186–193.

58 Ray, A. (1994), 187.

59 Beverley, H. (1874), 'The Census of Bengal'. *Journal of the Statistical Society of London*, 37 (1): 69–113.

60 Bahar, A. (2010), *Burma's Missing Dots: The Emerging Face of Genocide*. Bloomington: Xlibris.

61 Tahir Ba Tha (2007), 'A Short History of Rohingya and Kamans of Burma'. *Kaladan Press Network*, 13 September. Available online www.kaladanpress.org/index.php/scholar-column-mainmenu-36/arakan/872-a-short-history-of-rohingya-and-kamas-of-burma.html; Islam, N. (2012), 'Muslim influence in the kingdom of Arakan'. *ARNO*, 13 January. Available online www.rohingya.org/portal/index.php/scholars/65-nurul-islam-uk/293-muslim-influence-in-the-kingdom-of-arakan.html; Htay Lwin Oo (2013), 'Mr Htay Lwin Oo Speech in ANU on Rohingya History'. Available online www.youtube.com/watch?v=jE-JV4d1cx8; Siddiqui, H. (2008), *The Forgotten Rohingya: Their Struggle for Human Rights in Burma*. (n.p.): Author.

62 Ma Huan ([1433] 1970), *Ying-yai sheng-lan: 'The Overall Survey of the Ocean's Shores'*. (J. Mills, trans.). Bangkok: White Lotus Press, 160

63 Barbosa, D. ([1518] 1918). *The Book of Duarte Barbosa; an Account of the Countries Bordering on the Indian Ocean and Their Inhabitants*. (M. Dames, trans.). New Delhi: Asian Educational Services.

64 Ibid, 148.

65 Federici, C. (1971). *The Voyage and Travaile into the East India*. New York: Da Capo Press.

66 Manrique, S. (1927), *Travels of Fray Sebastian Manrique 1629–1643*. Oxford: The Hakluyt Society.

67 UNESCO (2019), 'Mrauk-U'. Available online https://whc.unesco.org/en/tentativelists/824

68 Bahar, A. (2010), *Burma's Missing Dots: The Emerging Face of Genocide*. Bloomington: Xlibris; Htay Lwin Oo (2013), 'Mr Htay Lwin Oo Speech in ANU on Rohingya History'. Available online www.youtube.com/watch?v=jE-JV4d1cx8; Siddiqui, H. (2008) Tahir Ba Tha (2007).

69 Suthachai Yimprasert (2004), 'The Portuguese in Arakan in the Sixteenth and Seventeenth Centuries'. *Manusya: Journal of Humanities*, 7 (2): 66–82.

70 Ibid.

71 Harvey, G.E. (1967); Yegar, M. (2002), *Between Integration and Secession: The Muslim Communities of the Southern Philippines, Southern Thailand, and Western Burma/ Myanmar*. Lanham, MD: Lexington Books.

72 Daehnhardt, R. (1994), *The Bewitched Gun*. Alfragide: Texto Editora.

73 Harvey, G.E. (1967), 143–144.

74 Collis, M. (1943), *The Land of the Great Image: Being Experiences of Friar Manrique in Arakan*. London: Faber & Faber.

75 Manrique, S. (1927).

76 De Vries, J. (1984), *European Urbanization 1500–1800*. London: Methuen and Co, 275, 277.

77 Aye Chan (2005), 'The Development of a Muslim Enclave in Arakan (Rakhine) State of Burma (Myanmar)'. *SOAS Bulletin of Burma Research*, 3 (2): 396–420.

78 Ibid.

79 Roberts, R. (1999), 'An account of Arakan Written at Islaàmabad (Chittagong) in June 1777'. *Aséanie*, Sciences humaines en Asie du Sud-Est, 3: 142–150.

80 Smith, S. (2011), *Creolization and Diaspora in the Portuguese Indies: The Social World of Ayutthaya 1640–1720*. Leiden: Brill.

81 Barbosa, D. ([1518] 1918)..

82 Dijk, W. (2008), 'An end to the history of silence? The Dutch trade in Asian slaves: Arakan and the Bay of Bengal, 1621–1665'. *IIAS Newsletter*, 46 (Winter): 16.

83 Ibid.

84 Dijk, W. (2004), 'International Institute for Asian Studies: Wil Dijk'. Available online www.iias.asia/profile/wil-dijk

85 Van Driem, G. (2019), *The Tale of Tea: A Comprehensive History of Tea from Prehistoric Times to the Present Day*. Leiden: Brill.

86 Dijk, W. (2008), 16.

87 Singh, A. (2018), *High Resolution Palaeoclimatic Changes in Selected Sectors of the Indian Himalaya by Using Speleothems*. Cham: Springer.

88 Galen, S. (2008), *Arakan and Bengal: the Rise and Decline of the Mrauk U Kingdom (Burma) from the Fifteenth to the Seventeenth Century AD*. PhD Thesis, Leiden University.

89 Alam, I. (2007), 'Indian Ocean Slave Trade: the Dutch Enterprise'. *Proceedings of the Indian History Congress*, 68 (Part Two): 1178–1190.

90 Galen, S. (2008).

91 Miller, J. (1988), *Way of Death: Merchant Capitalism and the Angolan Slave Trade 1730–1830*. Madison: University of Wisconsin Press.

92 Rennell, J. (1776), *An Actual Survey, Of The Provinces Of Bengal, Bahar &c*. London: Andrew Dury.

93 Hall, D.G.E. (1981), *A History of South-East Asia*. London: Palgrave.

94 Sherwood, M. (2007), *After Abolition: Britain and the Slave Trade Since 1807*. London: I.B. Tauris.

95 Allen, R. (2008), 'Slavery and the Slave Trades in the Indian Ocean and Arab Worlds: Global Connections and Disconnections'. In *Proceedings of the 10th Annual Gilder Lehrman Center International Conference at Yale University*. New Haven: Yale University.

96 East India Company (1813), 'Reports of Sir Robert Ker Dick on the practice, prevalent in Sylhet and elsewhere, of enticing away slaves and minors and subsequently selling them'. India Office Records and Private Papers IOR/F/4/566/13970, 10.

97 Wright, H.R.C. (1960), 'Raffles and the Slave Trade at Batavia in 1812'. *The Historical Journal*, 3 (2): 184–191.

98 Charney, M. (2019), *The Misuses of Histories and Historiography by the State in Myanmar: The Case of Rakhine and Rohingya*. In: *The International Conference on Protection and Accountability in Burma*. New York: Columbia University.

Chapter 2

1 Mratt Kyaw Thu (2018), 'Forsaken at the "western gate"'. *Frontier Myanmar*, 21 August. Available online https://frontiermyanmar.net/en/forsaken-at-the-western-gate

2 Hall, D.G.E. (1950), *Burma*. London: Hutchinson's University Library.

3 Shah, S. (2016), *The King in Exile: The Fall of the Royal Family of Burma*. New Delhi: Harper Collins.

4 Salem-Gervais, N. and Metro, R. (2012), 'A Textbook Case of Nation-Building: The Evolution of History Curricula in Myanmar', *Journal of Burma Studies*, 16 (1): 27–78.

5 Dijk, W. (2004), 'The Dutch East India Company in Burma: 1634–1680'. *IIAS Newsletter*. Available online http://iias.asia/sites/default/files/IIAS_NL34_13.pdf; Galen, S. (2008).

6 East India Company (1686), *Company Letter to King of Raccan*. India Office Records and Private Papers IOR/E/3/91 f. 42.

7 Symes, M. ([1800]2006), 'An Account of an Embassy to the Kingdom of Ava, Sent by the Governor-General of India, in the Year 1795'. *SOAS Bulletin of Burma Research*, 4 (1): 59–208.

8 Ibid.

9 Vicziany, M. (1986), 'Imperialism, Botany and Statistics in Early Nineteenth-Century India: The Surveys of Francis Buchanan (1762–1829)'. *Modern Asian Studies*, 20 (4): 625–660.

10 Buchanan, F. (2003), 'A Comparative Vocabulary of Some of the Languages Spoken in the Burma Empire'. *Asiatic Researches* 5 (1799): 219–240.

11 Ibid.

12 Tonkin, D. (2014), 'The R-word, and its ramifications'. *Democratic Voice of Burma*, 17 August. Available online www.dvb.no/analysis/the-r-word-and-its-ramifications-burma-myanmar-rohingya/43271

13 Buchanan, F. (1795), *Journal of Progress and Observations During the Continuance of the Deputation from Bengal to Ava in 1795 in the Dominions of the Barma Monarch.* India Office Records and Private Papers Mss Eur C12, 172.

14 Tonkin, D. (2014).

15 Leider, J. (2017), 'Transmutations of the Rohingya Movement in the Post-2012 Rakhine State Crisis', in Ooi Keat Gin & V. Grabowsky (eds), *Ethnic and Religious Identities and Integration in Southeast Asia.* Bangkok: Silkworm Books and EFEO, 191–239.

16 Leider, J. (2012a), 'The Muslims in Rakhine and the political project of the Rohingyas: Historical background of an unresolved communal conflict in contemporary Myanmar'. Available online www.burmalibrary.org/docs21/Jacques-P-Leider-2012-The_Muslims_in_Rakhine_and_the_political_project_of_the_Rohingyas-en.pdf

17 Leider, J. (2012b), '"Rohingya," Rakhaing and the Recent Outbreak of Violence – A Note'. *Bulletin of the Burma Studies Group*, Spring/Fall (89/90): 8–11.

18 Khin Maung Saw (2013), 'Analysis of Francis Buchanan's "Rooingas" and "Rossawns"'. Available online www.burmalibrary.org/docs21/Khin-Maung-Saw-NM-2013-Analysis_of_Buchanan_%20Rooingas_and_Rossawns-en.pdf, 7.

19 Khin Maung Saw (2013), 1.

20 Manrique, S. (1927).

21 Brown, R. (2004), 'Amsterdam in the Seventeenth Century, The Bourgeois Baroque Style'. Available online www2.uncp.edu/home/rwb/Amsterdam_l.html; Schouten, W. (2003), *De Oost-Indische voyagie van Wouter Schouten.* Zutphen: Walburg Press.

22 Ramachandra, G. (1978), 'The Outbreak of the First Anglo-Burmese War', *Journal of the Malaysian Branch of the Royal Asiatic Society*, 51 (2): 69–99.

23 East India Company (1800), *Deputation of Lieutenant Thomas Hill to Arakan to confer with the Burmese authorities.* India Office Records and Private Papers IOR/F/4/72/1592.

24 Pearn, B.R. (1944), 'Arakan and the First Anglo-Burmese War, 1824–25'. *The Far Eastern Quarterly*, 4 (1): 27–40.

25 Hall, D.G.E. (1950), *Burma.* London: Hutchinson's University Library.

26 Treaty of Yandabo, 24 February 1826. In Aitchison, C.U. (ed.) (1931), A Collection of Treaties, Engagements and Sanads: Relating to India and Neighbouring Countries, Volume XII. Calcutta: Government of India Central Publication Branch, 230–233. Available online www.assamtimes.org/sites/default/files/yandaboo-treaty.pdf

27 Leider, J. (2012a).

28 Aye Chan (2005), 'The Development of a Muslim Enclave in Arakan (Rakhine) State of Burma (Myanmar)'. *SOAS Bulletin of Burma Research*, 3 (2): 396–420.

29 Charney, M. (1999), *Where Jambudipa and Islamdom Converged: Religious Change and the Emergence of Buddhist Communalism in Early Modern Arakan (Fifteenth to Nineteenth Centuries)*. PhD Thesis, University of Michigan, 265.

30 East India Company (1800), *Report on the colony of Arakan emigrants in Chittagong*. India Office Records and Private Papers IOR/F/4/128/2381.

31 Ibid.

32 Leider, J. (2012a); Leider, J. (2013), 'Conquest and Resistance: When the Kingdom of Rakhine became a Province of the Myanmar kingdom. . .'. Seminar on the history of Rakhine/Arakan 2013, Bangkok, Thailand.

33 Buchanan, F. (1795), 176–177.

34 Buchanan, F. (1795), 88.

35 Thant Myint-U. (2007), *The River of Lost Footsteps*. London: Faber & Faber.

36 Christian, J. (1944), 'Thebaw: Last king of Burma', *The Far Eastern Quarterly*, 3 (4): 309–312.

37 Holmes, O. (2016), 'After 130 years of obscurity, Myanmar's forgotten royals make a comeback', *The Guardian*, 30 December. Available online www.theguardian.com/world/2016/dec/30/myanmar-burma-royal-family-monarchy-king-thibaw-comeback

38 Steinberg, D. (2010), *Burma/Myanmar: What Everyone Needs to Know*. Oxford: Oxford University Press.

39 Turnell, S. (2009), *Fiery Dragons: Banks, Moneylenders and Microfinance in Burma*. Copenhagen: NIAS Press.

40 Paton, C. (1828), 'Historical and Statistical Sketch of Aracan'. *Asiatic Researches*, XVI: 353–381.

41 Ibid.

42 Myanmar Information Management Unit (2019), 'The 2014 Myanmar Population and Housing Census'. Available online https://themimu.info/census-data

43 Paton, C. (1828).

44 Ware, A. and Laoutides, C. (2018), *Myanmar's 'Rohingya' Conflict*. London: Hurst.

45 Phayre, A. (1841), 'Account of Arakan'. *Journal of the Asiatic Society*, 117 (33): 679–711.

46 Duncan, H. (1875), *Report on the Census of British Burma Taken in August 1872: Appendix I Arakan Division*. Rangoon: Government Press.

47 Duncan, H. (1875), 6.

48 Duncan, H. (1875), 7.

49 Duncan, H. (1875), 6.

50 Duncan, H. (1875), 17.

51 Duncan, H. (1875), 30.

52 Copleston, F. and Burma Deputy Superintendent of Census Operations (1881), *Report on the Census of British Burma, taken on the 17th February 1881: Accompanied by a map.* Rangoon: Government Press, 39.

53 Charney, M. (2009), *A History of Modern Burma.* Cambridge: Cambridge University Press.

54 Egreteau, R. (2011), 'Burmese Indians in contemporary Burma: heritage, influence, and perceptions since 1988'. *Asian Ethnicity*, (12) 1: 33–54; Egreteau, R. (2014), 'The Idealization of a Lost Paradise: Narratives of Nostalgia and Traumatic Return Migration among Indian Repatriates from Burma since the 1960s'. *Journal of Burma Studies*, 18 (1): 137–180.

55 Baxter, J. (1941), *Report on* Indian *Immigration*. Rangoon: Superintendent, Government Printing and Stationery, Burma, 18.

56 Bennison, J. (1933), 'Census of India, 1931 Volume XI: Burma Part I – Report. Rangoon: Superintendent, Government Printing and Stationery, Burma, 49.

57 Biron, C. (2013), 'Myanmar Rohingya violence report assailed'. *Al Jazeera*, 2 May. Available online www.aljazeera.com/indepth/features/2013/05/20135111126387968.html

58 Islam, N. (2011), 'Anti-Rohingya campaigns, violations of human rights'. *The Sail*. Available online https://thesail.files.wordpress.com/2011/02/anti-rohingya-campaigns-violations-of-human-rights1.pdf; Kyaw Min (2014), 'Why not Rohingya an antiquity? [Part 2]: An assessment on Rohingyas' genuineness'. *Rohingya Blogger*, 30 April. Available online www.rohingyablogger.com/2014/04/why-not-rohingya-antiquity-part-2.html; Siddiqui, H. (2011), *Muslim Identity and Demography in the Arakan State of Burma*. (n.p.): Author.

59 Yunus, M. (1994), *A History of Arakan (Past & Present)*. Chittagong: Magenta Colour.

60 Kyaw Min (2014).

61 Turnell, S. and Vicary, A. (2008), 'Parching the Land: The Chettiars in Burma'. *Australian Economic History Review*, 48 (1): 1–25.

62 International Crisis Group (2013), 'The Dark Side of Transition: Violence Against Muslims in Myanmar'. Available online www.crisisgroup.org/asia/south-east-asia/myanmar/dark-side-transition-violence-against-muslims-myanmar

63 Nyi Nyi Kyaw (2016), 'Islamophobia in Buddhist Myanmar', in M. Crouch (ed.), *Islam and the State in Myanmar*. New Delhi: Oxford University Press.

64 Charney, M. (2009), *A History of Modern Burma.* Cambridge: Cambridge University Press.

65 Baxter, J. (1941), *Report on Indian Immigration*. Rangoon: Superintendent, Government Printing and Stationery, Burma, 4.

66 Baxter, J. (1941), 15.

67 Baxter, J. (1941), 98.

68 Keane, F. (2010), *Road of Bones: The Epic Siege of Kohima 1944*. London: HarperPress.

69 Aung San Suu Kyi (1984), *Aung San*. Brisbane: University of Queensland Press, 33.

70 Milko, V. (2019), 'Ethnic minorities across Myanmar protest against Aung San statues'. *Al Jazeera*, 29 March. Available online www.aljazeera.com/news/2019/03/ethnic-minorities-myanmar-protest-aung-san-statues-190328013321078.html

71 Kyaw Htut Aung (2019), 'Aung San statue controversy highlights vulnerability of ethnic minority identity'. *Frontier Myanmar*, 13 February. Available online https://frontiermyanmar.net/en/aung-san-statue-controversy-highlights-vulnerability-of-ethnic-minority-identity

72 Charney, M. (2009).

73 Slim, W. (1956), *Defeat into Victory*. London: Cassell and Company; Yegar, M. (2002), *Between Integration and Secession: The Muslim Communities of the Southern Philippines, Southern Thailand, and Western Burma/Myanmar*. Lanham, MD: Lexington Books.

74 Ibrahim, A. (2018), *The Rohingyas: Inside Myanmar's Hidden Genocide*. London: Hurst.

75 Center for Diversity and National Harmony (2015), *Rakhine State Needs Assessment*. Yangon: Center for Diversity and National Harmony.

76 Ibrahim, A. (2018).

77 Furnivall, J.S. (1967), *Netherlands India: A Study of Plural Economy*. Cambridge: Cambridge University Press.

78 Ware, A. and Laoutides, C. (2019), 'Myanmar's "Rohingya" Conflict: Misconceptions and Complexity'. *Asian Affairs*. 50 (1): 60–79.

Chapter 3

1 UNHCR (2020), Burma Citizenship Law [1982]. Available online www.refworld.org/docid/3ae6b4f71b.html

2 Republic of the Union of Myanmar (2008), *Constitution of the Republic of the Union of Myanmar*. Available online www.burmalibrary.org/docs5/Myanmar_Constitution-2008-en.pdf; Socialist Republic of the Union of Burma (1974), *The Constitution of the Union of Burma (1974)*. Available online www.burmalibrary.org/docs07/1974Constitution.pdf

3 Union Citizenship Act (1948). Available online www.burmalibrary.org/sites/burmalibrary.org/files/obl/docs/UNION_CITIZENSHIP_ACT-1948.htm

4 Union of Burma (1947), *Constitution of the Union of Burma* (1948). Available online www.ilo.org/dyn/natlex/docs/ELECTRONIC/79573/85699/F1436085708/MMR79573.pdf, Section 11.

5 Ibid.

6   Ibid.

7   Union Citizenship Act (1948).

8   Egreteau, R. (2014).

9   Union Citizenship Act (1948), s3.1.

10 Ibid.

11 Haque, M. (2017), 'Rohingya Ethnic Muslim Minority and the 1982 Citizenship Law in Burma'. *Journal of Muslim Minority Affairs*, 37 (4): 454–469.

12 Euro Burma Office (2009), 'Briefing Paper No.2. The Rohingyas Bengali Muslims or Arakan Rohingyas?'. Available online www.burmalibrary.org/docs6/EBO_Briefing_Paper_No._2_-_The_Rohingyas.pdf

13 Nay San Lwin (2012), 'Making Rohingya statelessness'. *New Mandala*, 29 October. Available online www.newmandala.org/making-rohingya-statelessness

14 Lintner, B. (2016), 'Militancy in Arakan State'. *The Irrawaddy*, 15 December. Available online www.irrawaddy.com/opinion/guest-column/militancy-in-arakan-state.html; Smith, M. (2006), The Muslim Rohingya of Burma. *Kaladan Press Network*, 11 October. Available online www.kaladanpress.org/index.php/scholar-column-mainmenu-36/36-rohingya/194-the-muslim-rohingya-of-burma.html

15 Than Myaing (1948), 'Activities of Moslem Pyaukkyas & Situation in North Arakan'. Rangoon: Inspector-General of Police, 1.

16 Ibid.

17 Ibid, 3–4.

18 Ibid, 1.

19 Nay San Lwin (2012).

20 Berlie, J. (2008), *Burma: The Burmanization of Myanmar's Muslims*. Bangkok: White Lotus Press; Yegar, M. (1972), *The Muslims of Burma: A Study of a Minority Group*. Weisbaden: Otto Harrassowitz.

21 Lee, R. (2017), Interview with Rohingya refugee from Myanmar (Participant 9), Kutupalong Refugee Camp (Bangladesh), 23 October 2017. (Unpublished).

22 Lee, R. (2015), 'Between the Devil and the Deep Blue Sea: The Rohingya's Dilemma'. *The Conversation*, 2 June. Available online https://theconversation.com/between-the-deviland-the-deep-blue-sea-the-rohingyas-dilemma-42359; Mathieson, D. (2015), Interview.

23 Lintner, B. (1990), *The Rise and Fall of the Communist Party of Burma (CPB)*. Ithaca: Cornell Southeast Asia Program; Smith, M. (1991), *Burma: Insurgency and Politics of Ethnicity*. London: Zed Books; Taylor, R. (1973), *Foreign and Domestic Consequences of the KMT Intervention in Burma*. Ithaca: Cornell University Library.

24 Callahan, M. (2003), *Making Enemies: War and State Building in Burma*. Ithaca: Cornell University Press.

25 South, A. (2008), *Ethnic Politics in Burma: States of Conflict*. London: Routledge.

26 Taylor, R. (2009), *The State in Myanmar*. Singapore: NUS Press.

27 Sadan, M. (2013), *Being and Becoming Kachin: Histories Beyond the State in the Borderworlds of Burma*. Oxford: Oxford University Press and the British Academy.

28 Socialist Republic of the Union of Burma (1974), *The Constitution of the Union of Burma (1974)*. Available online www.burmalibrary.org/docs07/1974Constitution.pdf

29 Yegar, M. (1972), *The Muslims of Burma: A Study of a Minority Group*. Weisbaden: Otto Harrassowitz.

30 Walton, M. (2013), 'The "Wages of Burman-ness:" Ethnicity and Burman Privilege in Contemporary Myanmar'. *Journal of Contemporary Asia*, 43 (1): 1–27.

31 Berlie, J. (2008), *Burma: The Burmanization of Myanmar's Muslims*. Bangkok: White Lotus Press; Holmes, R. (1967), 'Burmese Domestic Policy: The Politics of Burmanization'. *Asian Survey*, 7 (3): 188–197.

32 Chaturvedi, M. (2015), 'Indian Migrants in Myanmar: Emerging Trends and Challenges'. Available online www.mea.gov.in/images/pdf/Indian-Migrants-Myanmar.pdf; Egreteau, R. (2008), 'India's Ambitions in Burma: More Frustration Than Success?'. *Asian Survey*, 48 (6): 936–957; Holmes, R. (1967); Smith, M. (1991), *Burma: Insurgency and Politics of Ethnicity*. London: Zed Books.

33 Sen, A. (1983), *Poverty and Famines: An Essay on Entitlement and Deprivation*. Oxford: Oxford University Press.

34 Ware, A. and Laoutides, C. (2018), *Myanmar's 'Rohingya' Conflict*. London: Hurst.

35 Islam, N. (2006), 'Facts About the Rohingya Muslims of Arakan'. *ARNO*, 5 October. Available online www.rohingya.org/portal/index.php/learn-about-rohingya.html

36 Bangladesh Genocide Archive (2018), 'History'. Available online www.genocidebangladesh.org/history

37 Bangladesh Genocide Archive (2018), 'History'; Bangladesh Genocide Archive (2018), 'Refugees'. Available online www.genocidebangladesh.org/refugees; Curlin, G., Chen, L., and Hussain, L. (1976), 'Demographic Crisis: The Impact of the Bangladesh Civil War (1971) on Births and Deaths in a Rural Area of Bangladesh'. *Population Studies*, 30 (1): 87–105.

38 Sen, A. (1983).

39 Gunasekanan, S. and Mya Than (1988), 'Population Change in Burma: A Comparison of the 1973 and 1983 Censuses'. *Sojourn*, 3 (2): 171–186; Maung, M.I.K. (1986), 'The population of Burma: An analysis of the 1973 Census'. *Papers of the East-West Population Institute*. 97 (April 1986). Socialist Republic of the Union of Burma (1986), *Burma: 1983 Population Census*. Rangoon: Immigration and Manpower Department, Ministry of Home Affairs.

40 Smith, M. (2019), *Arakan (Rakhine State): A Land in Conflict on Myanmar's Western Frontier*. Amsterdam: Transnational Institute.

41 Human Rights Watch (2009), 'Perilous Plight: Burma's Rohingya Take to the Seas'. Available online www.hrw.org/report/2009/05/26/perilous-plight/burmas-rohingya-take-seas

42 Anand, J.P. (1978), 'Refugees from Burma'. *Economic and Political Weekly*, 13 (27): 1100–1101.

43 Government of Bangladesh, Ministry of Foreign Affairs (1978), 1978 Repatriation Agreement. Available online https://dataspace.princeton.edu/jspui/bitstream/88435/dsp01th83kz538/1/1978%20Repatriation%20Agreement.pdf, 1.

44 Nanda Htoo Thant (2019), 'NLD seeks charter changes to increase civilian control'. *Myanmar Times*, 24 July. Available online www.mmtimes.com/news/nld-seeks-charter-changes-increase-civilian-control.html

45 Burma Citizenship Law (1982), Chapter 2, Section 3.

46 Burma Citizenship Law (1982), Chapter 2, Section 4.

47 Al Jazeera (2017), 'Myanmar: Major ethnic groups and where they live'. *Al Jazeera*, 14 March. Available online www.aljazeera.com/indepth/interactive/2017/03/myanmar-major-ethnic-groups-live-170309143208539.html; Cheesman, N. (2017), 'How in Myanmar "National Races" Came to Surpass Citizenship and Exclude Rohingya'. *Journal of Contemporary Asia*, 47 (3): 461–483.

48 Htoo Thant (2016), 'Mone Wun (Bamar) national cards debated'. Myanmar *Times*, 5 May. Available online www.mmtimes.com/index.php/national-news/20123-mone-wun-bamar-national-cards-debated.html

49 Taylor, R. (2015), 'Refighting Old Battles, Compounding Misconceptions: The Politics of Ethnicity in Myanmar Today'. *ISEAS Perspective*, 2 March. Available online www.iseas.edu.sg/images/pdf/ISEAS_Perspective_2015_12.pdf, 8.

50 Ferguson, J. (2015), 'Who's Counting? Ethnicity, Belonging, and the National Census in Burma/Myanmar'. *Bijdragen Tot De Taal-, Land- En Volkenkunde*, 171 (1): 1–28.

51 Anderson, J. (1912), 'Sir Herbert Risley, K.C.I.E., C.S.I.'. *Man* 12: 1–4.

52 Risley, H. (1892), *The Tribes and Castes of Bengal*. Calcutta: Bengal Secretariat Press.

53 Walton, M. (2013), 'The "Wages of Burman-ness:" Ethnicity and Burman Privilege in Contemporary Myanmar'. *Journal of Contemporary Asia*, 43 (1): 1–27.

54 Taylor, R. (2015), 3.

55 Cederlöf, G. (2013), *Founding an Empire on India's North-Eastern Frontiers, 1790–1840*. Oxford: Oxford University Press; Chadha, V. (2005), *Low Intensity Conflicts in India: An Analysis*. New Delhi: SAGE Publications India; Harvey, G.E. (1967).

56 Baker, C. and Phongpaichit, P. (2014), *A History of Thailand*. Cambridge: Cambridge University Press; Wyatt, D. (2003), *Thailand: a Short History*. New Haven: Yale University Press.

57 Chatterji, N. (1956), 'The Out-break of the First Anglo-Burmese War on the Chittagong Frontier'. *Proceedings of the Indian History Congress*, 19: 338–341; Hayman Wilson, H. (1827), *Documents Illustrative of the Burmese War: With an Introductory Sketch of the Events of the War and an Appendix*. Calcutta: Government Gazette Press.

58 International Court of Justice (2019), 'Public sitting held on Wednesday 11 December 2019, at 10 a.m., at the Peace Palace, President Yusuf presiding, in the case

concerning Application of the Convention on the Prevention and Punishment of the
Crime of Genocide (The Gambia v. Myanmar): Verbatim Record'. Available online
www.icj-cij.org/files/case-related/178/178-20191211-ORA-01-00-BI.pdf, 14.

59 Burma Citizenship Law 1982 (Myanmar).

60 Radio Free Asia (2012), 'Call to Put Rohingya in Refugee Camps'. *Radio Free Asia*,
12 July. Available online www.rfa.org/english/news/rohingya-07122012185242.html

61 Ibid.

62 Ibid.

63 Wallace, J. (2016), 'Myanmar casts minorities to the margins as citizenship law denies
legal identity'. *The Guardian*, 3 November. Available online www.theguardian.com/
global-development/2016/nov/03/myanmar-casts-minorities-to-margins-
citizenship-law-denies-legal-identity

64 Advisory Commission on Rakhine State (2017). 'Towards A Peaceful, Fair and
Prosperous Future for the People of Rakhine: Final Report of the Advisory
Commission on Rakhine State'. Available online www.rakhinecommission.org/app/
uploads/2017/08/FinalReport_Eng.pdf

65 UN Human Rights Council (2018), 'Report of the independent international
fact-finding mission on Myanmar'. Available online https://ap.ohchr.org/documents/
dpage_e.aspx?si=A/HRC/39/64, 6.

66 Amnesty International (2004), 'Myanmar: The Rohingya Minority: Fundamental Rights
Denied'. Available online www.amnesty.org/en/documents/ASA16/005/2004/en

67 Lee, Y. (2014), 'Situation of human rights in Myanmar'. United Nations, 23 September.
Available online https://reliefweb.int/report/myanmar/report-special-rapporteur-
situation-human-rights-myanmar-yanghee-lee-a69398

68 Human Rights Watch (2015), 'Burma: Amend Biased Citizenship Law', Available
online www.hrw.org/news/2015/01/13/burma-amend-biased-citizenship-law

69 Amnesty International (2017a), '*Caged Without A Roof*': Apartheid in Myanmar's
Rakhine State. London: Amnesty International.

70 Dubow, S. (2014), *Apartheid, 1948–1994*. Oxford: Oxford University Press, 10.

71 Abdulla, R. (2016), 'Colonialism and Apartheid Against Fragmented Palestinians:
Putting the Pieces Back Together'. *State Crime Journal*, 5 (1): 51–80; Gordon, N.
(2017), 'How Israel's Occupation Shifted From a Politics of Life to a Politics of Death',
The Nation, 5 June. Available online www.thenation.com/article/israels-occupation-
shifted-politics-life-politics-death; Human Rights Watch (2008), 'China's Forbidden
Zones', *Human Rights Watch*, 6 July. Available online www.hrw.org/
report/2008/07/06/chinas-forbidden-zones/shutting-media-out-tibet-and-other-
sensitive-stories; King, C. (2001), 'Saudi Arabia's Apartheid', *The Washington Post*,
22 December. Available online www.washingtonpost.com/archive/
opinions/2001/12/22/saudi-arabias-apartheid/6dc54ab8-37bc-4a87-86f4-
c0b489fc8b8e/?noredirect=on&utm_term=.cf363c221867

72 UN General Assembly (1973), 'International Convention on the Suppression and Punishment of the Crime of Apartheid'. Available online https://treaties.un.org/doc/Publication/UNTS/Volume%201015/volume-1015-I-14861-English.pdf

73 Ibid.

74 Amnesty International (2017a).

75 Amnesty International (2017a); Human Rights Watch (1996), 'Burma: The Rohingya Muslims: Ending a Cycle of Exodus?'. *Human Rights Watch*, 1 September. Available online www.refworld.org/docid/3ae6a84a2.html

76 OHCHR (2019). 'Right to a Nationality and Statelessness'. Available online www.ohchr.org/EN/Issues/Pages/Nationality.aspx

77 Human Rights Watch (2015), 'Burma: Amend Biased Citizenship Law'. Available online www.hrw.org/news/2015/01/13/burma-amend-biased-citizenship-law

78 Cheesman, N. (2015), *Opposing the Rule of Law: How Myanmar's Courts Make Law and Order*. Cambridge: Cambridge University Press.

79 UNHCR (2010), 'UNHCR Global Report 2010'. Available online www.unhcr.org/gr10/index.html#/home

Chapter 4

1 Shwedagon Pagoda Official Website (2019), 'About Shwedagon Pagoda'. Available online www.shwedagonpagoda.com.mm/about-shwedagon-pagoda

2 Charney, M. (2009), *A History of Modern Burma*. Cambridge: Cambridge University Press.

3 Cockett, R. (2015), *Blood, Dreams and Gold: The Changing Face of Burma*. New Haven & London: Yale University Press, 53.

4 Al Jazeera (2011), 'The world's longest ongoing war'. *Al Jazeera*, 10 August. Available online www.aljazeera.com/programmes/101east/2011/08/201181073919760492.html

5 Nyein Nyein (2019), 'Timeline: 70 Years of Ethnic Armed Resistance Movements in Myanmar'. *The Irrawaddy*, 1 February. Available online www.irrawaddy.com/specials/timeline-70-years-ethnic-armed-resistance-movements-myanmar.html

6 Brown, I. (2013), *Burma's Economy in the Twentieth Century*. Cambridge: Cambridge University Press.

7 United Nations Economic Analysis & Policy Division (2018), 'Least Developed Country Category: Myanmar Profile'. Available online www.un.org/development/desa/dpad/least-developed-country-category-myanmar.html

8 Turnell, S. (2010), Finding dollars and sense: Burma's economy in 2010. In S. L. Levenstein (ed), *Finding Dollars, Sense, and Legitimacy in Burma*. Washington, DC: Woodrow Wilson International Center for Scholars, 20–39.

9 Asian Development Bank (2012), *Myanmar in Transition: Opportunities and Challenges*. Manila: Asian Development Bank.

10 Republic of the Union of Myanmar (2008), 'Constitution of the Republic of the Union of Myanmar'. Available online www.burmalibrary.org/docs5/Myanmar_Constitution-2008-en.pdf

11 Union Election Commission Law (Myanmar) (2010), Available online www.burmalibrary.org/docs16/2010-SPDC_Law2010-01-Union_Election_Commission_Law-en.pdf

12 Centre for Peace and Conflict Studies (2011), 'Observation Report 2010 Myanmar General Elections Learning and Sharing for Future'. Available online www.centrepeaceconflictstudies.org/wp-content/uploads/2010-Myanmar-Observer-report.pdf, 20.

13 Davies, J. and Weaver, M. (2010), 'Burma election turnout remains low'. *The Guardian*, 7 November. Available online www.theguardian.com/world/2010/nov/07/burma-election-turnout-low

14 International Crisis Group (2011), 'Myanmar's Post-Election Landscape'. Available online https://d2071andvip0wj.cloudfront.net/b118-myanmar-s-post-election-landscape.pdf

15 ALTSEAN-Burma (2011), 'Burma Issues & Concerns Vol 6 The Generals' Election'. Available online http://altsean.org/Issues%20and%20Concerns%20Vol%206.pdf

16 Al Jazeera (2010), 'Myanmar bars "outsiders" from poll'. *Al Jazeera*, 18 October. Available online www.aljazeera.com/news/asia-pacific/2010/10/2010101811659430825.html

17 Heyn, A. (2010), 'Burma election: polling day seemed just like a normal Sunday'. *The Guardian*, 8 November. Available online www.theguardian.com/news/blog/2010/nov/08/andrew-heyn-burma-election-day

18 Burma Fund UN Office (2011), 'Burma's 2010 Election: A comprehensive report'. Available online www.burmalibrary.org/docs11/BurmaFund-Election_Report-text.pdf

19 Charney, M. (2009), *A History of Modern Burma*. Cambridge: Cambridge University Press, 177.

20 Human Rights Watch (2010), 'Burma: Events of 2009'. Available online www.hrw.org/world-report/2010/country-chapters/burma

21 Banyan (2010), 'Myanmar's elections: Shades of drab'. *The Economist*, 20 October. Available online www.economist.com/banyan/2010/10/20/shades-of-drab

22 Bookbinder, A. (2015), 'U Shwe Maung, former USDP MP: "This is illogical and ridiculous"'. *Frontier Myanmar*, 31 August. Available online https://frontiermyanmar.net/en/u-shwe-maung-former-usdp-mp-this-is-illogical-and-ridiculous

23 McVeigh, T. (2010). 'Aung San Suu Kyi "released from house arrest"'. *The Guardian*, 13 November. Available online www.theguardian.com/world/2010/nov/13/aung-san-suu-kyi-released

24 Popham, P. (2011), *The Lady and the Peacock: The Life of Aung San Suu Kyi*. London: Rider Books.

25 BBC (2014), 'Profile: Myanmar President Thein Sein'. *BBC News*, 10 November. Available online www.bbc.co.uk/news/world-asia-pacific-12358204

26 Adams, B. (2009), 'The Lessons of Cyclone Nargis'. *Human Rights Watch*, 3 May. Available online www.hrw.org/news/2009/05/03/lessons-cyclone-nargis

27 Embassy Yangon (2004), 'TOUGH(ER) GUYS MOVE UP IN RANGOON: BIOGRAPHIC INFORMATION ON THE NEW PRIME MINISTER AND S-1'. Wikileaks Cable: 04RANGOON1372_a, dated 20 October. Available online https://wikileaks.org/plusd/cables/04RANGOON1372_a.html

28 Rogers, B. (2010), *Than Shwe: Unmasking Burma's Tyrant*. Chiang Mai: Silkworm Books.

29 Fisher, J. (2016), 'Myanmar: Thein Sein leaves legacy of reform'. *BBC News*, 30 March. Available online www.bbc.co.uk/news/world-asia-35916555

30 Banyan (2014), 'Don't count on it'. *The Economist*, 5 April. Available online www.economist.com/news/asia/21600119-myanmars-course-leading-wrong-direction-dont-count-it

31 Motlagh, J. (2014), 'When a SIM card goes from $2,000 to $1.50'. *Bloomberg*, 29 September. Available online www.bloomberg.com/bw/articles/2014-09-29/myanmar-opens-its-mobile-phone-market-cuing-carrier-frenzy

32 The World Bank (2018), 'GDP per capita (current US$)'. Available online https://data.worldbank.org/indicator/NY.GDP.PCAP.CD?locations=MM

33 Matsui, M. (2015), 'Foreign Providers, Price Competition Spur Growth'. *Nikkei Asian Review*, 7 April. Available online http://asia.nikkei.com/Business/Trends/Foreign-providers-pricecompetition-spur-growth

34 James, K. (2019), 'Plunging prices bring connectivity to the masses in Myanmar'. *DW*, 9 May. Available online www.dw.com/en/plunging-prices-bring-connectivity-to-the-masses-in-myanmar/a-48200452

35 Holliday, I. (2013), 'Myanmar in 2012: Toward a Normal State'. *Asian Survey*, 53 (1): 93–100.

36 Hodal, K. (2013), 'Buddhist monk uses racism and rumours to spread hated in Burma'. *The Guardian*, 18 April. Available online www.theguardian.com/world/2013/apr/18/buddhist-monk-spreads-hatred-burma

37 Tin Aung Kyaw (2013), 'Buddhist monk Wirathu leads violent national campaign against Myanmar's Muslims'. *GlobalPost*, 21 June. Available online www.pri.org/stories/2013-06-21/buddhist-monk-wirathu-leads-violent-national-campaign-against-myanmars-muslims

38 Beech, H. (2013), 'When Buddhists go bad'. *Time*, 181 (1): 14–21.

39 Wade, F. (2017), *Myanmar's Enemy Within: Buddhist Violence and the Making of a Muslim 'Other'*. London: Zed Books.

40 Human Rights Watch (2012), 'The Government Could Have Stopped This'. Available online www.hrw.org/reports/2012/07/31/government-could-have-stopped

41 Ibid, 18.

42 Wade, F. (2017).

43 Lee, R. and González Zarandona, J.A. (2020), 'Heritage destruction in Myanmar's Rakhine state: legal and illegal iconoclasm', *International Journal of Heritage Studies*, 26 (5): 519–538.

44 Republic of the Union of Myanmar (2013), *Final Report of Inquiry Commission on Sectarian Violence in Rakhine State*. Yangon: Republic of the Union of Myanmar.

45 Wade, F. (2017).

46 Human Rights Watch (2013), '"All You Can Do Is Pray": Crimes Against Humanity and Ethnic Cleansing of Rohingya Muslims in Burma's Arakan State'. Available online www.hrw.org/sites/default/files/reports/burma0413webwcover_0.pdf

47 UN Office for the Coordination of Humanitarian Affairs (2017), '2018 Interim Humanitarian Response Plan for Myanmar'. Available online https://reliefweb.int/report/myanmar/2018-interim-humanitarian-response-plan-myanmar

48 Lowry, D. (1976), 'Internment: Detention Without Trial in Northern Ireland'. *Human Rights*, 5 (3): 261–331.

49 Lee, R. (2019), 'Myanmar's Citizenship Law as State Crime: A Case for the International Criminal Court'. *State Crime Journal,* 8 (2): 241–279.

50 Stone, D. (2017), *Concentration Camps: A Short History*. Oxford: Oxford University Press, 4.

51 Pitzer, A. (2017), *One Long Night: A Global History of Concentration Camps*. New York: Little, Brown and Company, 362.

52 Bookbinder, A. (2014), 'Mandalay riots reveal splintered community, complex agendas'. *Democratic Voice of Burma*, 8 July. Available online www.dvb.no/news/mandalay-riots-reveal-splintered-community-complex-agendas-burma-myanmar/42144

53 Miles, T. (2018), 'U.N. investigators cite Facebook role in Myanmar crisis'. *Reuters*, 12 March. Available online https://uk.reuters.com/article/us-myanmar-rohingya-facebook/u-n-investigators-cite-facebook-role-in-myanmar-crisis-idUKKCN1GO2PN

54 Reuters (2018), 'Myanmar: UN blames Facebook for spreading hatred of Rohingya'. *The Guardian*, 13 March. Available online www.theguardian.com/technology/2018/mar/13/myanmar-un-blames-facebook-for-spreading-hatred-of-rohingya

55 Hatmaker, T. (2018), 'In Senate hearing, Zuckerberg faces blame over violence in Myanmar'. *Washington Post*, 10 April. Available online www.washingtonpost.com/news/the-switch/wp/2018/04/10/transcript-of-mark-zuckerbergs-senate-hearing/?noredirect=on

56 United States Department of State (2015), Trafficking in Persons Report. Available online https://2009-2017.state.gov/j/tip/rls/tiprpt/2015//index.htm

57 Lee, R. (2015), 'Between the Devil and the Deep Blue Sea: The Rohingya's Dilemma'. *The Conversation*, 2 June. Available online https://theconversation.com/between-the-deviland-the-deep-blue-sea-the-rohingyas-dilemma-42359

58 International Crisis Group (2016), 'Myanmar: A New Muslim Insurgency in Rakhine State'. Available online www.crisisgroup.org/asia/south-east-asia/myanmar/283-myanmar-new-muslim-insurgency-rakhine-state, ii.

59 Green, P., MacManus, T. and de la Cour Venning, A. (2015), *Countdown to Annihilation: Genocide in Myanmar*. London: International State Crime Initiative.

60 Ibrahim, A. (2018), *The Rohingyas: Inside Myanmar's Hidden Genocide*. London: Hurst, 1.

61 Zarni, M. and Cowley, A. (2014), 'The Slow-Burning Genocide of Myanmar's Rohingya'. *Pacific Rim Law & Policy Journal Association*. 23 (3): 683–754.

62 Fortify Rights (2015), 'Persecution of the Rohingya Muslims: is genocide occurring in Myanmar's Rakhine State? A legal analysis'. Available online www.fortifyrights. org/downloads/Yale_Persecution_of_the_Rohingya_October_2015.pdf, 3

63 Feierstein, D. (2014), *Genocide as Social Practice: Reorganising Society under the Nazis and Argentina's Military Juntas*. New Brunswick: Rutgers University Press.

64 Green, P., *et al.*, 15.

65 Ibid., 16.

66 Card, C. (2003), 'Genocide and Social Death', *Hypatia*, 18 (1): 63–79.

67 Green, P., *et al.*, 16.

68 Amnesty International (2017a).

69 Fortify Rights (2015).

70 Human Rights Watch (2012).

71 Médecins Sans Frontières-Holland (2002), '10 Years for the Rohingya Refugees in Bangladesh: Past, Present and Future'. Available online www.rna-press.com/data/item files/5ae98e43d068cb749b3060b002601b95.pdf

72 Physicians for Human Rights (2016), 'Where There is Police, There is Persecution – Government Security Forces and Human Rights Abuses in Myanmar's Northern Rakhine State'. Available online https://s3.amazonaws.com/PHR_Reports/Burma-Rakhine-State-Oct-2016.pdf

73 de la Cour Venning, A. (2017). 'Rohingya crisis: this is what genocide looks like'. *The Conversation*, 15 September. Available online https://theconversation.com/rohingya-crisis-this-is-what-genocide-looks-like-83924

74 UN Human Rights Council (2018), 'Myanmar: UN Fact-Finding Mission releases its full account of massive violations by military in Rakhine, Kachin and Shan States'. Available online www.ohchr.org/EN/HRBodies/HRC/Pages/NewsDetail. aspx?NewsID=23575&LangID=E

75 Ibid.

76 Dallaire, R. (2004), *Shake Hands With The Devil: The Failure of Humanity in Rwanda*. London: Arrow Books.

77 UN General Assembly (1948), 'Convention on the Prevention and Punishment of the Crime of Genocide'. Available online www.un.org/en/genocideprevention/genocide-convention.shtml

78 Power, S. (2002), *A Problem from Hell: America and the Age of Genocide*. New York: Basic Books.

79 Carroll, R. (2004), 'US chose to ignore Rwanda genocide'. *The Guardian*, 31 March. Available online www.theguardian.com/world/2004/mar/31/usa.rwanda

80 The Economist (2018), 'Can the world stop genocide?'. Available online www.economist.com/international/2018/12/08/can-the-world-stop-genocide

81 UK Parliament (2020), Genocide Determination Bill [HL] 2019–21. Available online https://services.parliament.uk/bills/2019-21/genocidedeterminationbill.html

82 International Court of Justice (2020), 'Application of the Convention on the Prevention and Punishment of the Crime of Genocide (The Gambia v. Myanmar)'. Available online www.icj-cij.org/en/case/178

83 Kean, T. and Aung Kyaw Min (2015), 'President backtracks on white cards'. *Myanmar Times*, 13 February. Available online www.mmtimes.com/national-news/13106-president-backtracks-on-white-cards.html

84 Bookbinder, A. (2015), 'U Shwe Maung, former USDP MP: "This is illogical and ridiculous"'. Frontier Myanmar, 31 August. Available online www.frontiermyanmar.net/en/u-shwe-maung-former-usdp-mp-this-is-illogical-and-ridiculous

85 Fuller, T. (2015), 'Myanmar Striking Rohingya From Voter Rolls, Activists Say'. *New York Times*, 23 August. Available online www.nytimes.com/2015/08/24/world/asia/myanmar-lawmaker-u-shwe-maung-barred-from-re-election-on-citizenship-grounds.html

86 Election Observation and Democracy Support (2015), 'EU EOM Myanmar General Elections 2015 Final Report'. Available online www.eods.eu/library/myanmar_final_report_en.pdf

87 Vogt, R.J. (2015), 'UEC puts election turnout at 69 per cent'. *Myanmar Times*, 3 December. Available online www.mmtimes.com/index.php/national-news/nay-pyi-taw/17948-uec-puts-election-turnout-at-69-percent.html

88 UN General Assembly (2015), 'Situation of human rights in Myanmar'. Available online https://documents-dds-ny.un.org/doc/UNDOC/GEN/N15/301/10/PDF/N1530110.pdf?OpenElement

89 Veash, N. (1999), 'Husband of Nobel heroine dies after "no" to reunion'. *The Observer*, 28 March. Available online www.theguardian.com/uk/1999/mar/28/theobserver.uknews6

90 Yunus, M. (2016), 'Open Letter to the President of the Security Council and Member Countries of the Council to End the Human Crisis of the Rohingyas in Myanmar'. Available online www.facebook.com/Professor.Muhammad.Yunus/posts/996372943802283:0

91   UN Human Rights Council (2018), 'Myanmar: Tatmadaw leaders must be investigated for genocide, crimes against humanity, war crimes – UN report'. Available online www.ohchr.org/EN/NewsEvents/Pages/DisplayNews. aspx?NewsID=23475&LangID=E

92   Ibid.

93   Al Jazeera (2017), 'Aung San Suu Kyi's speech, analysed'. *Al Jazeera*, 19 September. Available online www.dailymotion.com/video/x61aud9; Lee, R. (2014), 'A Politician, Not an Icon: Aung San Suu Kyi's Silence on Myanmar's Muslim Rohingya', *Islam and Christian–Muslim Relations,* 25 (3): 321–333.

94   Holmes, O. (2017), 'Fact check: Aung San Suu Kyi's speech on the Rohingya crisis'. *The Guardian*, 20 September. Available online www.theguardian.com/world/2017/sep/20/fact-check-aung-san-suu-kyi-rohingya-crisis-speech-myanmar

95   BBC (2017), 'Rohingya crisis: Suu Kyi speech criticised by global leaders'. *BBC News*, 20 September. Available online www.bbc.co.uk/news/world-asia-41329662

96   Ebbighausen, R. (2012), 'Aung San Suu Kyi's Sacrifice for Politics'. *DW*, 9 November. Available online www.dw.com/en/aung-san-suu-kyis-sacrifice-for-politics/a-16369029

97   Fisher, J. (2017), 'Hounded and ridiculed for complaining of rape'. *BBC News*, 17 March. Available online www.bbc.co.uk/news/magazine-39204086

98   Burma Campaign UK (2019), 'Rape and Sexual Violence Reports'. Available online https://burmacampaign.org.uk/reports-category/all-news/rape-and-sexual-violence

99   Yunus, M. (2016).

100 MacCharles, T. (2018), 'Canada revokes honorary citizenship for Aung San Suu Kyi'. *The Star*, 27 September. Available online www.thestar.com/news/canada/2018/09/27/canada-revokes-honorary-citizenship-for-aung-san-suu-kyi.html; Reuters (2017), 'City of Oxford strips Aung San Suu Kyi of human rights award'. *Reuters*, 4 October. Available online https://uk.reuters.com/article/uk-myanmar-rohingya-britain/city-of-oxford-strips-aung-san-suu-kyi-of-human-rights-award-idUKKCN1C91ZW; Sheffield City Council (2017), 'Agenda item, Notice of Motion Regarding "The Removal of the Freedom of the City Awarded to Aung San Suu Kyi"'. *Sheffield City Council,* 1 November. Available online http://democracy.sheffield.gov.uk/mgAi.aspx?ID=15897

101 Linehan, H. (2017), 'Geldof returns Freedom of Dublin in protest at "killer" Suu Kyi'. *Irish Times*, 12 November. Available online www.irishtimes.com/news/ireland/irish-news/geldof-returns-freedom-of-dublin-in-protest-at-killer-suu-kyi-1.3289438

102 Amnesty International (2018a), 'Amnesty International withdraws human rights award from Aung San Suu Kyi'. Available online www.amnesty.org/en/latest/news/2018/11/amnesty-withdraws-award-from-aung-san-suu-kyi

103 US Holocaust Memorial Museum (2018), 'Museum Rescinds Award to Daw Aung San Suu Kyi'. Available online www.ushmm.org/information/press/press-releases/museum-rescinds-award-to-daw-aung-san-suu-kyi

104 People's Alliance for Credible Elections (2019), 'Citizens' Political Preferences for 2020'. Available online www.pacemyanmar.org/2019-survey

105 Amnesty International (1997), 'Myanmar/Bangladesh Rohingyas – The Search for Safety'. Available online www.amnesty.org/en/documents/asa13/007/1997/en; Amnesty International (2004), 'Myanmar The Rohingya Minority: Fundamental Rights Denied'. Available online www.amnesty.org/en/documents/ASA16/005/2004/en; Amnesty International (2016), 'Bangladesh pushes back Rohingya refugees amid collective punishment in Myanmar'. Available online www.amnesty.org/en/latest/news/2016/11/bangladesh-pushes-back-rohingya-refugees-amid-collective-punishment-in-myanmar; Amnesty International (2017a); Human Rights Watch (1996), 'The Rohingya Muslims: Ending a Cycle of Exodus?' Available online www.hrw.org/legacy/summaries/s.burma969.html; Human Rights Watch (2000), 'Burmese Refugees in Bangladesh: Still No Durable Solution'. Available online www.hrw.org/reports/2000/burma/index.htm; Human Rights Watch (2002), 'Crackdown on Burmese Muslims'. Available online www.hrw.org/legacy/backgrounder/asia/burmese_muslims.pdf; Human Rights Watch (2009), 'Perilous Plight: Burma's Rohingya Take to the Seas'. Available online www.hrw.org/report/2009/05/26/perilous-plight/burmas-rohingya-take-seas; Human Rights Watch (2012), 'The Government Could Have Stopped This'. Available online www.hrw.org/reports/2012/07/31/government-could-have-stopped; Human Rights Watch (2013), '"All You Can Do Is Pray": Crimes Against Humanity and Ethnic Cleansing of Rohingya Muslims in Burma's Arakan State'. Available online www.hrw.org/sites/default/files/reports/burma0413webwcover_0.pdf; Physicians for Human Rights (2013), 'Patterns of Anti-Muslim Violence in Burma: A Call for Accountability and Prevention'. Available online https://physiciansforhumanrights.org/library/reports/patterns-of-anti-muslim-violence-in-burma.html; Physicians for Human Rights (2016), 'Where There is Police, There is Persecution – Government Security Forces and Human Rights Abuses in Myanmar's Northern Rakhine State'. Available online https://s3.amazonaws.com/PHR_Reports/Burma-Rakhine-State-Oct-2016.pdf; Refugees International (2014), 'Myanmar: A Tipping Point for Rohingya Rights'. Available online www.refugeesinternational.org/reports/2015/10/4/myanmar-a-tipping-point-for-rohingya-rights

106 Amnesty International (2016), 'Bangladesh pushes back Rohingya refugees amid collective punishment in Myanmar'. Available online www.amnesty.org/en/latest/news/2016/11/bangladesh-pushes-back-rohingya-refugees-amid-collective-punishment-in-myanmar, 7, 9.

107 Human Rights Watch (2013), 11.

108 International Crisis Group (2016), 'Myanmar: A New Muslim Insurgency in Rakhine State'. Available online www.crisisgroup.org/asia/south-east-asia/myanmar/283-myanmar-new-muslim-insurgency-rakhine-state

109 ARSA. (2019), 'It is, once again, reassured that #ARSA only legitimately and objectively operates as an #ETHNO-NATIONALIST movement within its ancestral homeland (Arakan) in #Burma & its activities had not & will not transcend beyond its country'. [Twitter post, 13 July]. Available online https://twitter.com/ARSA_Official/media

110 Arakan Rohingya Salvation Army (2019), 'Reviving the Courageous Hearts'. Available online https://issuu.com/arsapublisher/docs/report_1_final_2, 45.

111 Ibid., 45.

112 Nyein Nyein (2017), 'Muslims "Refuse to Accept" ARSA'. *The Irrawaddy*, 8 September. Available online www.irrawaddy.com/news/muslims-refuse-accept-arsa.html

113 The Economist (2018), 'Press freedom is waning in Myanmar'. *The Economist*, 8 March. Available online www.economist.com/news/asia/21738413-no-law-too-obscure-tool-silence-awkward-journalists-press-freedom-waning-myanmar

114 Article 19 (2018), 'Myanmar: Pattern of attacks on press freedom must end'. Available online www.article19.org/resources/myanmar-pattern-attacks-press-freedom-must-end

115 Shoon Naing and Aye Min Thant (2018), 'Myanmar court jails Reuters reporters for seven years in landmark secrets case'. *Reuters*, 3 September. Available online https://uk.reuters.com/article/uk-myanmar-journalists/myanmar-court-jails-reuters-reporters-for-seven-years-in-landmark-secrets-case-idUKKCN1LJ09D

116 AFP (2018), 'Myanmar security forces took part in killing 10 Rohingya: Army'. *The Straits Times*, 10 January. Available online www.straitstimes.com/asia/se-asia/myanmar-security-forces-took-part-in-killing-10-rohingya-army

117 Shoon Naing and Thu Thu Aung (2018), 'Seven Myanmar soldiers sentenced to 10 years for Rohingya massacre'. *Reuters*, 10 April. Available online www.reuters.com/article/us-myanmar-rohingya-military/seven-myanmar-soldiers-sentenced-to-10-years-for-rohingya-massacre-idUSKBN1HH2ZS

118 Wa Lone, Kyaw Soe Oo, Lewis, S. and Slodkowski, A. (2018), 'Massacre in Myanmar'. *Reuters*, 8 February. www.reuters.com/investigates/special-report/myanmar-rakhine-events/

119 Pulitzer Prizes (2019), 'Staff of Reuters, with notable contributions from Wa Lone and Kyaw Soe Oo'. Available online www.pulitzer.org/winners/staff-reuters-notable-contributions-wa-lone-and-kyaw-soe-oo

120 Paddock, R. and Wong, E. (2019). 'Who Was Most Opposed to Freeing 2 Reporters in Myanmar? Aung San Suu Kyi'. *New York Times*, 10 May. Available online www.nytimes.com/2019/05/10/world/asia/myanmar-reuters-aung-san-suu-kyi.html

121 UN News (2019), 'Release of prize-winning Reuters journalists in Myanmar welcomed by UN'. *UN News*, 7 May. https://news.un.org/en/story/2019/05/1038011

122 Stoakes, E. (2017), 'UN influence in Myanmar at a low after Aung San Suu Kyi cold shoulders envoys'. *The Guardian*, 18 July. Available online www.theguardian.com/ global-development/2017/jul/18/un-influence-myanmar-at-low-aung-san-suu-kyi-cold-shoulders-envoys

123 McPherson, P. (2017), 'Inside the "glaringly dysfunctional" UN mission in Myanmar'. *The New Humanitarian*, 17 July. Available online www. thenewhumanitarian.org/investigations/2017/07/17/inside-glaringly-dysfunctional-un-mission-myanmar

124 Adams, B. (2015), 'Dispatches: UN Falls Short in Helping Burma's Rohingya'. Available online www.hrw.org/news/2015/06/01/dispatches-un-falls-short-helping-burmas-rohingya; Lynch, C. (2017), 'For Years, U.N. Was Warned of Threat to Rohingya in Myanmar'. *Foreign Policy*, 16 October. Available online http:// foreignpolicy.com/2017/10/16/for-years-u-n-was-warned-of-threat-to-rohingya-in-myanmar; Stoakes, E. (2016), 'Leaked Documents Show How the UN Failed to Protect Myanmar's Persecuted Rohingya'. *Vice News*, 22 May. Available online https://news.vice.com/article/how-the-un-failed-to-protect-myanmars-persecuted-rohingya

125 Amnesty International (2017a).

126 Adams (2015); Amnesty International (2017a); Amnesty International (2018b), 'Myanmar's apartheid campaign against the Rohingya'. Available online www. amnesty.org.uk/myanmar-apartheid-campaign-against-rohingya-burma

127 World Bank (2016), 'World Data Bank: World Development Indicators'. Available online http://databank.worldbank.org/data/reports.aspx?source=2&country=MMR

128 Center for Diversity and National Harmony (2015), 'Rakhine State Needs Assessment'. Available online www.cdnh.org/publication/rakhine-state-needs-assessment; MacGregor, F. (2013), 'Economic focus for Rakhine relief'. *Myanmar Times*, 22 September. Available online www.mmtimes.com/business/8212-economic-focus-for-rakhine-relief.html

129 UN Human Rights Council (2018), 'Myanmar: UN Fact-Finding Mission releases its full account of massive violations by military in Rakhine, Kachin and Shan States'. Available online www.ohchr.org/EN/NewsEvents/Pages/DisplayNews. aspx?NewsID=23575

130 UN Security Council (2018), '8381st meeting'. Available online: www. securitycouncilreport.org/atf/cf/%7B65BFCF9B-6D27-4E9C-8CD3-CF6E4FF96FF9%7D/s_pv_8381_resumption_1.pdf, 4.

131 Ibid., 5.

132 Ibid., 27.

133 Nichols, M. (2018), 'China fails to stop U.N. Security council Myanmar briefing'. *Reuters*, 24 October. Available online www.reuters.com/article/us-myanmar-rohingya-un/china-fails-to-stop-un-security-council-myanmar-briefing-idUSKCN1MY2QU

134 UN Human Rights Council (2018), 'Independent Investigative Mechanism for Myanmar'. Available online www.ohchr.org/EN/HRBodies/HRC/IIMM/Pages/Index.aspx

135 International Criminal Court (2019), 'Ms Fatou Bensouda'. Available online www.icc-cpi.int/about/otp/who-s-who/pages/fatou-bensouda.aspx

136 UN Population Fund (2017), 'Horrific stories, urgent action: Addressing gender-based violence amid the Rohingya refugee crisis'. Available online https://asiapacific.unfpa.org/en/news/addressing-gender-based-violence-amid-rohingya-refugee-crisis-horrific-stories-urgent-action-0

137 International Criminal Court (2019), 'The States Parties to the Rome Statute'. Available online https://asp.icc-cpi.int/en_menus/asp/states%20parties/pages/the%20states%20parties%20to%20the%20rome%20statute.aspx

138 International Criminal Court (2019), 'Bangladesh'. Available online https://asp.icc-cpi.int/en_menus/asp/states%20parties/asian%20states/Pages/bangladesh.aspx

139 Safi, M. (2018), 'ICC says it can prosecute Myanmar for alleged Rohingya crimes'. *The Guardian,* 6 September. Available online www.theguardian.com/world/2018/sep/06/icc-says-it-can-prosecute-myanmar-for-alleged-rohingya-crimes

140 International Criminal Court (2019), 'ICC Prosecutor, Fatou Bensouda, requests judicial authorisation to commence an investigation into the situation in Bangladesh/Myanmar'. Available online www.icc-cpi.int/Pages/item.aspx?name=pr1465

141 International Criminal Court (2018), 'Statement of ICC Prosecutor, Fatou Bensouda, on opening a Preliminary Examination concerning the alleged deportation of the Rohingya people from Myanmar to Bangladesh'. Available online www.icc-cpi.int/Pages/item.aspx?name=180918-otp-stat-Rohingya

Chapter 5

1 Nyan Hlaing Lynn (2018), 'Rakhine political leader Dr Aye Maung arrested in Sittwe after Mrauk U violence'. *Frontier Myanmar*, 18 January. Available online https://frontiermyanmar.net/en/rakhine-political-leader-dr-aye-maung-arrested-in-sittwe-after-mrauk-u-violence

2 Min Aung Khine (2018), 'Trial of Mrauk-U Riot Suspects Opens in Special Jailhouse "Court"'. *The Irrawaddy*, 21 February. Available online www.irrawaddy.com/news/trial-mrauk-u-riot-suspects-opens-special-jailhouse-court.html

3　Ye Mon (2019), 'Aye Maung, Wai Hin Aung handed 20-year sentences for high treason'. *Frontier Myanmar*, 19 March. Available online https://frontiermyanmar.net/en/aye-maung-wai-hin-aung-handed-20-year-sentences-for-high-treason

4　Kaladan Press Network (2007), 'A Short History of Rohingya and Kamas of Burma'. *Kaladan Press Network*, 13 September. Available online www.kaladanprcss.org/index.php/scholar-column-mainmenu-36/arakan/872-a-short-history-of-rohingya-and-kamas-of-burma.html

5　Tahir Ba Tha (2007), 'A Short History of Rohingya and Kamans of Burma', (A.F.K. Jilani, trans.). *Kaladan Press Network*, 13 September. Available online www.kaladanpress.org/index.php/scholar-column-mainmenu-36/arakan/872-a-short-history-of-rohingya-and-kamas-of-burma.html

6　Yunus, M. (1994), *A History of Arakan (Past & Present)*. Chittagong: Magenta Colour.

7　Sloane Collection (1728), 'Trading Permit in Persian'. British Museum Sloane Collection, 3259.

8　East India Company (1783), 'Translation of letter from the Rajah of Aracan to Warren Hastings, Governor-General'. India Office Records and Private Papers Add MS 26583, 101.

9　Bahar, A. (2010), *Burma's Missing Dots: The Emerging Face of Genocide*. Bloomington: Xlibris; Islam, N. (2006), 'Facts About the Rohingya Muslims of Arakan'. *ARNO*, 5 October. Available online www.rohingya.org/portal/index.php/learn-about-rohingya.html; Islam, N. (2012), 'Muslim influence in the kingdom of Arakan'. *ARNO*, 13 January. Available online www.rohingya.org/portal/index.php/scholars/65-nurul-islam-uk/293-muslim-influence-in-the-kingdom-of-arakan.html; Htay Lwin Oo (2013), 'Mr Htay Lwin Oo Speech in ANU on Rohingya History'. *BRC Australia*, 17 March. Available online www.youtube.com/watch?v=jE-JV4d1cx8; Siddiqui, H. (2008), *The Forgotten Rohingya: Their Struggle for Human Rights in Burma*. (n.p.): Author.

10　Bahar, A. (2010); Htay Lwin Oo (2013).

11　Ibrahim, A. (2018), *The Rohingyas: Inside Myanmar's Hidden Genocide*. London: Hurst; Zarni, M. and Cowley, A. (2014), 'The Slow-Burning Genocide of Myanmar's Rohingya'. *Pacific Rim Law & Policy Journal Association*, 23 (3): 683–754.

12　Bahar, A. (2012); Siddiqui, H. (2011), *Muslim Identity and Demography in the Arakan State of Burma*. (n.p.): Author; Islam, N. (2012).

13　Paton, C. (1826), *A Short Report on Arakan*. London: Colonial Office.

14　Government of India (2013) Census of India Website. Available online www.censusindia.gov.in/DigitalLibrary/Browse_Presentation.aspx

15　Leider, J. (2014), 'Rohingya. The name. The movement. The quest for identity'. Available online www.burmalibrary.org/docs21/Jacques-P-Leider-2014-01-28-Rohingya-The_Name-The_movement-The_quest_for_identity-en.pdf; Leider, J. (2017), 'Transmutations of the Rohingya Movement in the Post-2012 Rakhine State

Crisis', in Ooi Keat Gin and V. Grabowsky (eds), *Ethnic and Religious Identities and Integration in Southeast Asia*. Bangkok: Silkworm Books and EFEO, 191–239; Ware, A. and Laoutides, C. (2018), Myanmar's 'Rohingya' Conflict. London: Hurst.

16 Gunasekanan, S. and Mya Than (1988), 'Population Change in Burma: A Comparison of the 1973 and 1983 Censuses'. *Sojourn*, 3 (2): 171–186.

17 Radio Free Asia (2012), 'Call to Put Rohingya in Refugee Camps'. *Radio Free Asia*, 12 July. Available online www.rfa.org/english/news/rohingya-07122012185242.html

18 Ibid.

19 Ibid.

20 Aye Chan (2005), 'The Development of a Muslim Enclave in Arakan (Rakhine) State of Burma (Myanmar)'. *SOAS Bulletin of Burma Research*, 3 (2): 396–420; Maung Tha Hla (2004), *The Rakhaing*. New York: Buddhist Rakhaing Cultural Association.

21 Bengali, S. (2017), 'Myanmar's long-suffering Rohingya Muslims hoped that Aung San Suu Kyi would make them full citizens. They were wrong'. *Los Angeles Times*, 9 April. Available online www.latimes.com/world/la-fg-myanmar-rohingya-2017-story.html; Wallace, J. (2016), 'Myanmar casts minorities to the margins as citizenship law denies legal identity'. *The Guardian*, 3 November. Available online www.theguardian.com/global-development/2016/nov/03/myanmar-casts-minorities-to-margins-citizenship-law-denies-legal-identity

22 Burma Citizenship Act (1982), Section 8(b).

23 UNHCR (2018), 'UNHCR and UNDP agree on text of MoU with Myanmar to support the creation of conditions for the return of Rohingya refugees'. Available online www.unhcr.org/news/press/2018/5/5b0fff7b4/unhcr-undp-agree-text-mou-myanmar-support-creation-conditions-return-rohingya.html

Chapter 6

1   Schug, A. (2019), Personal Communication, July 21.

2   United Nations (1992), 'Declaration on the Rights of Persons Belonging to National or Ethnic, Religious and Linguistic Minorities'. Available online www.ohchr.org/EN/ProfessionalInterest/Pages/Minorities.aspx, Article 2, Section 1.

3   Ei Ei Toe Lwin (2015), 'Election Commission rejects Muslim candidates en masse'. *Myanmar Times*, 1 September. Available online www.mmtimes.com/national-news/16240-election-commission-rejects-muslim-candidates-en-masse.html; Enlightened Myanmar Research (2015), *Important Data of 2015 General Election Myanmar*. Yangon: Enlightened Myanmar Research; Hein Ko Soe (2015), 'Democracy and Human Rights Party expels 1,000 white card holders'. *Mizzima*, 19 February. Available online www.mizzima.com/news-domestic/democracy-and-human-rights-party-expels-1000-white-card-holders

4   Clements, A. (2008), *The Voice of Hope: Aung San Suu Kyi*. London: Rider Books; Popham, P. (2011), *The Lady and the Peacock: The Life of Aung San Suu Kyi*. London: Rider Books.

5   Colombage, D, (2014). 'Buddhist monk to fight "jihad threat"'. *Al Jazeera*, 28 September. Available online www.aljazeera.com/news/southasia/2014/09/buddhist-monk-fight-jihad-threat-asia-2014928153512953861.html

6   Wa Lone and Lewis, S. (2017), 'Myanmar plays diplomatic card to avert U.N. censure over Rohingya'. *Reuters*, 6 September. Available online https://uk.reuters.com/article/uk-myanmar-rohingya/myanmar-plays-diplomatic-card-to-avert-u-n-censure-over-rohingya-idUKKCN1BH0HJ

7   Al Jazeera (2012), 'Ending Myanmar's Civil War'. *Al Jazeera*, 13 February. Available online www.aljazeera.com/indepth/opinion/2012/02/20122494825985895.html; Campbell, C. (2013), 'Is the World's Longest-Running Civil War About to End?' *Time*, 6 November. Available online http://world.time.com/2013/11/06/is-the-worlds-longest-running-civil-war-about-to-end

8   ARNO (2018), 'Who we are?'. Available online www.rohingya.org/~rohingya/portal/index.php/who-we-are.html; EdithMirante (2018), '1. This History Thread is background on the small-scale Rohingya armed resistance pre-2016. Rohingyas also resisted oppression by Burma (Myanmar) govt/military in nonviolent ways incl. information gathering, legal/political representation and lobbying for human rights support'. [Twitter post, June 21]. Available online https://twitter.com/EdithMirante/status/1009698604162793472

9   Colombage, D. (2014); Oppenheim, M. (2017), '"It only takes one terrorist": the Buddhist monk who reviles Myanmar's Muslims'. *The Guardian*, 12 May. Available online www.theguardian.com/global-development/2017/may/12/only-takes-one-terrorist-buddhist-monk-reviles-myanmar-muslims-rohingya-refugees-ashin-wirathu; Pyae Thet Phyo. (2017), 'MP wants to use label "Bengali terrorists" in Rakhine'. *Myanmar Times*, 17 August. Available online www.mmtimes.com/national-news/nay-pyi-taw/27303-mp-wants-to-use-label-bengali-terrorists-in-rakhine.html

10 ARSA Official. (2017), '#ARSA Denies Attacks on Burmese-speaking strangers at #GyunPaukPyoSuu in #Maungdaw North on Jun24, Blames on military for Inciting Violence'. [Twitter post, 29 June]. Available online https://twitter.com/ARSA_Official/media

11 Khin Maung Saw (2011), 'Islamization of Burma Through Chittagonian Bengalis as "Rohingya Refugees"'. *Burma Library*, 11 September. Available online www.burmalibrary.org/docs21/Khin-Maung-Saw-NM-2011-09-Islamanisation_of_Burma_through_Chittagonian_Bengalis-en.pdf

12 Barron, L. (2017). 'Rohingya and the "Paper Tiger" Insurgency. *The Diplomat*, 1 June. Retrieved from https://thediplomat.com/2017/06/rohingya-and-the-paper-tiger-insurgency/

13 Frontier Myanmar (2018), 'U Ko Ko Gyi: "What is important is how policies impact people's daily lives"'. *Frontier Myanmar*, 23 January. Available online https://frontiermyanmar.net/en/u-ko-ko-gyi-what-is-important-is-how-policies-impact-peoples-daily-lives

14 Solomon, F. (2016), 'Nine Police Have Been Killed in Border Post Attacks in Western Burma'. *Time*, 10 October. Available online http://time.com/4524441/burma-myanmar-border-attacks-rakhine-rohingya

Chapter 7

1 Amnesty International (2016), 'Bangladesh pushes back Rohingya refugees amid collective punishment in Myanmar'. Available online www.amnesty.org/en/latest/news/2016/11/bangladesh-pushes-back-rohingya-refugees-amid-collective-punishment-in-myanmar

2 BBC (2016), 'Myanmar wants ethnic cleansing of Rohingya – UN official'. *BBC News*, 24 November. Available online www.bbc.com/news/world-asia-38091816

3 Lewis, S., Siddiqui, Z., Baldwin, C. and Marshall, A. (2018), 'Tip of the Spear'. *Reuters*, 26 June. Available online www.reuters.com/investigates/special-report/myanmar-rohingya-battalions

4 ARSA Official. (2017). 'Urgent Statement: #Arakan State Situation We are defending against the #Burmese colonizing forces. Check out the attached file. #Rohingya'. [Twitter post, 25 August]. Available online https://twitter.com/ARSA_Official

5 Inter Sector Coordination Group (2017), 'ISCG Situation Update: Rohingya Refugee Crisis, Cox's Bazar, 26 December 2017'. Available online https://reliefweb.int/report/bangladesh/iscg-situation-update-rohingya-refugee-crisis-cox-s-bazar-26-december-2017

6 Human Rights Watch (2017b), 'Burma: New Satellite Images Confirm Mass Destruction'. Available online www.hrw.org/news/2017/10/17/burma-new-satellite-images-confirm-mass-destruction

7 Human Rights Watch (2017a), 'Burma: Military Commits Crimes Against Humanity'. Available online www.hrw.org/news/2017/09/25/burma-military-commits-crimes-against-humanity

8 Amnesty International (2017b), 'Myanmar: Crimes against humanity terrorize and drive Rohingya out'. Available online www.amnesty.org/en/latest/news/2017/10/myanmar-new-evidence-of-systematic-campaign-to-terrorize-and-drive-rohingya-out

9 UN News (2017), 'UN human rights chief points to "textbook example of ethnic cleansing" in Myanmar'. *UN News*, 11 September. Available online https://news.un.org/en/story/2017/09/564622-un-human-rights-chief-points-textbook-example-ethnic-cleansing-myanmar

10 Al Jazeera (2017), 'UN Security Council to discuss Rohingya situation'. *Al Jazeera*, 12 September. Available online www.aljazeera.com/news/2017/09/security-council-discuss-rohingya-situation-170912083144394.html

11 UN Human Rights Council (2018), 'Myanmar: UN Fact-Finding Mission releases its full account of massive violations by military in Rakhine, Kachin and Shan States'. Available online www.ohchr.org/EN/NewsEvents/Pages/DisplayNews.aspx?NewsID=23575

12 Ethnic National Council of Burma (n.d.), Panglong Agreement (1947). Available online https://peacemaker.un.org/sites/peacemaker.un.org/files/MM_470212_Panglong%20Agreement.pdf

13 Smith, M. (2006), 'The Muslim Rohingya of Burma'. *Kaladan Press Network*, 11 October. Available online www.kaladanpress.org/index.php/scholar-column-mainmenu-36/36-rohingya/194-the-muslim-rohingya-of-burma.html

14 Smith, M. and Allsebrook, A. (1994), *Ethnic Groups in Burma: Development, Democracy and Human Rights*. London: Anti-Slavery International, 56.

15 Selth, A. (2005), *Burma's Muslims: Terrorists or Terrorised?* Canberra: Strategic and Defence Studies Centre.

16 International Crisis Group (2016), 'Myanmar: A New Muslim Insurgency in Rakhine State'. Available online www.crisisgroup.org/asia/south-east-asia/myanmar/283-myanmar-new-muslim-insurgency-rakhine-state

17 Development Media Group (2020), 'AA says nearly 700 clashes with Tatmadaw in 2019'. *BNI Multimedia Group*, 7 January. Available online www.bnionline.net/en/news/aa-says-nearly-700-clashes-tatmadaw-2019

18 ARSA (2019), 'Reviving the Courageous Hearts: A Report by Arakan Rohingya Salvation Army', 5.

19 Ibid.

20 Amnesty International (2018c), 'Myanmar: New evidence reveals Rohingya armed group massacred scores in Rakhine State'. Available online www.amnesty.org/en/latest/news/2018/05/myanmar-new-evidence-reveals-rohingya-armed-group-massacred-scores-in-rakhine-state

21 The Irrawaddy (2018), 'Kofi Annan's Contribution to Myanmar's Pressing Rakhine Crisis'. *The Irrawaddy*, 21 August. Available online www.irrawaddy.com/news/burma/kofi-annans-contribution-to-myanmars-pressing-rakhine-crisis.html

22 Kofi Annan Foundation (2016), Towards a Peaceful, Fair and Prosperous Future for the People of Rakhine: FINAL REPORT OF THE ADVISORY COMMISSION ON RAKHINE STATE. Available online www.rakhinecommission.org/the-final-report

23 BBC (2016) 'Myanmar policemen killed in Rakhine border attack', *BBC News*, 13 June. Available online www.bbc.co.uk/news/world-asia-37601928

24 Republic of the Union of Myanmar (2017), 'Arakan Rohingya Salvation Army (ARSA) Declared as Terrorist Group', *The Global New Light of Myanmar*, 28 August.

Available online www.globalnewlightofmyanmar.com/arakan-rohingya-salvation-army-arsa-declared-as-terroristgroup/

25 ARSA Official. (2019), '#CLARIFICATION: It is, once again, reassured that #ARSA only legitimately and objectively operates as an #ETHNO-NATIONALIST movement within its ancestral homeland (Arakan) in #Burma & its activities had not & will not transcend beyond its country.' [Twitter post, 13 July]. Available online https://twitter.com/ARSA_Official

26 International Crisis Group (2016), 'Myanmar: A New Muslim Insurgency in Rakhine State'. Available online www.crisisgroup.org/asia/south-east-asia/myanmar/283-myanmar-new-muslim-insurgency-rakhine-state

27 Ye Mon, Eaint Thet Su and Durant, B. (2020), 'No exit: Rohingya jailed en masse for escaping Rakhine'. *Frontier Myanmar*, 15 January. Available online https://frontiermyanmar.net/en/no-exit-rohingya-jailed-en-masse-for-escaping-rakhine

28 Green, M. (2018), 'Faces of the Rohingya: "I have hope we will be looked upon as human"'. *SBS*, 15 May. Available online www.sbs.com.au/topics/voices/culture/feature/faces-rohingya

29 Harris, K. (2017), 'Canada's response to Rohingya humanitarian crisis tops $50M'. *CBC*, 13 December. Available online www.cbc.ca/news/politics/canada-aid-rohingya-myanmar-bangladesh-1.4446139

30 The Canadian Press (2017), 'Trudeau has "very direct" talk with Myanmar's Aung San Suu Kyi on Rohingya crisis'. *GlobalNews.ca*, 10 November. Available online https://globalnews.ca/news/3854982/rohingya-trudeau-aung-san-suu-kyi/

31 Vanderklippe, N. (2018), 'Top levels of Myanmar military responsible for crimes against Rohingya, report finds'. *The Globe and Mail*, 26 June. Available online www.theglobeandmail.com/world/article-myanmar-militarys-top-officials-responsible-for-crimes-against/

32 Trudeau, J. (2017), 'Prime Minister appoints the Honourable Bob Rae as Special Envoy to Myanmar'. Available online https://pm.gc.ca/en/news/news-releases/2017/10/23/prime-minister-appoints-honourable-bob-rae-special-envoy-myanmar

33 Genius, G. (2017), 'To The Critics: Rohingya Really Are The Victims'. *Huffington Post*, 10 October. Available online www.huffingtonpost.ca/garnett-genuis/to-the-critics-rohingya-really-are-the-victims_a_23235078; Mulcair, T. (2017), 'House of Commons Hansard #236 of the 42nd Parliament, 1st Session'. *Open Parliament*, 22 November. Available online https://openparliament.ca/debates/2017/11/22/thomas-mulcair-1

34 International Court of Justice (2019), 'Application Instituting Proceedings and Request for Provisional Measures: Republic of The Gambia v. Republic of the Union of Myanmar'. Available online www.icj-cij.org/files/case-related/178/178-20191111-APP-01-00-EN.pdf

35 UN General Assembly (1951), 'Convention Relating to the Status of Refugees'. *United Nations Treaty Series*, 189, 137.

36 UNHCR (2016), '*Global Focus Malaysia 2016 Report: People of Concern*'. Available online http://reporting.unhcr.org/node/2532?y=2016#year

37 The Straits Times (2017), '11 dead in landslide at Penang construction site'. *The Straits Times*, 23 October. Available online www.straitstimes.com/asia/se-asia/11-dead-in-landslide-at-penang-construction-site

38 Security Council Report (2017), 'Myanmar'. Available online www.securitycouncilreport.org/monthly-forecast/2017-12/myanmar.php

39 United Nations (2017), 'Security Council Presidential Statement Calls on Myanmar to End Excessive Military Force, Intercommunal Violence in Rakhine State'. Available online www.un.org/press/en/2017/sc13055.doc.htm

40 Reuters (2018), 'Massacre in Myanmar'. *Reuters*, 8 February. Available online www.reuters.com/investigates/special-report/myanmar-rakhine-events/

41 Mozur, P. (2018), 'A Genocide Incited on Facebook, With Posts from Myanmar's Military'. *New York Times*, 15 October. Available online www.nytimes.com/2018/10/15/technology/myanmar-facebook-genocide.html

42 Green, P., MacManus, T. and de la Cour Venning, A. (2018), *Genocide Achieved, Genocide Continues: Myanmar's Annihilation of the Rohingya*. London: International State Crime Initiative.

43 Green, P., *et al.* (2018), 28; Stanton, G.H. (2004), 'Could the Rwandan genocide have been prevented?', *Journal of Genocide Research*, 6 (2): 211–228.

44 OHCHR (2017), 'Brutal attacks on Rohingya meant to make their return almost impossible – UN human rights report'. Available online www.ohchr.org/EN/NewsEvents/Pages/DisplayNews.aspx?NewsID=22221&LangID=E, 1.

45 Klug, F. (2018), 'Rohingya say Myanmar targeted the educated in genocide'. *AP News*, 6 June. Available online www.apnews.com/3a486e94ea7e48d1bfa5a5e0e1bf0518

46 UN Human Rights Council (2019), 'Sexual Violence as a Tactic of War: The UN Independent Fact-Finding Mission on Myanmar'. Available online https://reliefweb.int/report/myanmar/fact-sheet-sexual-violence-tactic-war

47 Ibid.

48 Ibid.

49 Ibid.

50 Amnesty International (2018d), 'Myanmar: Military land grab as security forces build bases on torched Rohingya villages.' Available online www.amnesty.org/en/latest/news/2018/03/myanmar-military-land-grab-as-security-forcesbuild-bases-on-torched-rohingya-villages

51 Head, J. (2017), 'Rohingya Crisis: Seeing through the official story in Myanmar'. *BBC News*, 11 September, Available online www.bbc.co.uk/news/world-asia-41222210

52 BBC (2017), 'BBC reporter in Rakhine: "A Muslim village burning"'. *BBC News*, 7 September. Available online www.bbc.co.uk/news/world-asia-41189564

53 UN Human Rights Council (2018), 'Report of Independent International Fact-Finding Mission on Myanmar'. Available online www.ohchr.org/EN/HRBodies/HRC/MyanmarFFM/Pages/ReportoftheMyanmarFFM.aspx, 9.

54 Whiteside, P. (2017), 'Satellite images "Prove Rohingya villages were burned"'. *Sky News*, 18 October. Available online https://news.sky.com/story/satellite-images-prove-rohingya-villages-were-burned-11086627

55 Human Rights Watch (2018), 'Burma: Scores of Rohingya Villages Bulldozed'. Available online www.hrw.org/news.2018/02/23/burma-scores-rohingya-villages-bulldozed

56 Amnesty International (2018d).

57 Tribune Desk (2018). 'Mother of Humanity Award policy gets Cabinet nod'. *Dhaka Tribune*, 19 November. Available online www.dhakatribune.com/bangladesh/government-affairs/2018/11/19/mother-of-humanity-award-policy-gets-cabinet-nod

58 Amnesty International (2017a).

59 Radio Free Asia (2019), 'Myanmar Military Denounces New US Travel Restrictions on Top Brass'. *Radio Free Asia*, 17 July. Available online www.rfa.org/english/news/myanmar/myanmar-military-denounces-new-us-travel-restrictions-07172019160033.html; International Criminal Court (2019), 'Bangladesh/Myanmar'. Available online www.icc-cpi.int/bangladesh-myanmar

60 OCHA (2019), 'Rohingya refugee crisis'. Available online www.unocha.org/rohingya-refugee-crisis

61 World Bank (2019), 'GDP per capita (current US$)'. Available online https://data.worldbank.org/indicator/ny.gdp.pcap.cd

62 World Bank (2017), 'Bangladesh Continues to Reduce Poverty But at Slower Pace'. *World Bank*, 24 October. Available online www.worldbank.org/en/news/press-release/2018/09/19/decline-of-global-extreme-poverty-continues-but-has-slowed-world-bank

63 Thu Thu Aung, McPerson, P. and Ruma, P. (2019), 'Exclusive: Myanmar, Bangladesh agree to start Rohingya repatriation next week'. *Reuters*, 15 August. Available online www.reuters.com/article/us-myanmar-rohingya-exclusive/exclusive-myanmar-bangladesh-agree-to-start-rohingya-repatriation-next-week-idUSKCN1V51O5

64 Rahman, T. (2019), 'Rohingya repatriation attempt fails again'. *Dhaka Tribune*, 23 August. Available online www.dhakatribune.com/bangladesh/rohingya-crisis/2019/08/23/rohingya-repatriation-attempt-fails-again

65 Dholakia, N. and Frelick, B. (2018), 'An "Island Prison" is Not the Answer'. *Human Rights Watch*, 5 August. Available online www.hrw.org/news/2018/08/05/island-prison-not-answer

66 Al Jazeera (2019), '"Genocide Day": Thousands of Rohingya rally in Bangladesh camps'. *Al Jazeera*, 25 August. Available online www.aljazeera.com/news/2019/08/day-thousands-rohingya-rally-bangladesh-camps-190825055618484.html

67 McVeigh, K. (2019), 'Bangladesh imposes mobile phone blackout in Rohingya refugee camps'. *The Guardian*, 5 September. Available online www.theguardian.com/global-development/2019/sep/05/bangladesh-imposes-mobile-phone-blackout-in-rohingya-refugee-camps

68 Hasan, K. (2019), 'Govt turns to barbed-wire fencing to combat human trafficking from Rohingya camps'. *Dhaka Tribune*, 13 September. Available online www.dhakatribune.com/bangladesh/rohingya-crisis/2019/09/13/govt-turns-to-barbed-wire-fencing-to-combat-human-trafficking-from-rohingya-camps

69 Krishnan, M. (2019), 'India builds detention camps for Assam "foreigners"'. *DW*, 19 September. Available online www.dw.com/en/india-builds-detention-camps-for-assam-foreigners/a-50497835

70 Ministry of Law and Justice, India (2019), 'The Citizenship (Amendment) Act (2019)'. *The Gazette of India*, 12 December. Available online http://egazette.nic.in/WriteReadData/2019/214646.pdf

71 Reuters (2019), 'Explainer: Why India's New Citizenship Plans Are Stirring Protests'. *New York Times*, 23 December. Available online www.nytimes.com/reuters/2019/12/23/world/asia/23reuters-india-citizenship-explainer.html

72 BBC (2019), 'Citizenship Act protests: Three dead and thousands held in India'. *BBC News*, 19 December. Available online www.bbc.co.uk/news/world-asia-india-50833361

Chapter 8

1 Green, P. and Ward, T. (2004), *State Crime: Governments, Violence and Corruption*. London: Pluto Press, 2.

2 International Criminal Court (2018), 'Statement of ICC Prosecutor, Mrs Fatou Bensouda, on opening a Preliminary Examination concerning the alleged deportation of the Rohingya people from Myanmar to Bangladesh'. Available online www.icc-cpi.int/Pages/item.aspx?name=180918-otp-stat-Rohingya

3 People's Alliance for Credible Elections (2019), 'Citizens' Political Preferences for 2020'. Available online www.pacemyanmar.org/2019-survey

4 South, A. (2008), *Ethnic Politics in Burma: States of Conflict*. London: Routledge.

5 Advisory Commission on Rakhine State (2017), 'Towards A Peaceful, Fair and Prosperous Future for the People of Rakhine: Final Report of the Advisory Commission on Rakhine State'. Available online www.rakhinecommission.org/app/uploads/2017/08/FinalReport_Eng.pdf

6   Progressive Voice (2018), 'Apartheid Awaits for Rohingya'. *Progressive Voice*, 14 November. Available online https://progressivevoicemyanmar.org/2018/11/14/apartheid-awaits-for-rohingya; Progressive Voice (2018), 'ASEAN Leaders must Push Myanmar to End Rohingya Genocide'. *Progressive Voice*, 10 November. Available online https://progressivevoicemyanmar.org/2018/11/10/asean-leaders-must-push-myanmar-to-end-rohingya-genocide

7   Coconuts Yangon (2018), 'Protester Arrested Minutes After Calling for Arrest of Myanmar's "Murderous Generals"'. *Coconuts Yangon*, 31 August. Available online https://coconuts.co/yangon/news/protesters-arrested-minutes-calling-arrest-myanmars-murderous-generals

8   Dunant, B. (2018), 'Myanmar Democracy Activists Break Ranks With NLD Party'. *Voice of America*, 30 June. Available online www.voanews.com/a/myanmar-democracy-activists-break-ranks-with-nld-party/4460354.html; Generation Wave (2018), Generation Wave [Facebook page, 20 November]. Retrieved from www.facebook.com/generation.wave; Radio Free Asia (2018), 'Antiwar Protesters Charged With Violating Myanmar's Peaceful Assembly Law'. *Radio Free Asia*, 15 May. Available online www.rfa.org/english/news/myanmar/antiwar-protesters-charged-with-violating-myanmars-peaceful-assembly-law-05152018164336.html

9   Al Jazeera (2020), 'Internet blackout in Myanmar's Rakhine enters its second year'. *Al Jazeera*, 21 June. Available online www.aljazeera.com/news/2020/06/internet-blackout-myanmar-rakhine-enters-year-200621065709404.html

10 Reuters (2018). 'UN chief "shocked" by Min Aung Hlaing's latest comments on Rohingya'. *Democratic Voice of Burma*, 28 March. Available online http://www.dvb.no/news/un-chief-shocked-min-aung-hlaings-latest-comments-rohingya/80339

11 Lewis, S., Siddiqui, Z., Baldwin, C. and Marshall, R.C. (2018), 'Tip of the Spear'. *Reuters*, 26 June. Available online www.reuters.com/investigates/special-report/myanmar-rohingya-battalions/

12 UN Human Rights Council (2018), 'Report of the independent international fact-finding mission on Myanmar'. Available online https://ap.ohchr.org/documents/dpage_e.aspx?si=A/HRC/39/64

13 International Court of Justice (2019), 'Public sitting held on Wednesday 11 December 2019, at 10 a.m., at the Peace Palace, President Yusuf presiding, in the case concerning Application of the Convention on the Prevention and Punishment of the Crime of Genocide (The Gambia v. Myanmar): Verbatim Record'. Available online www.icj-cij.org/files/case-related/178/178-20191211-ORA-01-00-BI.pdf, 14.

14 Amnesty International (1992), *Union of Myanmar (Burma): Human Rights Abuses Against Muslims in the Rakhine (Arakan) State, May 1992*. London: Amnesty International; Corr, A. (2016), 'Secret 1978 Document Indicates Burma Recognized Rohingya Legal Residence'. *Forbes*, 29 December. Available online www.forbes.com/sites/anderscorr/2016/12/29/secret-1978-document-indicates-burma-recognized-

rohingya-legal-residence/#3cc89605a795; Human Rights Watch (2000), 'Burmese Refugees in Bangladesh: Still No Durable Solution'. Available online www.hrw.org/reports/2000/burma/index.htm

15 Hunt, K. (2017a), 'How Myanmar's Buddhists actually feel about the Rohingya'. *CNN*, 20 September. Available online https://edition.cnn.com/2017/09/19/asia/myanmar-yangon-rohingya-buddhists/index.html; Hunt, K. (2017b), 'Rohingya crisis: "It's not genocide," say Myanmar's hardline monks'. *CNN*, 26 November. Available online https://edition.cnn.com/2017/11/25/asia/myanmar-buddhist-nationalism-mabatha/index.html

16 Doyle, D. (2016), '"No Rohingya": Behind the US Embassy Protest in Myanmar'. *The Diplomat*, 29 April. Available online https://thediplomat.com/2016/04/no-rohingya-behind-the-us-embassy-protest-in-myanmar; Lee, R. (2014); Rigby, J. (2015), 'Aung San Suu Kyi aide: Rohingya are not our priority'. *The Telegraph*, 19 November. Available online www.telegraph.co.uk/travel/destinations/asia/burma/12006208/Aung-San-Suu-Kyi-aide-Rohingya-are-not-our-priority.html; Zaw, J. (2015), 'NLD official admits party snubbed qualified Muslim candidates for fear of Buddhist backlash'. *Coconuts Yangon*, 30 September. Available online https://coconuts.co/yangon/news/nld-official-admits-party-snubbed-qualified-muslim-candidates-fear-buddhist-backlash

17 Safi, M. (2017), 'Aung San Suu Kyi says "terrorists" are misinforming world about Myanmar violence'. *The Guardian*, 6 September. Available online www.theguardian.com/world/2017/sep/06/aung-san-suu-kyi-blames-terrorists-for-misinformation-about-myanmar-violence

18 UN Human Rights Council (2018), 'Myanmar: UN Fact-Finding Mission releases its full account of massive violations by military in Rakhine, Kachin and Shan States'. Available online www.ohchr.org/EN/HRBodies/HRC/Pages/NewsDetail.aspx?NewsID=23575&LangID=E

19 Ibid.

20 Hiroi, T. and Omori, S. (2013), 'Causes and Triggers of *Coups d'état*: An Event History'. *Politics & Policy*, 41 (1): 39–64.

21 Eckstein, D., Vera Künzel, Schäfer, V. and Winges, M. (2019), *Global Climate Risk Index 2020*. Bonn: Germanwatch.

22 European Union External Action (2018), 'EU-Myanmar relations'. Available online https://eeas.europa.eu/headquarters/headquarters-homepage_en/4004/EU-Myanmar%20relations; UK Foreign & Commonwealth Office (2017), 'Burma – Human Rights Priority Country'. Available online www.gov.uk/government/publications/burma-human-rights-priority-country/burma-human-rights-priority-country; US Department of State (2020), 'U.S. Relations With Burma'. Available online www.state.gov/r/pa/ei/bgn/35910.htm

23 Fieldview Solutions (2018), 'Time to break old habits: Shifting from complicity to protection of the Rohingya in Myanmar'. Available online www.fieldviewsolutions.

org/2-uncategorised/64-time-to-break-old-habits-groundbreaking-new-study-on-the-rohingya-crisis-in-myanmar, 1.

24 UN Human Rights Council (2018), 20.

25 Ibid.

26 Jones, L. (2015), *Societies Under Siege: Exploring How International Economic Sanctions (Do Not) Work*. Oxford: Oxford University Press.

27 UN News (2019), 'Genocide threat for Myanmar's Rohingya greater than ever, investigators warn Human Rights Council'. *UN News*, 16 September. Available online https://news.un.org/en/story/2019/09/1046442

Acknowledgements

1 Joyce, J. ([1922] 2011), *Ulysses*. London: Wordsworth, 32.

2 Johnson, J. ([1922] 1993), 'Explanatory Notes'. In Joyce, J. *Ulysses*. Oxford: Oxford University Press, 775.

Index

8888 Uprising 67, 84, 86–87, 138, 140, 152,
        157–158, 215, 218, 220
Election Bangladesh 203–205
Election 1948–1962 (Burma) 60
Election 1990 (Myanmar) 83, 139
    Kyaw Min elected 139
    Result annulled 83
    Rohingya elected 139
Election 2010 (Myanmar) 81, 83–86,
        101–103
    Aung San Suu Kyi boycott 83–84
    Election monitoring 83
    NLD boycott 83–84
    Rohingya elected 102–103
    Rohingya participation 101–102
    Shwe Maung success 85
    UEC 83
    Union Election Commission 83
    USDP victory 84
Election 2015 (Myanmar) 60, 101–102,
        111, 138–139, 141, 159, 174–175,
        181, 194, 217, 220
    Abu Tahay election ban 141
    Aung San Suu Kyi success 101–102,
        159, 220
    Chin voters 102
    DHRP 139
    Hindu voters 102
    Kyaw Min 139
    NLD Muslim exclusion 139, 174–175,
        194, 217
    NLD success 101–102
    Rakhine voters 102
    Rohingya avoid public space 101–102
    Rohingya disenfranchisement 60,
        101–102, 159, 181
    Shwe Maung election ban 102
    Union Nationals Development Party
        141
    Voter turnout 102
English, language 10–11, 36, 38–39, 103,
        119, 131–132, 142, 172, 180,
        194,
    Aung San Suu Kyi, speech using 103
    Official Language, Burma 131
    Traders in Arakan speaking 36
Ethnicity 3, 8–9, 55, 65, 67, 73–75, 77, 102,
        139, 142, 159, 169, 173, 186, 191,
        202, 209, 213–214, 222

Ethnic minorities 5, 8–9, 14, 19–21, 23–25,
        27, 29–30, 38–40, 42–43, 45,
        50–53, 58–60, 62–64, 67–68, 70,
        73, 76, 82, 85, 87, 89, 90, 94, 97,
        102–104, 107, 109–114, 116–117,
        122, 133, 141–143, 149–150,
        154–158, 163, 165–166, 168,
        171–172, 174–176, 179, 185–186,
        197–199, 201, 206, 210–214, 216,
        219–221, 227
    Chin 39, 58, 73, 102, 150, 211–212, 214
    Ethnic Armed Groups 68, 107, 114,
        163, 168, 171, 176, 197, 216, 219
    Kachin 58–60, 64, 68, 73, 114, 150, 158,
        163, 171–172, 176, 199, 211–212,
        214, 219
    Karen 39, 58–59, 68, 70, 73, 150, 158,
        211–212, 214
    Kayah 52, 58–59, 73, 150
    Mon 58–59, 73, 150
    Rakhine 5, 8, 14, 19–21, 23–25, 27,
        29–30, 38–40, 42–43, 45, 50,
        52–53, 59, 62, 67, 73, 76, 85, 90,
        94, 97, 102, 107, 110–114, 117,
        122, 126, 129, 133, 141–143,
        149–150, 154–157, 163, 165–166,
        168, 174–176, 185–186, 197–198,
        201, 210–212, 214, 216, 218–219,
        227
    Shan 20, 43, 58, 59–60, 64, 70, 73, 114,
        150, 163, 168, 171–172, 176, 199,
        212, 214
    Tatmadaw violence against 70, 114,
        168, 172, 199, 211–212
    See also Burmanization; Chin; Kachin;
        Karen; Kayah; Mon; Shan;
        Rakhine
Euro-Burma Office 64
Europe 15, 17–18, 21, 43
    Influence on Arakan 15
    Knowledge of Arakan coast 18
    Mariners 18, 21
    Sea trade to Asia 17
European Union 10, 135, 222–224
    Renting house from Ne Win's family
        223
European Rohingya Council (ERC) 129,
        147, 150
Ethiopia 82

www.ingramcontent.com/pod-product-compliance
Lightning Source LLC
Chambersburg PA
CBHW070559270326
41926CB00013B/2366